WHEN LONDON WAS CAPITAL OF AMERICA

WHEN
LONDON
WAS CAPITAL *of*
AMERICA

JULIE FLAVELL

YALE UNIVERSITY PRESS
NEW HAVEN AND LONDON

Published with assistance from the Annie Burr Lewis Fund

For information about this and other Yale University Press publications, please contact:
U.S. Office: sales.press@yale.edu   www.yalebooks.com
Europe Office: sales @yaleup.co.uk   www.yaleup.co.uk

Set in Minion by IDSUK (DataConnection) Ltd
Printed in the United States of America

Library of Congress Cataloging-in-Publication Data

Flavell, Julie.
  When London was capital of America / Julie Flavell.
    p. cm.
  ISBN 978-0-300-13739-2 (cl : alk. paper)
  1. Americans—England—London—History—18th century. 2. London (England)—
Intellectual life—18th century. 3. Americans—England—London—Biography.
4. Visitors, Foreign—England—London. I. Title.
  DA688.F57 2010
  305.813'042109033—dc22

                                                                  2009053163

A catalogue record for this book is available from the British Library.

10 9 8 7 6 5 4 3 2

To My Family
Andy, Eve, Paul

Contents

	List of Figures	*viii*
	Acknowledgments	*xi*
Prelude	An American City in Europe	1
Chapter One	The London World of Henry Laurens	7
Chapter Two	Upstairs, Downstairs: Master and Slave in Georgian London	27
Chapter Three	English Lessons in London: A Tale of Two Teenagers	63
Chapter Four	Young and Rich in Fleet Street: The Decadents Abroad	84
Chapter Five	A Long Island Yankee in the City	115
Chapter Six	'The Handsome Englishman'	143
Chapter Seven	London's American Landscape	165
Chapter Eight	Franklin and Son in London	189
Chapter Nine	'The most cautious man I have ever seen': Ben Franklin's London Career	209
	Epilogue	*235*
	Appendix	*249*
	Notes	*252*
	Further Reading	*288*
	Index	*291*

Figures

End papers Based on *A Plan of the Cities of London and Westminster, and Borough of Southwark, with the new buildings, 1767* reproduced by permission of MAPCO: Map And Plan Collection Online – archivemaps.com. Details appear on pages 6, 62, 114, 164, 188.

1. *Henry Laurens* (1724–92), by John Trumbull. Yale University Art Gallery, Trumbull Collection.   9
2. View of Fludyer Street, looking towards St James's Park, Whitehall by Thomas Hosmer Shepherd, 1859 © Trustees of the British Museum   15
3. *The Cricketers* by Benjamin West, courtesy of Peter A. Juley & Son Collection, Smithsonian American Art Museum   24
4. *Rare Mackerel*, from the series 'Twelve London Cries done from the Life, Part 1st' by Paul Sandby, 1760 © Trustees of the British Museum   31
5. *Bandy Bob*; a chimney-sweep's boy eating a piece of bread and holding a brush. Anonymous, *c.*1800. Courtesy of City of London, London Metropolitan Archives   33
6. *May Morning* by John Collet, *c.*1760. Courtesy of the Museum of London.   36
7. *The Third Duke of Richmond out Shooting with his Servant, c.*1765, by Johann Joseph Zoffany, 1733–1810. Courtesy of Yale Center for British Art, Paul Mellon Collection.   41
8. *A Mungo Macaroni*, published by Matthew Darly, 1772 © Trustees of the British Museum   43
9. Aston Hall, Shifnal, Shropshire, 2009 © Fiona Trenchard-Davies   56

10. *John Laurens,* (1754–82), a miniature painted by Charles Willson Peale in 1780, watercolor on ivory. Courtesy of Mr. John Laurens III   64

11. *The Staymaker,* engraved by Joseph Haynes (after William Hogarth), 1782. © Tate, London 2010   77

12. View of the Mall, St James's Park by Jean Baptiste Claude Chatelain, 1745. Courtesy of City of London, London Metropolitan Archives   78

13. *The Idle 'Prentice return'd from Sea, & in a Garret with a common Prostitute* from the series 'Industry and Idleness' by William Hogarth, 1747 © Trustees of the British Museum   88

14. *A Lawyer and his Agent,* etching after Robert Dighton, 1793 © Trustees of the British Museum   90

15. *The Middle Temple Macaroni. In Short I am a West Indian! Cumberland,* anonymous, 1773 © Trustees of the British Museum   91

16. View of houses on the corner of Chancery Lane and Fleet Street, also showing figures, by William Capon, 1798. Courtesy of City of London, London Metropolitan Archives   94

17. *View in Fleet Street,* published by Colnaghi, 1800 © Trustees of the British Museum   95

18. *High Life at Midnight,* anonymous, *c.*1769 © Trustees of the British Museum   97

19. *Stephen Sayre, A.B. 1757,* courtesy of Princeton University Archives. Department of Rare Books and Special Collections. Princeton University Library   117

20. *The Bank* by Thomas Malton, 1781 © Trustees of the British Museum   121

21. *The Royal Exchange* by Thomas Malton, 1798 © Trustees of the British Museum   123

22. *A View of the Mansion House appointed for the Residence of the Lord Mayor of London, during the Year of His Mayoraltry,* by Thomas Bowles III, 1751 © Trustees of the British Museum   124

23. *The Coffee-House Patriots; or News, from St Eustatia,* after William Henry Bunbury, 1781 © Trustees of the British Museum   126

24. *Watkin Lewes Esqr presenting the addresses from the counties of Pembroke, Carmarthen, and Cardigan, to the Lord Mayor, Alderman Wilkes, and Alderman Oliver in the Tower,* anonymous, 1771 © Trustees of the British Museum   152

25. *Mrs Baddeley*, print made by Robert Laurie (after Johann Joseph Zoffany), 1772 © Trustees of the British Museum   155

26. *A View of St James's Gate from Cleveland Row*, print made by Edward Rooker (after Paul Sandby), 1766 © Trustees of the British Museum 156

27. View of London from below the Tower; view from a height, looking up the river, with the Pool in the foreground left with a fleet of ships, and the Tower right under a setting sun, by William Daniell, 1805 © Trustees of the British Museum   171

28. View of Fulham Palace, with boats on the water in the foreground. Anonymous; engraved by Taylor, published by John Sewell, 1788. Courtesy of City of London, London Metropolitan Archives   173

29. *The Death of General Wolfe at Quebec* by Benjamin West, 1770. National Gallery of Canada, Quebec.   179

30. *A New Humorous Song, on the Cherokee Chiefs inscribed to the Ladies of Great Britain* published by Henry Howard, 1762 © Trustees of the British Museum   184

31. *Benjamin Franklin* by David Martin, 1767. Courtesy of the Pennsylvanian Academy of the Fine Arts, Philadelphia. Accession number:1943.16.1. Gift of Maria McKean Allen and Phebe Warren Downes through the bequest of their mother, Elizabeth Wharton McKean   191

32. *A Law Macaroni*, published by Matthew Darly, 1772 © Trustees of the British Museum   198

33. View of the old Middle Temple Hall, drawn by Charles Tomkins, copied from a painting attributed to Hogarth, *c*.1780 © Trustees of the British Museum   199

34. *House occupied by the Royal Society, Crane Court, Fleet Street*, print made by Charles John Smith, *c*.1840 © Trustees of the British Museum   206

35. *The American School* by Matthew Pratt, 1765. The Metropolitan Museum of Art, Gift of Samuel P. Avery, 1897 (97.29.3) Photographed by Geoffrey Clements.   212

36. *View of the Interior of the House of Commons during the Session of 1821–3*, print made by James Scott, published by Mary Parkes, 1836 © Trustees of the British Museum   215

37. *Peace Proclaimed at Charing Cross* and *Peace Proclaimed at Temple Bar* by Robert Dodd, 1783. Courtesy of City of London, London Metropolitan Archives   244

Acknowledgments

*W*hen *London Was Capital of America* reflects my longstanding interest in when and how Britons and Americans began to think of themselves as separate peoples. No book like this happens without the help and support of a number of people so, first and foremost, I would like to thank my family, Andy, Eve and Paul. Thanks to my husband Andy for supporting me in every way he could, both large and small, from criticising the text to improving my word processing skills. My daughter Eve and my son Paul were always proud of me, and gave me the benefit of their respective expertise in art and computer technology.

My mother, Susan Zorn, many times remembered back to her own years in publishing to give me the benefit of her experience as an editor. Her advice was invaluable to me in the early stages of the book project. My father, Bruce Richardson, was a warm and appreciative reader of several chapters. My friend Ruth Delfiner gave me the benefit of her tremendous skill as a critical reader, and also tirelessly talked through ideas and problems on many occasions. Bill Taylor never failed me when I needed encouragement, for which I will always be grateful. Sue Watts was a keen reader of the book at several stages.

I am grateful to a number of colleagues who have undertaken to read all or portions of the draft manuscript in one of its editions, and who have supported the project in various ways: Peter Marshall, Andrew O'Shaughnessy, Peter D.G. Thomas, John McCusker, Richard Dunn and Steve Sarson. Their valuable comments and corrections have enriched the book and rescued me from a number of errors. Peter D.G. Thomas generously assisted me with various points of research. Peter Marshall, John McCusker and Andrew O'Shaughnessy were always ready with advice on any aspect of the book project. Andrew O'Shaughnessy's enthusiasm took many forms. He and other colleagues at the

2005 Robert H. Smith International Center for Jefferson Studies conference held at the Salzburg Seminar helped me to sharpen my ideas.

I would like to thank Gordon Hay of the Centre for Drug Misuse Research at the University of Glasgow for having the patience to help me to apply a new statistical method to the problem of assessing the size of the colonial population in London. Unexpectedly, I learned from him that statistics can be enjoyable, and that numbers can open up a whole new way of looking at a subject.

I would also like to thank the staff at the Central Library, Wellgate, Dundee, who uncomplainingly processed scores of Interlibrary Loan requests.

Finally, I would like to thank my editor at Yale University Press, Heather McCallum, for always urging me to go that bit farther to achieve the very highest standard, both at the proposal stage and in the process of writing the book.

An American City in Europe

It was early May 1810. Doctor Benjamin Rush of Philadelphia sat at his desk in his imposing brick house on South Fourth Street. In the garden it was almost spring; the scorching summers of Pennsylvania had not yet arrived, the tender green weeks of May lay ahead. But Benjamin Rush saw none of this because in his mind's eye he was far away in time and space, harking back to his student days in London before the Revolution. His memory was stirred by the letter he was writing to his son James, who was about to follow in his father's footsteps, walking the wards of London's famous teaching hospitals.

Young James had left America the year before, in 1809, to study at Edinburgh University, one of Europe's finest medical schools. Relations with Britain were not good; President James Madison was resorting to trade restrictions in retaliation for British outrages against American shipping on the high seas. The second war between the United States and Britain, the War of 1812, was only a few years away, and Rush had cautioned James to use 'the utmost prudence' to avoid giving offence while in Scotland.[1] Yet he whole-heartedly endorsed his son's decision to prolong his trip abroad with a stay in London. 'That great city is an epitome of the whole world,' Dr Rush wrote enthusiastically. 'Nine months spent in it will teach you more by your "eyes and ears" than a life spent in your native country.' For any young man, even for a young citizen of the new American Republic, experiencing London was a rite of passage. The War of Independence had wrought no change in this respect.

No one knew better than Benjamin Rush the minefield that had been made of personal relations between Americans and their former countrymen by the decades of conflict. Rush had been in the thick of the patriot movement from the start, joining the Continental Congress and signing the Declaration of Independence in 1776. He served in George Washington's army as surgeon general. On the battlefield at Princeton he found the body of his Scottish friend Captain William Leslie of the British 17th Regiment of Foot, whose sister he had once, in happier days, hoped to marry. Undeterred by personal tragedy, he worked tirelessly in the ensuing years for the fledgling United States. He pushed for adoption of the U.S. Constitution. He helped to establish America's first medical school at the University of Pennsylvania. Just before his death in 1813 he performed a final service for his new country by bringing about a reconciliation between those two great Founders, Thomas Jefferson and John Adams, long estranged by politics.

But like Ebenezer Scrooge under the spell of the Ghost of Christmas Past, on this May morning Rush's student days in London suddenly seemed more real to him than all the ensuing years of conflict. He felt his youthful enthusiasm for the capital of his former mother country rekindling. In 1810 London was still the showcase of the English-speaking world, ten times the size of the largest city in the United States. It was the 'great metropolis' where could be seen the full spectrum of humanity: noblemen and commoners, merchants and shopkeepers, mechanics, clergymen, lawyers, soldiers and sailors, footmen, porters and beggars.[2] More than thirty years after signing the Declaration of Independence, Benjamin Rush still agreed with his old acquaintance Dr Johnson that 'when a man is tired of London, he is tired of life'.

Rush's salad days in London had been the time of his life. He frequented the wards of London's great teaching hospitals, where graphic scenes of sickness and amputation failed to put him off his chosen profession. He toured the Houses of Parliament, sitting on the king's throne 'with emotions that I cannot describe', and reciting a speech of Pitt the Elder before the empty chamber. He hobnobbed with the literary and artistic stars of the day, Dr Johnson, Oliver Goldsmith, the great actor David Garrick, and artists Benjamin West and Joshua Reynolds. He drank with the roguish City politician John Wilkes, enthusiastically toasting 'His Majesty and all the Royal Family'.[3]

For when Rush was in his prime, London was America's capital city. The London that Rush remembered was the largest city in the western world, its population more than twenty times the size of colonial towns like Boston and New York, and England's Bristol and Liverpool. London alone in the English-speaking world could muster the critical mass of talent necessary for greatness. From it flowed the best in theatre, retailing, publishing, art and music. It was the seat of government where Parliament met and the Royal Court of St James held its glittering assemblies. It was the financial centre of Britain's vast trading empire that spanned the globe from America to the West Indies,

Africa and Bengal. It was perhaps the greatest city America ever had, for it combined these centres of government, commerce and culture into a single mighty metropolis, the like of which would never be seen in the United States.

By the time Rush came there in the 1760s, London had been the capital of Britain's Atlantic empire for a century and a half, and it had taken on an unmistakably American cast. In the city of Dr Johnson, Garrick and Reynolds, the plants, products, people and exotica of the New World filled the taverns, streets, theatres and Court of the centre of empire. Cheek by jowl with the icons of Georgian London were the signs of its distant American hinterland. American trees – the darlings of Georgian landscape gardeners – swayed in the breeze in the Royal Parks. American curiosities were displayed in the newly opened British Museum, while crowds queued up in fashionable St James's Square to see a family of porcupines. At Mrs Salmon's famous waxworks in Fleet Street, figures of Cherokee braves were displayed alongside the usual likenesses of Royals and statesmen. Sugar from America's wealthy West Indian islands had become the favourite target for thieves at the docks near the Tower of London, who siphoned the precious stuff off into sacks or crammed it into pockets. Tobacco shops were everywhere in Georgian London, their exteriors decked with jaunty Indian kings, their interiors cloudy with the smoke of the New World's 'jovial weed'.[4] In Westminster Abbey new marbles commemorating Britain's recent military exploits at Quebec and Fort Ticonderoga were squeezed in among the revered monuments of ages past. In atmospheric St Michael's Alley, where seventy-five years hence Charles Dickens would imagine the fictional counting house of Ebenezer Scrooge, the Jamaica Coffee House was the best place to buy the American rum that was overtaking gin as London's favourite tipple. The first American-born sheriffs of London dined at the lord mayor's mansion. The slave trade that fed the New World's insatiable appetite for labour had given London its own population of blacks, London-born, African and American, and with them new and troubling questions about the reach of English liberty.

The story of London when it was the capital of America is a missing chapter in the history of the Great City, overlooked by the biographers of a nation who are inclined to forget that America was once part of its empire. It is also a missing chapter in the social and cultural history of Americans abroad. That history usually begins with the earliest American travel writers in the nineteenth century, but it was the score of years before independence that witnessed the first big wave of American visitors overseas, most of them bound for London.

Since the first settlers left Jamestown, Virginia, in 1607 to beg supplies for their starving settlement, American colonists had been returning to London, but their numbers rose sharply in the mid-eighteenth century. The empire was expanding; business and trade were on the rise, and the conquest of French Canada in 1763 was followed by a new, heightened movement of people throughout the British Atlantic. Merchants and merchant sailors, students, artists, clergymen, fashion retailers, lobbyists and land speculators, all those whose business had always taken them to the capital of empire now arrived there in ever greater numbers. And swelling their ranks came a new type, the first true American tourists, wealthy colonists on the Grand Tour, drawn to the Old World for pleasure just as much as business, endowed by their own growing wealth and sophistication with a new curiosity to see the world for themselves. With them came an unprecedented number of African Americans, servants to these wealthy visitors.[5] Most of the colonial Americans ever to visit London did so in the years just before independence. It was a trend that ran counter to the widening political rift over Britain's right to tax the colonies.

Their first big venture overseas took place at a time when these Americans were hardly Americans at all. Hector St John de Crèvecoeur's famous question 'What is an American?' would not be asked until the end of the War of Independence in 1782. British America was a string of seaports and provinces that stretched in a great arc from Newfoundland to Barbados. By the end of the Seven Years' War in 1763, the thirteen colonies that would eventually become the United States were only half of the total British possessions in the New World. To the north of them were the recently acquired colonies of Canada; to the south of Georgia were the two relatively unsettled colonies of East and West Florida. The Bahamas and Bermuda, and a string of Caribbean islands – Jamaica, Barbados and others, the smallest too numerous to count – brought Britain's dominion into America's tropics.[6] The colonial societies that spanned this vast territory were remarkably diverse, ranging from Nova Scotia through the Yankee heartland of New England, Pennsylvania with its Quakers and Germans, down to the slave-based colonies of exploitation in the southern mainland and the West Indies. For the inhabitants of these far-flung provinces, their colony was their home and their nation was Britain.

And London was their capital city. The story of the colonials who ventured there does not fit the traditional stereotype used to characterise American nationals in Europe after independence, of innocents encountering Old World corruption. Instead it is about a cornucopia of colonial types in a time when 'American' still meant something open-ended, and London was not yet a foreign place to the colonists: the wealthy tobacco and rice planters and their families who fitted into the fashionable West End neighbourhoods, the black slaves who integrated with the English servant classes and found new opportunities in the English capital, the fun-loving students, the Yankee businessmen eager to make good in the City, the ambitious scientists and artists, the agents and land speculators at Whitehall, the frontiersmen who gave a show to the cheering crowds. To Londoners these incomers looked exotic, occasionally sophisticated, or even decadent before they looked like innocents abroad.

How America's colonial forebears responded to their capital must be told through their many stories, stories that vividly recreate an all but forgotten world. That great advocate of American nationhood, Thomas Paine, would declare in 1776: 'There is something absurd, in supposing a continent to be perpetually governed by an island.' But these colonial visitors – including Benjamin Rush, who signed Paine's longed-for Declaration of Independence – saw nothing absurd in the arrangement. In the following pages we shall see a bygone alternative vision to Paine's patriotic geography – of the Atlantic Ocean as a highway rather than a barrier, with Americans as part of a far-flung world that stretched from the British Isles to Africa, the Caribbean and Canada, and was centred upon London when it was the capital of America.

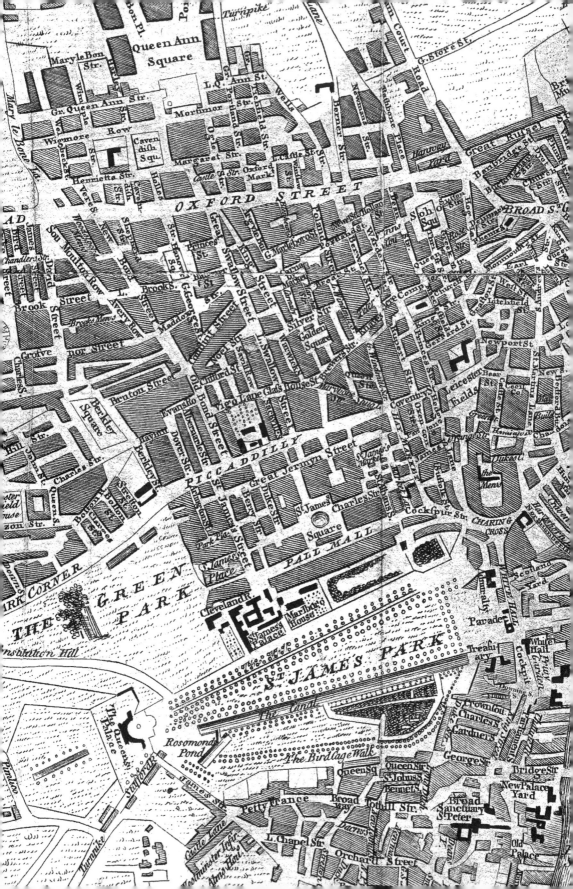

CHAPTER ONE

The London World of Henry Laurens

It was early April 1771 and the temperature in Charleston was poised to soar to the suffocating high of a South Carolina summer. Henry Laurens, rice planter, slave-keeper and transatlantic merchant was busy arranging the transportation of one small human across the ocean.

Henry, forty-seven years of age, at the peak of his success, was used to moving people around the British trading empire that was his world. He had consigned cargoes of men, women and children from Africa's west coast to his business associates in England and America. He had dispatched scores of male slaves to his remote plantations on the colonial frontier. He had sent dozens of enslaved women after them, on purpose to provide them with wives. He had ordered unhappy white overseers to the middle of nowhere to inspect conditions on his newly developed rice swamps.[1]

Now he was making arrangements for a cargo of a more precious kind, his own son Harry who was bound for school in England. For four days Henry composed a succession of letters to friends, schoolmasters and ships' captains, detailing every stage of Harry's journey from his embarkation at Charleston to his arrival at a boarding school in the London suburbs. Writing in the careful longhand used by businessmen of his day, he covered many pages in his meticulous care of his child. It must have been the labour of many hours. Harry was not to be suffered to waste his time while on shipboard – Harry was to remember his prayers – Harry had sixpence in his purse, and should have no more until he reached his school – Harry's clothes should be plain but fashionable – Harry must be screened against exposure to the smallpox that was endemic in England.[2]

Henry's care of his child was reflected in his great organisational skills. To an onlooker he might have seemed grossly insensitive in larger matters because Harry, aged seven, was being sent abroad alone within a year of the

death of his mother. Mrs Laurens – once the beautiful Eleanor Ball who
graced Carolina society – had died after giving birth to her twelfth child in
twenty years of marriage.

Despite his businesslike nature, Henry had given way to open grief. For ten
days after her death, he could not wield a pen; for months he confided to
friends that he could barely conduct his business. With the loss of his wife,
Henry was discovering what it meant to be a single parent. Eleanor had left
him with the care of the five surviving children, from John, the eldest at
sixteen, down to newborn baby Mary, whose arrival Henry had scarcely
noticed in the anxiety of her mother's final illness. The bereaved family lived
together at their suburban retreat, Ansonborough. Dozens of servants worked
about the place, but Henry still found the children tied him down – as he
put it graphically, 'they hang upon my breast and my knees, and look up with
eager cravings for education, and for that tender care in domestic life' which
they had always received from their Mama.[3] There was no replacement
for mother.

Henry was not one to wait about while the family completed the cycle of
grief. Before Eleanor's death he had hatched a scheme to send John to England
to finish his education. Now he took this up again with renewed interest. The
schools around Charleston were not very good. Why not take all three of his
sons to England? Harry, who wilted every summer under the South Carolina
heat, could go on his own, ahead of the others. Henry would personally escort
John and little five-year-old Jemmy later in the year.

The daughters, twelve-year-old Patsy and the infant Mary, would stay at
Ansonborough. Henry's brother James and his wife had promised to move in
and look after them. Patsy was an intelligent girl, acutely sensitive to family ties.
When her older sister Nelly had died seven years earlier, Patsy was inconsolable,
bursting into tears so often that the family made a joke of it. Much later in life she
would have a premonition of her brother John's death, although at the time they
were separated by an ocean.[4] But whatever Patsy felt at this particular separation,
Henry left no record. Activity was to be the antidote for his personal sense of loss.

If the girls were to stay, one other member of the Laurens household was
singled out to accompany Henry and the boys. The slave Scipio, Henry's body
servant, would complete the Laurens entourage in London. Bringing a slave
to London was a shrewd financial move, because it saved the cost of a highly
trained English servant. But Scipio – a young man – was not a passive figure
in the decision whether to include him or not. He begged Henry to take him
along, giving him 'ten thousand promises' of good behaviour. And Henry

1 Henry Laurens, 1791.

finally acquiesced, confiding to his brother that if Scipio behaved well, 'no stranger could serve me so acceptably as he can'.[5]

Master, children and slave, the Laurenses would be a typical grouping in London. Absentee American planters with slaves in tow had become a common sight in the Great City in the past ten years, and the colony of South Carolina – the wealthiest of Britain's mainland American colonies – led the trend. There were at least fifty Carolina families already in London when Henry planned his trip.

An upbringing in Charleston could only have whetted the appetites of the young people for London's famous attractions. At last they would see a real London play, instead of a travelling theatre troupe whose costumes and scenery – if one were lucky – were copied from Drury Lane originals. They would see the real Vauxhall Gardens, where at night one could wander through a labyrinth of mysterious walks that led past follies, cascades and pavilions, all brilliantly lit up by candles – a far cry from the imitation Vauxhall in Charleston that had only an orchestra and perhaps some card tricks.[6] Instead of settling for Charleston shops whose goods were advertised as 'lately arrived from London', they would be able to wander at will through all the shops of London itself.

For Henry, as family patriarch, the rewards of a trip to London were more subtle and more dignified. He had been there years before, under very different circumstances. Henry had not begun life as one of Carolina's gentry. His father was an industrious saddler who had acquired real estate in the booming South Carolina economy, and educated his children to rise in the world. Henry was an avid pupil. When he was in his late teens he went to London to serve as a merchant's apprentice. By his mid-twenties he was an established Charleston merchant. Determined to succeed, he worked a twenty-hour day. His marriage into the prestigious Ball family in 1750, and the acquisition of his first plantation six years later, put him firmly in South Carolina's upper crust. By the time Eleanor died he owned five plantations, an extensive suburban compound near Charleston and hundreds of slaves.[7] His return to London on an extended visit marked the apogee of his success, for only the wealthiest planters could afford to live as absentees in London.

Knowing London, experiencing it personally, was the crowning achievement for South Carolina's elite. As quickly as Carolinians made money hewing rice swamps out of the semi-tropical wilderness, they exchanged it for a façade of something English and genteel. In the days of wooden ships, with England three thousand miles away, that façade had to be constructed largely from imagination and by proxy. Planters wanted country retreats that looked like the leisured English seats represented in books and pictures. They wanted clothes that would look up-to-date in Bond Street. They wanted food on their tables, books in their libraries, furniture and accessories that would look suitable in the home of any English landed gentleman. They wanted gardens modelled after those that graced the villas that bordered the Thames.

A consumer revolution that was sweeping the English-speaking world in the eighteenth century helped make this possible. As never before, what could be bought in England could be bought in her American colonies. English textiles, clothing, porcelain, clocks, guns and instruments, books, prints, toys and trinkets of every kind adorned the bodies and houses of those who could afford them. Charlestonians consulted English gardening manuals to find out how to grow the radishes, rosemary and carrots necessary for English cuisine. When their semi-tropical climate ruled out potatoes and cabbages, they imported them from the northern colonies. Slaves might dine on cassava and plantain, but their white masters were determined to have an English menu. Eleanor Laurens created a garden that was a well-known showpiece, bringing together English kitchen produce, exotic tropical fruits and the features of a Georgian ornamental garden, all encompassed within a traditional red-brick wall.[8]

Following the fashions in English architecture incurred the biggest expense. South Carolina's country estates and townhouses replicated the

Georgian taste of the period, with its distinctive Palladian and neoclassical styles. All this involved importing many features of a house, from pilasters and doorways to cornices and panelling. Add to the list 'London made' wallpaper, paints and furniture, and the potential to spend was endless. The finished products were often given English names. Henry's kinsmen the Balls owned plantations named after London's fashionable parks – 'Kensington' and 'Hyde Park'.[9] Henry Laurens called his suburban Charleston retreat Ansonborough after Lord Anson, the English naval hero who had protected the Carolina coast from pirates early in the century. Like his native colony, Henry presented the world with a front of polish and refinement that concealed a lifetime of hard work and ambition.

It was fitting, then, that at the age of forty-seven Henry Laurens should join the galaxy of wealthy South Carolina planters who were living as absentees in London. Carolinians had always travelled to London for business and for pleasure. But after 1760 their numbers rose sharply. What had been an occasional practice was set to become an entrenched tradition for the well-heeled Carolinian.[10] More money and better transport meant more of them could see London for themselves. In taking to the sea, these rich colonists were doing what they had always done – they were copying the English gentry. In the process they were acquiring another indispensable accessory of the true English gentleman, one that had hitherto been beyond their grasp – they could make an appearance among the beau monde of London's social season.

The Laurens family reached Falmouth, England, on 9 October 1771. Their crossing had taken twenty-nine days. Henry, always stoical, confided to his brother: 'I had some dread of a September passage, though I suppressed my own feelings, in order to keep those about me in good humour.'[11] This was despite the fact that Henry had travelled first-class, in one of the packet ships established by Britain to improve imperial communications. The packet service was supposed to be comfortable; packets even carried their own milk cows.[12] It can be taken for granted that Henry had reserved a cabin for his family, but this sounded far grander than it was. Cabins were simply tiny spaces in the stern of the ship that gave the traveller a modicum of privacy. Even this was questionable, for travellers reported that they could hear the steerage passengers through the thin cabin walls. Two or three to a cabin was common, with two in bunks and a hammock lashed up for a third. Scipio probably slept on the floor, adding to the overcrowding. In the days when wooden ships were only ten to fifteen feet above the ocean's surface, mid-Atlantic waves could, and frequently did, wash into cabin windows. Even a moderate wave height could leave the passengers shaking uncontrollably, unable to write or lift a cup of tea to their lips.

But none of this discomfort would have seemed unacceptable to the Laurens family. They lived in an age when every traveller had to be hardy. All travel was dangerous, uncomfortable and unreliable. In the American colonies many roads were merely glorified Indian paths. Anyone who lived within sixty miles of the coast still turned to the sea as the best means of transportation.

In Britain things were not as different as one might expect. To be sure, the eighteenth century witnessed improved roads and more coach services. But this was relative. A stagecoach from London to Edinburgh still took ten to twelve days in the Laurens's time. The famous Shrewsbury Flying Waggon, which was supposed to be particularly fast because it changed horses, took five days to travel 152 miles from Shropshire to London. If one left the main roads for the byroads and country lanes, one took the risk that bad weather would dissolve them into a morass of impassable mud and ruts. Open moors were sometimes so poorly signposted that one needed a guide to cross them safely. And coaches and wagons could rattle incessantly, producing the Georgian equivalent of carsickness. A Devonshire landlady complained that the passengers from the mail coach that stopped at her inn were always so ill that they would not order dinner, resulting in a substantial loss of profit.[13] Chronic overcrowding, encouraged by greedy coachmen, added to the general discomfort. It has been said that if one thinks in terms of the trouble and the time, rather than the actual distances involved, Britons who emigrated to America in colonial times were only moving 'from one of London's provinces to another'. The far-flung parts of the British Isles were as remote from London as were Massachusetts and Barbados.[14]

It is no wonder that when they reached Falmouth, the Laurenses burst forth from their nautical prison in a holiday mood. They rose early to walk for hours over England's green fields and hilltops, no doubt glad to see something besides the empty blue sea. They saw the castles built by King Henry VIII to guard Falmouth Harbour. St Mawes and Pendennis were not so very old by English standards, but to the colonial boys any castle was unmistakable proof that they were really in England at last. They dined on fish unknown at home, such as John Dory, plaice and turbot. Despite a stay of only three days at Falmouth, they received many callers at their tavern, a mark of Henry's consequence. And Henry got a chance to resume his habit of furious letter-writing, which the relentless jostling motion of the ship had made impossible for so many weeks.[15]

'Jacky and Jemmy are both well,' wrote Henry to his brother in South Carolina, 'Robert (some time Scipio) is well too, and hitherto has behaved very well and promises fair to continue good and dutiful.'[16] Scipio got only one brief mention in the many pages Henry penned at Falmouth. But if his master had little time to think of his bondsman, his news reveals that Scipio was doing a great deal of thinking for himself.

For Scipio had decided to use the occasion of a trip to England to change his name. He was now Robert Laurens. The decision revealed him to be a young man who was aware of the world around him and his place within it. His old name, Scipio, was definitely a 'slave name'. One did not meet white people who were named Scipio or Pompey. To be sure, classical names were usually given to favoured house servants rather than mere field hands, but who cared for a distinction like that in a world where being any kind of slave made one into an object of derisory curiosity? Slaves with august-sounding Roman names were objects of fun in London. One London newspaper joked that plantation blacks were 'Princes in their own Country', depicting a satirical scene of a West Indian home in which the white master called out, '*Domitian, kill me that Fly.– Pompey, clean my Shoes – Caesar, hand me my Slippers – Caligula, gather me those Cockles – Nero, kick your Mother downstairs*'.[17] Robert wanted to be taken seriously in England. As the crowning touch to his new image, he gave himself a last name. Very few slaves had last names. Perhaps he chose 'Laurens' in order to reassure his master that he was not planning to run away. Runaway slaves would change their names to disguise themselves.[18]

Before he got to London, Robert knew his old name would be a liability. His prescience confirms how closely connected with the London scene were the great homes of wealthy Carolinians, since even an enslaved house servant was aware of London attitudes towards provincial types. In Charleston, 'London' was the constant buzz of the drawing rooms where black servants waited upon elegant whites. And the black manservants who had accompanied their masters on their jaunts to England were likewise able to display a metropolitan polish.[19] Robert would have heard from the mouth of experience how London society was prone to look upon an unpolished, plantation-bred black youth. The metropolitan stereotype took on a definite form in the character of Mungo, a black servant in a popular London play called *The Padlock*, which was a hit in Britain and the colonies. It was a typical comic love story, with the novelty that the go-between for the star-crossed English lovers was an irascible, muttering house slave from the West Indies named Mungo. 'Mungo' was to become a stock, low-burlesque black type on the English stage – servile, rude and funny. The name Mungo, with its African origins, became a derisive epithet for a servant who carried out his master's dirty work.[20] Robert did not want to be a 'Mungo' or a 'Scipio'.

If Henry's sons wanted to cut a certain figure in London, so did Robert. It may even be that as early as Falmouth, Robert was planning the challenge to Henry's authority that was to unfold in London. If so, Henry ignored this portent. The two colonial Americans were about to enter a world that was, in its own way, just as divided between extremes of wealth and poverty as the one they had left at home. But instead of planters' mansions and slaves' huts, the contrast manifested itself in elegant squares and squalid slums. The difference was that for Robert it was to be an empowering new experience.

The Laurens family reached the suburbs of the Great City on 21 October. There they stopped, for no well-informed (and well-to-do) colonial like Henry would venture into London itself without first protecting his household against smallpox. Smallpox was still a dreaded disease in the eighteenth century, but with the callous injustice of all microorganisms it was crueller to Americans than to Britons. It was endemic in Britain, which meant that a significant proportion of British adults were immune, although epidemics hit children hard. It had been completely unknown in America at the start of European settlement, and along with a Pandora's box of other European diseases it had played an important part in decimating the Native American populations. Over time, the descendants of European and African peoples who settled in America also came to have less resistance to smallpox than did their cousins back home.[21] When smallpox did occur, it wreaked havoc on the local population.

Patsy Laurens had almost died of the smallpox in 1759. In fact, the family thought she was dead until just before her burial, when a doctor noticed she was still breathing.[22] John had probably contracted the disease at the same time as Patsy, but Robert and Jemmy were still vulnerable. So Henry kept them in Chelsea just outside London for almost a month, putting them through the ordeal of an eighteenth-century inoculation. This was a rather horrible process that involved inserting the matter from a ripe smallpox pustule into an open cut. The usual result was that the patient contracted a very mild case of the pox, with all the subsequent benefit of immunity. But fatalities did occur.

The inoculations took place on 31 October. Henry was nervous, but by 9 November the doctor was declaring Jemmy safely clear of the disease. Jemmy 'went through the small pox without an hours confinement, and without any eruption except in the punctured part' where the skin had been pierced. Robert, on the other hand, was a textbook case, with three days of

2 Fludyer Street looking into St James's Park.

mild fever followed by a sprinkling of 'pustules' over his face and body. Jemmy's reaction was so mild compared to Robert's that Henry worried it had not been effective. Afraid for his son, he told himself that Robert's more usual 'larger crop' of pustules occurred because the servant had foolishly ignored the doctor's orders, indulging in 'irregular eating, smoking, and chewing, and hovering about the kitchen fire too much'. In his relief, Henry poked a little fun at Robert, diminishing the danger he had gone through. The black youth was never 'confined to bed or chamber a minute', but he nevertheless complained 'according to his way, abundantly'.[23] Cast in the role of comic faithful retainer, Robert Scipio Laurens was a virtual member of the family in Henry's eyes.

Death had been defied, and the Laurenses were ready to set up house in London at last. On 20 November they moved into the home of Mr Robert Deans, 'an old Carolina Acquaintance in a pleasant Part of the West End of the Town'.[24] Deans lived in Fludyer Street just around the corner from Downing Street, which was already the official residence of the prime minister and a fashionable address 'fit for persons of honour and quality'.[25] Fludyer Street was newer but equally fashionable. It was a short street of Georgian terraced houses, which connected Whitehall with St James's Park.

Fludyer Street no longer exists, but James Boswell – who rented rooms in Downing Street for a few months in 1762 and found them very expensive – has left a picture of what it must have been like for the Laurens family. Like them, Boswell had arrived in November. On one of his first evening strolls he saw 'the king and queen pass from the opera, and then saw the guards drawn up in the court of the palace while the moon shone and showed their splendour.' Both streets were within a few steps of Horse Guards Parade, so Boswell could view this splendour whenever he wished. Just across St James's Park was Buckingham House, the Royal residence for George III and Queen Charlotte. There was a Royal Cockpit in St James's Park where Boswell went to see the cruel spectacle of two birds 'armed with silver heels' fighting one another.[26] For little Jemmy Laurens of South Carolina, who had more pacific tastes, it was novelty enough to know that the park at the end of his street offered a daily chance of seeing 'the king and the swans'.[27]

The little household in Fludyer Street now settled down to a routine. Each day Jemmy went off to school, probably escorted by Robert. John had joined Harry at Mr Clarke's boarding school in Chelsea, but the two boys were often at Fludyer Street with their father. Robert admitted callers for Henry and ran errands. Henry must have rented at least three rooms in the Deans' house, because he entertained there, on one occasion having ten to dinner.[28]

The house Henry chose as his London home was at the very core of the venerable city he remembered from his youth. The west end of Fludyer Street opened onto the royal parks and palaces. The east end led to Whitehall, Parliament Street and the ancient medieval chapel that was home to the House of Commons. A five-minute walk in either direction could take Henry, Jemmy and Robert to St James's Palace or Westminster Abbey. If Henry chose, he could walk to Mr Clarke's school to inspect the progress of John and Harry, for Chelsea was only a mile or so beyond Westminster on the

King's Road. This had been Charles II's favourite route to Hampton Court. It took one out of the city, and gradually opened up among elegant houses and gardens.[29]

Turn from the green spaces of the west and head east towards the bustling city, and Fludyer Street was only a twenty-minute walk away from the crowded, noisy merchants' counting houses and coffee houses that Henry recalled from his youth. The Royal Exchange, ancient Cornhill with its countless tiny alleyways, and beyond it the Tower of London and the city's famous docks – this was the financial heart of the city that Henry had known as a merchant's apprentice.

Yet in the midst of what was old and familiar, much had changed since Henry had left in 1747. London was a city that never stopped growing, and its growth was most conspicuous in the fashionable new squares and houses that sprang up wherever there was space. The pressure for space was coming not from the poor but from England's wealthy classes – the nobility and gentry, who always spent part of the year in London, and the wealthy English provincials who aspired to be like them in all ways, and now began to find they could afford to follow their betters to London for the 'season'. Such people wanted to live in the elegant West End rather than the workaday, vulgar City, and space there was at a premium. Fludyer Street had not even existed when Henry was last in London. It had been a cul-de-sac called Axe Yard, lined with unimpressive buildings. Grosvenor Square and Mayfair next to the Royal Parks had been transformed into new developments for the beau monde early in the eighteenth century, but the London housing boom really took off after 1763.[30] Henry wrote home: 'The increase of buildings in and about this city since I was formerly in England is very amazing. The elegance of many of those buildings is not less wonderful.'[31]

The Peace of Paris in 1763 that ended the Seven Years' War ushered in a new phase of prosperity and optimism, not only for the British empire in general but for London developers in particular. It was inevitable that this would push the wealthy developments northward. At mid-century Oxford Street was still the northern boundary of the West End, with the villages of Marylebone and Paddington standing among farms and fields. Now the city would leap this boundary and a New Road to the north was designed, replacing Oxford Street as London's northern frontier and resulting in the engulfment of these villages. (It was naively contended that the New Road – part of it is known today as Euston Road, with its busy railway stations – would mark the end of London's advance on the countryside.)[32]

This is where Jane Austen would place the aspiring middle-class characters of *Sense and Sensibility*, written about forty years later. When Eleanor and Marianne Dashwood came to London with the good-natured Mrs Jennings, they stayed in Berkeley Street. Not far away in Conduit Street lived Mrs Jennings's pretentious daughter Lady Middleton, who was anxious to bury her family's associations with City merchants. Both ladies had Mayfair addresses. Mr and Mrs John Dashwood lived in Harley Street, Marylebone, and the faithless Willoughby was in Bond Street, also heavily developed during the century and a fashionable promenade.

The South Carolina families that came to London in such numbers after 1763 joined the English nouveau riche who were buying in these neighbourhoods. Henry spent many hours in Berners Street just north of Oxford Street.[33] Like Fludyer Street, it had come into existence since his last visit to London. The houses on Berners Street were particularly elegant, for some were designed by the architect Sir William Chambers, a royal favourite who had helped create some of the famous landmarks at Kew Gardens. Chambers himself lived at Number 53.[34] No fewer than five South Carolina families were living there during Henry's London sojourn.

Berners Street – still there today, although the Georgian architecture has entirely disappeared – is a short, straight street, and the little community of South Carolinians must have seen one another constantly. Shortly after reaching London, Henry had dined with the Steads, the Wrights and the Brailsfords. 'My friends in the City have got hold of me and have engaged me every day till Sunday next,' he wrote just five days after arriving in the city. As one of the wealthiest men in South Carolina, a merchant who also belonged to the colony's landowning and political circles, Henry could take it for granted that he would be embraced by the Berners Street set.[35]

The most famous of that set was Ralph Izard, a scion of one of South Carolina's founding families. His early years offer no clue as to what was in store for him after 1776, when he served first as a Revolutionary diplomat in France and then as senator for South Carolina. At a tender age Izard had inherited his father's vast South Carolina estate, which included over 500 slaves. When he was twelve he was sent to school in England. From Hackney and Eton he went on to Cambridge, where he was an avid sportsman. By his early twenties he was back in South Carolina. At home he showed his versatility in moving between high-style London life and the relative rusticity of his family's plantation by sowing his wild oats with various slave women. In 1767 he headed north and married Alice DeLancey of the wealthy New York

DeLanceys. Four years later Mr and Mrs Ralph Izard were back in London. There they took a house in Berners Street.[36] Nearby lived their cousins from South Carolina, the Fenwicks and the Middletons, who owned estates on both sides of the Atlantic. Ralph flirted briefly with the idea of running for Parliament, and indulged his love of art.[37] London life suited the Izards.

Ralph had relatives in England with aristocratic connections. His cousin Sarah Izard, a beautiful woman but shy according to the aristocratic Horace Walpole, had become 'Her Ladyship' through her marriage to Lord William Campbell. Campbell, the youngest son of the fourth Duke of Argyll, was to be the last royal governor of South Carolina. He was as colourful as his wife was quiet. A 'most gallant and humane sea officer', he on one occasion leaped into the River Thames to save a man trapped under a tree trunk while his terrified wife and her friend Lady Aylesbury watched from the safety of their boat.[38] Through Lady Campbell, Izard knew the Duke of Richmond. And through his marriage into the DeLancey family, Izard was connected to several prominent military figures: Admiral Sir Peter Warren, the hero of Louisbourg, and Sir William Draper (both married to DeLanceys) and General Thomas Gage, the second son of Viscount Gage, who is better known as the British commander-in-chief in Boston at the start of the Revolutionary War. Both Izards and DeLanceys called on the famous Horace Walpole at his retreat, Strawberry Hill.[39]

Ralph Izard was also related through marriage to most of his South Carolinian neighbours in Berners Street. His cousin had married a daughter of the merchant Benjamin Stead. The Steads were among the new, stylish merchant families (like Mrs Jennings of *Sense and Sensibility* and her daughter Lady Middleton), who lived off the premises of their business so that they could enjoy a more refined lifestyle. Stead's counting house was in bustling Threadneedle Street, near the Bank of England and the Royal Exchange; in the evening he would come home to his genteel Berners Street address.[40] Mrs Richard Beresford and her daughter Elizabeth took a house in Berners Street a few months after the Laurens family settled in Fludyer Street. Elizabeth had married Alice Izard's rather wild brother Peter DeLancey in 1771, only to be widowed a few months later when he was killed in a notorious duel in Charleston. The duel took place just weeks before the Laurens family embarked for England, so it would have been the talk of every drawing room in Berners Street well before the Beresfords' arrival.[41] And James Wright, Jr., of South Carolina, who was in London studying law at the Middle Temple, married Miss Elizabeth Izard. He lived on the street with his father, Sir James

Wright, who became governor of Georgia.[42] Of the Berners Street set, only Samuel Brailsford and his family, whose fortune had been made importing African captives into South Carolina, had no Izard connections to boast of.[43]

The South Carolina community that Henry Laurens and his sons joined in London had not existed twenty years earlier. Yet by 1771 Berners Street was just the tip of the iceberg. The Laurens family's arrival meant reunions with various old friends and relations. George Appleby and George Austin, once Henry's business partners in Charleston, were now settled with their families in Shropshire. George Appleby was the godfather of Henry's son John Laurens. George Austin's daughter had married one of the Moultries of South Carolina, and young Moultries attended school with the Laurens boys in London.[44] All of these were only part of a colourful planter community that flowered in London just before the Revolution. The colonists who met in the empire's capital were destined to divide over the cause of American independence, but for now that conflict cast no shadow over the close-knit group.

With all these comings and goings between Charleston and the centre of empire, it is not surprising that native South Carolinian gossip was alive and well in London. A particularly spicy story was connected with a young friend of John Laurens, Francis Kinloch, already in England when the Laurens family arrived. Francis was the ward of Thomas Boone, former governor of South Carolina. Boone had also brought another charge of a very different kind back home with him when he left his royal post in 1764. Sarah Tatnall Peronneau, the wife of a South Carolina planter, had abandoned her husband and eloped with Boone to England. They lived together until her husband's death in 1768 enabled them to marry.[45]

The scandal did not make them social outcasts. Perhaps they followed the path outlined by Mary Crawford in Jane Austen's *Mansfield Park*, when she suggested to the shocked Edmund Bertram that Mrs Rushworth and her brother Henry Crawford (now adulterers) could still marry and mix in society: 'In some circles, we know, [Mrs Rushworth] would never be admitted, but with good dinners, and large parties, there will always be those who will be glad of her acquaintance.' Henry Laurens was not one of these modern types. He reported that he did not visit Governor Boone: 'he was polite to me at my first arrival, I believe I omitted an enquiry after Mrs. Boone, either not knowing or not thinking of their marriage and may have given offence.' Henry was touching on a sore spot and no doubt his innocence was put on. Back home, Governor Boone had tried to get Mrs Peronneau accepted in Charleston social circles as the governor's lady, introducing her under the name of 'Mrs Worthington', but she had been mercilessly snubbed. Strangely, the news of their marriage in England was not reported in the *South Carolina Gazette* until August 1771, three years after it took place. Henry had departed for England just before, so he could pretend not to have heard of the marriage when he met Governor Boone in London. A couple of young Peronneau lads were studying law at London's Inns of Court at this time; one wonders whether they came to their Aunt Sarah for Christmas.[46]

Henry was dragged into more of his countrymen's fights and feuds after he had settled down in Fludyer Street. One of the Brailsford children from Berners Street was a scholar at Mr Clarke's boarding school in Chelsea with John and Harry Laurens.[47] This Master Brailsford was a pugnacious lad who got into a duel with Alexander McQueen, another Carolina scholar at Clarke's. The boys agreed to meet at Hyde Park at dawn – the favourite spot for London duellists. Schoolboys didn't have guns but they had fencing lessons, so they agreed to use swords. Poor Henry Laurens heard about it the night before, and, not knowing where they had appointed to meet, set out on horseback to track them down. 'It cost me almost one whole night, and the walking eight or ten miles and riding twelve or thereabout, in order to find out the gentlemen and prevent it,' he complained. He dispatched young Brailsford back to Berners Street, where his father was shocked when he heard how close the boys had been to bloodshed. Henry promptly sent a full account of it all back home, lest some overblown version 'from the mouth of fame' should be the first to reach the ears of poor Mrs McQueen in Charleston and frighten her out of her wits.[48] Even in the days of wooden ships, three thousand miles was not enough to separate Henry from the scandals and quarrels of his native colony.

But Henry Laurens's American set in the Great City was still broader than the transplanted South Carolina community. Before American independence created a national government and America's own capital, London was where wealthy Americans from all over the empire were most likely to meet. Henry knew merchants and planters from New York, Philadelphia, Virginia and Maryland, but also from the British West Indies. West Indians were counted as Americans. They were, after all, part of Britain's American empire. Youthful West Indians registering to study law at London's Inns of Court signed themselves in as 'of the island of Antigua, in America', or 'of the island of Jamaica, in America'.[49] West Indian absentees were even more plentiful than South Carolinians. They too bought up houses in the new West End developments. The parish of Marylebone in particular was associated with West Indian grandees.

Marylebone had become a fashionable part of London since the middle of the eighteenth century. In *Mansfield Park* the fictitious Mrs Rushworth stayed in Marylebone's Wimpole Street, in a house formerly owned by 'Lady Lascelles'. The real Lascelles family had made its fortune from West Indian sugar.[50]

A short walk from Wimpole Street was Soho Square, where lived eighteenth-century London's most famous West Indian, William Beckford. Member of Parliament for London and twice its lord mayor, Beckford was a man of his time with a West Indian twist, who indulged in his proverbial English 'bottle and wench' and hailed traditional English liberties, while earning the soubriquet 'negro-whipping Beckford' for keeping slaves. He left a string of illegitimate sons behind him, to whom he bequeathed substantial legacies. His one legitimate son, William Beckford junior, scandalised English society in the 1780s with his homosexuality. Beckford junior had a sufficient fortune from his father's sugar plantations to live as a recluse at his Gothic monstrosity, Fonthill Abbey in Wiltshire.[51]

Living in the same neighbourhood as they did, Carolinians and West Indians mixed socially. They had much in common. South Carolina had originally been settled by English colonists from Barbados. They imported their slave system and their lavish lifestyles. Barbados grew sugar; South Carolina grew rice. Lowland South Carolina had four black people to every white person, a ratio similar to that of Barbados.[52] Eighteenth-century visitors to Charleston, South Carolina, called it 'the center of our beau monde', one of the gayest cities in America, where rich (and somewhat decadent) West Indians joined South Carolinians in a 'round of pleasure', all looking very much like one other.[53]

In London the conviviality continued. Henry Laurens was a constant visitor at the house of William Manning, a West Indian merchant whose family had long been established in St Kitts and who had extensive business ties with South Carolina. Manning lived in Broad Street (present-day Broadwick Street) in the heart of Soho. There Steadman Rawlins's sons from the island of St Kitts played with young Harry Laurens during school holidays. As the Rawlinses lived in North Street, a stone's throw from Fludyer Street, the two families probably met regularly in St James's Park.[54]

DeLancey, Manning, Laurens, Izard, Moultrie, Rawlins, Wright, Brailsford – all of these families were members of the wealthy elites of Britain's American empire before 1776. These well-to-do colonists, whose trade and social networks criss-crossed the Atlantic, lived in an arc that stretched from Boston and New York to the Caribbean. Of those who travelled to the mother country for education and pleasure, the numbers increased with the proximity of their native provinces to the tropics. The Caribbean colonies probably sent as many absentees again as the total from America's mainland. Only after independence would they cease to be counted as 'Americans'.

In this colonial American social geography it was not the Caribbean islands but New England that was out of place. New England did not yet have the leading role in defining American identity that it would come to have after American independence. Its homespun image was seen as just that. In Henry Laurens's time, far fewer gentlemen came from New England.[55] Henry knew few New Englanders and those he did know were Bostonians with trading connections to the American South or the West Indies. In London the wealthy planters residing in the West End, whether from the American mainland or the Caribbean, were seen as the 'typical Americans'. Other colonists were there, and in large numbers, but American planters and American slaves, like Henry and Robert, were what stood out in the streets of the Great City.

All of this mixing and matching between families from different parts of Britain's eighteenth-century Atlantic empire had escalated sharply after the Seven Years' War, when an embryonic tourist industry began in the colonies. Wealthy colonists began travelling strictly as a leisure pursuit.[56] The well-to-do from all of Britain's American colonies got together and became acquainted at fashionable resorts on the mainland of America. A popular colonial resort that is still going strong today is Newport, Rhode Island. Southerners and West Indians came north in the summer to escape the terrible heat, which wreaked havoc on their health. The arrivals of Izards, Middletons and Wrights were all announced in the Newport newspapers of the 1760s. And rich Philadelphians and New Yorkers wanted to leave the dirty city during the hot summer months.[57]

But the total numbers at these American resorts were nothing compared to the numbers found in the empire's capital. Newport might boast just a couple of hundred at the height of its summer season compared to London, where there were never fewer than a thousand wealthy mainland Americans and West Indians to be found all the year round.[58] These were the first American tourists. They were the beginning of a trend that has never stopped. By the end of the Napoleonic Wars 5,000 Americans ventured to Europe annually. The advent of steam travel after 1850 bumped the numbers up nearer to 30,000 – still far short of the millions who go abroad today, but pushing the limits of available technology.[59] Americans were drawn back to revisit the Old World after 1763 in an impulse that contradicted the growing political row between the colonies and their mother country. When the American

3 Benjamin West, *The Cricketers*, *c*.1764. Ralph Izard stands holding a cricket bat, facing (right to left) Andrew Allen, Ralph Wormeley and James Allen of Pennsylvania. The figure to the right of Izard has been variously identified as Arthur Middleton of South Carolina, or an unknown member of the Beckford family. The latter is more likely, as Middleton's departure from London in late 1763 barely gave him time for a sitting.

Revolution began twelve years later the individual colonists who met so congenially in their original capital city would for the first time split ranks over the war.

Benjamin West's painting *The Cricketers* is an attractive illustration of the cross-colony sociability to be found in London during the heyday of Britain's American empire. It was painted for Ralph Izard in 1763 or 1764, when he was just a young man. 'The conversation piece' as Izard called it, hung over the chimney in his Berners Street parlour. He is shown leaning on his cricket bat – he was reputed to have been an excellent sportsman – accompanied by young Andrew Allen of Pennsylvania, Virginian Ralph Wormeley, Andrew's brother James, and a member of the numerous Beckford clan of Jamaica.[60] These were young men in England for their education. The Allens were studying law at the Inns of Court when they joined Ralph Izard and his circle.

The Cricketers shows Ralph and his friends about to play the most popular competitive sport of the time. Mainland Americans hadn't turned to baseball yet; cricket still united the English-speaking Atlantic. The earliest mention of baseball in America dates from after the American Revolution, in Massachusetts in the 1790s, at a time when cricket was still widely played.[61] Cricket was played in all the colonies, from New England to Georgia (and of course the West Indies, where today it is the national sport).

Confident, at ease and at least half British, the group of Americans portrayed in *The Cricketers* epitomises the plantation community that was making London its own just before the Revolution. Ralph Izard and his set were not the self-styled 'doomed aristocrats' of the antebellum period, supposed upholders of a gracious, dying order that would end with the American Civil War. The planters of the late colonial period had a cosmopolitan outlook. Their economic world was just as urbane, an Atlantic system whose geographic scope was focused on coastlands and sea lanes rather than the American interior.[62] As far as they were concerned, they were not part of a dying breed, but British colonials who fit into a modern, expanding British empire. Eleven years after they sat for the picture these five colonists would part company over the American rebellion, some choosing to remain loyal to their king, others joining the patriot cause. *The Cricketers* – a picture that could not have been painted in another fifty years, when the old Atlantic colonial world had faded out – lingered in the Izard family until the end of the Civil War when, by family tradition, it was sold to a Yankee carpetbagger.[63] It had become an artefact of a bygone era.

It was this wealthy and colourful set that were Henry Laurens's new neighbours in his London home. But Henry, always a hard worker, was somewhat scornful of their leisured lifestyles. He had better things to do than live 'an idle and what is called genteel life in London'. There was merchant business every day at the Carolina Coffee House in Birchin Lane, where he met up with Samuel Brailsford and Benjamin Stead. Henry kept his finger on the pulse of the market for indigo, rice and of course slaves. A young business associate back in Charleston, John Lewis Gervais, wanted to turn 'Negro merchant'. When Henry reached London he used his business contacts to help Gervais, who vended his first cargo of 218 Sierra Leone captives just a few months later.[64]

But Henry's main concern was his children's education, and this was keeping him busier than he'd expected. All was not as it should be at Mr Clarke's boarding school. An acquaintance at Chelsea had hinted to him 'that it was not a proper place, for gentleman's children'. Jacky Petrie, the son of a friend back in South Carolina, was one of Mr Clarke's scholars. He complained to Henry about the 'ill natured behaviour' of one of the teachers. Worse was what happened to Harry. He arrived home at Fludyer Street one day with a 'horrible burn' on his cheek caused by a younger 'vagabond brother' of Mr Clarke's. The Clarke boy was an apprentice and had left his master. According to Henry, he 'wantonly and maliciously' thrust a candle into poor Harry's face during a quarrel. A typical parent, Henry saw it as all the fault of the Clarke boy, who was entirely too rough. He could have put out Harry's eye![65]

Little Jemmy certainly could not board at Mr Clarke's when Henry went home to South Carolina. Other arrangements would have to be made. And despite the children having their friends from home about them (all the boys at Clarke's were from South Carolina), Henry did not want to keep John and Harry at Chelsea either. In his methodical way he began to research England's schools. As always he was exacting and hard to please. What he particularly dreaded was the prospect of his boys 'rambling the streets of the City' on their days off school. 'I hate the thoughts of his being in, or so near London, as to be able to get there by virtue of his own will', he wrote of his eldest, John. His concern extended to the children of his friends back in South Carolina. He sent their parents reports on their progress, and on one occasion kept a young South Carolinian busy in his lodgings, copying business letters, to prevent him 'strolling about the streets or sauntering in a coffee house'.[66]

London, the pleasure capital of the world! How many parents dreaded setting their sons loose there. Geneva in far-off Switzerland had become a popular choice for boarding the sons of wealthy English families, in part because it was safe from the temptations of home. Henry began to have thoughts of travelling there to see for himself and taking his two eldest boys with him. 'God forbid', he wrote to a friend, that the 'tainted air of this kingdom' should infect his sons' morals.[67]

But what about that other young South Carolinian who passed his days right under Henry's nose? Were Robert's morals being infected? Henry said little about his bondsman in his letters, but there were signs of trouble. The Great Metropolis offered very different temptations to Robert from those it offered the Laurens boys, but the temptations were real nonetheless. As one American colonist expressed it, London was a place 'where there are so many occasions of spoiling servants, if they are ever so good'.

CHAPTER TWO

Upstairs, Downstairs: Master and Slave in Georgian London

'Saucy and impertinent', 'insolent, impertinent, saucy', 'idle, luxurious', 'impudence, discontent, extravagance' – these were the sort of epithets that were applied daily to the servant class of Georgian London.[1] Some called their sturdiness English spirit, but most deplored it as a symptom of the decadent modern living that prevailed in the nation's capital. 'Servant trouble' was the talk of the town, not only in aristocratic circles but among the middle classes. It was plain Ben Franklin who had complained that the metropolis was 'spoiling servants', however good.

What was so bad about London servants, and was Robert susceptible to the same pernicious influences? London servants were simply too hard to control because they had more jobs to choose from, more money and less direct supervision than country servants. The same middle classes that had filled up the new, elegant housing developments in the west end of Georgian London created a new demand for servants – and it kept on growing right through the century. Servants were an absolute requirement for those who wished to look genteel. An ordinary middle-class London home required three or four servants; those with pretensions required more. The biggest complaint about servants was that they quit at the drop of a hat, 'for every idle disgust', as Daniel Defoe put it. Servants 'have very little attachment to those they serve; ... self is the sole motive', lamented one disillusioned contemporary. In hard terms, three or four years was the average time that a London servant kept a place. It was not uncommon for it to be less. And in so many ways that frustrated their employers, London servants evaded the direct supervision of their lives and work that was possible in remote rural households. It was said that a London servant who ventured into the English countryside laughed at the homespun ways and 'patient submission to labour' of his rustic fellow servants, calling it 'plodding and slavery'.[2]

What, then, would they call an American youth from the plantations like Robert, for whom 'slave labour' was not merely a figure of speech? Robert had changed his name. Could he change his behaviour to fit in with his new fellow servants? Of all the members of the Laurens household, Robert was surely faced with the steepest learning curve when he first arrived in London. He was not a member of the tiny colonial elite who were raised to look at home in an English drawing room, but one of the hundreds of thousands of black slaves who formed a fifth of the population of the American colonies. Robert, however, was not a field worker who spent his days cultivating exotic American crops. He was a house servant. As such he would find a numerous brotherhood in London.

Robert's history before London is shadowy, emerging as it does by chance in Henry Laurens's letters. Six years before the London trip he makes his first appearance, carrying messages for Henry on foot and by horseback between the various branches of the South Carolinian plantation, and even on one occasion hauling 100 pounds of oakum – an indication that he was used to outdoor labour as well as the light work of the house. On Henry's plantation Robert was much like an English rural household domestic, who could find himself outdoors making hay on occasion if the weather required it.[3]

In London, Robert was Henry's body servant. Probably the term 'footman-valet' best describes his role, a personal servant with the multifarious duties of a footman. Since Henry was in lodgings in London, the other servants were in the employ of the landlord, Mr Deans. This probably brought the two Americans together more than ever. Robert assisted Henry with the business of rising in the morning, helped him to dress, and escorted the children to school or to the park. He admitted Henry's callers. As in South Carolina, he delivered messages for Henry and undertook other minor tasks out of doors. He most likely waited at table. He also probably went everywhere with Henry – to the play, to the coffee house at noontime, on visits and to the shops.

Footmen had a conspicuous role as escorts for their masters.[4] Henry's West Indian friend John Baker had brought with him from St Kitts a slave named Jack Beef. Beef made himself so indispensable to Baker that he achieved a kind of fame in the neighbourhood. 'He attends his master on horseback, goes messages and does commissions in London, takes the boys to school at Winchester when they run away, and is much in request amongst John Baker's friends and neighbours for cooking the turtles and bottling the wines. He goes out with the hounds.' Jack Beef died just before Robert came to London – a tragic denouement, as he had just been granted his freedom and was about to return to the West Indies with his savings.[5]

With ties in St Kitts to return to and a wealth of sophisticated job skills, Jack Beef must have been older than Robert. Robert probably started working for Henry Laurens in his teens. In 1765 when Robert (then Scipio) first appears in his master's letters, Henry was calling him 'the boy'; by the time they reached London he was invariably 'my black man', but he was assuredly a young man.[6] Robert was the very type of the 'laborious and simple youth' from the country whose character would be ruined by exposure to London life.[7]

Sir John Fielding, the eminent Westminster Justice of the Peace, described the progress of corruption of American slaves who came to London: 'they no sooner arrive here than they put themselves on a footing with other servants, become intoxicated with liberty, grow refractory', and begin to expect wages. They sometimes become so troublesome to their masters, warned Fielding, that they are finally discharged; they then proceed to 'corrupt and dissatisfy the mind of every black servant that comes to England'. But the corruption did not stop there, according to Fielding. '[T]here is great reason to fear', he wrote, 'that those blacks who have been sent back to the plantations' have inspired insurrections.[8] In a similar vein English servants were thought to export decadent London lifestyles and attitudes to their country cousins – to use the historian's term, to serve as 'social nexuses' between a certain class of people in the metropolis and the provinces.[9] American slaves threatened to have the same deplorable cultural impact in their native colonies, and with even more dangerous results, in the minds of contemporary authorities. Would Robert be ruined by exposure to the Great Metropolis?

Out and about, running errands for Henry Laurens, Robert must have quickly learned his way around the Great City. From Fludyer Street to the Carolina Coffee House with a message for Mr Stead or Mr Brailsford would take him past the most famous landmarks of Georgian London. Down Whitehall he would go, past the government buildings and Banqueting House where Charles I was executed. From thence his route took him to the Strand where stood old Somerset Palace, a Renaissance royal residence, then through Temple Bar to Fleet Street with its law scholars, pubs and winding lanes, and on to St Paul's Cathedral, the defining feature of London's Georgian skyline. From here the merchant coffee houses were just a short distance away. Taking a message to Berners Street was another adventure altogether, as it took one through St James's Park and the elegant, decorous squares of the new West End. Robert's errands would leave him with plenty of time to explore independently, away from his master's scrutiny, for Henry reckoned that it took two to three hours for a servant to deliver a message from Fludyer Street to the City and return with a reply.[10]

Back in the colonies there was nothing to equal what Robert saw. What buildings, what monuments, what dress, display and equipage! The town-houses and the plantations of the Carolina rich only gave a foretaste of the reality. But at the same time – what poverty, what deprivation! Even the slave quarters at home probably did not prepare him for what he encountered on his solitary perambulations through the Great City.

What he saw were some of the poorest white people in the empire, degraded, half-starved, stinking and desperate, stripped of all dignity, people whose condition was enough permanently to change his idea of the white race. '[T]hey learn here to despise the whites'. So wrote a West Indian planter of the plantation slaves who were brought to London.[11]

How would London's poorest look to one who was unused to the sight of white people at the 'bottom of the barrel'? Andrea Levy in her novel *Small Island* conjures up the shock that black West Indians experienced when they came to Britain during the Second World War, using terms that suggest what Robert might have felt a century and a half earlier. The West Indian RAF volunteers arrived in the land they called their mother country – a place they had known from afar as 'refined, mannerly and cultured' – to find that 'Mother has a blackened eye, bad breath and one lone tooth that waves in her head when she speaks'. They shook their heads at their 'first long look at England' – 'it was the squalid shambles that made them frown so'. They wondered 'how so many white people come to speak so bad – low class and coarse as cane cutters'. They marvelled at 'white women who worked hard on the railway swinging their hammers and picks like the strongest man'. They saw the English slum children, 'white urchin faces blackened with dirt, dryed snot flaking on their mouths'. They saw white women in public wearing worn-out, undersized clothes.[12] It was this that worried the West Indian planter of Robert's day, the revelation of a white underclass that eroded the slave's 'terror' of his masters, giving him 'new and enlarged notions' of the 'weaknesses of the whites'. The deference to the white race that was deliberately cultivated in plantation slaves would be gone forever.[13]

Even in Whitehall, the Strand and Fleet Street, the main arteries of the city that Robert knew well, the very poor and the desperate were everywhere in evidence. Right around the corner from Fludyer Street in King Street, there was a cookshop where unskilled kitchen help worked for food only. The

4 A ragged woman aggressively pedals fish on the doorstep of a genteel London home, frightening its inmates.

basket-women who carried loads in Fleet Market just off Fleet Street worked for the same wages. They were not unknown to starve to death. Thin, worn and humble, the people who lived these hand-to-mouth existences would have made a sharp contrast in Robert's eyes with those who chose to beg or thieve instead. Georgian London still had the 'sturdy beggars' of the days of Henry VIII, fantastic, ragged figures who deliberately created open sores on their faces to arouse the sympathy of passers-by. The stocks at Charing Cross were on Robert's way to the Carolina Coffee House. In the pillories petty criminals were pelted with filth and rocks, and humiliated by a jeering mob. London had more prostitutes than any city in Europe, and on the Strand girls as young as twelve solicited passers-by. And the children of London's poorest, set to work as mindless drudges in apprenticeships that amounted to virtual slavery, would routinely pass through the Laurens's neighbourhood. The maids who cried 'milk' and the chimney sweeps all grew up in abject ignorance, not even taught housework, taken on by masters who hoped the value of their labour would amount to more than the cost of their food and clothes. Chimney sweeps needed to be very small, so they started young, sometimes as early as five years. When their masters did not bother to wash the coal dust off them for three or four years, they succumbed to a form of skin cancer. They were literally 'used up'.[14]

'White trash' – the term was not used in Robert's world, but the destitute of London were indeed treated as refuse by their countrymen. The social reformers of the Georgian era were still only lone voices crying in the wilderness. Robert Laurens, like the other plantation slaves he knew in London, was a significant cut above these portionless folk. For Robert met many fellow American slaves in the West End homes of Henry Laurens's South Carolina friends. At the Mannings's in Broad Street there was 'black George'.[15] The Austins, who moved between London and their country home in Shropshire, had at least two slaves.[16] Cato lived with the George Applebys, the friends and former business partners of Henry from Charleston. In Berners Street there was July, the slave of Carolina planter Peter Manigault who was visiting the Stead family.[17]

It is impossible to know how many plantation slaves like himself Robert met in the London homes of absentee planters, because they make only very occasional appearances in the letters and papers of their white masters. Certainly after 1760 Londoners had the impression that the number of black servants in London was rising markedly, as they accompanied wealthy Americans on their jaunts to the metropolis. As one put it, planters were bringing 'swarms of Negro attendants into this island'.[18] This impression squares with the fact that the number of white planters was rising sharply at that time.

One could hazard a guess that it was the norm for wealthy mainland Americans and West Indians to bring at least one slave with them to London. Proving this is another matter because of the serendipitous manner in which

Bandy Bob _

5 Chimney sweeps covered from head to toe with black soot were a common sight in Georgian London. This barefoot boy is eating a crust of bread which he tries to hold clear of the soot.

black servants emerge in old letters and records. To illustrate, the wealthy John Baker of St Kitts, who kept an exhaustive diary, made a number of fleeting mentions of slaves in England. For example, he went riding one April in the English countryside with a West Indian planter and his 'Black Jack'. In another entry he mentioned a lady friend of his from Jamaica who was poisoned by 'Abba, the wench' because Abba had learned that she would be set free when her mistress died (Baker's friend survived but was 'vastly altered').[19]

The story of Thomas Windsor is another illustration of just how difficult it is to reconstruct the community of fellow slaves who inhabited Robert's London world. Windsor's existence, and his sad fate, only came to light because he was tried at the Old Bailey for robbing another black servant just a few years before the Laurens family arrived in London. At his trial he stated that he lived with 'Esquire Spooner, in Cavendish-square', Marylebone. This was Charles Spooner of St Kitts, who lived in the West End's Harley Street and was another of the West Indian absentees mentioned in Baker's diary. The Laurens family may have known him, as they knew so many West Indians in that neighbourhood. Spooner's bondsman Windsor had robbed John Shropshire, whom he met in a pub in the same gentrified neighbourhood. Esquire Spooner did not appear in court to defend his black servant, and Windsor was sentenced to hang.[20] Many, perhaps most of the black people living in London were household domestics like Windsor and Shropshire, and a large number must have arrived in the city as servants of the well-to-do. Trained black manservants advertised for positions in the newspapers, frequently giving West End or Soho addresses.[21] Given these examples, it seems probable that every South Carolina household on Berners Street visited by Henry and Robert had a black member.

If the numbers of black American servants were on the rise after 1760, they still did not constitute the majority of London's black population. By the time Robert walked London's streets, it was estimated that there were 15,000 blacks living in London. Some of them were first-generation Africans who were off-pourings of the slave trade (London had been a slaving port since the seventeenth century). Some had been born there, native Londoners. Some were part of the city's shifting seafaring population. Both slave and free black mariners came and went in ever greater numbers during the eighteenth century, making London 'the hub of the black Atlantic'. Many of the blacks who lived there were in any case among the city's very poor. They could be found sharing some of the worst slums with the white population that had been there since time immemorial.[22] However poor many of them were, London still had the attraction of having the biggest urban black population in the empire. It had a thriving black community that held parties, balls and public gatherings. Robert would have known London taverns and clubs that were identified as places where black servants 'herded together'.[23]

In Fludyer Street, Robert worked alongside white servants. The Deans probably had five or six servants. That was a typical number for a comfortable West End home that was still modest enough to take in a lodger. Since Robert Deans was from South Carolina, he may have brought a black servant to London with him, but on this the record is silent. The only member of the Deans' household staff who emerges in Henry Laurens's correspondence is Kitty, an English maid who made daily enquiries on Henry's behalf about the fate of a lottery ticket. When it failed to win, Henry noted, 'the poor maid seemed to be a good deal affected', because Henry had promised her twenty guineas if it won – a princely sum.[24]

Robert must have come to know Kitty well, because all the servants at the Deans' would have worked and lived at close quarters. The servant quarters in the new West End developments were typically below street level, with windows facing out at the back of the house. Clustered in this area below stairs were the kitchen, the storerooms and the servants' bedrooms. Servants usually shared rooms, sometimes two to three sleeping together, but their waking hours were in any case always spent elsewhere. The heart of the house for the servants was without a doubt the kitchen, the one communal room that offered relative privacy from the master and mistress. Unsurprisingly, tales of servants carousing in the kitchen abound. Beer, a fiddle and a dance for the fun-loving, tea and card tables for the more pretentious – servants in the kitchen echoed the round of socialising carried on by their masters upstairs.[25] This was the close-knit world Robert joined when he came to London.

And how did Mr Deans' servants take to having a 'Blackamoor' among them? In a country that adhered to a rigid social hierarchy, servants had ranks of their own. Housekeepers and cooks outranked chamber maids; gentlemen's valets outranked footmen. Then there were less substantial (but nonetheless real) gradations in rank between servants who worked for a nobleman, a wealthy merchant, or a mere tradesman. And the personal background of the servant himself had an effect on his standing. The social backgrounds of servants were extremely variable in Georgian England. They could be from the parish poor, but they could also be offspring of the lower gentry. Farmers and tradesmen with comfortable incomes, even on occasion clergymen, sometimes sent their younger children to be servants in well-to-do homes. With genteel manners, a bit of education and skills that were of use in the stables, the kitchen and the dressing-room, this 'better class' of servant could command a bit more respect within the employer's household.[26]

6 A traditional London May Day procession. A black servant in livery has joined a street procession made up of other servants and members of the lower orders, including a milkmaid, ragged children, a beggar, and a hurdy-gurdy player. A soldier looks on in amusement. The Lord and Lady of May are on the left-hand side of the picture.

Robert could handle horses, and he could read and write, so his skills far exceeded those of the unwashed, untrained English poor. But, after all, he was a slave from the American plantations. That would not cut much ice below stairs. There is plenty of evidence of racism in the servants' quarters, in Georgian prints and theatricals that depict black servants as at the bottom of the pecking order. But these things are relative. Black servants may have been serving the tea in the servants' kitchen, but they were still one of the gang in an occupation that was known for its sense of solidarity. And some of the demeaning aspects of being a house slave were shared by free servants in Georgian London. White servants too were sometimes assigned names that were not their own by their employers.[27] Even their personal freedom was sometimes threatened. Young girls were sometimes entrapped into prostitution by people pretending to hire them as domestics; young men following up advertisements for places were sometimes ensnared by the press gang and forced into the British navy.[28] It was a rough life in many ways, but a life that made it easy for servants and slaves to develop a sense of camaraderie despite the differences in their situations. English servants were very willing to marry black Americans, as numerous instances show.[29] Interracial unions were common enough in Britain to give rise to a Scots version of the old plantation joke about the cuckolded husband:

> 'I have known a lady, John, who was delivered of a blackamoor child, merely from the circumstance of having got a start by the sudden entrance of her negro servant, and not being able to forget him for several hours.'
>   'It may be, sir; but I ken this;- an I had been the laird, I wadna hae ta'en that story in.'[30]

Back in America, of course, most of the colonies strictly outlawed interracial marriage – it threatened to overturn the colonial social order – and white colonial visitors like Henry Laurens have left behind testimonies to the shock they felt at seeing black and white couples in London.[31] Henry was disgusted by the numbers of mulatto children he saw there. He found the 'gust' of Englishwomen for black men incomprehensible (there was an imbalance in the sex ratio in favour of black men in Britain, so most couples were white woman/black man). Henry predicted darkly that at the present rate of interbreeding, by 1780 'there will be at least 20,000 mulatties in London only'.[32] Henry was not alone; mixing between the races in England was conspicuous enough to cause concern in certain circles that the lower orders would become 'mongrelized'.[33]

While Henry deplored sex between the races, Robert busied himself getting to know his new workmates. London servants were particularly notorious for their group loyalty, which, seen from the master's point of view, translated as organised insubordination.[34] Less than five months after his arrival in Fludyer Street, Robert had evidently achieved solidarity. Henry wrote a complaining letter to a friend in South Carolina: 'I have suffered through the winter under one misfortune, the dark and wet mornings, and the universal practice here of sitting up late at night and rising late in the morning, obliged me to be confined to bed, many hours when I would gladly have been employed in writing or walking abroad. The servants even my black servant would all comply with the fashion, if I quitted the bed it must be to starve in a cold room.' Just a week later Henry was apologising to a friend for the late repayment of a loan 'owing to a great error in my black servant'. Robert had been careless.[35] Already he was adopting the easy ways of a London servant. We can assume that for every note of displeasure that made its way into Henry's correspondence, many more were relayed to his bondsman verbally. Trouble was brewing. But Henry was a man who knew how to handle his slaves, and in particular Robert – or so he believed.

Back home in South Carolina, he managed his slaves through a fine-tuned 'carrot and stick' approach. On his remote outback plantations, where he barely knew the hands, he allowed hard-working slaves to grow small crops of their own which they sold to him. In return he sent them a small selection of consumer goods, chosen by him at fixed prices. This was to be the safety valve for those who had ambitions to improve their lot. For those who were just plain troublesome or lazy, there was the lash. As a last resort they could be sold on. Back on the home plantation at Ansonborough, Henry had favourite house slaves – 'Town Negroes', he called them, as opposed to the plantation drudges he barely saw. Dealing with the 'Town Negroes' gave the opportunity for a more personal touch. Henry treated them much as an English country gentleman would look after a faithful family retainer. For example, there was 'Mulatto Sam' Massey, who was a talented bricklayer and carpenter. Henry had bought him for £1,200 (three times the price of a field hand). In order to keep 'Mulatto Sam' sweet, as the expression goes, Henry gave him handouts of rum, sugar and cash. Then there was 'old Daddy Stepney', the gardener, who ended his days as an alcoholic, still under Laurens's protective wing. He cried tears of joy when Master Henry returned from England in 1774.[36]

Henry Laurens knew that the institution of slavery was one that could not be defended, and late in life he asserted that to 'save the honor' of the new United States, the abolition of slavery was necessary. But at the same time he seemed to indulge in a mind game whereby he convinced himself that his own slaves were so well treated that they didn't want to leave. His 'Town Negroes' undoubtedly played an important role in feeding his illusions. Once or twice he experimented with offering freedom to a few individual slaves, who by his own account refused it, saying they were happy in his service. 'I will venture to say, the whole are in more comfortable circumstances than any equal number of peasantry in Europe', he confidently pronounced.[37]

Robert was part of Henry's close-knit Ansonborough household staff. But men like Mulatto Sam – a skilful builder with a wife and family – and the aging and deferential Daddy Stepney would not be compelling role models for young Robert as he pondered his future. Closer to home in his mind was probably the experience of a young black footman at Ansonborough whom Henry had purchased only to find him hopelessly lazy – 'some smart flogging' would sort him out.[38] Robert, too, showed signs of a high spirit early in Henry's service. Glimpses of this emerge in Henry's correspondence. When Robert delivered a chaise and three horses to a nearby homestead, Henry warned the neighbour not to ask 'but order him to do what you would have done. Please to remember that those are the only terms upon which you are to expect his service.' Robert had to be driven. And above all Robert (still Scipio at that time) was not to be given money for his trouble: 'If you give Scipio more than meat and drink you contribute to root out the very little superficial goodness that I have endeavoured to plant in his thorny soil.'[39] There is no evidence that Henry ever flogged Robert, but the threat was always there. By the time they departed for London four years later, Henry believed he had taken the measure of Robert. He was a young man who needed to be kept firmly in his place to forestall trouble.

Much of Henry's system of management would go by the wayside once they reached the Great Metropolis. Henry could not command the nice control over rewards and punishments that he had back on the plantation. Like all London servants, Robert had too much time and money of his own to be fully under his master's control. Fraternising in the Deans' kitchen, waiting in a coffee house or tavern for Henry while he conducted his business, visiting downstairs with the servants in Berners Street – there were plenty of places and spaces where Robert could do and speak as he liked. When he carried messages for Henry he could go where he liked, too, and there was little Henry could do about it. And there was plenty that was new to see and hear in the Great City.

'Money does him no good', groaned Henry.[40] But Robert received no wages, so where could he get money unless from Henry? The practice of tipping servants was widespread in Georgian London, so much so that there had been several public campaigns to stamp it out. Servants in wealthy homes where there was frequent entertainment expected to receive a constant flow of tips from guests. This was such an established practice that an estimate of the tips to be expected was commonly included when reckoning a servant's salary. These tips were known as 'vails', and they were blamed as a root cause of the insolence of London servants. Effectively, they meant that servants only looked to their masters for part of their income, undermining their loyalty to the household they served.[41]

Robert would have received vails regularly as he carried out tasks for Henry around London. But there were still other ways to get money. Servants had to be given board money for their meals when they travelled alone or followed their masters to dinner in a coffee house or tavern, and it was common practice to pocket this and eat the master's leftovers, or make do with very plain fare.[42] Robert travelled often, with or without Henry, and he had plenty of chances to pocket some spare change in this way. On at least one occasion Henry tried to pay Robert so sparingly for his meal that he would have no change.[43] But he must have known it was in vain. He simply could not stop Robert from getting money.

If, in Henry's opinion, money did Robert no good, what was the young man doing with it? London had pubs that were dedicated servant hang-outs, where drinking and gaming took place. Then there was Vauxhall Gardens, the famous pleasure ground where music and entertainment could be had in a verdant setting of trees and walkways. Everyone ventured there, both high and low. Servants went to the play in Covent Garden, enjoying the spectacle from the gallery. Henry never specified what Robert did with his money that displeased him so much. One is tempted to think that if he were drinking or gaming, that would have come out. It's just as likely that when Robert had money, he simply found better things to do with his time than to be at Henry's beck and call. That was the experience of the generality of London masters.[44] It fits in with a grumpy remark Henry made to the effect that Robert did 'not work enough to earn his meat'.[45]

One wonders whether a 'smart flogging' would have sorted Robert out, but Henry probably felt more inhibited about this last resort in London than at Ansonborough. One could still beat servants in Georgian England, but the attitude was changing in the latter half of the century. The better sort of servants were taking masters to court if they thought their punishment was excessive – and winning. Henry's friends the Mannings had taken in their former maid after she was beaten by her new mistress. The maid received between £20–£30 in damages in a court action.[46] The occasional scandalous cases of English servants who were beaten to death that got into the newspapers always concerned poor, friendless apprentices. As we will see, American slaves in London were beaten, but the practice probably wasn't entirely respectable and hence less common than in the colonies. A contributor to the *Gentleman's Magazine* complained that the 'rigour and severity' required to 'make [blacks] useful' was 'impracticable' in London. In one respect this could be said to work to the advantage of the slave owners, because one of the 'excuses' for slavery

7 An English gentleman out hunting, accompanied by his liveried black servant, *c.*1765. The sportsman is Charles Lennox, third Duke of Richmond (1735–1806), who knew many absentee planters in London, including Ralph Izard and the West Indian John Baker.

that was commonly put forward in the metropolis was that slaves lived under far better conditions than the English poor. At least one historian has suggested that the sight of healthy, well-dressed servants from the plantations in the streets of London was a contributory factor in the general complacency of the English public towards slavery in this period.[47]

The notion that planters in London had to refrain from administering as many 'smart floggings' as they would have liked is borne out in a letter from a tobacco planter to his slave soon after returning to Virginia. It is dripping with the frustration he felt at having to hold off from his usual plantation system of management while abroad: 'You were very saucy while you were in England, and resisted me twice. There must be no more of that'. Back on the plantation, the man was warned, he would be 'tied up and slashed severely', and fitted with an iron collar if he persisted in such behaviour.[48]

The Virginia planter would no doubt have heartily agreed with Ben Franklin that London was a place 'where there are so many occasions of spoiling servants, if they are ever so good'. When Franklin wrote those words, he was referring to his own slave, King. King and another slave, Peter, had accompanied Franklin to London in 1757, when he crossed the Atlantic to act as agent for the colony of Pennsylvania. A year into the 'Electrical Doctor's' sojourn, King ran off. Franklin explained the situation to his wife:

> King, that you enquire after, is not with us. He ran away from our house, near two years ago, while we were absent in the country; but was soon found in Suffolk, where he had been taken in the service of a lady that was very fond of the merit of making him a Christian, and contributing to his education and improvement. As he was of little use, and often in mischief, Billy consented to her keeping him while we stay in England. So the lady sent him to school, has him taught to read and write, to play on the violin and French horn, with some other accomplishments more useful in a servant. Whether she will finally be willing to part with him, or persuade Billy to sell him to her, I know not.

'In the meantime,' concluded Franklin, with a hint of sour grapes, 'he is no expense to us.'[49]

King was not a charity case. The lady in Suffolk had hired him, probably as a footman. Employers sometimes taught servants to read and write. Learning the French horn was a fantastic bonus for King. The newspapers advertised £10 for an ordinary footman, and £15 if he could play the French horn.[50] Footmen who blew a French horn often rode behind carriages, and black footmen were probably sought after as a smart accessory.[51] King was picking up some priceless job skills, and he was undoubtedly working in a larger establishment than Franklin's plain London lodgings, which meant better vails. By running away, King had certainly bettered his position, but Franklin – although he had once been a runaway apprentice himself – did not extol the virtues of self-help.

When King started looking around for a better place, he surely perceived that there was a demand for black servants in England. Since the seventeenth century it had been fashionable for the English aristocracy to have black attendants. Fantastically dressed black serving boys were social accessories for the beau monde. Having a black servant started as a fad, but it was an established practice by the middle of the eighteenth century. Not only rich American planters but also aspiring middle-class English people increasingly regarded black servants as a badge of gentility.[52] By the time of the American Revolution, a British observer commented that 'it is no uncommon thing to see a British member of parliament have his *Negro slave* following him'.[53] But not all black servants were slaves.

One of London's most famous black servants was Soubise, the Duchess of Queensberry's favourite. Soubise's career demonstrated that in London it was possible for a black person – even a servant – to become a 'figure about town', a thing that would have been unthinkable in the colonies. Catherine Hyde, the Duchess of Queensberry, publicly lavished attention on her West Indian slave, Julius Soubise. She trained him as a riding and fencing master, gave him an expense account and brought him everywhere with her. Soubise became a perfumed dandy who hosted lavish dinners and kept a horse and a mistress of his own. Henry Laurens wrote home in disgust of 'him whom the Duchess of Queensberry delighteth to honour', suggesting (with a hint of paranoia) that the Duchess might purchase Soubise a seat in Parliament, if she could arrange for him to be elected 'sight unseen'.[54] Soubise ran up huge debts and was finally dispatched by his mistress to Bengal, where he headed a riding and fencing academy. He died there in a riding accident.[55]

8 A caricature of a stylishly dressed black dandy, possibly modelled after Julius Soubise.

Under the circumstances, the temptation to stay in Britain must have crossed Robert's mind. Running away like King would of course be the ultimate disobedience, and in one respect it looked easy. England had no laws for apprehending runaway slaves. Only criminals could be forcibly seized and detained; the slave codes of the colonies did not apply in their mother country. But as Robert knew, escape was not so simple. Many slave owners who came to Britain kept their slaves in bondage by simply flouting the law.

There were men in London who made a living recapturing runaway slaves.[56] Slaves were sometimes bound, gagged and dragged away in public when their masters deemed it necessary.[57] Unpleasant scenes could occur. A woman embarking for the West Indies from Britain recalled that when she first came on board, her brother 'warned us not to be alarmed if we heard a noise and screaming on deck, for that the boat had gone off to bring Ovid, our owner's poor devil of a Negro man on board, who was to be laid in irons, 'till we were fairly out at sea'.[58] The captain of the ship was taking no chances with Ovid who, knowing he was returning to the West Indies, might flit before he could be secured below decks. The story was a familiar one.

As the numbers of slaves on London's streets increased after 1760, the more unlovely aspects of the 'peculiar institution' gradually seeped into everyday London life. English law did not legitimate slavery, but slaves were nevertheless bought and sold on English soil in a legal twilight where slavery's status remained undecided. Slaves were routinely advertised for sale in the newspapers. Some were the spin-offs of London's slave trade, as in the case of two 'fine Negro boys' who could be viewed 'on board the Molly . . . from Africa', at anchor at Horsleydown opposite the Tower of London in 1756. Some were from the colonies: '[A] fine healthy Negro boy, between ten and eleven years of age', ran a 1769 advertisement offering for sale a lad who had been born in America and had lived in England for the past five years.[59] There were many such advertisements. A 'Negro girl, aged about fifteen years' was advertised for sale in the *Public Ledger* in 1767. A *'well made, good-tempered black boy'* who had 'lately had the smallpox' was advertised for sale to 'any Gentleman' in a London paper of 1769. Runaway slaves were also openly advertised in the London papers. A slave girl ran away from her mistress in Hatton Garden, and a reward was offered for her return.[60] In 1768 one of the numerous Beckford clan, living in Pall Mall, published an advertisement for a slave boy who had disappeared.[61] Sometimes 'wanted' ads appeared for slaves. A prospective buyer in fashionable Conduit Street in Mayfair sought a 'Blackamoor boy, of eight or nine years of age', perhaps to train as a footman.[62]

Many, probably most, Londoners looked the other way, but one, Granville Sharp, decided to challenge this alien import from the colonies. Less than a year after Robert reached London, Sharp became involved in a landmark legal battle that would challenge the plight of slaves in the capital. Its outcome would deepen the sense of uneasiness between Robert and his master as Henry felt his control slipping away.

Granville Sharp was an English civil servant living in London. He became interested in the plight of slaves in the empire's capital in 1765, when he met a young man named Jonathan Strong. Strong had appeared one day, badly beaten, at the surgery of Sharp's brother in Mincing Lane (where also lived the West Indian Vaughan family, friends of the Laurenses). Strong was from Barbados and had been brought to London by his master, planter and lawyer David Lisle. One day Lisle beat Strong with a pistol until he was almost dead. Thinking him lamed and useless, Lisle threw Strong out. Now destitute and in need of immediate medical attention, Strong heard of Dr Sharp's surgery, which offered free medical care for the poor in the mornings. For the next few months the Sharps arranged for Strong to be cared for in hospital. When he was released, he found a job running errands for a surgeon in Fenchurch Street.

Two years later Lisle spied young Strong, now restored to health, running in the street. Here was an opportunity to make some money. Lisle arranged for Strong to be kidnapped and locked up in a City holding place for persons who had been accused of crimes. He then sold Strong for £30 to a new master, Jamaican James Kerr, who arranged for Strong to be transported out of the kingdom to the West Indies by one Captain Laird. But Granville Sharp took the matter to the lord mayor. The lord mayor determined that as Strong had committed no crime, there was no basis on which to hold him against his will, and he was released. Captain Laird then attempted to lay claim to Strong as Kerr's personal property. Sharp threatened to charge him with assault if he tried.[63]

This was the crux of the matter. Either Strong was a slave and someone's property, or not. English law did not specifically recognise slavery. Furthermore, even if Strong were a slave in England, there was no law entitling anyone to hold him against his will unless he had committed a crime. The case of Jonathan Strong ended inconclusively. But he remained in London, a free man, and Granville Sharp was primed to take up the issue again.

The legal predicament was that although slavery was embedded in the laws of the American colonies, it was not explicitly recognised in English common law. Were American slaves, then, still slaves when they stepped onto the shores of England? Or was slavery nonexistent in the mother country? And even if they were still slaves, did the colonial laws providing for the control of slaves apply in England? Did English law permit slaves to be apprehended and forcibly returned to the colonies with their masters, whenever those masters should decide to return to their plantations? These same issues would be battled out in the United States between the North and the South in the years leading up to the American Civil War, as northern, free states resisted Federal fugitive slave laws, and slaves like Dred Scott attempted to win their freedom through the courts on the grounds of residency in a free state.

The case of Jonathan Strong was only a prelude. In February 1772, just a few months after Henry and Robert reached London, the famous Somerset Case had its first hearing. The case would stir up hope on both sides of the Atlantic that slaves could gain their freedom. It began when an American slave in England, James Somerset, went to court to challenge his master's right to return him forcibly to his home in the colonies. Somerset was the servant of a Scotsman, Charles Stewart, who had been residing in Boston, Massachusetts. In late 1769 Stewart had taken Somerset with him on a business trip to London. After two years Somerset ran away. Stewart had him recaptured, clapped in irons and put on board a ship bound for Jamaica, where he was to be returned to slavery. But the story didn't end there. Witnesses had seen Somerset overpowered and forced by Stewart's men. They obtained a writ of habeas corpus, Somerset was released, and a trial was set for January. Charles Stewart and the captain of the Jamaica ship, John Knowles, declared that they were the injured parties; Somerset had 'without any lawful authority' run away from his master. They wanted to reclaim their property. Somerset, on the contrary, saw himself as the aggrieved party; he had been unlawfully seized and held, in effect assaulted and kidnapped.[64]

Granville Sharp, by now a known advocate for the rights of the black population in London, quickly became involved. Sharp engaged legal counsel for Somerset. The case, which dragged on for months, was widely canvassed in the newspapers, and stirred up a great deal of popular antipathy to slavery. But the presiding judge, Chief Justice Mansfield, did not want to make a landmark decision on the issue of slavery and slaves' rights in England. On 22 June 1772 he delivered his final decision. On the question of whether a slave remained a slave in England, he said that it was too weighty a matter to be inferred from existing laws, and only a positive Act of Parliament could establish it for certain. But there were no English laws that empowered a master to force his servant out of the kingdom, even if that servant had deserted the master.[65] 'No master was ever allowed here to take a slave by force to be sold abroad because he deserted from his service', the Chief Justice summed up, 'or for any other reason whatever; we cannot say, the cause set forth by this return is allowed or approved by the laws of this kingdom, and therefore the man must be discharged.'[66]

Lord Mansfield's decision was hailed as ending slavery in Britain. And he has gone down in history for just that. But Mansfield himself was exasperated by this misreading of his very narrow, carefully worded judgement. He did not want to have to rule on the legality of the institution of slavery itself, which was a can of worms. Britain's colonies had laws recognising slavery, and these laws had been approved by His Majesty's Privy Council. Mansfield carefully side-stepped the central issue.

Despite Mansfield's cautious approach, at the heart of the Somerset Case lay the eternal principle that a human being cannot be property. But the case also crystallised the way the American colonies looked from their capital city. It established once and for all that slave owning was a colonial thing. Britain remained an asylum for liberty, untainted by the unsavoury practices of its New World possessions.[67] What deepened this impression was the wide-spread misunderstanding of Mansfield's ruling, that it abolished slavery in the mother country. It did no such thing; the status of slavery in England remained in a kind of legal limbo until 1833, when the Slavery Abolition Act ended slavery in the British colonies. But that was too fine a point for public consumption, and the English mood in the wake of the decision was distinctly self-congratulatory. Slaves 'touch our country, and their shackles fall', wrote the poet William Cowper inaccurately and melodramatically. Mansfield in his decision had labelled slavery 'odious', and the mud stuck.[68]

Where slavery was concerned, Londoners tarred all the colonies with the same brush. The clear distinction between North and South, slave and free states, that was to be so important in the years leading up to the American Civil War had not yet been drawn in the metropolis. Ben Franklin, the leading advocate for the colonies in London, had tried to correct this impression in the London papers, mapping out slavery in the colonies thus: 'what slaves there are belong chiefly to the old rich inhabitants, near the navigable waters, who are few compared with the numerous families of back-settlers, that have scarce any slaves among them. In truth, there is not, take North America through, perhaps, one family in a hundred that has a slave in it.'[69] Franklin was provoked to write this in response to a public jeer from Granville Sharp that 'The *boasted liberty* of our American colonies' had not so much as a right 'to that sacred name' as long as the practice of slavery continued.[70]

Franklin's newspaper defence failed to correct the metropolitan image of the colonies. Most Londoners did not know a great deal about America, but what they did know squared with the impression of a land of slave compounds and 'Negro-drivers'. In part this arose from a confused knowledge of American geography. To many Englishmen in the eighteenth century the northern and southern colonies were a jumbled blur. As one traveller put it, the English were 'eccentric upon the New World's geography and social arrangements, transporting the backwoods to the seashore, linking New England to the slave states', and peopling it all 'indiscriminately with Yankees, blacks, and savages'.[71] A London merchant asked a visitor from New York whether Boston 'was not the capital of Philadelphia'.[72] A Connecticut man was disgusted when a 'respectable counselor-at-law' asked whether Philadelphia was in the East or West Indies.[73] A single newspaper article from Ben Franklin would not make much of a dent in all this.

But even if they couldn't point to them on a map, the people of London were nevertheless very aware of the southern plantation colonies, far more so than they were of the colonies to the north. They had good reason, for the products of the plantation colonies had transformed Britain's economy and way of life in the past 150 years. Evidence of their existence greeted one everywhere in London's streets. They were eaten, smoked, snorted and drank daily in the empire's capital. Sugar, tobacco and rum were everywhere, advertised in the newspapers, sold in shops, puffed and consumed in taverns, coffee houses and drawing rooms. Snuff-taking was at an all-time high, even among the ladies. Most of the tobacco came from the Chesapeake. Most of the rum came from the West Indies. Portrayals of the blacks who cultivated these crops were traditionally included in the London signboards and advertisements selling these goods. Such portrayals were so widespread that one art historian has described Georgian London as ' "swamped" by images of blacks'.[74] The port of London was the main point of departure for English emigrants looking for a better life in America, and almost all of these emigrants were destined for the tropical and semi-tropical colonies whose goods were continuously being unloaded at London's busy wharves – Maryland, Virginia, the West Indies, South Carolina and Georgia. Of the northern colonies, only Pennsylvania was a popular choice.[75]

And since 1760, as we have seen, the numbers of wealthy planters with slaves who walked the streets of London had risen sharply. The fact that West Indians were classed as Americans in pre-Revolutionary London added to the confusion. One English writer in support of colonial rights complained: 'How many people are there, and those too of no small figure, who know no difference between the inhabitants of *North America*, and those of the *West-India* Islands?'[76] But even he had to admit that colonists from the southern colonies *were* rather like West Indians, with their 'show and extravagance' and their retinue of 'dark attendants'.[77] These were the colonial Americans that Londoners actually noticed in their streets. To Georgian Londoners, typical Americans were the mixed-race folk of the mainland and West Indian plantations, not Franklin's white homespun 'back-settlers'.

Some white Americans complained that Englishmen thought Americans were all black. There is plenty of evidence that this was a widespread impression in England at the time, no doubt the result of the fact that most ordinary Englishmen, when they thought of the settled parts of America, thought of plantations and slave gangs. Marylander Daniel Dulany, Jr., in England in the 1750s, commented sarcastically: 'Perhaps in less than a century, the ministers may know that we inhabit part of a vast continent, and the rural gentry hear that we are not all black . . .'[78] Thomas Ruston of Pennsylvania met an Englishman who claimed that the people of Pennsylvania practised 'a promiscuous copulation between white and black' in order to boost the colony's population.[79] Just before the start of the American Revolution, Bostonian Josiah Quincy was told by a British army officer that two-thirds of the people of Britain 'thought the Americans were all Negroes!' English crowds who came to gawp at American prisoners of war at the beginning of the American Revolution were astonished to find them all white. 'Why,' cried one, 'they look like our people.'[80] Bostonian James Otis, one of the Sons of Liberty, fumed that 'the common people of *England*' pictured the colonists as 'a compound mongrel mixture of *English, Indian, and Negro*'. Just as bad, he wrote, New England, New York and Virginia were commonly taken in Britain to be West Indian islands.[81] He spluttered to his English audience: 'You think most if not all the colonists are Negroes and mulattoes – You are wretchedly mistaken – Ninety nine in a hundred in the northern colonies are white, and there is as good blood flowing in their veins, save the royal blood, as any in the three kingdoms.'[82]

But colonial writers like Otis and Franklin expostulated in vain. Try as they might to sink the black population of the mainland colonies into the background, success eluded them. Whatever misconceptions Londoners might have about life in the colonies, they knew that African Americans were an integral part of the colonial scene. The evidence was right before them in the growing black presence in London's streets. The vast majority of Londoners in

Franklin's day were most certainly not human-rights activists; the anti-slavery movement would not get going until the late 1780s. Granville Sharp's voice was a lone one at this time. But Londoners simply knew what some white colonists wished they would ignore, that the American colonies were a place where slavery was central to the way of life, not an exception, and the Americans themselves were a colonial, multi-racial people. Franklin's implication in the London papers that slavery was a dying institution was very far from the truth. The real figure for slave-owning households in America was more like one in ten, not one in a hundred as he had claimed.[83] Overall, the black population in the mainland colonies during the century made up about a fifth of the total population, and was growing faster than the white population.[84] Slavery was not sectional; it was found throughout the colonies. True enough, there were fewer slaves in the north, but they were still a visible presence in every seaport. Somerset and his master, Charles Stewart, were from Boston, Massachusetts, not Virginia or South Carolina.

In the twenty-first century an American journalist would write that in today's America, 'anything all-white' is now 'deficient, inappropriate, un-American'.[85] His statement is the culmination of more than half a century of racial conflict and struggle. But two centuries earlier, eighteenth-century Londoners had known that 'American' did not necessarily equate with 'white'. Americans were a colonial people, English, Scottish, Irish, European and African, direct spin-offs of Britain's Atlantic trading empire. Most Georgian Englishmen, if asked to picture a colonial American, would probably conjure up an image of a planter with a slave at his heels rather than a homespun farmer. Robert and Henry were the typical Americans of Georgian London. Their very different adventures in the Great City were two sides of the same coin.

Dozens of black Londoners had crammed into Westminster Hall to hear the final decision on the Somerset Case on 22 June 1772, and they openly celebrated afterwards.[86] What they were to discover was that (like the Brown Decision against segregation of schools in 1954) court rulings were mere paper unless they were enforced. Long after the Somerset case blacks continued to be bought and sold in England, and forced out of the kingdom to the colonies by their masters.[87] But that was far from clear on the day of the ruling and for months afterwards.

Henry was not in London to hear Mansfield's decision. At the end of May he left for the continent to take Harry and John to their new school in Geneva. Robert was to stay behind, to fetch little Jemmy from his new boarding school near Birmingham and escort him to Shropshire, where he would spend the school holidays. By the eve of Henry's departure, there had been four hearings in Westminster Hall right around the corner from Fludyer Street, and the newspapers were full of the business. Henry was taking it all very lightly. 'They say supper is ready, otherwise I was going to tell a long and comical story, of a trial between a Mr. Stuart and his black man James Somerset, at King's Bench, for liberty', he wrote to a business associate and slave trader in South Carolina.

The fact was that Henry's West Indian friends in London, who had become very involved in the case, were confident that the court would decide in favour of the slave owners. Slavery had to be legitimate in England, they reasoned, because it was legitimate in the colonies, and colonial laws were required to conform to those of England. The King's Privy Council had from the beginning approved every colonial law relating to slavery. Parliament itself had sponsored the creation of the Royal African Company a century ago, whereby English traders could carry slaves from Africa to the American colonies. With such a history, how likely was it that the British legal establishment would make a decision that hurt the property rights of wealthy colonists like Henry and his friends?

But if the outcome was so certain, why, in the months leading up to the trial, did Lord Mansfield repeatedly urge Mr Stewart voluntarily to liberate Somerset in order to avoid a ruling? The ominous sign was ignored; Stewart would do no such thing. After his final refusal, Mansfield was said to have remarked fatalistically: 'If the parties will have judgment, "fiat justitia, ruat coelum" ["let justice be done though the heavens fall"]'.[88]

Henry was not expecting the heavens to fall. In May he had some sort of confrontation with Robert, in which he came out on top. He alluded to it in the same letter about the 'comical' Somerset case: 'My man Robert Scipio Laurens says, that Negroes that want to be free here, are fools', he wrote gleefully. 'He behaved a little amiss one day, and I told him I would not be plagued by him. If he did not choose to stay with me, to go about his business. He said he would serve no body else, and has behaved excellently well here ever since.'[89] What had triggered the argument between Henry and Robert? It sounds as if Robert's heedless behaviour had come to a head. Henry had resorted to brinkmanship, and won. Henry's mood was triumphant; with his good humour restored, his paternalistic feelings reasserted themselves. Writing to friends in Shifnal in Shropshire, where Robert and Jemmy would spend the holidays, he detailed Robert's duties in an indulgent tone:

Jacky, Harry, and myself will leave London at 4 o'clock this afternoon. Robert will go tomorrow evening in the Birmingham Fly, and wait upon Jemmy, if Mr. Austin desires it to Shifnal for the Whitsun holidays. I have enjoined him to be careful of the child, and believe he will be so. You should have timely notice of my intended return to London, in order to send Robert to meet me. I have paid his passage in the coach, and given him ten shillings in his pocket. If you should find it necessary to give him a further supply, I will thankfully repay that, and all the expenses which may be incurred on his account. He has promised to attend the plough very diligently. If any old woman in your neighbourhood will make a couple of strong dowlass shirts for him, I will pay for these also. I gave him two yesterday, but he craves more.[90]

The old, familiar relationship of master and slave was restored in Henry's mind. He waxed generous about the shirts and the spending money. But Robert probably knew that Henry was simply up to his old trick of threatening a slave with freedom in order to be told what he wanted to hear. Robert was not an Ansonborough 'Town Negro' for nothing. He roundly disclaimed all desire for freedom. As we will see, Robert knew his man.

Jemmy would be spending his school holidays at the home of George Austin in Shifnal, Shropshire. Austin, a former business partner of Henry, had lived in South Carolina for a number of years before returning to England in 1762. The fortune he amassed from his Carolina plantations enabled him to purchase Aston Hall, an elegant Georgian mansion. Nearby lived another of Henry's former business partners, George Appleby. Henry visited both men frequently during his sojourn in England, taking Robert with him. In fact, he and Robert had been to Aston Hall just a few weeks before his departure for Geneva.[91] But Robert had never travelled to Shifnal alone before. It would be a journey of four or five days by coach, first to Winson Green near Birmingham to collect Jemmy from his school, and then on to Shifnal itself.

Shifnal was a place that Robert would come to know almost as well as London. In the summer of 1772, while the Somerset Case was making the news in London and Henry and his two oldest sons were touring the continent, Robert and Jemmy spent over two months in this quiet Shropshire village. An ancient settlement dating back to Saxon times, Shifnal was set in the green countryside, a far cry from the lights of London. Its medieval churches and half-timbered houses were atmospheric enough for Charles Dickens to depict them in his *Old Curiosity Shop*.[92] By Georgian times it had livened up enough to boast several coaching inns and a number of fine

Georgian houses, but it must have nevertheless been a profound sea-change for those used to London. Yet even here Robert had the company of fellow slaves from the plantations. Here at Shifnal were Appleby's Cato and at least two other slaves who lived at Aston Hall with the Austins.[93] In this sleepy village, then, the four black Americans must have heard word of Lord Mansfield's final ruling back in London – 'The man must be discharged.'

By the time Henry returned from the continent in early August, Lord Mansfield's decision had been out for over a month, and the West Indians in London were making a fruitless attempt to draft a Parliamentary Bill to give legal recognition to slavery in England.[94] Slave owners everywhere were feeling insecure. The London newspapers, never noted for their accuracy, reported the decision as ending slavery in England. Some slaves took it as a cue to run away. A few weeks after Mansfield's judgment was published, a Bristol slave owner wrote to Charles Stewart (Somerset's 'owner'), saying his own black servant had run off and declared himself now to be free.[95] Charles Carroll, Barrister of Annapolis, Maryland, in London with his wife in 1772, had 'servant trouble' within months of the case. His manservant Adam left him after listening to 'ill advisers'. Finding that he couldn't survive on his own in the metropolis, Adam returned to the household through the intercession of Joshua Johnson, a Maryland tobacco merchant in London whose daughter would one day marry John Quincy Adams and live in the White House.[96]

Far away in the colonies, slave owners worried that their runaway slaves would make for Britain. Examples appeared in the colonial newspapers. In one, a Georgian slave owner advertised for his runaway man Bacchus, whom he feared had found a berth on a ship bound for England. In the remote backwoods of Georgia, Bacchus had heard of the Somerset decision and believed he would be free if he could set foot on English soil.[97]

Naturally, Henry Laurens did not like the ruling, but he was guarded in his opinion in letters home.[98] Characteristically, his disapproval was expressed in actions rather than words. Less than a month after returning to England from the continent, Henry was helping George Appleby to dispatch his man Cato to South Carolina. A visit to Shifnal in early September ended abruptly and Henry 'posted to town faster than I had intended greatly on account of your man Cato'. With his usual efficiency Henry arranged to have Cato put on board the brig *Charming Polly*, then lying in the Thames. She was bound for Savannah, Georgia. Such was the haste to get Cato safely on board that he did not wait for a Charleston-bound vessel. Once in Savannah, Cato would be 'conveyed to Charleston' by Joseph Clay, a business associate of Henry.

Writing to Mr Clay, Henry explained that the 'Negro man named Cato' was 'the property' of the Applebys, and would Clay please ensure 'that proper precautions may be taken immediately upon arrival at Savanna to prevent elopement'.[99] In bundling Cato back to the plantations, Henry did not hesitate to act in contravention of the Somerset decision. Lord Mansfield was simply wrong as far as he was concerned.

Cato, who had been living in Shropshire for the past ten years, had probably expressed himself too freely at a time when slave owners in England were feeling insecure. Now he was to be sent home. Perhaps Cato had been away from the plantation for too long and had lost touch with the harsh realities of the master–slave relationship. Robert had shown greater wisdom back in May, when he reassured Master Henry that 'Negroes that want to be free here, are fools'. In light of what happened to Cato, it is hard to believe that Henry really meant it when he told Robert 'if he did not choose to stay with me, to go about his business'. At any rate he certainly was in earnest about helping the Applebys to keep hold of Cato. Getting away from Henry Laurens would not be that easy.

There were three typical routes for one who wanted to escape from slavery in England: to somehow start getting wages and then 'certify a free status'; to marry an English person; or to simply run away.[100] None of these was guaranteed to work. All carried risks. Running away, if not planned properly, could leave one starving in the streets.

We do not know whether Robert was meditating upon a means of escape in the summer of 1772, but for now his relationship with his master was running smoothly. In early October Henry left for another trip to Geneva. He travelled with George Appleby, one of the young Austins, and John Faucheraud Grimké, a South Carolinian who was studying at Cambridge. 'We shall fill a genteel hired coach', wrote Henry to Grimké, 'and be attended by an interpreting servant and my black man.'[101] So Robert was to see Europe. Geneva was the destination, but on their return journey they took in the south of France, stopping at the Mediterranean seaports of Marseilles and Toulon. Henry's Huguenot ancestry no doubt influenced him to visit La Rochelle on France's west coast as well – and Nantes, which at that time was France's biggest slaving port.

Henry had not brought Robert along on his previous continental jaunt. This, then, was a sign that his bondsman was currently in his good graces. But good feeling never seemed to last long between the two Americans. Back in London by Christmas, Henry set off almost immediately on another tour, this time a very English one: Oxford, Stratford-upon-Avon, Bristol – and of course Birmingham and Shifnal. Robert did not go with him. The day after he left London, Henry wrote to his landlord, Mr Deans, instructing him, 'If Robert is not come away from London when this reaches you let him remain till you hear from me again. I desire he may not have access to my trunks between you and me.'[102] It sounds as if he did not trust Robert with his baggage. We know Robert craved money and Henry tried to prevent him from getting it. Was Robert resorting to theft? Whatever was going on, Henry did not want Robert with him.

And that inclination persisted for the remainder of his stay in England. In April 1773 Henry was off to the continent again to see his sons in Geneva. It would be an absence of almost three months. Robert was to be banished to Shifnal. 'I accept your kind permission to let Robert stay at Aston until my return from Geneva,' wrote Henry to George Austin. 'I have admonished him to behave well and it will vex me exceedingly if he should be troublesome.'[103]

Was Robert troublesome? The record is silent. Henry soon had other things to think about, for shortly after Christmas he began planning his return to South Carolina. His three sons were safely settled, John and Harry at Geneva and Jemmy at Winson Green, and his plantations needed his personal attention. There were many loose ends to be tied up before he left England. 'I have money, rice, and deer skins scattered in several hands here and in Bristol,' he wrote from Fludyer Street. A Charleston merchant was pressuring Henry to secure him 'several cargoes of Negroes' for next summer, and Henry was talking to his associates in London.[104] In the midst of all this the momentous news of the Boston Tea Party on 16 December 1773 arrived in London. Draconian plans to close the port of Boston as a punishment for the riot were being mooted in government circles. Soon Henry would be involved in an ambitious plan to organise a petition to the Crown and Parliament on behalf of beleaguered Boston, a foreshadowing of the leading role he would play in the American Revolution.

Master Henry was busy, and he kept Robert busy too, running errands back and forth in the city and the countryside. It was while he was on an errand to Henry's old friends in Shifnal in February 1774 that the thunderbolt fell. 'Foolish rascally Robert', raged Henry when he heard the news. For Robert had been arrested for burglary. He had broken into Aston Hall, the home of Henry's friends the Austins, and stolen a gammon and 'other things of value'. Or so it said in the papers, for the *Shrewsbury Chronicle* ran the story two days before Henry heard it.[105] Henry was livid.

9 Aston Hall, Shifnal, Shropshire.

In a lengthy letter to George Appleby, Henry poured out the history of his relationship with Robert. 'I paid a valuable consideration for him', he recalled, 'and at his own earnest petition too to save him from transportation to the West Indies, where he would probably have felt the weight of slavery in a degree which he has been quite unacquainted with in my hands.' Henry had treated Robert with humanity, even indulgently at times, 'exempting him from punishment for capital faults, from a consideration of instances of past merits admitted, and the security of his own promises of amendment. I brought him to England in consequence of his *own* entreaties, founded upon his *own* apprehensions that he should not be so well used if I left him behind me . . .'

By this account of things, Robert owed his master a lot. Henry had stood between Robert and the horrors of a slave compound in the West Indies. He had brought his young bondsman to England to save him from unspecified ill usage were he to remain at Ansonborough. And he had refrained from meting out to Robert the same fate as befell the unfortunate Cato. For he now admitted that he had had thoughts of spiriting Robert, too, back to the plantations. 'I have had frequent opportunities of sending him to America and have been more frequently advised by my friends to that measure,' he wrote.

Henry was no doubt disburdening himself of months of pent-up frustration, and defending himself at the same time. He had no great desire to retain Robert as a slave, he claimed, and his refusal to force the youth back to America was proof. 'Unhappy wretch, I should have been much better pleased to have heard, that his life and conversation were daily refuting my predictions and that his crimes had ended with his ingratitude to me.'

And yet Master Henry was not ready to let Robert go. He thought the situation over. Burglary was a hanging offence in England. 'Bad as he has been, I would not wish him hanged for stealing bacon, which a Negro counts a crime, to be cancelled by a flogging,' he wrote. George Appleby thought Robert might only receive 'the light penalty of transportation' instead. If that was the case, Henry had an idea. Transportation would of course mean he was sent to the colonies. If Henry were to contract with government officials to carry out the sentence, he could take personal charge of Robert's transportation. He knew of an instance where this had been done before. And Robert would still be his! 'If he is transported to America it will be impossible for him to escape slavery and no man in the world has so just a claim upon him as I have. He is my property according to the laws of this land as well as of that country.'

What had prompted Robert to steal from Aston Hall, a place where he was well known? Robert, as we have seen, had always wanted more money than Henry was willing to give him. But there was more behind the burglary than that. When he first heard of Robert's arrest, Henry was told that there was to be an additional charge of bigamy. In the event, Robert was never charged with bigamy, and Henry never mentioned it again.[106] What the hint of bigamy reveals is that Robert had an English sweetheart in Shifnal. In his initial burst of outrage at Robert's disaster, Henry marvelled at the taste of English ladies in favouring 'Negroes', and the indolence of English gentlemen in tolerating it.[107] As there is no reason to think that Robert was ever married (slave marriages in any case had no legal standing in the colonies[108]), the would-be bigamist must have been the lady in the case.

Bigamy was a common crime in Georgian England, because divorce was not an option for most. Ordinary people sometimes got out of a bad marriage by simply moving away from their homes and remarrying, hoping and expecting that former spouses would never hear of them again. Parish records were notoriously hard to access, and communications in country areas were still rather basic. For these reasons bigamy charges, where brought, were often dropped. A bigamous marriage between Robert and an Englishwoman, if the couple got away with it, might have paved the way for Robert to escape slavery. Such a scheme would need money. Perhaps that is what drove Robert to take the risk of breaking into Aston Hall and helping himself to a few things.

Henry did not speculate about Robert's motives, but it could not have escaped him that the young man was chafing badly under his authority. Yet Robert, it seemed, could never do enough to convince Henry to give up on him. The trial was set for 19 March. Robert awaited it in the county gaol, going under the name of John Moreton. Once again his name had been changed, probably at the insistence of the Applebys. Genteel eighteenth-century families did not like to have their household affairs made public in a courtroom.[109] Nine days before the trial, Henry wrote to George Appleby with fuller instructions on how to assume responsibility for Robert's transportation to the colonies. 'His value will not be very great even if I recover him,' reflected Henry. 'He is a sad rascal, unprincipled, ungrateful, and will never be better.' But Henry was convinced that under his firm hand Robert's ways could still be mended. 'Though he is not prompt in good deeds, yet there may be ways and means devised for restraining him hereafter from committing gross evils and compelling him to earn more than barely his own bread by labour.'[110] Perhaps Robert's reclamation would involve the 'smart flogging' from which he had been exempt in England.

Why had Henry brought Robert to England with him in the first place? He had surely proved to be more trouble than he was worth. The usual reason given, that a slave from the plantations was cheaper than a London servant, falls apart under a closer inspection of the finances. In 1772 an English footman-valet was paid 15 guineas a year.[111] It had cost Henry half that just to inoculate Robert against the smallpox. He had also been obliged to pay Robert's passage to England. The total cost of the Laurens family's passage to England had been £100 – no small sum, whatever Robert's share of it.[112] Once in England, Robert's 'market value' automatically dropped. Granville Sharp reckoned that a trained house servant brought to England from the West Indies could only be sold for half his value once he set foot in the mother country.[113] And there were Robert's expenses. Free English servants had their room and board paid for by their employers, but they usually paid for at least some of their clothes.[114] If servants from the country came down with the smallpox when they reached London, they were often kicked out into the streets. But Henry had to cover all of Robert's expenses, large or small – clothes, doctor's bills, travel, even when unrelated to his work. When Henry banished Robert to Shifnal, in April 1773, simply to get him out of the way during another jaunt to Europe – a circumstance that would surely have led to a white servant's dismissal – the cost of the trip one way was at least a guinea, and Henry was bound to cover his bondsman's expenses while in Shifnal.[115] Bringing Robert to England was hardly a bargain.

Granville Sharp suggested that a planter brought a slave with him to England simply because the planter 'prefers the constrained service of slaves to the willing attendance of freeman'.[116] There were American planters who confessed to finding white servants intimidating; it was harder to keep them in their place.[117] And perhaps nouveau riche Londoners felt the same way, judging by the growing popularity of black servants in the metropolis. James Fenimore Cooper, in England in the early nineteenth century, gave as his opinion that 'The negro, bond or free, is treated much more kindly and with greater friendship, than most of the English domestics; the difference in colour, with the notions that have grown up under them, removing all distrust of danger from familiarity.'[118] Cooper probably did not have much first-hand knowledge of a slave's life, but he had identified the same predilection for black over white servants that Sharp had described in more judgemental terms. The racial divide made it easier for each party to know its place.

But for Henry Laurens the old, comfortable plantation dynamic fell apart in England. He discovered the bitter truth of the words of an English contemporary who wrote that London servants had 'little attachment to those they serve; . . . self is the sole motive'.[119] If Henry had looked more critically at Robert instead of taking him for granted, he might have noticed that the young man had shown considerable purpose and enterprise in directing his own life. At the start of their relationship it was he who had prevailed upon Henry to purchase him in a bid to escape being sold to the West Indies. Next he had convinced Henry to take him to England. Even before he set foot in Falmouth, Robert knew that he wanted to cultivate a certain image in the capital. He changed his name; he made new friends; he avoided the fate of his fellow slave Cato by reassuring Henry that he did not want his freedom. Now, for the first time, Robert's initiative had landed him where he did not want to be. He was locked in the county gaol, awaiting trial.

But where Robert's enterprise failed him, he was going to be saved by a fantastic stroke of luck. For 'John Moreton' was not sentenced at the Assizes to hanging or transportation. Instead, he was branded on the hand and imprisoned for twelve months.[120]

Detained at His Majesty's pleasure, Robert was finally where Henry could not get him. Henry would have heard the full details of the verdict when he came to Shifnal two months after the trial. Robert's name (or rather, any of his names) never appeared in Henry's correspondence again.

In November 1774 Henry Laurens embarked for America. The start of the War of Independence was only a few months away, and Henry would soon figure prominently in the patriot cause. By the next year he was the president of South Carolina's Provincial Congress. He rose to become president of the Continental Congress in 1777. Two years later he was sent abroad to negotiate an alliance between the new United States and Holland. Captured en route, he found himself in London once again, this time as a prisoner in the Tower. His fifteen-month confinement in England's most famous prison was well publicised in the press. Henry had come back to London as a famous rebel rather than the private, prosperous and respectable British merchant who had brought his sons to school in Chelsea in 1771.

Did Robert hear of his former master's incarceration? It is impossible to tell, because once he disappeared from Henry's correspondence, he effectively disappeared from the pages of history. But for one brief moment the mists of time clear, and we are left with a final glimpse of Scipio Robert Laurens John Moreton. On 10 September 1777 'John Moreton (a Black)' testified against one Mary Slugg at London's Old Bailey. For once we can have the story in Robert's own words:

> I came from High Wickham to see after a place; I was disappointed of the place, and did not know where to go for a lodging; I met a young man in the street, who took me to a public house, and asked the landlord if I could lodge there; he said, no, his house was full; the prisoner and another woman came in; she said she could lodge me; I went home with her, and went to bed; I told her I was not able to give her any money, I would give her my handkerchief I had on my neck; I pulled off my things and laid them by my bedside; when I waked in the morning I missed my waistcoat, my hatband, and also a knife out of my pocket; there were some women there in the morning; they laughed at me; I saw the prisoner at the door about two hours after, and took her up.[121]

This sounds like the Robert we have come to know, gregarious and competent. Mary Slugg claimed 'John Moreton' gave her his waistcoat to pawn, but the court took Robert's word over hers and she was sentenced to a whipping. So fewer than two and a half years after Robert's release from gaol, he was back in service, and managing without Henry. If he was not rich, he was at least making ends meet, for at the Old Bailey trial he had a silver hatband, a knife and clothes that would do for service in a London home. And he was free. We don't know whether he had his Shropshire 'wife' with him, or how he fared in London. But we wish him well as he disappears from our view.

CHAPTER THREE

English Lessons in London:
A Tale of Two Teenagers

The warm afternoon sun sifted through the window upon the boy's fair hair and the olive-green shell of the turtle. The boy was concentrating all his skill on the paper before him as he carefully sketched the lines and curves of the animal. The turtle was lethargic, trapped in surroundings where it had no glimpse of the slow-moving water and lush green foliage that was its home. Both were caught up in their separate American reveries, the boy of South Carolina's unexplored natural world, the turtle of the Altamaha river snails and crayfish it craved after weeks at the mercy of captors who did not know what it liked to eat.

Neither could know that in a few months they would become objects of intense interest thousands of miles away in a narrow, dim room off a noisy London courtyard. In humble Crane Court met the illustrious Royal Society, the premier club for Georgian England's great philosophers and scientists. For them the Florida softshell was a miracle, a wonderful new addition to the fifteen species of hard-shell turtles already classified by their Swedish colleague Carolus Linnaeus. The boy, John Laurens, was an American natural whose gift for copying the world around him would prompt them to invite him to join their select company.

John was fifteen when he drew the softshell turtle in the Charleston home of his tutor, Dr Alexander Garden. Dr Garden was an eminent naturalist who had corresponded with the Royal Society before. In his day the existence of soft-shelled turtles was at the frontier of European knowledge. When Garden got hold of two 'by chance' in 1770, he observed them in his home for several months and wrote a detailed description for his colleagues in London. And he set his young pupil John Laurens to work drawing one, as best he might.

But John needed no prompting from a schoolmaster. The urge was spontaneous. When he was three years old 'he began of his own accord to draw',

10 John Laurens, 1780.

choosing the natural world as his subject, recalled his father Henry Laurens.[1] John's vocation took firm root as he grew up on his family's plantation surrounded by the unspoilt semi-tropical rivers, swamps and forests of colonial South Carolina.

In early May 1771 John's art work was appraised by the gentlemen of the Royal Society in their unassuming headquarters in Crane Court. The occasion was the reading of Dr Garden's paper on the Florida softshell. John was not the first American colonist whose combined love of nature and budding artistic talent had brought him to the attention of this learned group. Pennsylvanian William Bartram's sketches of the New World's flora and fauna were winning him the patronage of a select circle of aristocrats, merchants and men of science. When the Laurens family reached London late in 1771, young John was invited to meet Dr John Ellis, a naturalist who had been to Florida and the West Indies. Dr Ellis called upon Henry first, 'showed me a drawing of a softshelled turtle, asked me if that was not the performance of a son of mine. Yes. It is exceedingly well done indeed, and has been much admired at the Royal Society', Ellis told the proud father, concluding: 'You must send that son to see me.'

So John went to see Dr Ellis one December morning. He arrived early and alone, sitting over a leisurely breakfast with the Doctor so that they could talk 'without interruption'. In that short time vast new horizons opened to John. Ellis knew Dr Daniel Solander, a naturalist who had just returned from a round-the-world voyage with Captain James Cook in the *Endeavour*. Solander's adventures had made him the talk of the town. He had been presented to the king and fêted by the Royal Society. Would John like to accompany him on Cook's next voyage to the South Seas?[2] John's artistic skills and keen powers of observation were highly prized in a day when photography was nonexistent.

At seventeen, John was very young to have an opportunity of such magnitude unfolding before him, one that gave him an exciting outlet for his own natural talents. If he accepted, he would enter a cosmopolitan world of scientists, philosophers, statesmen and men of business from all over Europe who were united by their curiosity about the natural discoveries that were opening up to western explorers. But Henry did not think the time was right for his son to take such a step. 'If he had two years more school learning, I should cultivate the hint of his attending Doctor Solander,' he wrote to his brother James back in Carolina.[3]

Privately, Henry may have been glad of the excuse to decline Ellis's offer, because he was not happy with his eldest son's childish vocation. John had declared that he wanted to study medicine when he was still back in Charleston drawing the softshell turtle. He was drawn to the profession of his tutor, Dr Garden. Henry hoped John would follow in his own footsteps, but he admitted that his son 'had not any inclination to merchandise', and that he was unlikely ever to give up his interest in science. From the age of three he had been fascinated by the natural world. '[L]et his profession be outwardly what it may', Henry conceded, 'he will at least be a smatterer in the medical sciences.' But Henry hoped he would remain only a smatterer. 'I don't altogether like his turn to physic, but I will do nothing to obstruct it. I would rather he should study divinity, the law, or apply himself to trade and commerce.'[4]

Henry's words revealed that he was socially ambitious for his son. Henry thought of himself as a gentleman; well, and so he was. In eighteenth-century England, genteel status no longer required the rigid qualifications of a landed estate or a coat of arms. It was more a matter of opinion. One needed a good income, evidence of the right sort of taste, and if one had to have an occupation it must be a gentlemanly one. Henry qualified on all these counts. He was a great merchant who engaged in overseas commerce. He owned plantations, and he lived in a genteel style that conformed with London standards. But there was still something more to be desired. By his own admission, Henry could not express himself 'however good my cause may be, like a scholar and a man of letters'. What he lacked, John would have. John would have a surer foothold in the polite world. A physician could be a gentleman (although surgeons and apothecaries were dubious). But physicians were not so gentlemanly as barristers or clergyman.[5] Or John could follow his father into trade. Henry was not apologetic about his self-made status. He'd sooner see John an Atlantic merchant than a doctor who poured over leaves and seed-pods in his spare time.

The Army, the Navy, the Law and the Church – these were the gentleman's professions in Georgian England. Provided one were at the top of any of them, one could 'cut a figure' in society, as so many of Jane Austen's leading characters declaimed. Henry Crawford, the unprincipled flirt of *Mansfield Park*, confessed that he never listened to a distinguished preacher without feeling 'a sort of envy' and 'half a mind' to preach himself, as long as it was to a sophisticated London audience. The awkward Edward Ferrars of *Sense and Sensibility* practically went through the whole list. He was the despair of his family for refusing a career in the army – 'it was a great deal too smart for me' – and the navy – 'it had fashion on its side, but I was too old'. All that was left was to become a barrister. 'The law was allowed to be genteel enough; many young men, who had chambers in the Temple, made a very good appearance in the first circles, and drove about town in very knowing gigs.' But modest Edward would have none of it; in the end genteel idleness 'was pronounced to be the most advantageous and honourable'.

Henry would have none of that. He wanted his sons to have useful professions. A career in the British regular army or Royal Navy was unusual for colonial Americans, who lived far from the fountain of patronage and activity. John did not have any inclination for the Church, so only the law remained. Although his son appeared to have just one choice, Henry insisted John himself must make the final decision whether to give up medicine.

While he was deciding, an English education could only improve John's prospects. English schooling peaked in popularity among wealthy colonists in the score of years before American independence. Uncounted numbers of school-age colonial boys like the Laurenses were sent across the ocean to school. Oxford or Cambridge often followed. Colonial students at the Inns of Court – 'the Temple' as Edward Ferrars called it – tripled in number after the middle of the century. The Inns formed the highest level of training for Britain's barristers and judges. The instruction actually received at them was often thin on the ground, as we shall see, but association with them gave one a definite social purchase.[6]

By sending their sons away for their education, these rich colonists were following an English trend. Once upon a time education at home by private tutors had been the norm for the children of the rich. Now, increasingly, they were being shipped off to boarding schools instead. For the English gentry, all this meant frequent trips to private schools and academies in London or the countryside, university, and, ideally, continental travel. The Grand Tour as the completion of a gentleman's son's education was de rigueur.[7] For wealthy American colonists, the expectation was much the same.[8] School in England, followed by Oxford and Cambridge or the Inns of Court, a trip to the continent if it wasn't too expensive – this was the pattern of an English education for the sons of America's rich.

What was at stake was not mere fashion. An education away from home was seen as an antidote to provinciality; one lost the traces of rusticity that came with an upbringing on a remote estate, be it in Yorkshire or Virginia. Yet Henry Laurens could not contemplate parting with his children without a tinge of regret. 'Such separation', he lamented, 'happens every day even between parents and children in this land of universities and schools.' He named the Brailsfords of Berners Street, whose eldest daughter was at a boarding school in London and whose son was destined for a merchant apprenticeship in Amsterdam, and an English friend who had just left for Geneva in order to put his children to school there. Henry would make the same sacrifice as these conscientious parents. 'I consider what is the most likely method to make my children happy in being useful to society and I pursue that method, in spite of all the strong affections and inclinations of nature.'[9]

Behind Henry's regret was real anxiety at sending his boys away, for the new trend in education brought its own risks. Boarding school was controversial because it meant that children were exposed to all sorts of influences, some of them highly undesirable – and parents could do very little about it. During the century there was an ongoing debate over the merits of private versus public education. Was it better to keep a child at home, insulated from corrupting influences, and risk him turning into a bashful clown? Or send him out to acquire the polish necessary for polite society, and take the risk that he would also acquire its vices? The debate was carried on in newspapers and pamphlets throughout the century. *The Spectator*, widely read in America, granted that a private education was the best way to safeguard a child's virtue; on the other hand, leaving home was essential if the child was to acquire 'manly assurance, and an early knowledge in the ways of the world'.[10] It was a dilemma that worried many parents, Henry Laurens among them.

Yet the need to assume genteel manners and deportment was also very real. A gentleman's manners were essential to gain an entrée into social and business circles in eighteenth-century Britain and her American colonies.[11] The affability and polish attained from a polite education was the established character of a man of business.[12] As Henry Laurens put it: 'It seldom happens that a private education qualifies a man to shine in public life.'[13]

Jane Austen caricatured the difference between a private and a public education in the characters of Edward Ferrars and his dandified brother Robert in *Sense and Sensibility*. The fashionable Robert Ferrars explained to Eleanor Dashwood that his brother's 'extreme *gaucherie* which he really believed kept him from mixing in proper society' was not due to any natural deficiency, but to 'the misfortune of a private education; while he himself, though probably without any particular, any material superiority by nature, merely from the advantage of a public school, was as well fitted to mix in the world as any other man'. Granted, Austen was creating a caricature, but it reflected a very real issue. Young men of a certain social level were under immense pressure to acquire the correct manner and air if they wished for advancement.

Not all succeeded. The ordeal of Edward Tilghman of Maryland, who studied at the Inns of Court in 1772, illustrates what some went through in pursuit of a 'gentlemanly air'. Tilghman, the son of a prominent Marylander, was an eager legal student, but like the hero of *Sense and Sensibility* he lacked the 'graces of person and address' required to cut a figure in public life. His family hoped that study in London would cure him. A year into his stay, Tilghman confided that he was having trouble overcoming his 'vile awkwardness'. '[D]ecent fashionable words of common civility do not come from me as from others,' he wrote sorrowfully. 'All is too constrained, my very legs and arms refuse genteel postures, a dancing master shall chasten them and unless my bad habits are bred in the bone they shall be rooted out.'[14] Tilghman senior lamented that his son was missing the main point of his trip to London – 'the polish, the something not to be expressed, only to be acquired by mixing with the world & c & c. – I give up'.[15] ('A certain *je-ne-sais-quoi*' was the good Gallic expression old Mr Tilghman was groping for; polite manners, like good cooking, were of French origin.) Young Tilghman's quest ended in failure; a lack of charm remained a conspicuous part of his personal make-up for the rest of his life, despite having a distinguished legal career.[16] But if Tilghman failed, hundreds of other sons of wealthy colonial families succeeded, and returned to the colonies as 'pretty gentlemen' (in the words of one critical New York parent), with all the polish of fashionable London.[17]

Not only young gentlemen but young ladies from the colonies came to the imperial capital to acquire the fashionable graces. Although wealthy American families sometimes sent their daughters to English boarding schools, more often the young ladies simply came to London for a season or two to mix with fashionable society. Whether they attended school, or simply enjoyed the advantages of London dancing and music masters, a stay in London was a chance for these colonial girls to take on a metropolitan polish. Clothes, curtsies, elegant deportment, all were to be studied and perfected. It was not work, but fun. 'London takes off the rawness, the prejudices of youth and ignorance,' wrote one enthusiastic young American. 'It would be impossible to enumerate all the benefits to be acquired in London, but it cannot be disputed that more is learnt of mankind here in a month than can be in a year in any other part of the world.'[18] There was always the risk that this accelerated growing-up process would result in a loss of innocence. But it was a risk that was worth taking, for America's imperial capital set the standard in manners, dress and taste for English-speaking people everywhere.

What all wealthy colonial Americans wanted – whether destined to be Whig or Tory – was to seem like the gentrified English, and the evidence is that they succeeded. Just ten years before American independence, there is not a whisper of the development of an 'American character' among this crowd, even those who went on to become leading patriots. Indeed, they were taken for English wherever they went. Walter Jones of Virginia, studying medicine at Edinburgh University in Scotland in 1766, reported to his brother that the medical students there were divided into three 'ranks, or orders', with Englishmen and Americans classed together:

> 1st. The fine gentlemen, or those who give no application to studies, but spend the revenues of gentlemen of independent fortunes. 2ly. The gentlemen, or students of medicine. Strictly speaking these live genteelly and at the same time apply themselves to study. 3ly. The vulgar, or those who, if they are not indolent, are entirely devoid of every thing polite and agreeable . . . Now the two first orders which I mentioned, are chiefly composed of Englishmen and Americans, who are reckoned here much the same. The last is chiefly of Scotsmen . . .[19]

A spicy story circulating in Edinburgh at about the same time was of a 'wild Englishman' who had arrived from London with a young lady whom he 'locks up when he goes out and often threatens to shoot: she is a very pretty young lady'. He 'sometimes says that he is married to [her], and sometimes not; but the latter is to be feared, as he is of the most fiery and ungovernable temper.' In fact the young man was not English; he was Cyrus Griffin of Virginia, who would one day be president of the Continental Congress. The young lady was the daughter of the Earl of Traquair. Griffin did marry her, after all.[20]

And on the continent the same mistake was made. When Henry Laurens was in France in 1773, he was considered an Englishman by the French innkeepers and beggars he met on his journey. The innkeepers regularly over-charged him. Henry explained to a friend that Englishmen were known to live well while on the road, and so the bills were always 'pretty extravagant for Mi Lord Angloise'. Henry beat them down. 'Beggars', he found, 'will hardly go near a French voiture when there is an English carriage in the way.' They all seemed to take for granted 'the liberality of an Englishman'. A hopeful French beggar boy called Henry 'his good – his adorable – noble English lord'. For as long as John Laurens was at school in Geneva, the English students there were classed as his 'countrymen'.[21]

Genteel Americans blended into London society. An instructive comparison is the experience of the Scots – even the educated classes – who were 'specially conscious of being Scots when they were in London'. The Scots were very unpopular. Since the Act of Union in 1707 there had been two Scottish rebel-lions, and an influx of Scots into London who competed with the local English for jobs. They were something of a Londoner's pet hate by mid-century. Scots in London were the objects of mob aggression at times. James Boswell was at the opera in Covent Garden when the audience hissed at the sight of two Scots soldiers. 'No Scots! No Scots!' was the general cry. Boswell wrote angrily that the audience were 'bullying and being abusive with their blackguard tongues'. But abuse was hard to avoid, because Scots on the streets could be detected by their accents. Some Scots resorted to elocution lessons.[22] In 1764 the renowned Scottish philosopher David Hume poured out his anger at his sense of exclu-sion in a letter to a fellow Scot, asserting that he could never settle in London:

> Some [English] hate me because I am not a Tory, some because I am not a Whig, some because I am not a Christian, and all because I am a Scotsman. Can you seriously talk of my continuing an Englishman? Am I, or are you, an Englishman? Will they allow us to be so?[23]

White American colonists like the Laurens family *were* allowed to be Englishmen. They looked and sounded like Englishmen. Well-to-do colonial youths sent to England for their education acquired English accents. It was said in the eighteenth century that Virginia's first families sounded like educated Londoners.[24] As late as the 1820s James Fenimore Cooper, on a visit to England, declared that New Yorkers sounded English. He found that his English friends could not distinguish between the speech of an American and that of an Englishman. Cooper boasted that he could, but only if he were able to listen for five minutes.[25] Distinguishing an educated American accent from an English one in Cooper's day was probably like trying to distinguish a Canadian from an American accent today – it required an effort.[26]

Henry Laurens certainly wanted his boys to be genteel and English, and he was doing everything in his power to make them so. But being Henry, he was also very worried about leaving them within striking distance of London after he returned home to South Carolina. Even before they arrived in England, Henry was anxious about the trouble his three sons might get into in Europe's largest city. He fretted that Harry, the son he had sent to England ahead of himself and the other two, would 'ramble in the City'. He preferred that the lad 'be kept a *boy* under the eye of his tutor'. Along the same lines, he worried about John: 'I hate the thoughts of his being in, or so near London, as to be able to go there by virtue of his own will'.[27] Clarke's school in Chelsea would put the two boys several miles' distance from the city. But was that far enough away? Scholars from Clarke's school had been seen recently by another South Carolinian in London, 'rambling the streets of the City, in half holidays'.[28]

And in the City, the boys might fall in with some undesirable company. Privately, Henry did not want them to spend too much time with 'my good friends in the City, to whom I consign rice and indigo, because I have seen very ill fruits spring from their superabundant kindnesses to some of our American youth'. True enough, his merchant friends did not seem to have a very good record on controlling their own young people. George Austin, whose Shropshire home Aston Hall had been robbed by Robert Scipio, had a son with a serious drinking problem. George junior went on binges, on one occasion disappearing during an afternoon visit 'as if he was only going in the garden', according to Henry, not to show his face again until the next day.[29] The Mannings had a son, John, who was the same age as John Laurens. John Manning was a wild youth who ran away from his school at Winchester and was continually in and out of trouble. Henry thought he needed a firmer hand.[30]

It was probably difficult for busy City merchants like Mr Manning to keep track of teenage boys who had only to walk out the front door to gain access to all the coffee houses and prostitutes of Georgian London. Wandering around the largest city in the British empire with money in one's pocket could give an intoxicating sense of freedom. The potential for getting into trouble was endless. Under these circumstances, young American boys in England who strayed from the straight and narrow became something of a cliché. Typical was a story run by the *London Chronicle* (probably an apocryphal one) of a sixteen-year-old boy from Antigua who stole £400 from the counting house of his merchant host and ran away to Paris. He was last sighted with a prostitute in Greenwich.[31]

By the time the Laurens family reached London, America's young people had a very bad reputation, as Henry was all too aware. He wrote with chagrin of 'the general censure which the people here pass upon American youth'.[32] The Americans meant here were of course the juvenile offspring of wealthy merchants and planters. Some came to London without parental supervision, tempting them to give full indulgence to the 'let-off-the-leash' syndrome. A Pennsylvania student who was a friend of young Ralph Izard wrote home in frank terms that 'Americans are particularly remarkable for being wild and extravagant'.[33] Virginian William Lee, who worked in London as agent for his family's tobacco interests, had to act *in loco parentis* to a kinsman whom he described as having unspecified 'strong and ungoverned passions' that amounted to 'the full American idea of extravagance and dissipation'.[34]

This was not going to happen to the Laurens brood! When worrying stories about the discipline at Clarke's boarding school started to trickle into Fludyer Street, Henry began to research alternatives. He visited a number of private academies, and checked out Oxford and Cambridge as universities for John. He found something to worry about everywhere. Most of the problems were down to lack of discipline. In the end he decided to send John and Harry to Geneva in Switzerland, a popular destination for the children of well-to-do English families. Its educational standards were reputed to be excellent, and the city of only 25,000 was a stark contrast to London. Geneva's local laws promoted frugal lifestyles, and even without these there was simply less opportunity for young people to get into trouble. Henry, John and Harry Laurens travelled to Geneva to see for themselves, reaching it by mid-June 1772. Liking what he found, Henry left John and Harry in the home of a respectable Huguenot.[35]

John was left in Geneva to ponder his future career. He was to let Henry know his decision, but it was already obvious that his father wanted him to be a merchant, with law as an acceptable second choice. John, on the other hand, was very sure he didn't want to be a merchant, and very sure he loved 'physick'.[36] In the manner of Jane Austen's heroes, John agonised over the list of gentlemen's professions.

On the clergy: 'When I hear a man of improved education, speak from the goodness of his heart, Divine truths with a persuasive eloquence which commands the most solemn silence and serious attention from all his audience, my soul burns to be in his place.' On lawyers: 'When I hear of one who shines at the Bar, and overcomes chicanery and oppression, who pleads the cause of helpless widows and injured orphans, who at the same time that he gains lasting fame to himself, disperses benefits to multitudes, the same emulous ardour rises in my breast.' And finally, still in the running at this stage, medicine: 'When I hear of another, who has done eminent service to mankind, by discovering remedies, for the numerous train of disorders, to which our frail bodies are continually subject . . . I can't refrain from wishing to be an equal dispenser of good.' In John's pantheon of worthwhile professions even the military got a look in, although this was an unusual choice for a colonial. The unifying theme in all this was obviously 'lasting fame'. 'No particular profession is in itself disagreeable to me; each promises some share of fame.'[37] John wanted very much to cut a figure in the world and to feel a sense of higher purpose in the process. Beyond this, though (and to his father's immense frustration), he could not decide.

But John had once known very clearly what he wanted, when he was back in South Carolina drawing the turtle in Dr Garden's study. His childhood interest thwarted, he badly needed an equally engrossing substitute. He found it in a craving for distinction. One day his new ideal would cause him to make fatal choices.

For Henry, meanwhile, back in London, things had never looked better. John and Harry were ideally situated in Geneva. Henry congratulated himself on hitting upon the perfect solution for their schooling, a place that was away from the vices of a big city but with all the requisite influences for a genteel education. John would eventually decide on his career, and Henry would then place him at one of the universities or the Inns of Court. Little Jemmy was at his well-conducted boarding school in Winson Green near Birmingham. And Henry had just returned from a little post-Christmas tour of Oxford, Stratford-upon-Avon, Bristol, Birmingham and Shifnal, where he had visited his friends the Austins. This time he had prudently left the troublesome Robert Scipio behind. Henry was getting the hang of living in England. 'I am at present, thank God!' he wrote to John, 'as happy as this world can make me. Enjoying the most perfect health, in the center of a circle of letters all abounding with good news from my dear children.'[38] The letter to John was written on 26 January 1773. Like the proverbial jinx, Henry had spoken too soon. The very next day everything would fall apart.

For the next day brought Captain William White of the *Carolina Packet*, knocking on Henry's door in Fludyer Street with news that his teenage niece Molsy had arrived unexpectedly from Charleston – and had given birth to an illegitimate child during the passage. Molsy was in desperate straits. Would her uncle help her? She had taken refuge in the house of her cousins the Parsons in Union Court. For the next few days Henry was so upset that he could not eat, drink, or sleep.[39] Mary Bremar, or Molsy as she was known, was the youngest daughter of Henry's sister. By 1769 both her parents were dead. Left an orphan, she had been taken in by her older sister Martha, who had a prosperous marriage to Egerton Leigh, the attorney general of South Carolina. As 'eldest daughter', Molsy was made welcome in her sister's numerous family.[40]

Egerton Leigh was someone Henry did not get on with. Marriage had made them kinsmen, but although Egerton was in London when Henry arrived in late 1771, the two families did not meet. At the start of Egerton's marriage to Martha Bremar in 1756, he and Henry had been companionable in-laws. Just a few years later they were public enemies. Back in South Carolina they had crossed swords over a legal case which went before the Vice-Admiralty Court, involving the seizure by customs of one of Henry Laurens's ships. Leigh, the presiding judge, had incensed Henry with his decision, and the two had publicly insulted one another in an exchange of pamphlets. The quarrel, which pitted Henry against a royal official at a time when the patriot movement was gaining momentum in the colonies, had actually helped to put Laurens firmly into the patriot political camp, and had probably improved his reputation in influential Carolina circles. But each man felt the other had betrayed family values, and the relationship was over.[41]

Now Egerton's character was about to sink to unexpected depths, because the buzz of the Charleston drawing rooms was that he was the father of Molsy's baby. 'The perjured, adulterous, incestuous, murderer – Egerton Leigh' spluttered Henry. He could not find adjectives sufficient to express his indignation. But still Henry couldn't quite believe in Leigh's guilt.[42] After all, the Bremar orphans had turned out rather wild since their mother's death in 1769.

Molsy had been allowed to grow up leading a dissipated life in her sister's home. She had little or no useful education, being trained up in 'sloth, pride, and idleness' as critical Uncle Henry put it.[43] Such feminine incapacity was not taken for granted, even among the gentrified classes. Planter's wives and daughters had to have the skills requisite for heading a great household. Eleanor Laurens, Henry's wife, elegant and accomplished as she was, had been no fine lady but cured hams, oversaw an extensive kitchen garden, sewed with her own hands infant clothes for expectant slave women, and managed the production of clothing and linen for use throughout Henry's domains. Henry's eldest girl Patsy was in a fair way to follow in her mother's footsteps. She could read and write, studied arithmetic and English history, understood French and played the harpsichord. By the time she was ten she had learnt 'women's work' as well, was accomplished with her needle, and an excellent cook.[44]

Molsy could not sew to save her life, and presumably knew nothing of women's work, since her Uncle Henry declared her 'incapable of any employment for earning a livelihood'. According to Henry, she was 'accustomed to ridicule' the industry of girls like her cousin Patsy.[45] No doubt she would have joined in the joke when Mrs Bennet of *Pride and Prejudice* sneered that Charlotte Lucas had gone home because 'she was wanted about the mince-pies'. '*My* daughters are brought up differently,' she assured Mr Bingley, and indeed the fate of her daughter Lydia – whose love of mindless gaiety would have just suited Molsy – was to prove her point.

Molsy's brother Frank had turned out much the same. He kept bad company, led a 'loose disorderly life', and was as work-shy as his sister, 'skulking about in idleness' in Charleston. But Frank at least had flashes of good intention when he talked about finding gainful employment. Worse than either Molsy or Frank was their older brother John, who controlled the family estate, and who made no bones about casting his younger siblings off when they were too much trouble. Four years after their mother's death, in 1773, John threw Frank out, obliging the youth to go in quest of a position. This proved to be impossible, because his unnatural brother had added insult to injury by blackening Frank's name around Charleston. Finally, Uncle James Laurens rescued poor Frank by convincing the merchant firm Hawkins Petrie & Co. to take him on in their counting house. Unbeknownst to Frank, his wages were secretly paid by Uncle James, at least until Mr Hawkins was satisfied the young man was worthy of his hire.[46]

John Bremar treated his sister Molsy no better. In spring 1771 the Leighs had left on a trip for London, leaving her with her brother. Some sort of breach occurred between the brother and sister – no great surprise given John's total lack of family feeling – that drove Molsy to undertake a December crossing in order to follow her adopted family to London. Henry assumed that she had 'acted amiss' and 'in despair of aid' from her brother had decided to join the Leighs there, with Henry as a last resort if that did not work out.[47] But Henry never saw Molsy after he reached London in October 1771. She had joined the Leighs in their home in elegant Pall Mall, a stone's throw away from St James's Palace and the royal parks.

Henry did not see his niece, but he heard about her. By the time she left London, in April 1772, he had the impression that she was an 'unfortunate, ruined girl'. 'Ruined' sounds very strong, and in such cases it usually hinted at a sexual indiscretion. And in fact, within just a three-month stay, Molsy's name had been linked in scandal with a young man Henry would not name, although he alluded to 'a certain young nobleman who used to frequent [the Leigh's] house in Pall Mall'.[48] As far as Henry was concerned, Sir Egerton and his wife had not kept a tight enough rein on their teenage charge while in London. But within the Leigh household itself Molsy aroused other, more insidious suspicions.

Molsy was still classed as a child when she first came to London in 1771. She would find a large circle of Carolina girls with whom to associate. There was Peggy Stevens, the niece of the Gibbeses. There was Betsey Barnwell, who was engaged to be married when she arrived, and stayed long enough to have the thrill of a London wedding in 1772. The Brailsfords in Berners Street had a daughter at school in London. And the Mannings from St Kitts had three daughters ranging in age from fourteen to seventeen.[49] Whole families of West Indian girls were sent to school in London, and some of these would have formed part of Molsy's circle.[50]

Molsy joined the young set long enough to attend the annual Children's Ball given by her London dancing school. On the night of the ball Egerton Leigh's sister saw something that gave her the gravest suspicions that her own brother was tampering with his orphaned sister-in-law. Other suspicious circumstances followed, blatant enough so that even Egerton's own mother could not ignore them. The climax was an ugly scene in which Molsy's sister Martha – Mrs Egerton Leigh – threw out 'some strong expression of her jealousy'. Egerton's own sister had to intercede to prevent him from striking his wife with such brutality that it 'might have killed her on the spot'.[51]

The Stay-Maker
From an Original Sketch in Oil by Hogarth in the Possession of Mr. Sam. Ireland
Etched by Jas. Haynes, Pupil to the late Mr. Mortimer

11 A young woman is having her ball gown fitted by a stay-maker. She twists her head to peer at herself in a mirror while younger members of the family play in the room.

Under the circumstances it was not surprising that Molsy went back to South Carolina after only a three-month stay. In the third week of April 1772 she was at Gravesend boarding the *Portland* for Charleston, with Egerton Leigh there to see her off. He and his family were not to return to Charleston until the autumn. Henry Laurens was disgusted with the news that Molsy was to be left to make another solo crossing, seeing it as a betrayal of Egerton's promise to care for her. 'This may be what he calls treating her as his eldest daughter', wrote Henry sarcastically, but in fact it was another instance of Leigh's 'perfidy'.[52]

What Henry didn't know was that Molsy was one month pregnant. The rushed return voyage to Charleston was the first phase of an incredibly clumsy effort to conceal it. By October, when Molsy was visibly pregnant, the Leighs were back in South Carolina. Rumours got around about her condition, but when she was confronted by Henry's brother, her Uncle James, she swore earnestly and convincingly that she was suffering from a medical condition that affected her appearance. Uncle James was taken in, at least for the time being. In the meantime she tried to terminate the pregnancy by whatever means were available in colonial Charleston, but to no avail.[53]

A few days before Christmas, with the baby due any moment, Egerton Leigh hurried Molsy on shipboard once more, this time Captain White's *Carolina Packet*. She was bound for London. Egerton's master plan was that she would give birth out at sea, away from prying Charlestonian eyes. Captain White did not know she was pregnant, and Leigh pressured him – probably with bribes – to keep quiet about her presence on board. Egerton's plan seemed to be going smoothly. The *Carolina Packet* put to sea at once, but with what must have seemed infernal bad luck to Leigh, contrary winds obliged her to return within two hours. That night Molsy went into labour. Molsy had a slave girl to help her, but no midwife, and a 'very scanty stock' of provisions laid on by Uncle Egerton. Nevertheless, she gave birth to a full-term male child, '*hearty and stout*' according to Captain White.[54]

Although Leigh had sworn Captain White to secrecy, enough was enough, and White went to James Laurens with his tale. 'I would give 50 Guineas that I had never taken her on board my ship,' he raged. Molsy was offered every inducement of support and assistance to return to shore and go to the home

12 St James's Park, very close to Pall Mall, where Molsy Bremar stayed with Sir Egerton Leigh and his family during her first visit to London.

of her Uncle and Aunt Laurens, but she refused. Provision had been made for her in London, she said, and she excused the appearance of her illegitimate child with 'such a stupid improbable tale as never was heard of' – namely that she had been raped the previous March in St James's Park 'by an unknown person, who had stifled her cries by thrusting a handkerchief into her mouth', and that only her Uncle Egerton knew of it. Molsy appeared very sure of herself, but Captain White reported that privately she 'bewailed herself and wished to be on shore again'.[55]

So Molsy set out to sea again, undaunted by the prospect of a winter passage. Her infant did not prove to be so hardy. The little boy died six days after his birth. Despite his good start, his mother 'had no milk and nothing proper to feed the child'. It was common practice for genteel South Carolinian women to have their infants suckled by slave women, so the boy might have been saved had he been delivered ashore and at home. With some justification, Henry conjectured that Egerton Leigh had been hoping that the child (and perhaps its mother as well) would perish during the voyage.[56]

It was a short passage. By 27 January 1773 Molsy was lodged in London at the home of her cousins the Parsons. Mrs Parsons was related to Molsy through the Bremars. The Parsons, though genteel, were not as wealthy as Henry Laurens and his Berners Street set. Like most South Carolinian families in London they had their 'Negro girl' servant, but their address in Union Court was close to the Bank of England and the crowded, noisy business district. When Molsy reached their doorstep, Mrs Parsons learnt for the first time of her pregnancy and the loss of her baby. Two days later Molsy, 'after struggling under a most violent agony which seemed to threaten her life', confessed that Egerton Leigh was the father of her child, that he had 'composed the fable of the rape and adventure in the park', and had promised to marry her as soon as the present Mrs Leigh – Molsy's elder sister Martha – had died, 'which he said would soon happen'.[57]

Now, friendless and in trouble, Molsy was on Henry's hands. Henry began to discover that the whole story was 'too well known in London', and that he was cast in the rather foolish role of the family member who was the last to know. The day after Molsy's arrival, while Henry was still in denial over the idea that Egerton Leigh was the father, a friend said bluntly, 'depend upon it, Sir, Leigh was the father of that child'. For the next two months Henry and his brother James agonised over whether to take Leigh to the law and publicly expose him. He had a wife and seven children in America. In London he had a sister and an aged, infirm mother. To add to his sins, it came to light that he had been 'defrauding his mother' for years, keeping back income that was her due. 'Good God,' exclaimed Henry upon hearing this, 'which is the blackest of his numerous crimes?'[58] Leigh's sister frequently came to visit Henry, understandably anxious about the outcome of the case, but she must have made his situation still more awkward. Henry arranged for Molsy to swear a deposition before the lord mayor, but beyond this he abandoned legal proceedings.[59] There were simply too many people who could be hurt.

At this point an unexpected figure appeared, a young man named Edwards Pierce. His identity remains obscure, but he evidently knew Molsy from happier times. He now wrote to Henry Laurens, asking for her hand in marriage. He was persistent. Even when Henry informed him about Molsy's past, Pierce did not withdraw his offer. Henry's brother James back in Charleston thought this was Molsy's best hope of happiness. But Molsy was not interested. She told Henry that she wanted some solitude, to get away by herself to recover from 'the horror and blackness' of her experiences. Henry respected this. When he left in April 1773 for the continent to visit his boys John and Harry at Geneva, he took Molsy with him. At her request he left her at an Ursuline convent in Boulogne, France. The Ursulines were a teaching order, and Henry had, in effect, put Molsy into a secluded boarding school where she would be removed from the worldliness of London. There, he hoped, 'she will learn, or at least see examples of, humility and be out of this scene of endless temptation to expense and folly'.[60]

And what did Molsy make of all this? That is difficult to uncover. Like Lydia Bennet and Maria Bertram, the two 'fallen women' of Jane Austen's novels *Pride and Prejudice* and *Mansfield Park*, Molsy was apparently 'trained up in sloth, pride, and idleness', and 'accustomed to ridicule' a sober, industrious life.[61] From such a description, she presumably felt at home with the fashionable, pleasure-seeking beau monde of London. Her uncle James, when he confronted her about her pregnancy, reported that she lied very glibly, adeptly covering up her foster-father's crime.

Perhaps at the start Molsy did not take the situation too seriously, but she must have quickly realised that she was trapped. Henry feared that if left to fend for herself, she would end up as a common prostitute on the streets of London. She needed someone to support her, and the list was growing very thin. Egerton Leigh, back in Charleston, revived the old gossip about Molsy and the nobleman in Pall Mall, whom he pointed to as the real father. Molsy had her own promiscuity to blame for her predicament, claimed Egerton, who declared himself hurt by the girl's ingratitude. Mrs Egerton Leigh forgot the jealousy she had felt in London and backed her husband's version of events, declaring before company, 'thank God, she never had the least cause of jealousy'. Molsy's eldest brother John Bremar – a truly evil character – backed up Egerton's slanderous stories. He was probably also blackmailing Egerton, or so thought his younger brother Frank, who noticed that ever since Molsy had been shipped aboard the *Carolina Packet*, John had acquired an inexplicable 'influence' over his brother-in-law. John knew 'too much of the hellish secret', speculated Frank, and was receiving 'large wages' to keep quiet.[62]

Molsy's reputation was ruined in South Carolina, so James Laurens did not advise her to return. In London she could stay with her cousins the Parsons in Union Court. But they were of limited means, and Henry Laurens had to pay for her room and board. Then there were her uncles, Henry and James. But the Laurens brothers were not going to help her if she did not mend her ways. That was clear.[63] How difficult it must have been to seek help from relations whom she had never lived with as family, and among whom there was no older kinswoman to act as a mother figure.

Whatever Molsy Bremar was looking for, it was not simply a good time. It had been her own idea to go into seclusion in France. When she returned to London in 1774, she rejected Edwards Pierce's offer of marriage. Pierce was 'miserable', wrote Laurens; 'I never saw anything like it.'[64] When she turned down Pierce, she was left with few options. Henry thought that Egerton Leigh had 'so effactually ruined her reputation as to make it necessary for her to live recluse', like Maria Bertram, the adulteress in *Mansfield Park*.

Unlike Maria Bertram, Molsy was not sent to live in a remote farmhouse, but she did end up a virtual recluse. After Henry Laurens returned to South Carolina in the autumn of 1774, Molsy stayed with her cousins the Parsons. Uncle Henry continued to pay for her room and board. Her allowance from Henry was so frugal that she could not afford the clothes necessary to 'visit in the same families' with Mrs Parsons herself, even though Mrs Parsons' circle was not as smart as the Berners Street set. In 1775 her cousin John Laurens, by then studying law in London, apprised his father Henry of her situation. She is only bored for 'want of company and amusement', wrote cousin John somewhat scornfully. Her 'dejectedness', which the worried Henry had seen as a symptom of depression, arose in John's opinion from restlessness under the quiet lifestyle she was now forced to lead rather than 'a real sense of her misfortune'. Henry wrote angrily to Mrs Parsons that he could not afford to increase her allowance. 'She shall not wallow in frolic and idleness at the expense of my own children,' he wrote in plain terms.[65]

But events were to show that John and Henry Laurens had misjudged their kinswoman. Some time after her appeal to John for financial help, Molsy made an attempt to strike out on her own and support herself. The West Indian barrister John Baker, who knew Molsy, recorded that 'with only four or five guineas in her pocket [she] went off in stage to Plymouth, and there worked with a mantilla maker and came back in a small vessel by sea'. Molsy had evidently tried apprenticing herself to a mantua maker. This was an aspect of dressmaking, one of the very few gainful employments open to women of good family in the eighteenth century. But the experiment failed. She was 'a strange girl, discontented and flighty', mused Baker. In December 1777 Molsy committed suicide by an overdose of laudanum.[66] Thus ended her bid for freedom.

Egerton Leigh suffered too, though in keeping with the double standard of the day not as tragically as Molsy. Egerton's star in South Carolina had been falling ever since he sided openly with royal authority in his conflict with Henry Laurens in the late 1760s. A cultured man who enjoyed refined living, wrote poetry and filled his home with expensive *objets d'art*, Leigh's quest for gentility culminated in a baronetcy. His purpose in going to London in 1771 had been to become 'Sir Egerton'. In the end he was obliged to purchase the honour himself, which was awarded in September 1772 – three months before Molsy's baby was due. His triumphant return to Charleston as a baronet was tarnished by the Molsy scandal, which broke simultaneously. Rather than awing everyone with his baronetcy, Leigh's seduction of Molsy sealed his character as a villain, prompting him to be called 'the greatest rascal among all the King's Friends'.[67]

Leigh was perhaps one of the first royal officials to be cast in the role of the archetypal wicked Englishman that has graced so many American novels and films, from James Fenimore Cooper's *The Spy* to Mel Gibson's *The Patriot*. He was labelled a decadent epicurean and the seducer of 'his innocent foster-child'.[68] No one believed his protests that he was the victim of a scheming teenager. And the gossip spread. A story that made an English high official out to be so thoroughly wicked at such a juncture in Anglo-American relations was too good to ignore. John Adams heard it from Thomas Lynch, the congressional delegate from South Carolina, when they met in Philadelphia in 1774.[69] Leigh limped back to London for much of the War of Independence but died in Charleston in 1781, where he was trying to resume his royal post after the British reconquest of the city.[70]

Sir Egerton Leigh might take on the stock character of an English villain, but Molsy fit into a Georgian Londoner's notion of a typical American. As Henry

Laurens knew to his chagrin, America's youth were often stereotyped as 'wild and extravagant'. A common cliché was that they had been corrupted by a life spent among slaves. In the nineteenth century the story of an American going to Europe would always be a story of New World innocence encountering European worldliness. A century earlier in Georgian London, this 'innocents abroad' motif was reversed. Young people from the colonies supposedly brought the taint of plantation life to the metropolis. In English plays and novels the image of a colonial youth who must come to the metropolis to regain his or her essential Englishness would become an enduring motif. It had a powerful appeal to London chauvinism. The planters who made London their home before the Revolution offered no objection to being thus caricatured from time to time as prodigal sons. Their feelings would not change until after the American War of Independence, when they found themselves positively demonised in the anti-slavery campaign. But even before the first shots of the Revolution had been fired, there was a certain planter's son who would prove himself highly sensitive to the London stereotype.

CHAPTER FOUR

Young and Rich in Fleet Street:
The Decadents Abroad

John Laurens returned to London from Geneva in August 1774. He had finally decided, in the most reluctant terms possible, to abandon medicine ('my favorite') and study law 'considering that my dear Papa and the majority of our judicious friends give a preference to' it. His letter was so half-hearted that Henry lectured him on it, reminding him that he only wanted his children's happiness. He had already registered John's name at the Middle Temple, but he could withdraw it if John preferred. The lad had only to say the word.[1] Like Robert Scipio and the Ansonborough 'Town Negroes' who were obliged to assure Master Henry that they did not want to be free whenever freedom was offered, John must now tell his father that he wanted to study law, and sound like he meant it.

Henry was reassured, and John became the first Laurens to undertake higher education. He was also part of a wider trend, because more and more colonial boys of his generation were going to college or university. In response, the choice of colleges in the mainland American colonies was increasing. Until the 1740s there had only been New England's Harvard and Yale, and William and Mary in Virginia. But in 1746 Princeton opened its doors (it was first known as the College of New Jersey). From that time until the start of the War of Independence, a whole litter of future Ivy Leagues were born: the College of Philadelphia (later the University of Pennsylvania), King's College (Columbia), Queen's College (Rutgers), the College of Rhode Island (Brown), and Dartmouth.[2] But no matter how many colleges opened in the colonies, the number of American youths going to Oxford, Cambridge, the Inns of Court and Edinburgh University (the best medical school in eighteenth-century Britain) continued to rise.[3]

As the offspring of rich planter and merchant families who were already making the pilgrimage to England, the colonial students in London had a distinctly southern bias.[4] Of over one hundred colonial students attending the Inns of Court (John's destination) between 1755 and 1775, almost three-quarters were from the colonies of Maryland and southward. The study of law was a popular choice among the South Carolinian gentry. That colony sent forty-three students to the Inns in the score of years leading up to the War of Independence. For West Indians an English education was mandatory, as the islands had no college of their own; the West Indian students at the Inns slightly exceeded the number of mainland American students.[5]

A typical route to study at the Inns of Court was a stint at Oxford or Cambridge or one of the great public schools, or an apprenticeship in an attorney's office. But in practice the only real qualification was financial. Could one afford the admission fees and termly duties? Once accepted, a student needed to be a firm self-starter to benefit from his time there. There was almost no formal instruction, and there was no bar examination until the nineteenth century. All that was required of a student was that he keep a certain number of terms. To be credited with a single term's attendance, one had merely to reside at the Inns and eat at least three dinners in hall. It was said sarcastically that gentlemen were called to the bar only for paying the fees and producing 'a certificate of having dined a certain number of times in the hall of the inn'. From the parents' point of view it was an expensive and risky business. Yet this was the only route to becoming a barrister in England's royal law courts.[6]

In hard terms the expectation was that students would study dull legal texts and primers in their chambers, and visit the court at Westminster Hall to see barristers in action. They might obtain a placement in a barrister's chambers, but this was unsupervised and optional. There were many complaints about the lack of guidance, and more than a few drop-outs.[7] But this did not have to matter to those (and there were many) who attended the Inns for the 'half-social purposes' of acquiring a smattering of law and a set of London connections befitting a gentleman.[8] Some young Southern gentlemen at the Inns never intended to practise law. They had no need to earn an income, and if they chose instead to enjoy the sights of London they would find plenty of company among their fellow students.

Such a one was Charles Carroll of Carrollton, who as the son of Maryland landowner Charles Carroll of Annapolis was heir to one of the greatest fortunes in the colony. Because the Carrolls were Catholic, and Catholic schools were not permitted in Maryland, Charley was sent to school in France at the tender age of ten. He did not return home for seventeen years. As a

Catholic, Charley was debarred from political activity until the creation of the United States and the beginning of full religious liberty in America. In 1776 he signed the Declaration of Independence and went on to have a distinguished political career.[9]

Seventeen years earlier Charley Carroll was in London, living in chambers at the Inns and defending his new expenses to his parents. He must have a servant, he told them (he brought no slave with him), money for parties, riding and going to plays, new furniture for his rooms and more: 'a set of China cups and saucers a few plates and dishes, glasses, punch bowls a dozen of silver tea spoons tongs and etc (all which I assure you are necessary for no young gentleman that has a mind to appear genteel can go without them)'. His list paints a picture of the student life of the wealthy American youth in the Temple. All these things Charley (who was a dutiful son and careful about appearances) required, despite finding his fellow students rather indifferent company. 'Few young gentlemen are here to be found of sound morals', he complained. 'I could pardon a little obscenity, provided it were not too barefaced and extended no farther than words' – his silence implying that it often did extend further.[10]

Another American abroad, John Dickinson, has left a vivid record of life in student chambers. The son of a tobacco planter, Dickinson grew up in Delaware and Pennsylvania in comfortable homes where much of the work was carried out by slaves. Dickinson was to become a champion of American rights in the 1760s, famous for his *Letters from a Farmer in Pennsylvania*, which set out clearly the basis for colonial resistance to British taxes. But he is best remembered as one of the few leading patriots who opposed declaring American independence in 1776. His reluctance to break entirely with the mother country earned him the rage of fellow congressman John Adams. But Dickinson, whom Adams once (in a calmer frame of mind) described as 'tall, but slender as a reed – pale as ashes', had the resolve to undertake military service against the British later in the war.[11] Dickinson's lukewarm attitude towards American independence has been attributed to the time he spent at the Inns of Court, which supposedly led to 'a dangerous love affair with his mother country'.[12] But this does not hold up; Dickinson was no different from many young colonists at the Inns, whose loyalties in 1776 would fall into no particular pattern.

As a young man Dickinson was an avid student of the law, and in the 1750s his father had sent him to the Inns of Court to give a London finish to his education. There he settled into chambers in the Temple which he shared with a friend from Maryland. By 'chambers' was signified a set of rooms in an apartment or flat, rather than lodgings in a private house. It sounds more private to modern ears, but in the days when servants were critical to domestic comfort, chambers had distinctly less to offer than the average middle-class home. Dickinson's service was limited to a morning call by a housemaid: 'A laundress attends by seven in the morning, lights our fire, brings the bread, milk and butter, and puts on our tea kettle. We wait on ourselves at breakfast, which is no manner of trouble, and after that she returns, makes our beds and sweeps the rooms.' As Dickinson and his room-mate were entirely unable to cook for themselves, they were obliged to go out for their evening meals.[13] They usually studied until three or four in the after-noon, headed to a chophouse for dinner, then took a break in the nearest coffee house before returning to study for the evening.

It is not hard to see that the ten or more hours John Dickinson devoted to study each day could easily be passed in other ways. 'Every person lives without control in his chambers', he admitted, 'and according to his disposi-tion may either prosecute his studies with the greatest quiet in them, or employ them to the worst purposes.'[14] Charley Carroll summed up the careers of these latter types in Hogarthian terms:

> Nothing can be more absurd than the usual manner of young gentlemen's studying the law: They come from the university, take chambers in the Temple, read Coke upon Littleton: whom they cannot possibly understand, frequent the Courts whose practice they are ignorant of; they are soon disgusted with the difficulties and dryness of the study; the law books are thrown aside, dissipation succeeds to study, immorality to virtue; one night plunges them into ruin, misery, and disease![15]

The career of Charley's imagined student usually ended with an encounter with a prostitute and a bout of venereal disease. He wouldn't have to stray very far to meet his fate, because the route to the law courts at Westminster Hall passed through the Strand. This was Georgian London's most notorious haunt for pros-titutes. Strand prostitutes were described as 'absolutely void of all sense of modesty or shame' in the quest to attract clients. One pair achieved a kind of fame for their double act, in which they sang an obscene ditty and concluded it with suggestive pelvic motions and shammed orgasms.[16] For the first-year law student, the Strand was the broad, smooth road that led to Westminster Hall.

So how did John Laurens cope with the new-found freedom of legal studies at the Inns of Court? His liberty was increased by his father Henry's

13 A London prostitute gleefully examines the jewels she has just received from her client, while the client, a young man, gazes in horror at his sordid surroundings.

departure for South Carolina less than three months after his own arrival in London in August 1774. At first he sent a bare but dutiful account to Henry: 'I have worn my black gown twice at the Temple, and shall break bread there as often as is necessary for keeping my terms. I have attended the court of King's Bench, but have heard nothing of consequence . . .' He soon began to sound as if he were on the path to ruin so graphically described by Charley Carroll. He referred to his legal textbooks as a disgusting 'chaos of jargon'. Another couple of months led to the cautious admission that 'the unavoidable interruptions to study here are great and numerous'.[17]

To his uncle James, John was fuller and more frank. 'Law is the knotty study which I must endeavour to render pleasant,' he wrote. 'And a horrible prospect it is, that I am to get my bread by the quarrels and disputes of others.' John wrote these words to his uncle in September 1774. In another month he had moved in with Charles Bicknell, an attorney in Chancery Lane.[18] The new acquaintance did not work any improvement on John's impression of his chosen profession. '[M]y friend with whom I eat and drink, is the merest machine in the world, the most barren in conversation and least calculated to improve, of any man I ever was connected with', he complained.[19] Disillusionment was setting in.

When John Laurens called Bicknell a 'machine', he did not choose his words at random. Practitioners of law were often stereotyped as mere 'mechanicks' in the eighteenth century. Attorneys like Bicknell were seen as glorified clerks who handled the tedium of paperwork and procedures. They were looked down upon by would-be barristers like John Laurens.[20] By contrast, there was a glamorised image of barristers as 'tribunes of the people' who defended the poor and oppressed from their betters. It was this that had caught John Laurens's imagination in far-off Geneva, when he had pictured himself as 'one who shines at the bar', 'who pleads the cause of helpless widows and injured orphans'. Some radical barristers did make names for themselves as defenders of liberty, for example in the Somerset Case. Courtroom oratory made good reading in the newspapers, and the public hungered for heroes.[21]

But only a very few barristers became celebrities, and even they had a rather negative image in London. The alternative to the champion of widows and orphans was that of a grubbing race, tied to their work, not above chicanery, 'insular, unlearned, and unpolite', in short entire strangers to the aristocratic virtues that young Laurens's education had taught him to value. Once he reached London, John would have encountered this sordid charicature everywhere, for lawyers as a breed were often parodied in jokes, plays, ballads and novels.[22]

And law studies was not fun. The law was complicated and practical. The world John was now entering was at variance with any of his former educational experiences. Lawyers who took their practice seriously had to work hard, and much of their work was inevitably dry and detailed.[23] John's dismissive comments about his landlord Bicknell reveal his desire to distance himself from it all. He did not want to be identified with a set of men who were sometimes called 'mechanics' and sometimes 'the devil's playmates'.

But by enrolling at the Inns of Court, John had moved into a part of London where the sordid business of getting ahead counted for more than good breeding. Legal studies brought one into the ancient City of London, where men were in earnest about making money. The change was not only one of location, but of social geography. Wealthy young colonists at the Inns made no bones about their preference for the fashionable West End. Charley Carroll wrote to his father, 'the genteelest company is confined to the upper end of the town at a great distance from the Temple'. John Dickinson put it

14 A lawyer examines his legal papers while the devil looks over his shoulder. Lawyers were often depicted with the devil at their side in satirical prints.

more bluntly. 'Nothing within Temple Bar can be as it should be,' he wrote. The men of business in the City 'are so ignorant of everything from their counter that they are not fit to converse with people of fashion and breeding . . .'[24]

When John Dickinson ghettoised the undesirables of the City within the boundaries of Temple Bar, he was referring to a medieval gate that stood at the west end of Fleet Street. By the eighteenth century, Temple Bar was the last of London's ancient city gates still standing. The original wooden edifice had burnt in the Great Fire of London in 1666, and Dickinson and his fellow students would have passed through the arched stone replacement designed by architect Sir Christopher Wren. Temple Bar was well-known as a portal between the very different social milieus of Westminster and old London.

Unsurprisingly, wealthy young Americans and West Indians like John stood out in the business end of town. A cartoon of the period called 'The Middle Temple Macaroni' gives us a picture of how they looked walking along Fleet Street. 'Macaroni' was a slang term for a dandy who imitated the fashions of the continent. The cartoon shows a modish youth with a sword, and is below scribed 'In short I am a West Indian' – a line from a popular play of the time.

Just as in the case of the West End neighbourhoods that had been infiltrated by wealthy colonists, Fleet Street came to have its own visible black population as ever more colonial students arrived at the Inns bringing their slaves. William Franklin, who was registered at the Inns of Court in the 1750s, owned a slave called King before that enterprising individual ran away. John Dickinson had a servant named Cato. Dr Johnson's famous black servant Francis Barber, who lived in and around Fleet Street, had come to him through his great friend Richard Bathurst, the son of a Jamaican planter and a student at the Middle Temple.[25] Advertisements for runaway slaves in the neighbourhood appeared in the newspapers. A slave girl ran away from her mistress in Hatton Garden near Fleet Street, and a reward was offered for her.[26] A 'Negro Man' named George Stewart, formerly the property of Colonel Samuel Adams of Barbados,

The MIDDLE TEMPLE MACARONI

In short I am a West Indian !
                              Cumberland.

15 'The Middle Temple Macaroni', 1773. 'In Short I am a West Indian!' reads the caption. The print caricatures the wealthy West Indian and American law students of the Temple.

absconded from his new master's residence near Temple Bar, and was prom-ised 'all the good usage he has hitherto experienced' if he would return.[27] No doubt many of the well-dressed young American Templars made their wealthy origins still more obvious by having black servants in tow.

So what objection did these Middle Temple Macaronis have to the neigh-bourhood on the 'wrong side' of Temple Bar? The City was teeming with lesser merchants and tradesmen (the 'second rate gentry', as one American visitor called them).[28] Like attorneys, these poor souls were supposed to live lives so completely chained to their counting houses that they had no time to acquire the polish and the worldliness that were associated with a gentleman. '[A]nimals gross and barbarous' they were called by the denizens of the West End. London traders, in turn, traditionally saw themselves as no-nonsense, true-born Englishmen who despised the French-loving foppery of the polite end of town. But attitudes in the City were changing. By mid-century there was a growing trend for the really wealthy merchants – like Samuel Brailsford of Berners Street – to decamp to better parts of town.[29]

Young Americans at the Inns, of course, had taken great pains with their education, and that could not be for nothing. Even those who were to become leaders in the American Revolution were not egalitarian. In fact, John Laurens was becoming a bit of a snob. When he attended a Lord Mayor's Ball in the busi-ness heart of the City in late 1774, he carefully distanced himself from the other guests. There were only two noblemen present, he told Henry, a thing never heard of before! As it happened, he knew both. Lord Mahon had been at Geneva with him; the other was Viscount Mountmorres, an Irish peer who had friends in the Carolina set from his Oxford days. 'Never was so poor a show of Gens comme il faut,' John wrote rather grandly, 'nor such a number of the Polisson order collected upon any public occasion.' He was careful to show off his conti-nental education by abusing the ill-breeding of his fellow guests in French.[30]

The Middle Temple Macaronis had only to pass through Temple Bar to be on the high road to the spacious houses of the West End, where many of them had relatives. But there is great truth in the adage 'location is everything', and John and his friends found ample compensations for staying in the vicinity of the Temple.

The Temple is just off Fleet Street, between that busy thoroughfare and the Thames. Two of the Inns of Court are found here, the Middle Temple and the Inner Temple. They are so-called because they stand on land originally owned by the Knights Templar. The Inns of Court – there are four in total – are a set of independent societies of lawyers, founded in the fourteenth century. 'Inn' originally meant a hostel where the students lived while they undertook legal studies at the nearby courts of law. John Laurens was registered at the Middle Temple (the most popular choice for colonial students), but his lodgings in Chancery Lane were on the other side of Fleet Street near to Lincoln's Inn. All of these places and spaces were within easy walking distance of one another, and the great Fleet Street, like the 'lost river' it was named for – not really lost, but covered over by the 1760s – roared through the midst of it all, a vital artery connecting the old City with the Strand and the wealthy West End.

Fleet Street was a place where the worst and the best of Georgian London stood side by side. Its famous association with printing and publishers was already more than two centuries old when John Laurens arrived. The young Benjamin Franklin, on his first trip to London in 1725, undertook a printer's apprenticeship in nearby Lincoln's Inn Fields.[31] In the next century Fleet Street would become the generic name for the British press as the nation's biggest newspapers crowded in. But there was far more to Georgian Fleet Street than the print industry. Noisy Fleet Market was built over the 'lost river', and hard by that was Fleet Prison, famous as a debtors' prison and the source of the dubious 'Fleet marriages' of the early part of the century. Gentlemen law students who poured out of the alleyways of the Inns of Court into the street would mix with every level of London society. Coffee houses and curiosity shops beguiled passers-by of every rank. The famous Mrs Salmon's Waxworks – forerunner of Madame Tussaud's – stood near Chancery Lane. Not far away was Rackstraw's Museum of Anatomy, which included a wax 'reproductive-organ department' and such curiosities as stuffed crocodiles and the skeleton of a whale. If one could not afford the price of a ticket to these establishments, one could watch for free the spectacle of the lifesize wooden savages on St Dunstan's Church, striking the hour with their wooden clubs.[32]

In the manner of the old City of London, elegance could be found squeezed in among the businesslike and the sordid. There were still some fine merchant's houses in and around the area during the Georgian era. One of these was the house where the Royal Society met, in Crane's Court, an alley just off Fleet Street.[33] It was here, in May 1771, that the Fellows of that learned group had studied John's drawing of the Florida softshell turtle. Three and a half years later John was living a stone's throw away. Did he know that the American naturalist William Bartram had recently sent another drawing of the softshell to London? John seemed to have forgotten all about the scientists and naturalists whose world had once meant everything to him. His life had been diverted into a very different, much worldlier channel.

16 Chancery Lane looking into Fleet Street. The sign for Mrs Salmon's Waxworks in Fleet Street can just be made out on the building on the left.

The old City's answer to the splendour and fashion of the West End was the witty and intellectual culture that throve in its gritty coffee houses. London's coffee houses were famous, not for the beverages they served – which could be found in any European or American town – but for what went on in them. They were vibrant social institutions where politics, culture and social issues were talked over by all ranks of Englishmen. If the fashionable society of the West End gathered together at Court and in glittering assembly rooms, the earthy and intellectual City social life was carried on in coffee houses that were open to all. This gave celebrated Georgian Londoners an accessibility that is almost unthinkable today. The literati practically lived in coffee houses. One had only to find out their favourite haunts in order to see them in person. An introduction did not always follow, but one could at least get a good look at them and bring home a store of anecdotes.

The neighbourhood around the Temple and Fleet Street was the stomping-ground for Dr Johnson and his famous Literary Club. Dr Johnson himself had

17 View of Fleet Street. Temple Bar can be seen in the distance, with the Strand just beyond.

earned a place in Mrs Salmon's Waxworks, but it was just as easy to see the real thing walking in the street outside the museum, a recognisable figure with his wide girth, shuffling gait and scruffy appearance. And where the Doctor was, one might see other members of the Club: the great actor David Garrick, Johnson's faithful biographer James Boswell, the MP and orator Edmund Burke, author Oliver Goldsmith and artist Joshua Reynolds, all at home in their favourite coffee-house milieu. On Fleet Street the Cheshire Cheese, the Mitre and the Devil Tavern (where Dr Johnson threw a party for the American novelist Charlotte Ramsay Lennox that lasted until eight o'clock the next morning) were regularly patronised by this celebrated set. The famous Grecian Coffeehouse was around the corner in Devereux Court near Middle Temple Lane. The Grecian was a favourite with Goldsmith. It was also the haunt of Ben Franklin's Learned Society.[34] All of these establishments were minutes away from John Laurens's digs in Chancery Lane. John and his fellow law students went regularly to the Devil Tavern to 'meet and harangue upon different subjects'.[35] Those who had chambers in the Temple were even closer. Edward Tilghman, the American Edward Ferrars, lodged in Devereux Court itself. Charley Carroll lived within the Temple at 5 King's Bench Walk.[36]

William Franklin once commented that American colonists, 'when we go to England have as much curiosity to see a live author as Englishmen have to see a live ostrich, or Cherokee Sachem'.[37] The record shows that colonial students, finding themselves at such close quarters with England's literati, took full advantage of the opportunity. Edward Gibbon, Dr Johnson, Boswell, Goldsmith, the artist Francis Hayman and others all appear in letters home. The great actor Garrick knew many colonial Americans and even arranged a benefit performance for the College of Philadelphia (later the University of Pennsylvania).[38]

One could argue that all this sauntering about in coffee houses was educational. Certainly, encounters with the prestigious Literary Club gave it that gloss. But it tipped too easily into mere partying. There was a fun-loving 'Carolina set' at the Inns who had a reputation for spending beyond their means and wasting their time. Chief of these young Americans was Jacob Read, son of a wealthy South Carolina planter. He had started his studies at the Inns a year ahead of John, and knew his way around London's theatres and taverns. Read was involved in a notorious incident in which he and two other young Carolinians were arrested in a brawl. The threesome got drunk at a tavern in Covent Garden and kicked the waiter downstairs. Although they used their swords to resist arrest, eventually they were locked up for the night in a typical London gaol. There they were allowed to purchase unlimited alcohol of whatever sort they liked, 'from champagne . . . to humble porter'. Sir John Fielding, brother of Henry Fielding the author of *Tom Jones*, released them the next morning on good behaviour.[39]

Henry Laurens knew the young men in question. Before he left London he aired his views on them and their kind in no uncertain terms to his eldest son. John – no doubt prompted by the same insight into his father's unyielding disposition that had guided Robert Scipio – agreed with every word. How to account, then, for the fact that just one month after Henry had departed England, John's letters were telling of jaunts with this very set to Gravesend and Cambridge, even mentioning the awful Jacob Read by name? How could John be keeping company with youths whom 'inwardly you disapprove of', raged Henry from a distance of 3,000 miles. 'Are you so poor in valuable acquaintance, in books, in ideas?' Why the sudden about-face, so hard on the heels of Henry's own departure, 'like a bird after long confinement fled from her cage?' Hadn't John been sincere last September when he 'penetrated and marked with so much justice and severity' the flawed principles of the Carolina set? 'Some of your new associates have been eminent in squandering

18 'High Life at Midnight', *c*.1769. A street brawl has erupted between two drunken gentlemen with swords and a group of night watchmen.

large sums,' Henry warned, 'they are adepts in every thing which wise men wish to be ignorant of.' But he closed the subject more in sorrow than in anger: 'If your first month has given rise to such admonition I should tremble for the effects of eleven more, had I not great confidence in your understanding and docility'.[40]

Henry was trying as hard as he could to control his eldest son, who was now well out of his reach. The situation might have looked hopeless were it not for the fact that he had saddled John with several heavy responsibilities that would retard the path of pleasure-seeking. For a start, he had left Jemmy and Harry in England, with John *in loco parentis*. Jemmy was still at the boarding school in Winson Green, but Harry had been in Geneva with John, and he started at Westminster School when they returned to London. Westminster School was next to Westminster Abbey, a mile and a half from John's digs in Chancery Lane. Harry lodged with a family in Fludyer Street but John was supposed to keep an eye on his brother, who was now eleven years of age. The boy often came to John for weekends and holidays. On Sundays he sometimes accompanied John to Temple Church, which, as a Middle Templar, John was obliged to attend. Afterwards there was Sunday dinner at the Mannings. In April,

Harry was with John for his three-day Easter break. Then the subject of rowing came up – all the boys at Westminster went rowing on the Thames in the spring, and Harry wanted to join in. The school would not allow him without Henry's permission, which, as little Harry pointed out, might not reach London until the end of the season. So John agreed to supervise his brother's rowing sessions whenever he could.[41] Having Harry around was a substantial tie for a young man who aspired to the free-and-easy student life.

And John was responsible for managing the budget for both himself and his two brothers. Henry had left a specified sum, to be drawn upon Mr Manning when needed. Behind his son's back he prompted his friend Manning to keep John on his toes about the budget, as 'the more money is spent the more time also, and the less study will be taken'.[42] Money would be a means of curtailing John's activities. By March 1775 he was already panicking, protesting that he had 'not the least recollection' of his father mentioning £400 as his annual budget. He had already exceeded it, he confessed. In the process he called himself all sorts of names, such as imprudent, 'irresolute', 'unworthy', and swore to make amends by immuring himself in London all summer, keeping his nose in his books, and spending not a penny more. The panic proved unnecessary; upon speaking to Mr Manning, he found his spending was still comfortably within his budget.[43]

It was a happy ending, but one that illustrated John's impulsive character. Nothing shows this side of his nature better than the story of the circumstances under which he returned to London from Geneva in August 1774. Hearing that his father planned to set out for Geneva to discuss John and Harry's future there, John rushed to London hoping to spare Henry – who was then troubled with gout – the trip. It was a daft plan. Henry of course had already left, and John had to backtrack from London all the way to Paris on horseback to meet up with him and prevent him going any further. It was dismissed as youthful impetuosity by Mr Manning, who said John 'rode night and day like a young man . . . at all hazards to himself'.[44] Perhaps so, but it was also the mark of a highly strung personality given to extremes, and one that was not ready to assume so much responsibility.

John was barely twenty when Henry left him in London. That was a small stock of experience to draw upon for handling the matter of his cousin Molsy Bremar, another legacy Henry left behind him. John was expected to call upon Molsy from time to time and assess the situation for Henry. With so much pressure from Henry about money, no wonder John played down his cousin's request for a larger allowance. Moreover, there was the Leigh family. That troublesome tribe returned to London in the summer of 1774. Egerton Leigh and his wife were trying to woo Molsy back into their company, probably in an attempt to alleviate the scandal. They tried to draw John into their scheme. When John saw Egerton in the lobby of the House of Commons and unthinkingly tipped his hat to him, Egerton seized upon it as an opening to call on John in Chancery Lane. John was so worried by the whole encounter that he described it in a lengthy letter to Henry, going into detail on what prompted him to tip his hat in the first place, how Egerton responded (he had the sun in his eyes and didn't return the civility at first), how John felt about that, and so forth, ending with Egerton's unsolicited visit to Chancery Lane. He pressed John to come to dinner, and John, with all the deference of youth, tried politely to get rid of him. He stood booted and ready for a ride with Mr Manning, but still Sir Egerton would not go![45] The bad blood between Henry and Egerton was indeed a minefield that wiser heads would be reluctant to enter, and John's insecurity about the entire transaction was obvious.

For the first time in his life John was no longer under the daily eye of a parent or schoolmaster; he had his own rooms and he had money. In these circumstances his father was pressuring him to leap from schoolboy to adult in a single bound. What John needed was the chance to learn to be responsible to himself, away from his controlling father. His family duties and his own extreme conscientiousness compromised that. But the reality of his young life was that he hated the new career path he had chosen, and he needed desperately to find something to replace it.

John was apologetic about his jaunts with the Carolina set. But he quickly found English company that would cause his father bigger headaches. If the attorney Charles Bicknell was an insufferable bore, his older brother was not. John spent many hours in the company of the elder Bicknell (also a law student), and it was through him that he made another very significant friendship, with the author Thomas Day. Day had begun his studies at the Inns of Court some years before John. He was a man of strong opinions, and great causes were his watchword. Six years older than the twenty-year-old John, Day was of independent means, an eccentric-looking man who scorned fashion and was noted for his slovenly clothes and uncombed, unpowdered hair.[46]

Day counted himself among the ranks of Innsmen who never intended to practise law. He was open about his contempt for the profession. On one occasion in his chambers his roommate cried out 'Kill that spider, kill that spider!' at the sight of one of the tiny creatures rushing out from behind some dusty books (there were probably a lot of dusty books in the chambers of this particular pair of law students). Day asked him fancifully how he should like it if a 'superior being' were to cry 'Kill that lawyer, kill that lawyer!' 'And I am sure,' he added 'to most people, a lawyer is a more noxious animal than a spider.'[47] How Henry would have cringed to hear his son's new companion going on in this vein. From far-off South Carolina, Henry preached vainly to John that those who protested 'I hate the Law I never could abide it' were talking about something they knew nothing about.[48] Day was destined to become a strong influence on young John. Accustomed to deferring to his father, John found in his new friend an exciting (and equally opinionated) substitute.

Thomas Day surely fed John's urge to be part of something greater and more glorious than the legal profession. He was a poet, but he also shared John's childhood interest in science. He was a member of the Lunar Society, a group of intellectuals and natural philosophers centred in Birmingham which included Erasmus Darwin (grandfather of Charles), James Watt, Joseph Priestley and Josiah Wedgwood. They frequently met at Darwin's house. The 'Lunatics' (as they were called) were interested in everything from chemistry to steam engines.[49] Day was also a great exponent of the 'cult of feeling' that was popular in the latter half of the Georgian era. The movement had a pretentious, even narcissistic, streak to it, but was associated with the laudable rise in reform movements and public charities after the middle of the eighteenth century. Those who styled themselves 'men of feeling' liked to discover that they had acute sensations of generosity or sympathy for the sufferings and misfortunes of others. In the case of Thomas Day this took many forms. As an earnest man with a great deal of time on his hands he did not stop at mere feeling, but translated his compassion into action. His championing of the spider, for example, was no passing whim. Day became a lifetime defender of the feelings of animals, and was to end his life being kicked to death by a colt he was endeavouring to train using kindness rather than whips.[50]

Day was also an admirer of Jean-Jacques Rousseau, convinced by the Frenchman's critique of civilised society as a corrupting influence that distorts man's natural goodness. Entranced by the novel *Émile*, which illustrated Rousseau's notion of a proper education – allowing a child to grow up entirely without formal instruction, following the dictates of his own nature while overseen by a benevolent guardian – Day determined to conduct a practical experiment of his own. He adopted two orphan girls, aged eleven and twelve, and undertook to raise both according to his own methods in order to qualify one of the fortunate fair ones as his wife. His methods included inculcating stoicism in one of the girls by dripping hot sealing wax on her arm (she screamed) and firing pistols into her petticoats (they were blanks but she still went into hysterics). Needless to say, the experiment in parenthood was exhausting – the girls got ill and demanded lots of attention – and in the end Day married neither.[51] By the time he met John Laurens the experiment had been abandoned. But he must have converted John to his ideas on female education. When John's sister Patsy Laurens arrived in England in the summer of 1775, John submitted her to a test worthy of Thomas Day. He arranged for their coach to drive through the countryside at top speed, and watched his sister closely to see whether she would betray any 'womanish fears'. He was apparently satisfied with her reaction.[52] And perhaps Patsy, at age fifteen, did not resent a big brother who played such a ridiculous trick.

John was impressionable. And his new friend's stance on slavery made a very lasting impression. As a man of feeling, Day naturally hated it. Several years before he met John, he and his friend Bicknell had published a poem called 'The Dying Negro'. Based on a true incident, the poem told the story of a slave in London who fell in love with a white servant girl in his master's household, and before he could marry her was forced on board a ship in the Thames bound for the West Indies. In desperation the man shot himself. The incident took place one year after the Somerset decision, in 1773, and attracted a great deal of public sympathy. The poem was a huge hit. When it was reprinted in 1775, close to the start of the War of Independence, Day struck out at American hypocrisy in the dedication: 'Let the wild, inconsistent claims of America prevail, when they shall be unmixed with the clank of chains, and the groans of anguish. Let [America] aim a dagger at the breast of her milder parent, if she can advance a step without trampling on the dead and dying carcasses of her slaves.'[53]

Under the influence of his friend, John Laurens began to go about arguing against slavery among his American acquaintance in London. 'I have often conversed upon the subject,' he wrote to his father, 'and I have scarcely ever met with a native of the southern provinces or the West Indies, who did not obstinately recur to the most absurd arguments in support of slavery; but it was easy to perceive that they considered only their own advantage arising from the fact, and embarrassed themselves very little about the right.' One can picture John in a Fleet Street coffee house or a Berners Street drawing room, earnestly arguing away. Day described John as one who 'endeared himself to all who knew him, by his abilities and affectionate temper', and indeed John made friends everywhere he went. One hopes that this naive charm protected him as he pressed his arguments into the unwilling ears of his fellow

Americans, for by his own record he did not let them off easily. '[W]hen driven from everything else' by his arguments, he noted scornfully, 'they generally exclaimed_ Without slaves how is it possible for us to be rich_'.[54] John did not hesitate to expose their shabby morality.

Henry Laurens probably did not like this. He had privately expressed his own reservations about slavery as inconsistent with Christian precepts. But he was always cautious not to fly in the face of public opinion. His private principles did not trump his awareness of the social ostracism and humiliation facing anyone who spoke out against slavery in South Carolina. And Henry always had a practical side. Without slaves, he admitted, it was not possible to be rich.[55] But he could not hush up John from the other side of the Atlantic. Henry is believed to have been the author of a letter Thomas Day received from an American plantation owner in 1775, challenging his forthright anti-slavery stance. The letter has not survived, but Day wrote a spirited reply entitled 'Fragment of an Original Letter on the Slavery of the Negroes (1776)'. Its publication was held back until after the American Revolution because Day supported the American cause.[56]

What must have exercised John the most in his quest for his new friend's approval was Day's opinion of whites like himself who were raised on slave plantations. In fact, the achievement for which Thomas Day is best remembered is a book called *Sandford and Merton*, one of the earliest examples of literature written for children. It tells of Tommy Merton, the privileged son of a Jamaican sugar planter living in England, and his friendship with a simple farmer's son named Harry Sandford. Both boys are being educated by the Reverend Mr Barlow, whose unusual methods are designed to remove his pupils from any taint of luxury and modern living. Unluckily for Tommy, the result is a set of educational experiences in which Harry constantly emerges on top. *Sandford and Merton* was written at a time when there were virtually no competitors in the field of children's literature, hence Day could assume a relatively uncritical audience. Tommy Merton is so relentlessly exposed as a flawed character by the behaviour of his humbler playmate that the modern reader is left with a sneaking sense of sympathy for the planter's son, coupled with surprise at how he could endure it. When Tommy refuses to help in the vegetable garden, Mr Barlow tells him that those who won't work don't eat. The Reverend and Harry sit down to a good lunch, then go out on an educational nature walk. At the evening meal, when Tommy still has not earned his hire, the soft-hearted Harry gives the pampered rich boy his own dinner. The starved Tommy gulps down the food eagerly, only to have it turn to dust and ashes in his mouth as Mr Barlow saddles him with a massive guilt rap.

Most germane to the tale of John Laurens is the exhilarating learning moment when Tommy discovers that he can read, and incautiously boasts that none of the six slaves in his father's house can do so. 'Pray, who has attempted to teach them any thing?' asks Mr Barlow gravely. Tommy's elation is brought down to earth with a thump by his teacher's righteous reproof.[57] The incident is an object lesson in the Rousseauist principles followed by Day. The world had to wait until 1783 for *Sandford and Merton*, but John Laurens would have had the benefit of the author's opinions eight years earlier. The lessons were not lost on him. Back in America in 1778, and under very different circumstances, John would argue strongly that the slaves on his father's plantation were capable of the same 'noble exertions' as white people; it was the debased environment created by their bondage that caused them to appear deficient.[58]

Although Day liked to think of himself as an original, his portrayal of Tommy Merton was hardly that. It was a commonplace amounting to a cliché on both sides of the Atlantic that life on a plantation corrupted the character of the white slave owner. Planters' sons were assumed to be tyrannical in their homes and dissolute in society. This was what produced a Tommy Merton. The wild American youths who rioted in Covent Garden taverns or eloped to Edinburgh with noblemen's daughters were easily explained.

It was not that Londoners knew so very much about the day-to-day conditions in America's plantation colonies, but it did not take much imagination to picture a life of oriental despotism in that far-off realm of masters and slaves. In fact, Londoners made a habit of picturing Britain's peripheries as places that repressed true English spirit. Servants of the East India Company in Bengal were subjected to a similar caricature. They were presumed to be unprincipled plunderers who got rich from booty acquired by 'rapine and oppression' while on service in the east. In Bengal they were supposedly waited on hand and foot, living in splendour, keeping seraglios and drinking champagne and claret all day. At home their countrymen gave them the epithet 'nabob', derived from the Indian princely title nawab.[59] But in the minds of the English one did not have to go as far as Bengal or America to be corrupted by a hoard of slavish attendants. Even in green, rural Ireland dangers lurked for the young grandee. The hero of Maria Edgeworth's Regency novel *The Absentee* is a wealthy young Anglo-Irishman who spent his early years 'at his father's castle in Ireland, where, from the lowest servant to the well-dressed dependant of the family, every body had conspired to wait upon, to fondle, to flatter, to worship this darling of their lord'. His character was saved from destruction by a stint in an English boarding school followed by Cambridge. At a young age, 'before he had acquired any fixed habits of insolence or tyranny, he was carried far away from all that were bound or willing to submit to his commands, far away from all signs of hereditary grandeur'. Set among his equals he became 'a spirited school-boy', and eventually 'a man'.[60] The moral was clear. A life spent in the company of deferential inferiors, whether in America, India, or Ireland, destroyed one's character. But redemption was possible for these sons of Britons. They could get all that nonsense knocked out of their systems by a stay at an English boarding school with boys of their own class, or by exposure to the bluff, outspoken English spirit one met with in all types and classes of people in the nation's capital.

It was a theme that pandered to London chauvinism, and as such it was popular. While the Laurens family was in London, a hit play called *The West Indian* opened. It was about the adventures of a young planter's son named Belcour, on his first trip to London. Belcour proves himself to be haughty and imperious, striking honest English labourers with his rattan cane as if they were slaves on his plantation. But underneath it all he is also warm-hearted and brave. After a series of adventures in the metropolis he learns to respect the assertive, liberty-loving spirit of Englishmen and the well-bred modesty of English women.[61] If the play confirmed a certain smug view of London's place in the British empire, it also admitted that wealthy American planters could be English heroes with a difference. They were flawed, but they could be redeemed. Scratch the surface and their English traits appeared. *The West Indian* was a hit in the colonies too.[62]

But John Laurens did not want to be a Belcour. Four years abroad had taught him to question his native country too deeply for that. He no longer wanted to be defined by his plantation origins. Whatever he did with his life, he wanted it to live up to the standards of the wider cosmopolitan world he had come to know. And the chance was coming swiftly. John would be able to vindicate his American roots and be an English hero at the same time, for the War of Independence began only eight months after he returned to London.

News of the start of the fighting on Lexington Green reached London at the end of May 1775. The crisis leading up to it had begun seventeen months earlier with the Boston Tea Party. The British government had responded harshly to the destruction of the tea with the Coercive Acts, which altered the charter of the Massachusetts government to make it less democratic. Town meetings in the colony were restricted, and British soldiers were sent to Boston to close the port until the town made reparations for the damage. So draconian was the response of Lord North's administration to the tea riot that southern colonists, many of whom initially were disgusted with the Boston mob, took steps to show solidarity with Massachusetts.

In London the Berners Street set organised a protest against the punitive legislation. Led by Henry Laurens and Ralph Izard, petitions signed by thirty-eight 'native Americans' in London were sent to the king, the House of Lords and the House of Commons.[63] The Americans in these petitions were mostly the wealthy absentee types from the southern colonies. Almost half of the petitioners were South Carolinians, students at the Inns of Court, or members of Ralph Izard's ubiquitous network of relatives. Some of these would decide that they were Loyalists once the fighting began, but in early 1774 signing a protest against the Coercive Acts did not yet have the taint of rebellion. The genteel Berners Street set had no reservations about joining in. And a few West Indians signed too, still counting themselves as Americans.[64] Almost half of the thirteen colonies that would shortly declare independence weren't even among the signatories. Just four signatures were from beleaguered Massachusetts itself, the only New England colony to participate. Ben Franklin showed up for Pennsylvania, along with two others.

The rakish Jacob Read and Thomas Pinckney, who had been one of John Laurens's companions on the jaunt to Gravesend, signed along with half a dozen other Innsmen.[65] When John registered at Middle Temple a few months later, the pubs around the Temple were ablaze with the American crisis. The thirteen mainland colonies were calling a Congress in Philadelphia to decide whether to embargo British goods in protest against the Coercive Acts. There were rumours that the Congress would back up Boston if fighting broke out with the troops there. Much of the autumn was spent waiting for news from America. When the Congress decided to ban British imports until the British government retracted, London responded by restricting the trade of New England. The crisis was escalating.

The Anglo-American dispute over colonial rights had been rumbling along ever since John Laurens could remember, but for the first time in his life he was at an age where he could get involved. This was a lot more interesting than law books. '[T]he Robin Hood resounds with the harangues of American Patriots,' John wrote gleefully to Henry. The Robinhood was a debating society that met at the Robinhood Tavern near Temple Bar. By February 1775 John's letters home were full of the American crisis, declaring that the colonists had constitutional law on their side. But even if they didn't, he asserted roundly, 'it would be base in us to submit'; 'if a British Parliament may prescribe to us the mode and quantity of our taxes, we are but slaves'. With his characteristic impetuosity, John declared, 'putting all right out of the question, I would join them in fighting for it'. In the same letter he gleefully announced that 'if bills of attainder pass against the Americans, I am likely to be ranked among the rebels'.[66] Meaning, presumably, that he thought he had talked long enough and loud enough around the taverns of Fleet Street to be declared a rebel and have his property forfeited. John wasn't saying anything original in all this, but he was trying to sound like he meant it.

Henry became annoyed. Why were John's letters so full of the American crisis? In a rebuke that must have cut his son, Henry pointed out that merely 'talking and writing' of risking one's life had never been taken as proof of bravery. '[Y]ou read of nothing but America? You converse perhaps with none but Americans[?].' 'Your spirited declarations of readiness to bleed in your country's cause may sound well enough late at night in the Falcon', admonished Henry (the Falcon was another Fleet Street tavern). '[M]ind your chosen business study to be quiet and do not neglect the proper means which lie before you for serving your country – or rather for qualifying you in due time to serve it'. The message was clear. John should keep his nose in his books; his empty protestations of patriotism and sabre-rattling in far-off London were a little ridiculous to his father, even though by this time Henry himself was taking an active lead in South Carolina's resistance.[67]

But John's mood was not the product of a feverish imagination. It chimed in exactly with the atmosphere in London. There was a distinctly warlike mentality in the metropolis by 1775, an unattractive willingness to resort to force to settle the dispute with the colonies. This was new; in the two previous crises over taxation, the problem had remained the domain of politicians and merchants' lobbies. Perhaps this time around British politicians, tired of complicated arguments over rights and constitutional law, were looking for a quicker, cleaner resolution. Parliamentary orators openly jeered at the idea that colonial militia could face crack British troops. In the House of Lords the Earl of Sandwich sneered: 'Suppose the colonies do abound in men, what does that signify? They are raw, undisciplined, cowardly men'. In the House of Commons, Colonel James Grant, who had served in America during the Seven Years' War, told his fellow MPs that he 'knew the Americans very well, was certain they would not fight; they would never dare to face an English army, and that they did not possess any of the qualifications necessary to make a good soldier'.[68]

Grant, who had been governor of East Florida, was a friend of Henry and John Laurens. He had even offered, back in 1770, to escort John to London for his education, before learning that Henry was about to do it himself.[69] Shortly after his provocative speech an article appeared in the *Public Advertiser* challenging Grant to a duel. 'There is hardly a day or an hour', ran the article, 'in which the Honourable Gentleman does not meet with an American.' Grant probably had in mind the rank and file of the colonial provincial armies, ordinary Americans whom he would never encounter in his London circles. But his insults were couched in terms that certain Americans in London took personally. 'Does he insult any of them with impunity? Has he, or will he put their spirit to the proof?' cried the newspaper opponent.[70] Grant never responded.

John's own reaction is not recorded. But he commented, in general terms, 'much talk and many bugbears thrown out from each side. When the day of trial comes if that fatal day must come, we shall see "who's afraid", an expression which is attributed to Lord North, whenever he is questioned about American affairs.'[71]

'We shall see "who's afraid".' John may have even felt the sting of that taunt when he was with his friend Thomas Day. While he was calling the colonists hypocrites for keeping slaves, Day called them other things as well, 'inglorious soldiers, yet seditious citizens' who had no military triumphs to their credit.[72] After all, it had been British arms that had driven the French from Canada twelve years earlier.

But Day had written those words before the American Revolution had really begun. After that John's friend dropped his attacks on American slave owners. Now that the colonies were faced with armed repression, their situation was simply too precarious to allow British radicals like Day to continue to take potshots at the planters. Day began writing poems against the government (not very good ones). He did not take up his pen again on the slavery issue until after the peace in 1783. He was not alone. Granville Sharp, that champion of the rights of slaves such as Robert Scipio, wrote a pamphlet in support of the American cause that pleased Ben Franklin so much he bought fifty copies.[73] For these British radicals America's cause was England's cause too; both peoples were threatened by an overpowerful government. Slavery with all its injustices would have to wait while liberty was being defended on another field.

Here at last was a cause that validated John in his own eyes and the eyes of his most valued friends, a cause that made him proud of his native country and at the same time a champion of English liberties. 'Oh how I shall glory to be an American,' he wrote, if we 'continue to struggle with our adverse fortune, and act like men deserving that freedom which perhaps they may vainly fight for to the last'.[74] His words were tinged with a melodramatic fatalism, but even the staunchest American patriot or British radical had trouble believing that colonial militia could beat seasoned British soldiers. Yet John asserted over and over his willingness to die in the cause.

Were these empty words? Three years earlier, while still in Geneva pondering his career, he had written with admiration of soldiers whose 'valiant acts' and whose 'admirable bravery have rescued the liberties of their countrymen . . .' It had been a history lesson then, but now it was an imminent reality. At last John had found a path he wanted to follow as passionately as the one that had opened briefly to him years ago at Dr Ellis's breakfast table, when he had been invited to sail with Captain Cook.

From then on John kept asking Henry for permission to come home. In August he wrote desperately that 'every intelligence I receive gives me fresh cause to wish I were in America'. A few weeks earlier the news of the Battle of Bunker Hill on 17 June 1775 had reached the capital. Government supporters were shocked; the battle was a technical British victory, but the British suffered over a thousand casualties. It was to prove one of the bloodiest engagements of the war. What was more important was that it cast the first shadow of doubt over the notion that the colonies would be an easy conquest.[75]

'We shall see "who's afraid".' At the Inns of Court the hot patriots among the American students were gleeful. Pennsylvanian Jared Ingersoll, who was at the Middle Temple with John, wrote that 'the New-Englandmen' had 'fought like lions' and that 'more regular officers fell in this engagement, than in the Battle of Minden'.[76] But soon a rumour spread that dampened student spirits. The government was going to declare the colonies in rebellion. That meant there was the risk of getting trapped in London for the duration of the war. Fewer ships would be sailing for America, and those who wanted to return would have to apply for leave from the British government.[77] John had been afraid of getting trapped in London as far back as December. In late August 1775, three days before the Proclamation of Rebellion was issued, John wrote to Henry: 'I have written to you by the last two packets upon the subject of my return, and if conveyances were as swift as my wishes, should have been with you long before this time. What have I to do here in the present circumstances of my country? What have I not to do at home?'[78]

A month later John was urging his father that it was 'the duty of every American who is absent from home, to return'. In November he put his feelings in starker terms, telling Henry that he chafed under his character as an American law student in London; 'Baseness seems to lurk under every duty, and I feel like a man avoiding the service of his country because his father tenderly commands him to be out of danger.' His self-consciousness was no doubt deepened by the fact that by this time his father's leading role in the rebellion in South Carolina had been reported in the London papers and was known all over town.[79] But John's words reflected his own state of mind as much as anything, for not all the students at the Inns were patriots. There were many Loyalists as well. A number of these young Tories and rebels were kin to one another, and they continued to mix despite the war raging on the other side of the Atlantic. In London, far from the bloodshed, social rank was more decisive than politics in determining the society one kept. John was even on a friendly social footing with Governor Thomas Hutchinson (referring to him as 'our Pall Mall friend') and his two sons, who had been driven out of Massachusetts by angry patriots the previous year.[80] Ralph Izard's cousins the Middletons were divided over the cause, some eventually settling permanently in England and others returning to South Carolina to join the rebellion.[81] Of the Berners Street set, the DeLanceys and the Wrights were all Loyalists. John Laurens had plenty of people to mix with who would not criticise him for getting on with his legal studies instead of going home and joining up.

And Henry himself steadily insisted that John's place was in London. John had his two younger brothers to think of, he wrote. His law studies should not lightly be given up. It may have been in Henry's mind that if the cause of liberty in America took a turn for the worse, it would be good to have an (apparently) loyal eldest son in London to whom the property could revert if Henry as a rebel forfeited his estates.[82] There were other planter families who pursued this prudent strategy.

But John's responsibilities were shrinking. In July 1775 Uncle James and Aunt Mary, together with John's two sisters, Patsy and Polly, arrived in London. James was travelling ostensibly for his health but he also had no stomach for civil war.[83] Couldn't Uncle James represent the family interests in London just as well as John?

Soon after the arrival of Uncle James all the joys and tribulations of watching over little Jemmy Laurens came to a devastating end. The headmaster of Jemmy's school at Winson Green had suffered a stroke, and things there had not been running smoothly. John began looking around for another school. In early September he inspected two schools, one in Brompton and the other at

Greenwich. In his usual impulsive way he tried to carry out the whole business in a single day. Greenwich was just a day trip from the City, an hour to get there and an hour back, but Brompton was further, past Gravesend on the way to Canterbury. John rode a circuit of at least fifty-five miles. He must have been up at dawn. He decided in favour of the Greenwich school, and rushed back to London. He wanted to reach the Carolina Coffee House in Birchin Lane on time to get a letter off to Henry that very evening, informing him of his decision. He was in a hurry to wrap it all up. He had left Jemmy at the Mannings' new house in St Mary Axe for the day. It was only a short detour on the way to Birchin Lane, so he decided to look in briefly with his news.[84]

One of Mr Manning's clerks met him outside the house with a grim face. Jemmy had fallen from the upper storey of the house while skylarking on a window ledge, and had received a serious blow to the head. For two days the little boy languished, suffering gentle convulsions and drifting in and out of consciousness.[85] He died on 7 September. John did not write to Henry with the news for a month. When he did, he told his father that Jemmy's fatal leap had been 'a matter by no means so dangerous, as many to which his active spirit led him, and from which I found it difficult even in my presence to restrain him.' Was John taking the blame upon himself with these words? Henry seemed to think it was partly his fault. He responded with the terrible, ambiguous lines: 'I blame you not, if in aught you have been remiss, your own reflections will be too severe; henceforward take heed.'[86]

No mention was made of who exactly, in John's absence, had been responsible for Jemmy on that fatal day. Mr and Mrs Manning had five daughters, the youngest being eighteen years of age. They had servants, among them the black footman George and a maidservant. The property was both a home and a counting house, so Mr Manning's clerks were on the premises. With all these adults around, it is difficult to see why Jemmy was playing about on the window ledges without any supervision. But not a whisper of enquiry was ever made.

In the eyes of all concerned, Jemmy had been John's responsibility. John confessed that he had been unable to stop his brother on other, earlier occasions when he had tried such dangerous stunts. It is no wonder that John – who was a month short of twenty-one – should find it difficult to restrain his active nine-year-old brother. That is hard work. John himself was restless and distractible. He had trouble keeping track of money, he frequently acted on impulse, and he commonly carried out tasks in a hurried, careless way. Jemmy may have had the same hyperactive nature.

But John blamed himself. He confided to a friend that guilt compounded his sense of loss.[87] Perhaps he also sought consolation with one who was intimately connected with the tragedy and his own role in it, for within months of his brother's death he was having a secret love affair with Martha, the youngest Manning girl. By May or June 1776 she was pregnant. Was John reverting to type? Did he, after all, have a streak of the decadent planter's son within him?

It went without saying that he would have to marry Martha. Now was the time for John to seize his own destiny. Fate was closing in around him. If Mr Manning found out in advance, John suspected he would make it a condition of the marriage that the newlyweds settle permanently in London.[88] The combined forces of a wife, a child and demanding in-laws would trap him in London more surely than ever the British government could with its Proclamation of Rebellion. Knowing ones had anyway found they could get around that restriction by crossing the English Channel and embarking from France to America.[89]

In late October 1776 John secretly married Martha, telling Mr Manning only after the deed was done. To Henry he simply wrote: 'Will you forgive me Sir for adding a daughter in law to your family without first asking your consent? I must reserve particulars till I have the pleasure of seeing you.' 'My wife Mr Manning's youngest daughter promises soon to give you a grand child.' Without leaving Henry a moment to get over the shock, he announced in the next paragraph that he planned to 'take my passage immediately for Carolina.'[90] John glossed over his filial disobedience by seizing hold of some ambiguous expressions in Henry's latest letters that seemed to hint that he might now be allowed to come home. In early January 1777, without his wife, he left London for France in company with another young American who was keen to enlist, Pennsylvanian John White. The two youths experienced a close call when, two days out of Bordeaux, their ship was stopped and searched by a British frigate, but though the English officers spotted Laurens and White as Americans, they were ignored.[91]

John had become the hero of his own life. He had chosen a path and he had acted decisively. He never looked back. He never saw his wife again, never saw his daughter at all. She was born a few weeks after he left for America. He joined the Continentals and became one of Washington's most trusted aides. With respect to physical courage he proved that he was as good as every word that he had said back in the Fleet Street taverns. Washington wrote of him, 'he had not a fault, that I ever could discover, unless intrepidity bordering on rashness could come under that denomination'.[92] And as John took charge of his life, he became more self-assured. Still only in his twenties, he followed in his father's footsteps by being elected to the South Carolina Assembly, but quickly returned to soldiering. His cultivated manners and his knowledge of French saw him appointed envoy extraordinary to France a few years later, where he successfully pressed American interests at the French Court. This was not the John who had stood uneasily in his Temple chambers, waiting for Sir Egerton Leigh to go away.

Henry Laurens's decision to give his progeny a London education had brought with it an unexpected denouement. The younger members of the Laurens household would never be the same. Three would not return: little Jemmy, tragic cousin Molsy and the enterprising Robert Scipio. Young Harry, whom Henry had always accounted rather slow, spent the war in London, returned to South Carolina and lived to inherit his father's estate.

If the aim of an English education was to give one the character of a gentleman, John Laurens was the unqualified success of his father's experiment. His early and eccentric interest in amphibians and seedpods was happily thwarted, and he was transformed into the *beau idéal* of a soldier-hero, refined, educated and a man of action all in one. To be sure, there was a hint of pretentiousness in his new character. He was apt to describe people rather grandly as 'deficient in that grace of deportment which gives splendour to every action'. A streak of egotism never let him stop chasing after fame.[93] And his original impulsiveness never deserted him. So keen was he to harass and engage the enemy wherever possible during the war that he brushed aside Henry's appeals to think of his young wife and child back in London.[94] 'The love of military glory made him seek it upon occasions unworthy of his rank,' wrote General Greene of Lieutenant-colonel Laurens. And thus it was that John died, in an insignificant skirmish fought when the war was all but over.[95]

But John had done more than just learn his lessons well while abroad. He had learned to see his native province through London eyes – had seen clearly for the first time the full disgrace of slavery – and had never forgotten it. He went on to prove that he was not just a product of a tug-of-war between colonial and metropolitan influences, between his father Henry and his friend Thomas Day. He was his own man. The lesson of conscience proved as enduring as the lessons of ambition and worldly status. He acknowledged the hypocrisy of a people who contended for liberty while so grossly denying it to others. During the war he repeatedly promoted a scheme to enlist soldiers from among the slave population of Georgia and South Carolina by offering them their freedom, in the process risking derision and unpopularity. Though the scheme was defeated by both state legislatures, Laurens continued to stake his reputation on it.[96] Other Carolinian Innsmen – John and Edward Rutledge and the pleasure-loving Jacob Read to name a few – did not show such sensibility to the stigma of hypocrisy. They steadily opposed John's scheme.[97]

Although he had forsaken his early love of art and nature, John had found another path that still allowed him to be an individual. By breaking with his father's authority, returning home and joining the Continentals, he had died young. On the other hand, he had escaped the doom of a career in the legal profession. And despite his English manners, his West Indian wife and views on slavery that he picked up in a London coffee house, John Laurens had become one of that new breed – an American hero.

And Henry? Henry was not changed, either by London or by the example of his son's deep-felt new beliefs. After John's death, Alexander Hamilton wrote to Henry with the news that a slave named Frederic, who was in a New York gaol, claimed to have been freed by John. Henry replied that that was impossible. Frederic was Henry's own, and John would never trifle with another man's property. In words almost identical to those he applied in Robert Scipio's case, he wrote, 'he is according to the law of the land my property, I paid a valuable consideration for him'. Frederic came back to the Laurens plantation. Despite flirting with the idea of emancipating his slaves during the war, Henry only ever freed one, George, a youth who had attended him in London during his imprisonment in the Tower.[98] George had not tried to run away like that other. He should have his reward. And perhaps, to Henry's way of thinking, this belated display of magnanimity gave him the last word in the matter of Robert.

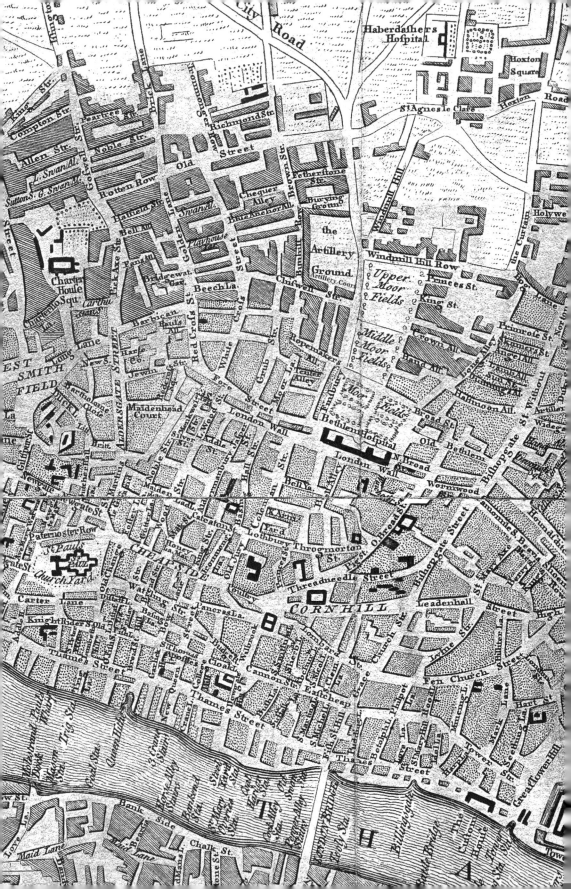

CHAPTER FIVE

A Long Island Yankee in the City

W ho has not heard the tale of Dick Whittington, the poor country boy who set out for London to make his fortune? There he became a servant in the house of a wealthy merchant until ill-usage and beatings obliged him to run away. When he reached the crest of Highgate Hill, he was stopped by the sound of the famous Bow Bells ringing a message to him to 'turn again', for he would one day be lord mayor of London. The fable ends with a rags-to-riches story of how Dick made his fortune by putting his cat in the hands of a canny London ship's captain. Puss proved to be worth her weight in gold to an oriental king whose palace was overrun with rats.

The real Richard Whittington was a medieval merchant of wealthy parentage who was four times lord mayor of London (that part was true), and was in no wise exceptional apart from his many good works. But his legend contained a very real moral for the English audiences who loved it over the centuries. London was where the plucky and the enterprising could make their fortune. It was a perennially dynamic, bustling place, the only British city that could be called 'metropolis'. And this was truer than ever in Georgian times, when it became the biggest city in the western world. 'The greatest Emporium in the known world', the government census boasted in 1801, 'a monument to man's material achievement'. It was the biggest port in the empire, home to one in ten Englishmen, the centre of aristocratic culture and the nursery of an alternative, vibrant middle-class culture that produced innovations in art and literature.[1]

For an ambitious colonial American of a certain stamp the opportunities of London seemed a greater lure than the limitless prospects of the New World. Such was Stephen Sayre, a farmer's son from Long Island whose adventures seemed for a time to mirror the career of the fabled Dick Whittington. Starting from scratch, Sayre skilfully worked his way into the most fashionable ranks of London society. Just as he got his foot in the door of the lord mayor's mansion, the War of Independence brought his achievements tumbling down.

Stephen Sayre was a New Englander by heritage, the descendant of Massachusetts Puritans who had settled in Long Island in the seventeenth century. His birthplace was the remote, quiet village of Southampton on the southeastern shore of Long Island. By the time of Stephen's birth in 1736 it had been settled for a century, but it remained a rustic place. The native Shinnecock Indians were still part of the neighbourhood.[2] His father, in addition to his farm, was a prosperous tanner and a deacon in the local Presbyterian church. The family was respectable but unremarkable. They were typical of ordinary colonial Americans, hardworking Yankee stock who made their livings as artisans and farmers.

But even Southampton felt the long reach of fashionable London. The old pioneer days when people like the Sayres wore homespun and ate off wooden plates were long gone. Without the money and the opportunity of families like the Laurenses, the Sayres aspired to at least a touch of gentility. With New York City nearby they would have no trouble getting hold of a cornucopia of store-bought goods from England: scented, flowered and silken gloves, soap (even the most rural ladies preferred not to use the homemade variety any more), wallpaper, textiles, lace, fans and hats.[3] The Sayre ladies bought the gloves, the hats and the trimmings, and of course mirrors to see the effect of all their imported finery. No doubt they decked themselves out for Sunday meeting. They bought tea and chocolate, and probably went through the middle-class ritual of the tea party with their occasional guests. Stephen's father even took a literary turn and bought three books.[4] But for most of the family these were only occasional luxuries in a life centred around hard work and country concerns. The Sayre boys, like their father, grew up to be farmers and artisans.

Except for Stephen. With echoes of Daniel Defoe's indomitable maid-servant Moll Flanders, Stephen wanted to be a gentleman. Perhaps the seeds of his ambition were planted in the glimpses of a more exciting, pleasurable world afforded by his sisters' store-bought frivolities and the chatter of the New York newspapers. These were full of London news, from Court presentations to notorious street crimes.[5] The colonial American thirst to know about London would only be equalled in the nineteenth century by the demand for stories about New York, the 'big city' of the young Republic.

Or perhaps Stephen was spoiled by exposure to too much book learning. Like that other, more famous son of a colonial artisan, Ben Franklin, Stephen

19 Stephen Sayre.

was counted a bright lad by his father and sent to school, probably under the tutelage of the local minister. He must have been an able scholar, for at age twenty he was enrolled at Princeton. This was late to enter college in a day when graduates were commonly in their teens. It may be that Stephen was having trouble choosing a career, and Princeton was a last-ditch effort. When he graduated in 1757 he did not become a clergyman as so many of his class-mates did. Instead he joined the army; the French and Indian War had begun at Fort Necessity three years earlier, and by now Britain was launching an aggressive attack on French fortifications in Canada. Stephen became the captain of a company of provincials bound for Fort Niagara.

Officers were expected to be gentlemen in those days. Stephen had prob-ably been polishing up his manners at Princeton, where he mixed with lads from wealthy colonial families. But his excursion to Niagara put him in the company of real British officers. For the first time Stephen saw up close bona fide metropolitan manners and what they could get you. The professional redcoats who came over during the war were said to be introducing England's 'polite national vices' into the wilds of America. But they also commanded respect and admiration. Even John Adams conceded their 'very engaging and agreeable' manners and conversation when he dined with some of them in Boston – this after speechifying elsewhere on their 'shocking impiety' and 'shameless, abandoned Debauchery'.[6]

Stephen saw more violence and probably worked harder than he ever would again in his life on the Niagara campaign. But the war was effectively over, and with it the possibility of a career as an officer and a gentleman. Provincial troops were disbanded. He went back to Princeton to add an M.A. to his qualifications. By 1761 he was working for New York merchant William Alexander. Stephen leapfrogged from connection to connection for his entire life, but, as we shall see, he always kept his eye on his main goal – to become a leisured gentleman.

William Alexander was an extraordinary individual whose career would serve as a road map for young Sayre's own aspirations. He was only in his thirties by the time Stephen came to work for him, but he had already built up a successful provisioning business, married into a prominent New York family, and – what was much more glamorous – had journeyed to London to lay claim to his right to the earldom of Stirling. Alexander was the nearest male heir to this vacant title, which came with rights to extensive lands in Nova Scotia and Long Island. But he wasn't just after the land. He hoped to buy the residence of the first earl of Stirling in Scotland, join the aristocracy and settle permanently in Britain.[7] When his claim was only partly successful, he returned to New York and called himself Lord Stirling for the rest of his life. He and Lady Stirling, together with their little ladyships his daughters, lived the life of the English gentry with a country estate in New Jersey.[8] But Alexander was no mere popinjay. He continued to be a successful merchant and went on to serve as a general on the American side in the Revolution, where he was remarkable for his bravery.

Stephen did not learn much about merchandising from his mentor. Ten years after his start in Alexander's counting house, he was described as 'a man of pleasure and unacquainted with business'.[9] What was much more interesting to Stephen than working up a balance sheet were Alexander's stories of the years he spent in Scotland and England in pursuit of his earldom: the castles he stayed in, the noblemen he befriended, his social life in London, and, in short, what having the airs of a gentleman and a bit of brazenness could get one in the metropolis. Alexander had been entertained at Gordon Castle, a magnificent palace in Morayshire, Scotland. He had dined at the home of a Scots friend whose wife, on seeing him, exclaimed in broad Scots and much to his amusement 'Mie God! The awnimal is wheete', expecting her husband's American guest to be red or black. He kept a house in London, in Portugal Street near Lincoln's Inn, and went shooting at the country house of Charles Townshend, a scion of the powerful Townshend family, who was soon to be a rising star in English politics.[10]

Perhaps Alexander recounted to Stephen the story of New Yorker Staats Long Morris, whom he met while in Scotland. If so, that must have made Stephen's ears prick up. Morris had married a widowed Scottish duchess ten years his senior, won over her outraged family with his youthful charm, and lived as a grandee in Britain for the rest of his life.[11]

Why couldn't something like that happen to Stephen? And the place to start was with Lord Stirling. He knew how to do things and had valuable connections in England. In New York everyone who could applied to him for letters of introduction before setting out for London. Lord Stirling knew rich students at the Inns of Court; he knew the DeLanceys, Ralph Izard and other South Carolinians who by the early 1770s would make up the Berners Street set. Even more useful were the powerful men of his acquaintance, Lord Shelburne and Charles Townshend, both of whom were becoming involved in colonial administration, and the Earl of Bute, who was soon to be very unpopular but was still prime minister and the king's favourite in 1762.[12]

Stephen's chance to see what he could do for himself in London came very quickly. In the spring of 1762 Lord Stirling sent him to Connecticut to check out the intentions of a land company called the Susquehanna, which schemed to establish a new western settlement on lands claimed by the colony of Pennsylvania. The Susquehanna Company had sent an agent to London the previous year to argue their case, and the governor of Pennsylvania (who was a friend of Stirling) was anxious to protect his interests. Sayre seemed a plausible young man; by August he was in London, testifying before the Board of Trade on behalf of Pennsylvania.[13]

Stephen's debut in London came at a momentous time in Anglo-American relations. The French had just been defeated in Canada, and in 1763 the Treaty of Paris gave Britain all of Canada, together with all land west of the colonies as far as the Mississippi. Pristine wildernesses teaming with unknown plants and animals now beckoned irresistibly to land speculators. Land speculation in the west was the favourite 'get-rich-quick' scheme of the day, and both British and American investors were bitten by the bug. A gaggle of eager colonial lobbyists had materialised in London by the early 1760s. It was only the beginning. For a century after American independence, the British would remain *the* major foreign investors in the development of the American west.

But this Anglo-American partnership in profit did not flourish immediately, for in the closing years of the war British officials were more concerned about keeping the peace on the frontier. Already the rumblings of Native American discontent that would end in the Pontiac uprising had drawn the attention of London policymakers to the problems of uncontrolled westward expansion. The British government hoped that a west sealed off from encroachments by whites, and where traders had to operate under the watchful eye of a British army detachment, would bring about good relations with the Indians. To the great discontent of speculators, in 1761 it was announced that all applications for land grants now had to go to London; no colonial government could approve them. The Proclamation of 1763 banned westward settlement altogether and instead encouraged colonists who wanted new lands to settle to the north in Quebec, and to the south in Florida. Within just a few years British ministers would be retreating from the Proclamation and granting western lands. But in 1763 it came like a thunderbolt to those who were eager to profit from the newly acquired west.

There is no evidence, though, that Stephen was unduly worried by the problems of would-be western investors in 1762. He impressed the Board of Trade with his indiscreet remarks on behalf of his patron, then seemed to forget about his mission. He had his own agenda, to set himself up as a merchant. Years later Stephen wrote that he had come to London with capital borrowed from friends in New York, who then sat on the goods he sent them, leaving him in debt.[14] In practice, it is doubtful that Stephen ever worked hard at the desk of his counting house. Much as he coveted the wealth of great Atlantic merchants, the thought of working twenty hours a day like Henry Laurens did not appeal. What spurred him to enterprise was the sight of London itself. 'I can't bear the thoughts of living in America or starving in England,' he wrote to a friend.[15] With those words he summed up what was to be his abiding ambition for the next fifteen years.

How did the Great City look to a Long Island farmer's son, that it should make such a powerful impression? Stephen set up business in Tokenhouse Yard, one of the many tiny courts and alleyways that criss-cross the old City of London. This particular location was 'up a court behind the Bank of England', where Charles Dickens placed the office of the seedy stockbroker Wilkins Flasher in *The Pickwick Papers*. Here was the very heart of the City's

20 The Bank of England in Threadneedle Street as it appeared in Stephen Sayre's day,
seen from the junction with Cornhill. The Bank is to the right of the church of
St Christopher-le-Stocks with its conspicuous square tower (demolished in 1782). Sayre's
route from Tokenhouse Yard into the heart of the business district would be via Prince's
Street, whose entrance can just be glimpsed behind the figures of men loading a
horse-drawn cart in the foreground.

business district. Commerce, of course, had an international flavour, and the
Yard had an association with England's long-standing trade with Portugal.
Prosperous Portuguese and English merchants had elegant residences in the
crowded courtyard. But an address in Tokenhouse Yard was not the West End,
and it was not out of the reach of aspiring small traders like Stephen. One
could keep a counting house there, giving one 'the consequence a merchant
merits' with clients, and have lodgings in another, cheaper part of town. Still
cheaper – and Stephen may have resorted to this – would be to rent a couple
of rooms, use one as an office, and cram all the signs of one's private living
arrangements into the other.[16]

From Tokenhouse Yard, Stephen had only to turn the corner from Lothbury
into Prince's Street, and within minutes exit into Threadneedle Street, where he
would find himself facing the entrance to the most famous bank on earth. The
Bank of England was one of the world's first purpose-built banks. It had been
constructed less than thirty years earlier, in 1734, by architect George

Sampson. Banks as a whole were a relatively new phenomenon in the eighteenth century, which meant the Bank of England was a tourist draw for curious visitors, who wandered in to inspect its public offices.[17] But it was not only its novelty that attracted tourists. The Bank of England was seen as a pillar of national greatness. Britain alone among the five Great Powers of Europe based her power on a happy blend of trade, finance and representative government. In contrast to her rivals, she had a constitutional monarchy and maintained only a small standing army. The other four – France, Russia, Austria and Prussia – were absolute monarchies with huge armies to enforce their power. The British saw themselves as a world power with a difference, whose success derived from the twin assets of a liberal political system (ensuring a healthy relationship between the British government and British businessmen) and the revenue derived from the vast British trading empire that was in the interest of both. The result? With a third of the population of France, Britain could boast the same government revenues, extracted from her thriving trade. She could buy her way to victory in any war, pushing her enemies into debt and hiring foreign armies if necessary. The French philosophe the Baron de Montesquieu had sung the praises of England's modern, free system to all of Europe in his *The Spirit of the Laws* in the 1740s, and British liberty was admired by progressive thinkers everywhere. Napoleon would in later years deride the British as a nation of shopkeepers; but for many Britons he was only underscoring the difference between his own conscripted army of peasants and the liberal prosperity of British society.[18] The Bank of England, which played a key role in loaning money to the government, could claim a distinctly patriotic gloss in all this.

That other pillar of British liberty and prosperity, the Royal Exchange, was only a stone's throw away from the Bank. The Royal Exchange stood in the triangular space where Threadneedle Street converged on Cornhill. Cornhill had been a place of commerce since the Romans built the forum of Londinium in the first century AD. Under Queen Elizabeth I the first Royal Exchange was erected so that merchants no longer need conduct their business in shops, taverns and even under the open skies. It was designed by Thomas Gresham, who decorated it with his family crest: a grasshopper. The original grasshopper weathervane became a recognisable symbol of commerce throughout the English-speaking world; it has gone on to adorn many public buildings, such as Boston's Fanueil Hall. It was also an apt symbol for the unsinkability of this temple of British commerce, for the Elizabethan Royal Exchange burnt down in the Great Fire of 1666, only to be quickly

21 The central courtyard of the Royal Exchange, where men from 'all considerable nations' met to conduct business.

rebuilt, then rebuilt again in the nineteenth century after once more being destroyed by fire.[19] Joseph Addison left a memorable picture of the central courtyard of the Exchange during peak business hours, in which men from 'all considerable Nations' – Frenchmen, Danes, Swedes, Dutchmen, Russians, even traders from the Far East – disputed, haggled and reached commercial agreements in a babble of languages, 'making this Metropolis a kind of *Emporium* for the whole Earth'.[20] London was already gaining its reputation as the business capital of the world.

Just around the corner from the City's foremost financial institutions was another new structure, Mansion House, built to host the lavish entertainments of London's lord mayors. It had been customary for lord mayors to live in their own homes and use the City Halls for official events, but by the eighteenth century lesser cities such as York and Dublin had acquired dedicated lord mayors' mansions. London must not lag behind these provincial towns. Completed in 1752, Mansion House was a grand structure built in the Palladian style, designed by architect George Dance. Its famous Egyptian Hall, splendid with its gilt cornicing and velvet draperies, could seat hundreds of guests for the lord mayor's proverbial banquets. Though the finished

22 The lord mayor's Mansion House (right), looking towards Cornhill and Lombard Street. To the left can be glimpsed the entrance into Threadneedle Street, with the spire of St Christopher-le-Stocks just in view.

product was liable to criticism, the building had 'an exciting touch of millionaire enormity' about it that added to the district's dynamic, modern atmosphere.[21]

Monumental as was the triumvirate of buildings at the junction of Cornhill and Threadneedle Street, it was not enough to contain all the merchant business that went on in the Great City in a day. That spilled over into the coffee houses and taverns that were thickly sprinkled throughout the neighbourhood. Eighteenth-century businessmen routinely used coffee houses as their offices. City merchants, who mostly worked in their counting houses, met together every day at prearranged hours in their local coffee house to transact collective business. So well established was this practice that it was Egerton Leigh's avoidance of the Carolina Coffee House during the usual business hours that first aroused Henry Laurens's suspicions against him.[22] Coffee houses were used by merchants to buy insurance, pick up and drop off mail, and transact business with ships' captains and planters. For confidential business, private rooms could be rented. People looking to emigrate to the West Indies or America could make enquiries in the relevant coffee house. Letter bags from the packet ships hung on the wall in such places and the latest newspapers were on the tables.[23]

Coffee houses sound convenient and they were, but they were also incredibly noisy and smoky. Not everyone was there on business; cards and chatter went on at many tables. A Bostonian complained of the 'intolerable racket of dice-boxes' that surrounded him as he tried to pen a coherent letter home. A young South Carolinian summed up the smells and the crowds when he wrote to his mother: 'Where do you think I am? At the Carolina Coffee House, smoked to death with tobacco, between two very greasy old gentlemen, who perhaps are at this moment looking at what I am writing.'[24] Still worse, one was not safe from the criminal element, as the different ranks of society mixed freely in the coffee houses of Georgian London.[25]

Most of the coffee houses where businessmen and merchants met were near the Bank and the Royal Exchange. Merchants whose business was with the American colonies tended to go to coffee houses named for the provinces with which they traded. Hence in Georgian London there was once a New England Coffee House at 60 Threadneedle Street, where it joined Old Broad Street. There was also a Georgia Coffee House, a New York Coffee House, and a Virginia and Maryland Coffee House. The Virginia and Maryland was in Newman's Court off Cornhill. A second Virginia Coffeehouse, better known as the Virginia and Baltick, was in Threadneedle Street near the Royal Exchange. All were just a few minutes' walk from one another, making business quick and easy.[26] Ben Franklin's regular, the Pennsylvania Coffeehouse, was in Birchin Lane, as was the Carolina Coffee House, where Henry Laurens met his planter and merchant friends while Robert Scipio loitered with the other servants. Directly off Birchin Lane in St Michael's Alley stands the Jamaica Coffee House, which still does business under the name of the Jamaica Wine House. In the eighteenth century it was known for the quality of its rum. Near the Jamaica Wine House is the George and Vulture. Now described as a pub, in the eighteenth century this was a chop house where Benjamin Franklin went every week to his Monday Club.[27]

At the height of business hours in the heart of the City, the merchants gathered 'on 'Change', crowding the neighbourhood as they 'hurried up and down, and chinked the money in their pockets and conversed in groups, and looked at their watches, and trifled thoughtfully with their gold seals'. This vivid description from Charles Dickens's *A Christmas Carol*, written eighty years after Sayre's arrival in London, still holds good for our period. Some of these busy traders had the appearance of gentlemen, but others retained the traditional bluff manner of the London businessman, and betrayed a hint of defiance at the growing pretentiousness of their associates. If some wealthy

23 Gentlemen confer in a coffee house, while behind them one man dozes and in the foreground another tucks into a meal. The bird climbing from its cage may indicate that this is the George and Vulture, which at one time was known for keeping a vicious parrot.

merchants escaped every evening from the social pollution of the City to their homes in the West End, others who were equally successful continued to live over their shops and wash themselves each morning in the pumps outside their front doors.[28]

Adding to this eclectic mix were businessmen from all over the American colonies. There were many of them. Business and trade in the empire had been on the rise throughout the century, with the colonies taking an ever greater share. By the 1770s the American colonies were the single fastest-growing market for English goods, more than quadrupling the English exports they consumed since the beginning of the century.[29] Colonial merchants and businessmen in their hundreds were constantly in the streets of London. Some were southern absentees like Henry Laurens who mixed a little business with pleasure while they enjoyed a prolonged stay in the capital. But there were many northerners like Stephen Sayre, from Pennsylvania, New

York and New England, who typically came alone and kept their visits short.[30] These northern businessmen in the City had none of the ostentatious wealth or the black attendants that caused absentee planters to stand out in the streets. In London they were difficult to distinguish from English provincials who came into the capital on business.

'I can't bear the thoughts of living in America or starving in England.' Stephen did not want to leave the dynamic world that lay just outside the door of his new address in Tokenhouse Yard. London's business district had the same exhilarating atmosphere that would be associated with Wall Street in the twentieth century. There was nothing to compare it to in any colonial port. And unlike the elegant West End, the City was a place where a Long Island country lad like Stephen would find fewer obstacles to fitting in.

This was just as well, for Stephen's background would not assist his project of becoming a leisured gentleman. It was not only his humble origins but his New England heritage that placed him at a disadvantage. New Englanders had a reputation as an underbred people, engrossed with the sordid business of making money. And they had an insular streak. John Adams, deploring the 'awkward and bashful' manners of his countrymen, attributed it to 'the little intercourse we have with strangers, and . . . our inexperience in the world.'[31] The rolls of the Inns of Court, where other colonies sent their sons to learn metropolitan ways, backed up Adams's words. Barely a name appeared from the colonies of Massachusetts, Connecticut, or New Hampshire.

Colonial absentees like Henry Laurens and his friends in the City knew very few New Englanders.[32] In fact, Henry's London acquaintance included far more West Indians and Englishmen than it did 'Yankees'. He and his merchant friends indulged in a traditional prejudice against the people of New England, labelling them a 'confederacy of smugglers' who were without the social hierarchy that was thought indispensable to polite society in the rest of England's Atlantic empire. New England was a land of small farmers that lacked the great estates of the colonies to the south, making it as undeveloped as the back country settlements in the eyes of Henry and his friends.[33]

Indeed, the chief sectional divide of colonial British America was not North versus South, or slave state versus free state, as it would be in the United States fifty years later. It was New England versus everyone else.[34] This was the general view. Ralph Izard's friend, the MP Edmund Burke, called the people of New England 'a mean shifting peddling nation' in 1775, even as he spoke up for colonial rights.[35] And they were widely compared with the Scots in a period when that was no compliment. In metropolitan eyes there was a resemblance between the Scots and the Puritans who had settled New England. Both peoples seemed fanatically religious, rustic and underbred; both regions were notorious for having persecuted witches well past the date when the more enlightened, modern England had given it up.[36] New England's cultural heyday, when Emerson, Thoreau and Melville would dazzle the world, was still far off in the future. What Robert Frost would later eulogise as a 'higher provincialism',[37] most eighteenth-century Anglo-Americans saw as simply countrified or uncouth.

It was in vain for Son of Liberty James Otis of Boston to point out that the New Englanders were the most English of all the colonists. 'Ninety-nine in a hundred in the northern colonies are white, and there is as good blood flowing in their veins, save the royal blood, as any in the three kingdoms.'[38] Speaking strictly of New England, that was more or less true; most of its population had migrated from England, the rest were from elsewhere in the British Isles. In contrast, the colonies to southward could with justification be branded a 'motley' people.[39] The middle colonies had a hefty mix of Dutch, German, French, Irish, African and Swedish added to their British population. The slave colonies had, of course, a substantial African population. But that was not the point. It was not racial purity but similar manners that best greased the wheels of social harmony in the eighteenth-century British empire. And in any case, Londoners themselves were also susceptible to the label 'motley'. Like many of the American colonies, London by the reign of George III was a mix of English, Scots, Scotch-Irish, Welsh, Irish, French Huguenot, Dutch, African, and Jews and Gentiles from Germany and Poland – all the peoples who had been swept into the enormous British trading system that encircled the Atlantic.[40]

In London, New Englanders did look rustic. Contemporary descriptions paint them as 'of rough manners', 'uncultivated', dressed in outdated country clothing that looked 'a leetle sarvanty' in the capital.[41] Even a wealthy Massachusetts merchant who dined with good company when he was in the City was mistaken for a servant at a wayside inn (merely because he had thriftily refrained from ordering the usual traveller's fare!). And he found himself rebuffed on several occasions when he tried to strike up conversations with strangers without benefit of an introduction. He dismissed them with a shrug as 'too proud or too refined to mix with those they don't know'.[42]

Rustic they might be, but when in London New Englanders couldn't be distinguished from their equally rustic English counterparts, for example Yorkshiremen (with whom they were sometimes compared).[43] Nor would their accents give them away. Although the Yankee twang had emerged by the eighteenth century, there is no evidence that Londoners could recognise it or any other colloquial colonial speech as American.[44] After all, there were enough dialects spoken in the British Isles alone to confound the average London shopkeeper.

So Stephen Sayre did not have to worry unduly about his background. A man of his character could easily play it down when necessary. It was more important simply to seem like a gentleman. And besides, as we shall see, there were circles – some of them quite influential ones – in which New Englanders were seen as the very best sort of Americans. Moreover, Stephen Sayre was a man who could play many roles, and who never ever overlooked an opportunity.

'I can't bear the thoughts of living in America or starving in England.' Stephen Sayre did not miss the rustic life he had left behind in Long Island. He never wanted to return. He did not want to starve, or experience any sort of deprivation whatsoever. Hopscotching from Princeton to a counting house in New York, and from there to London, he had found the place where he wanted to stay. His ambition was not only to live, but to live well. It required at least £600 a year for a single man to live 'in a style perfectly genteel' in London.[45] Stephen wanted the lavish lifestyle of an independent gentleman, and he did not wait to build up his own fortune before diving in. A few years after arriving in London, while he had yet to earn his fortune, he confessed to a friend: 'I am afraid to say a word of the luxurious paths of pleasure that I have for so many years rolled along.'[46] These paths were expensive; to ensure that they would forever be open to him, Stephen needed to find a steady and substantial income that didn't leave him working long hours in an office or counting house.

In just a few years Stephen had come a long way from his humble beginnings as a farmer's son on Long Island. Through his own unassisted efforts, he had raised himself to the situation of the younger sons of the English gentry and nobility, a class who were 'bred to no business and born to no estate', and were therefore obliged to cast around for a means of maintaining their idle lifestyles. These were a numerous brood in Georgian England.[47] Their predicament was summed up succinctly by the pleasant-mannered Colonel Fitzwilliam in *Pride and Prejudice*, who explained the trouble with 'younger sons' to Elizabeth Bennet: 'Our habits of expense make us too dependent, and there are not many in my rank of life who can afford to marry without some attention to money.' At least Colonel Fitzwilliam was the son of an earl and had a pedigree to make him attractive to a family that had money but no breeding. Poor Stephen more closely resembled Mr Wickham – charm and good looks in abundance, a favourite with the ladies, 'the handsomest man in England' some called him – but of obscure birth, and without even a Mr Darcy in the wings to blackmail into financial aid.[48] Like Dick Whittington, Stephen must try for what he could get by his wits and his luck.

From the start of his residence in London, Stephen kept company with the type of wealthy young colonists who had been groomed from their childhood to fit in to metropolitan society. If he needed to polish up his own manners, London was the best place to do it. Fortunately for Stephen, getting the knack of genteel speech and deportment depends more on innate ability than genteel parentage. Evidence is that he learned quickly – more quickly than some of the privileged youths who formed part of his circle. His quickness reflected not inborn sensitivity but the instincts of a charlatan.

Genteel manners were a cheap accessory for those who had the knack of imitation. If you could perfect your manners and acquire a good suit of clothes, it was very difficult for people to guess your social status. That opened up a window of opportunity for those who were sharp enough to take advantage of it. In a period when England's own King George III was widely regarded as awkward and unfashionable, wealthy ladies and gentlemen sometimes had the mortification of seeing their domestics equal or outdo them in putting on airs. The period abounds with stories of servants who were indistinguishable from those they served. Continental visitors sometimes complained that they couldn't tell English servants apart from their masters and mistresses. Even maidservants wore silk on their days off, observed a Frenchman, and the upper servants dressed in relative finery throughout the week.[49] American colonists were also bemused by this peculiar London form of 'servant trouble', for the first ever play written and produced in America was a comedy in which a rustic Yankee mistook a London valet for his master.[50] George Bernard Shaw's Professor Henry Higgins accomplished nothing with Eliza Doolittle that many of her class could not have done on their own, given the examples and the opportunity.

Naturally, all this opened the door to various types of fraud. In London, where genteel folk were often obliged to engage strangers as servants and were dependent on testimonials, a brisk trade in false references arose. For a fee a common swindler would impersonate a former master by donning a fine coat and adopting the appropriate air, and give a glowing account to a prospective employer.[51] In 1771 a young woman who had served as a lady's maid at the Court of St James was transported to the southern colonies for theft. With her knowledge of Court names and Court manners (and a few stolen gems to add to her credibility) she passed herself off in Virginia and South Carolina as Queen Charlotte's sister. She was invited into the homes of the 'best gentry', and American planters vied to kiss her hand before she was exposed as an imposter.[52] A truly horrifying story that became a proverb for the unwary was that of Sir Samuel Morland, a baronet who in the late seventeenth century was duped into marrying a beautiful, demure and well-dressed young lady after meeting her just once in Hyde Park. He believed her to be a wealthy and virginal heiress, but she proved instead to be some-one-or-other's discarded mistress, now fallen on hard times.[53] This sort of fraud worked best in London, where the anonymity of the big city provided additional cover for the imposture.

All of this worked to the advantage of a chameleon-like character such as Stephen Sayre. London had everything, and everything it had could be obtained by wits alone if one were willing to overcome certain scruples. Stephen's project was to marry an heiress, or any other get-rich-quick scheme that he could hit upon. He soon learned that London and Bath had the best marriage markets, certainly better than anywhere in the colonies. In America one could only find 'girls of fortune' in the colonies south of Pennsylvania, 'but believe me they are no where so frequent as in London', asserted a knowing one in Stephen's circle.[54] Stephen did not exactly lie about his identity – he never changed his name, and he kept his American contacts – but he allowed his rustic origins to sink so far into the background that he could speak grandly of a fellow Yankee in London as 'unpolished' and as one who gave 'great disgust' to polite society.[55] This from a farmer's son!

One could not live off manners, and within a year of arriving in London, Stephen had worked his way into the confidence of a wealthy merchant, Dennis De Berdt. That merchant, his family and his two homes would provide the backdrop and resources for the part Stephen would play for the next seven years. In Mr De Berdt, Stephen found at last a use for his rigid Presbyterian upbringing, for the elderly merchant was one of those Englishmen who, far from despising New England rusticity, idealised it as a throwback to an original and purer English way of life.

Dennis De Berdt was a leading export merchant who had been trading with the American colonies for many years.[56] He was also deeply religious, and it was this above all that defined him. His father had fled to England from Flanders to escape religious persecution; De Berdt remained true to his heritage. International relations he understood as a conflict between Catholic and Protestant nations. He spoke of the recent Seven Years' War in messianic terms: Pitt the Elder and Divine Providence had ended French power in Canada. He used biblical names for the French enemy, like 'Assyrians' and 'Amalekites'. This stuff peppered his advice to government ministers, which was sought during the war because of his extensive knowledge of America. He believed that Providence had cleared the American continent of the 'French vermin' after 1763 in order to open the way for 'the light of the gospel' to 'dawn among the benighted savages'. He was a strong supporter of Eleazar Wheelock's School for Native Americans, later to become Dartmouth College.[57]

But threats to the liberty of such as De Berdt did not only come from abroad. De Berdt was a religious dissenter, a Protestant who refused to conform to the established Church of England. In both New and Old England, dissenters felt threatened by the Anglican establishment. Dissenters were tolerated in England, but they lived under the disadvantage of certain discriminatory legislation which restricted their political life. In their own self-defence they developed a heritage of organised political opposition. In London the three principal denominations of Protestant dissenters (there were Catholic dissenters, too) – Presbyterians, Congregationalists and Baptists – formed a lobby called the Protestant Dissenting Deputies, of which De Berdt was a member. One of the causes they took up was the prevention of the establishment of Anglican bishoprics in the colonies, something the nonconforming New Englanders in particular opposed as a threat to their religious freedoms.[58] De Berdt and the Dissenting Deputies identified closely with New England's attempt to evade what each believed would be a prelude to ecclesiastical oppression in America.

Mr De Berdt and his circle of religious dissenters and nonconformist thinkers had far stronger personal ties with the northern colonies, and particularly New England, than with the plantation colonies. For them the rusticity found in the northeastern provinces was no dishonour, but marked them out as the preserve of an earlier, simpler and less consumer-oriented way of living that had once prevailed in England. England, they argued, was in a moral decline, but in her New World settlements one could still find true English values. In the view of men like De Berdt it was the northern colonies, with their small farms and relative social equality, that typified American society. As one historian put it, 'it is scarcely an exaggeration to say that in their eyes America was New England writ large'.[59] It was one of these pro-American dissenters, the Quaker Dr John Fothergill, who wrote angrily in defence of

American rights during the Stamp Act Crisis: 'How many people are there, and those too of no small figure, who know no difference between the inhabitants of *North America*, and those of the *West-India* Islands?'[60] This was what he and his circle of nonconformists hated, that for most Londoners 'American' signified the mixed-race incomers from the plantation colonies whose lifestyles were a corrupt mixture of luxury and degradation.

When the British government tried for the first time to tax the colonies in 1765, De Berdt and many of his fellow dissenters unhesitatingly supported colonial opposition. Seen from the government's pragmatic point of view, the Stamp Act seemed only fair. The British people, with a population four times the size of the colonies, paid about a hundred times more in taxes. Now the nation was staggering under a debt incurred by the late war in Canada, and the new American west required policing by British troops. Why shouldn't the colonists help out? But what most Americans saw was that their taxes were about to go up by about 50 per cent, and they hadn't had any say in the matter.[61] 'No taxation without representation' became the catchphrase.

De Berdt identified with the plight of the colonies in highly coloured religious terms. The colonists were descendants of English subjects who had fled during the bad old days, when English soil itself was polluted by the threat of Popery and tyranny. These 'brave and free' Englishmen had 'preferred an inhospitable desert to their native soil' in order to escape 'the arbitrary power of the faithless Stuarts'. Now the descendants of these hardy folk, living peacefully in their rustic settlements, found themselves once again threatened with 'acts of arbitrary power' emanating from a mother country that would make them 'slaves instead of Englishmen', their rights swept away and themselves loaded down with taxes that ignored their own constitutional arrangements.[62]

This folkloric view of the origins of the British settlements in America entirely ignored the rage to cultivate cash crops that had fuelled much of England's early colonisation, and its unlovely legacy of widespread slave keeping.[63] It was difficult to reconcile the notion of the colonists as victims of tyranny with the prevailing metropolitan stereotype of them as wealthy planters who imported their decadent lifestyles and slaves into London. As John Laurens's friend Thomas Day put it so vividly: 'If there be an object truly ridiculous in nature, it is an American patriot signing resolutions of independency with one hand, and with the other brandishing a whip over his affrighted slaves.' But Dennis De Berdt was less worried about the prospect of decadent planters importing their degraded lifestyles into London than he was about the moral impact of a British army stationed in America, officered by a 'dissolute set of men' who (according to his lights) would 'deprave the manners of the people' in the 'infant colonies'.[64] It is no surprise that the colony of Massachusetts appointed De Berdt as their London agent in 1765 to lobby for repeal of the Stamp Act, which occurred the following year.

We already know that Stephen Sayre hoped to become as dissolute and depraved as any British officer. So what could he and Dennis De Berdt possibly have in common? That was easy. Stephen's father back on Long Island was a Presbyterian deacon; Stephen had grown up listening to pious discourses, some of them no doubt directed in tones of concern or censure at the lifestyles of the Native Americans who lived in the neighbourhood. Nothing so simple as to talk the same talk to old Mr De Berdt, who was approaching seventy by the time they met. Stephen was as persuasive as ever; the old merchant described him as 'a man after my own heart who will take my son by the hand and animate him to fill up my place in the church and the world when I shall be no more . . .'[65]

Stephen quickly became commercial agent for the house of De Berdt, assuming important responsibilities at a troubled time. Dennis De Berdt reckoned that he was owed a staggering £50,000 by his American customers. Stephen made several extensive trips to the West Indies and America to collect debts and drum up business for the ailing firm. It was a difficult post, but he was philosophical about the trouble it gave him. '[T]he old codger must soon pop off,' he quipped to his cousin.[66] There are signs that he did not take his overseas commission too seriously, for by one account he 'did not behave well' while in Virginia.[67] And there were probably compensations. There has been a persisting question mark over Stephen's honesty. A rumour that he stole commission money during his service in the provincial army has never entirely died away. As agent of the house of De Berdt, he was accused by Philadelphia merchants of overcharging for goods (an accusation that he said gave him 'a good deal of pain'). Various angry creditors in New York were still demanding their money seven years after he'd left for England.[68]

Meanwhile, Stephen made himself at home with the 'old codger's' family and his town and country residences. The De Berdts lived in Artillery Court off Chiswell Street, not far from the business district and the Bank of England, but outside the ancient City walls, where the green spaces of Moorfields and Artillery Ground gave his home a breath of fresh air.[69] In addition, Mr De Berdt was one of the wealthy merchants who could afford to keep a rural retreat, at Enfield north of London.[70]

Stephen ingratiated himself with the rest of the family through a very different tack from the one he used with the head of the household. They were not so strict and serious. There was young Dennis De Berdt, Jr., 'gay, volatile and lively', a pleasant lad who was 'brought up in the expectation of a handsome fortune', good natured and 'agreeable rather than useful'.[71] There was the lovely Esther De Berdt, Dennis junior's older sister. 'Older' is a relative term; Miss De Berdt (known as Hetta to her family) was petite, lively, blond and just seventeen in 1763.[72] She might have been the heiress Stephen was looking for, but for the fact that she was already pledged to Pennsylvanian Joseph Reed, a distant cousin of Stephen and a fellow Princeton alumnus who was studying law at the Inns of Court. (Also, it would transpire that Stephen knew a good deal more about De Berdt's real financial state than Reed did, knowledge which perhaps disqualified Hetta as the future Mrs Sayre.) Nevertheless, Hetta and Stephen enjoyed a standing flirtation, as we will see.

Hetta De Berdt was an up-to-date young woman in a period when marriage for love was becoming the fashion in England and America. There were still plenty of arranged marriages and overbearing fathers who stood in the way of love-matches, but they were increasingly subjected to public disapproval. Novels and plays glamorised romance, and encouraged filial disobedience on the score of love.[73] In September 1764 Mr De Berdt opposed a marriage between Hetta and Joseph Reed. He did not like the idea of his only daughter being packed off to the colonies, and besides Joseph Reed had yet to earn his fortune. When the merchant forbade the young people to see one another or even to correspond, Hetta unhesitatingly entered into a secret engagement. Her father's orders, together with his outdated notions, were easily over-ridden. A ship's captain who came regularly to Artillery Court was taken into the secret and persuaded to carry letters between the lovers behind the back of his senior business associate. 'My parents have not the least suspicion', wrote Hetta with a precocious self-assurance. Mrs De Berdt – who must have been much younger than her husband, given the children's ages – soon took her daughter's side. Stephen quietly sided with his cousin Reed, taking a dig at the merchant for his hypocritical 'lectures on the uselessness of money which I have so often heard'. Eventually Mr De Berdt succumbed to the inevitable.[74]

A visitor to the De Berdt household in 1766 observed that Merchant De Berdt was 'a good man, but old and quite under the influence of his wife and two flirting children'.[75] He might have added Stephen Sayre to the list; Stephen pretty much came and went as he pleased, getting a home welcome in the drawing room at Artillery Court when he returned from business trips. 'We are vastly happy in our connection with him', wrote Hetta, 'and he seems, and I hope is so with us. Indeed, I do not know any other person that could have been so perfectly agreeable' – evidently forgetting that she was writing to her fiancé, who had by now returned to America and was starting up his law practice. She addressed Stephen familiarly as 'Sayre'; he returned the compliment, calling her Hetta, rather than Miss De Berdt. Stephen apparently assumed a brotherly role, as he escorted Hetta on a two-day jaunt to Windsor with no mention of any chaperone. Small wonder that there were rumours on both sides of the Atlantic that they were engaged.[76]

When Mr De Berdt had a minor stroke in the same year, Hetta covered it up. 'We wish my father's indisposition may be kept a secret', she wrote to Joseph Reed.[77] Was the household at Artillery Court conspiring to prevent the old man's retirement? Sayre was soon made a salaried assistant to the aging agent for Massachusetts. Whatever the truth, public criticism mounted of Mr De Berdt's performance as an agent. One observer wrote scornfully that he accepted without question every scrap of political gossip he picked up in the coffee houses or at the levees of government ministers, interpreting each polite 'squeeze *by the hand and come tomorrow*' as proof of support for his colonial clients. 'I don't imagine the agency of the colonies which was in his hands can come into worse', wrote a dissenting clergyman just after his death.[78] As a merchant, too, his best days were over; 'quite exhausted and worn out, he has given little attention to business for some time past', wrote his future son-in-law.[79]

Given the absence of any effective adult supervision at the De Berdt house in an era when adult interference was very hard to evade, it is not surprising that Artillery Court became something of a drop-in for young Americans. Most were Pennsylvanians because of Mr De Berdt's extensive colonial trading connections in that province. As well as Joseph Reed, whose merchant father did business with the De Berdts, there was John Morgan, a medical student who would help found the first American medical school at the University of Pennsylvania.[80] But not all were a credit to their native colony. There were James and Andrew Allen, the sons of William Allen, chief justice of the colony. These were the same Allens who were painted with the young Ralph Izard – posing with his cricket bat – and other wealthy planter friends in 1764.[81] They and their circle seemed intent on proving that northern boys could be just as decadent as their southern peers. Their father was one of the wealthiest men in Pennsylvania, and James and Andrew could afford to live the high life in London.[82] Andrew Allen frankly admitted that he had 'a disposition not much averse to pleasure' and neglected his studies. James Allen wrote almost boastfully of the 'wild and extravagant' behaviour of Americans at the Temple.[83] Years later Hetta De Berdt, having witnessed their entire 'want of application' at the Inns of Court, was astonished to learn that they actually intended practising law.[84] Their father complained about their expenses, comparing them to his own youthful stint in London, and grumbling: 'I am sure they are more, by near one half, than I was allowed, and *I lived handsomely*, and kept as good company as they do, and never left any tradesmen's bills unpaid.'[85] One hopes he had kept better company; in addition to Ralph Izard and the fun-loving planter's sons, the Allens' circle included New Yorker Peter DeLancey, who was later to marry one of the Beresfords of Berners Street and die in a Charleston duel. Peter came over to study at the Inns of Court in the same year as Stephen Sayre, and like Stephen brought letters of introduction from Lord Stirling.[86] Within a year he had contracted a venereal disease, no doubt through contact with London's ubiquitous prostitutes. New York merchant John Watts was deputised to tell the parents about 'the accident that happened to the branch' in London. '[T]hey received it very properly,' he recalled, 'the old gentleman though could not help now and then to throw up an ejaculation from the gizzard.'[87]

One member of the Artillery Court crowd, Thomas Ruston of Pennsylvania, was a particular intimate of Stephen. They had gone to Princeton together, and by 1763 Ruston was in London to attend the teaching hospitals, armed with a letter of introduction to Dennis De Berdt. Ruston was not as well off as some he met in the De Berdt's drawing room; he lodged for free in the home of a chemist named Jonathan Jacobs, who lived opposite the Monument in the business district.[88] He was obliged to go to Edinburgh for a time for his medical studies, but he preferred London, and by early 1766 he was back there. London was a great place; like his classmate Stephen he wanted to stay. After a brief and unsuccessful attempt to set up a smallpox house in Hackney (the locals threatened legal action and broke the windows of his infirmary[89]), Ruston set out in quest of a wealthy heiress. He informed his father that he hoped for no less than £10,000 – the same sum that had awed Mrs Bennet into silence when she contemplated her daughter Elizabeth's marriage to Mr Darcy in *Pride and Prejudice*. Ruston's project was backed by Ruston senior in Pennsylvania, who sent him sufficient funds to assume the appearance of 'a man of substance'.[90] Success was delayed, but in the end Ruston won through. In 1772, after several years of trying, he married the niece of a governor of the Bank of England. His office hours were 11 a.m. to 3 p.m., a sufficiently short working day to allow him still to qualify as a gentleman in the eyes of London society.[91]

Stephen Sayre had his association with the De Berdts to give him the appearance of a 'man of substance', and like Thomas Ruston he was keen to bag a rich heiress. But he was not as single-minded as his friend; why not look around a little before committing oneself? The world was his oyster during those first years in London. Early on he had engaged the affections of Charlotte Nelthorpe, daughter of a Lincolnshire baronet. Charlotte was only twenty, young, charming and impressionable, and her wealthy father was dead. On the down side, her fortune was not at her own disposal; a watchful mother held the purse strings, making an elopement futile. Stephen must watch and wait for an opportunity to convince Lady Nelthorpe that he was a suitable son-in-law. Meanwhile, the network of young people at Artillery Court worked for him. Joseph Reed carried letters for Stephen to Miss Nelthorpe, probably through her cousin John Nelthorpe who was at the Inns of Court with Reed. Sayre's letters to Reed hint that there may have been a secret engagement.[92]

But bright prospects in one area did not stop an enterprising young man from following up other opportunities. In 1765 Stephen was on St Croix in the Caribbean, on business for Mr De Berdt, when he spotted a beautiful, charming, childless young wife 'whose husband lies at death's door'. Once he 'popped off' (to borrow Stephen's own phraseology) she would be worth £10,000. If Bathsheba were 'half so fair and tempting' as this young widow-to-be, he confided to Reed, he could understand David's sin against Uriah. But this St Croix Uriah remained alive and at his wife's side, 'forever . . . watchful', lamented Stephen.[93] The lovely young wife disappeared from Stephen's letters (perhaps her husband recovered), and he spotted another opportunity. There was a plantation on the island going cheaply that he was sure would yield £2,000 a year in the right hands. Sayre was not thinking of turning businessman-farmer, but rather absentee sugar planter, like the ones he saw living so comfortably in London. He tried to interest Lady Nelthorpe's business adviser Mr Neate in the scheme (Neate was another useful De Berdt contact), in hopes he would persuade her ladyship to advance money for the estate. It was characteristic of Stephen's brand of impudence to try to cast himself in the light of an eligible son-in-law by soliciting money from his fiancée's family.[94]

Charlotte Nelthorpe wisely did not marry him. By 1768 she had married a highly respectable clergyman named Robert Carter Thelwall and later gave birth to a daughter who eventually married the eighth Duke of St Albans.[95] Nothing daunted, Stephen was soon pinning his hopes on a very different sort of liaison. Like Staats Long Morris, whose story had inspired Stephen when he was starting out back in New York, he took up with an 'old duchess'. According to Stephen, she was willing to marry him and was worth £3,000 a year – 'the connection would greatly gratify my ambition, mortify my enemies, and fix me in an independent station'. But he was a romantic at heart – 'I can't well quit the dear expectation of refined love and mutual enjoyment, with some sweet girl'. Instead, he made some sort of business proposition to the duchess, which she refused – 'though we have taken a friendly parting upon her refusal to advance a good sum for our trade, yet she has again sent me a kind invitation to come often to see her'. The relationship hinted of prostitution. The duchess remained in the picture, despite Stephen's unwillingness to tie the knot, and he confided to Joseph Reed that he was keeping the possibility of marriage in reserve in case of a crisis: 'I must confess myself rascal enough to play her off in case of absolute necessity'.[96]

What sort of man was Stephen Sayre, that he should write so freely of such matters? Frank and spicy letters like his are unusual, and give a flavour of what his conversation must have been. In his letters to his friend and former classmate Joseph Reed he seemed always to be playing the part of an eighteenth-century 'man of pleasure', an elegant, worldly playboy. The fact that he committed such confidential matters to paper suggests that he was extremely gregarious, and liked the company of his fun-loving peers. He was clearly popular with his circle at Artillery Court. But his letters show only how he wanted to look; Stephen's real feelings remain elusive. After 1770, when his correspondence with Reed broke off, we do not even have these breezy missives to give us an insight into his plans and motives. His actions must explain him.

At any rate, despite the opportunities that came his way, he remained unmarried throughout his years with the De Berdts. Perhaps he adopted a view widely held by Georgian England's gentrified younger sons, whose lifestyles he emulated, that marriage brought only expense. One was 'clogged with a wife and family' and marriage was best avoided until late in life, or side-stepped altogether.[97] Uncomplicated sexual satisfaction could be bought very cheaply in a variety of ways in London, which was notorious for its prostitutes in the eighteenth century.[98] James Boswell left a frank record of his sexual adventures as a young bachelor, which ranged from a sordid fumbling with a girl on the Strand for just a shilling to a voluptuous affair with a beautiful young actress.[99] The 'luxurious paths of pleasure' Stephen admitted he rolled along undoubtedly included dalliances with low-born girls. Meanwhile, he had other schemes for getting money.

For a while during the crisis surrounding the Stamp Act, Stephen looked to be a high flyer in political circles. Dennis De Berdt had political connections in high places as agent for Massachusetts. Stephen signed the petition of

London merchants praying for repeal of the new tax, which his employer and others had organised. Through the agent he met Lord Dartmouth, then president of the Board of Trade, and MP Charles Townshend, who was involved in organising the process of repeal for the government. Dartmouth he tried to impress with a scheme for imperial reform that would end Anglo-American disharmony (many such schemes were to be passed on to British ministers over the next ten years).[100] Townshend considered him as a possible witness to appear before a parliamentary committee investigating the effects of the Stamp Act. These House examinations were carefully rehearsed, and Sayre's written questions and answers are still lying among the Townshend papers, but he probably never testified.[101]

By the late spring of 1766, with the Stamp Act repealed, Stephen set off on another extended business trip to the colonies. This time he was armed with a commission from Charles Townshend (soon to be chancellor of the exchequer) to keep him informed on American affairs. Or so Stephen thought. Shortly after he embarked for America, Townshend told De Berdt that 'he was sorry I was connected with such an impertinent fellow'! The loyal Mr De Berdt dismissed Townshend as a 'mere weather cock'. Meanwhile Stephen, unconscious of the betrayal, could go about garnering American support for his scheme of obtaining a vast grant of land in Niagara (then still Indian territory), naming the powerful Townshend as a backer. Mr De Berdt was to be busy bringing Dartmouth in on the business during Stephen's absence.[102]

The faithless Townshend was in any case dead by the time Stephen returned in October 1767. Mr De Berdt immediately took his young protégé in his coach to Whitehall to meet Lord Shelburne, secretary of state for the southern department, who had an open mind towards western settlements and so could be the focus of all sorts of greedy speculations.[103] Stephen had been pushing himself on both sides of the pond as one who knew all about American affairs and had impeccable political connections. If he played it right he could become a colony agent like Mr De Berdt. There was his home colony of New York and, given his work for Mr De Berdt, inheriting the Massachusetts agency seemed another possibility. He wrote a pamphlet called *The Englishman Deceived* which chimed in with Mr De Berdt's views.[104] Americans, Stephen informed the reader, were true Englishmen who would never submit to unjust taxes. In a pleasant bit of fantasy, he promised his readers that rather than lose their rights, all three million colonists would banish English finery, wear 'the skins of beasts' and live in bark huts.[105] The notion that the colonists were so rustic that they would revert to a primitive state and stop consuming British goods, if provoked, was not dismissed as quickly as it deserved by the London reading public.[106]

Mr De Berdt probably footed the bill for Stephen's foray into publishing, as he did other such projects.[107] But it availed nothing. Stephen did not have a chance of the Massachusetts agency, which went to the eminent Benjamin Franklin after De Berdt died in 1770. And in New York they knew too much about Stephen (apparently some members of the New York Assembly thought him a 'young giddy foolish coxcomb'). There the post went to Edmund Burke. That would have been disappointing for Stephen, for agencies often earned between £200 and £300 a year plus expenses.[108] In return, agents were required to look after their constituent colony's political business in London, a charge that could be burdensome during a political crisis, but at other times called for only a bit of correspondence and some genteel trips to the government offices at Whitehall. '[T]he only idea of duty an American agent has', wrote a scornful member of Sayre's Artillery Court crowd, 'is to make a formal and very humble visit to Whitehall with any paper his assembly sends him, and leaving it to the good pleasure of the minister, thinks his business done.'[109] That would have been work enough for Stephen, who as Mr De Berdt's assistant seemed not to take his post too seriously. Given the charge of gathering political intelligence for the elderly agent, he conveyed such absurdities as that Lord Hillsborough, the American secretary, had plans to kill all the Indians in the colonies and put British soldiers in every American seaport, and that his lordship 'would rather see every man to 50 in America put to the sword than the Stamp Act repealed' – reports that Mr De Berdt appeared to take seriously.[110]

Stephen had many balls in the air, but they all fell abruptly to the ground with the death of Dennis De Berdt. Joseph Reed, who was returning to London to marry Hetta at last, arrived just in time to hear of his death. His letters record the chaos that ensued. Mr De Berdt proved to be insolvent: 'When I came I found every thing in confusion and the family buoyed up with those hopes which their own wishes suggested, but upon looking over the lists of debts, I found immediately that there was no reason to expect one shilling for the family.' Mrs De Berdt was forced to give up her coach immediately; Hetta sacrificed her horse. Everything was in disarray. '[I]t is impossible to describe to you the wretched management of this counting house,' Reed wrote. 'Upon looking into the books I can discover thousands lost by negligence and ignorance, and am not the least surprised at the event. Mr Sayre neither understands nor attends to business, though he was taken into the partnership purely on this account.'[111] Joseph Reed was not alone in laying the blame at Stephen's door. His reputation was damaged in the City, though not fatally as we will see.[112] Reed married his Hetta, and took her and her mother back to Philadelphia. They cut all ties with Stephen, who had once been almost a member of the family. Dennis De Berdt junior eventually set up as a City merchant himself, and succeeded at it. But Stephen's comfortable years as a hanger-on at the De Berdt establishment were well and truly over.

CHAPTER SIX

'The Handsome Englishman'

'I can't bear the thoughts of living in America or starving in England.' For eight years this thought had led Stephen Sayre on like a pillar of cloud. Was his abiding ambition over? By no means, for by the time of Mr De Berdt's death in 1770 he had another string to his bow through his association with the celebrated English political figure John Wilkes. In an age that was ripe for reform, Wilkes highlighted to the British public the shortcomings of their political system in a way that struck a chord with British subjects on the other side of the Atlantic as well, and for a while it seemed as if the two could make common cause.

John Wilkes had come into the political limelight at the end of the Seven Years' War in 1763, when as a Member of Parliament he had attacked the ministry in his scurrilous newspaper, the *North Briton*. His was the popular cause; the new king, George III, and his prime minister, Lord Bute, were bringing about what many saw as a premature end to the war. Wilkes harried Bute mercilessly in his weekly rag, accusing him of selling out England's interests to the French, and even resorting to ethnic slurs against Bute's Scots origins. With the publication of the particularly offensive issue Number 45 (soon to be notorious), Wilkes was arrested for seditious libel and confined to the Tower of London. Celebrity suited Wilkes; theatre was part of his tactics. He managed to turn the tables on his enemies in the law courts, successfully claiming that he was arrested with an illegal warrant. He became a popular figure, a victim of ministerial intrigue in the eyes of the London mob, but despite this he was ultimately obliged to flee to France to avoid further arrest.

It was his return to London in 1768 that secured for all time his role as a popular hero. He got himself elected as MP for Middlesex, a county on the outskirts of London that was becoming part of the London sprawl. He then gave himself up to the authorities (he was technically an outlaw, but the government at first studiously ignored his return to England). Wilkes made certain that he was not ignored for long. He was committed to King's Bench Prison and fined £1,000. He was also expelled from the House of Commons. Nothing daunted, Wilkes continued his opposition to the government from his prison cell. (We should not picture the likes of Henry David Thoreau or Martin Luther King in this instance; King's Bench Prison had luxury accommodation for those who could afford it, including the services of barbers, tailors, cooks and prostitutes.[1]) In the course of three months, starting in February 1769, Wilkes was thrice more elected MP by the voters of Middlesex and repeatedly expelled by the House of Commons.

The name of John Wilkes was to become forever linked with one of the towering radical political issues of the day, the controversy over parliamentary reform. The electoral system of Britain was one that cried out for reform. The electoral districts and voting qualifications had not been changed since the Middle Ages. Deserted villages like Old Sarum in Wiltshire returned candidates to Parliament, hand-picked by the local landowner. Big cities like Birmingham and Manchester that had mushroomed in size during the eighteenth century had no representation. Many elections were carefully managed by local grandees, who liberally dispensed bribes. In an age when few MPs adhered to any party, ministers relied on the support of members called placemen. These were government office-holders of various kinds who could be counted on to vote in favour of the government's policies. To modern ears it sounds utterly corrupt, and radical critics like Wilkes denounced it as such, but in the absence of party discipline, eighteenth-century government leaders needed such a system to ensure some kind of stability. The placemen were never more than a substantial minority, but they attracted persistent charges of corruption.[2] In addition, during the eighteenth century, government became more and more expensive. Despite their boasted representative government, English people paid more taxes than their downtrodden couterparts in France.

A new, rising middle class of professionals and businessmen in London and the growing commercial cities had become heartily tired of this system. They wanted a greater say in the politics of the nation, and John Wilkes became their hero. His expulsion from the House of Commons was an all too blatant attack on voters' rights. As if to add insult to injury, the Commons declared his opponent, Henry Luttrell, the duly elected Member for Middlesex. Wilkes himself warned ominously: 'If ministers can once usurp the power of declaring who *shall not* be your representative, the next step is very easy, and will follow speedily. It is that of telling you whom you *shall* send to Parliament, and then the boasted Constitution of England will be entirely torn up by the roots.'[3] The issues were so stark that a mass petitioning movement occurred, protesting the outcome of the Middlesex election. Petitions flooded in from all over the kingdom. The issue would never entirely die down in England until the great political reforms of the nineteenth century.[4]

But however pure Wilkes's cause might have been, the man himself left much to be desired. He was a member of Sir Francis Dashwood's notorious Hell Fire Club, also known as the Monks of St Francis. The Club met on the site of a former Medmenham Abbey, where its members – all male, and accompanied by prostitutes dressed up as nuns – conducted mock black Sabbaths that ended in sexual orgies.[5] Wilkes had deserted his wife early in their marriage, preferring the company of prostitutes. He wrote a ribald poem called 'Essay on Woman' that was so obscene (he rashly published it for a select private audience) that the government was able to use it in its campaign to outlaw him in 1764. The eighteenth-century diarist Horace Walpole spoke for many when he concluded: 'Though he became the martyr of the best cause, there was nothing in his principles or morals that led him to care under what government he lived'.[6] Yet Wilkes continued to have many staunch supporters on both sides of the Atlantic.

In the colonies the cause of Wilkes and Liberty struck a strong responsive chord. There the protest against parliamentary taxation had started up again, with the passing of the Townshend Acts in 1767 (the legislation was Charles Townshend's brainchild, but he died before he could see the trouble it caused). The Acts laid a new tax on various colonial imports, including – fatefully – tea. A sinister development was that the new colonial taxes were also intended to pay the salaries of royal officials in each colony, freeing them from local control. Wilkes's rhetoric against a corrupt government that was laying oppressive taxes to feed its army of placemen and tools seemed to have resonance on both sides of the Atlantic.[7] And wasn't the British army in on it, too, that tool of tyrants that had grown in size throughout the century? In London there was a bloody incident in 1768 when British troops (the city's ham-fisted police force), sent out to quell a riot in support of Wilkes, killed seven people. Eager to escalate the atmosphere of crisis, Wilkes had labelled this the 'massacre of St George's Fields', a 'hellish project' that he claimed had been perpetrated deliberately by some of his majesty's ministers, who were keen to use armed force to repress London's English spirit.[8] Two years later Boston featured its own bloody clash between redcoats and an angry mob. When five civilians were left dead, the Sons of Liberty followed Wilkes's lead, naming it 'the Boston Massacre'.

From the start of Wilkes's troubles in 1768, colonial sympathy had been forthcoming. The Boston Sons of Liberty sent Wilkes a gift of two turtles, one weighing 45 pounds (this was intended as a symbolic reference to the infamous issue Number 45 of the *North Briton*). Further south, Maryland and Virginia each sent forty-five hogsheads of tobacco. In South Carolina, Liberty Boys downed forty-five bowls of punch – not much help to Wilkes, but still an expression of solidarity.[9] On a more practical note, the Assembly of South Carolina made the handsome gift of £1,500 to Wilkes and his cause. Wilkes was hailed in the colonies as a brother in adversity, whose cause would stand or fall alongside theirs.

But it was Massachusetts that made the most of it. No other colony was as adept at resorting to intrigue in London to attack an unpopular governor.[10] And the Massachusetts Assembly was very keen to get rid of its current governor, Francis Bernard. He had had the bad luck to preside over some key moments in the escalation of Anglo-American discord. When the British ministry under Prime Minister Lord Grafton threatened all the colonial assemblies with closure if they did not rescind certain letters opposing the Townshend Acts, the odious Bernard had the job of enforcing the unpopular decree in the Bay Colony. When Britain sent troops to Boston to enforce customs laws there, Governor Bernard had to find quarters for them and listen to an unending stream of complaints and protests from the people of Boston. Of course, Massachusetts had brought some of this on itself. The Bay Colony was gaining a reputation as the most troublesome province in North America. It was the Massachusetts Assembly that had kicked off the letters protesting the Townshend Acts, and it was Boston mobs who had brazenly defied the customs officers. But Bernard was a particularly clumsy governor of a particularly troublesome colony at an impossible time, and he had to go.

Support for Massachusetts could be garnered in London from those in and out of Parliament who opposed the current administration. In the House of Commons opposition MPs Edmund Burke and the West Indian William Beckford supported a petition from Massachusetts calling for Bernard's removal. After all, an attack on Bernard was an attack on cabinet member Lord Hillsborough, who had become American Secretary in 1768. The opposition took the opportunity to force the Grafton administration (already mired down with the Wilkes crisis) onto the defensive for its all too controversial American policy.[11] Outside Parliament the Boston Sons of Liberty kept up a brisk correspondence with John Wilkes, whose cause, now electrifying the country, might lend some publicity to theirs.

Naturally, Stephen Sayre and Dennis De Berdt were in the thick of all this. De Berdt was there as agent for Massachusetts, his support for that beleaguered colony given an additional goad by Hillsborough's refusal (on a technicality) to recognise his agency appointment. And to anyone like Stephen who harboured dreams of wealth from American land speculation, Hillsborough was anathema, for he stubbornly refused to endorse new western colonies.[12] But Dennis De Berdt had only months to live when he finally appeared before the Privy Council in late February 1770 to substantiate the allegations against Governor Bernard. Small wonder he 'foundered' before the committee, showing himself to be inadequately prepared, and the petition was dismissed as 'groundless, vexatious, and scandalous'. Nevertheless Bernard, who by now had returned to London, was removed from office and kicked upstairs, as the saying goes, with a baronetcy. He never returned to Massachusetts (a circumstance that would give him no cause for regret).[13]

At about the time that Stephen Sayre became involved with John Wilkes, in 1768, a new figure appeared who would remain an important presence in his life long after the Artillery Court years. This was Arthur Lee, another young American with an ambition to live in London. Lee's background was very different from that of the Long Island farmer's son. He was one of the Virginia Lees, wealthy tobacco planters whose family seat, Stratford Hall, would one day be the birthplace of Robert E. Lee, Confederate general in the American Civil War. But Arthur was hampered by the fact that he was the youngest of ten children, and shared the fate of all younger sons – the need to earn a living. 'Good God what trouble does the not having been born to a fortune give me', was his ungrammatical shriek of despair several years into his career.[14]

Arthur Lee's early education followed the usual pattern. All the Lee children were sent to England for school, and after a shining career at Eton, Arthur went to Edinburgh to study medicine in 1761. But in between medical studies he was in London long enough to get a taste for the Great City that would remain with him for the rest of his life. Italian opera ('exquisite', he recalled), the theatres of the West End, 'elegant concert rooms' where he could listen to his favourite composers, Bach, Abel, Fischer – all these things were not to be had back home in Virginia. And still more to his taste, the politics; Lee was in London at the height of the Stamp Act Crisis in early 1766. The hothouse politics of the City coffee houses, he discovered, was exactly what suited his contentious disposition. He was a breathless spectator in the gallery of the

House of Commons. He managed to get introduced to Lord Shelburne, an advocate of repeal, and even had breakfast with him and Lady Shelburne. It was fun. But it couldn't last forever. By the end of the year, Lee was back in Virginia trying to earn a living, but medicine called for too much 'perseverance, of which I have very little', as he put it. He probably found it boring, for in other matters he had application enough. Politics was exciting; in between visiting patients he wrote angry pieces for the colonial press against the injustices of the Townshend Acts.[15]

The fact was that Lee wanted to live in London. By 1768 he was back. With him came one of his older brothers, William, who was looking after the London end of the family's tobacco interests. Like Stephen Sayre, Arthur Lee kept many balls in the air in his search for a living in the Great City. He acted as agent for the Mississippi Company, a land-speculation venture fostered by his brothers. He hoped to get the Virginia agency whenever it became vacant. He worked unsuccessfully to get a government place or pension for another older brother, Richard Henry, who would one day sign the Declaration of Independence.

Arthur Lee soon befriended Stephen Sayre and joined the crowd at Artillery Court. He enmeshed himself in the war against Governor Bernard, writing fiery pieces for the London press in support of Massachusetts. Now the prospect of inheriting the Massachusetts agency from old Mr De Berdt came into his sights. He augmented his political contacts, striking up a friendship with John Wilkes, joining his dinner parties in King's Bench Prison, and introducing him to visiting Americans like Benjamin Rush. That was not the full extent of his political ambitions. Under the pseudonym 'Junius Americanus', he attacked Lord Hillsborough in the newspapers with such ferocity that the colony agent for Connecticut shrewdly – and correctly – guessed that Lee hoped for a government post if opposition leader Lord Shelburne should ever become prime minister. With the examples of Stephen Sayre and Thomas Ruston before him, Lee probably thought of marrying for money. He sighed out his feelings for a 'Miss Talbot' and a 'Miss Palmer' to Hetta De Berdt, but all to no avail.[16] His shyness around the opposite sex was to keep him single all his life.

Land schemes, government posts, colony agencies, wealthy heiresses – Arthur Lee pursued the same avenues as his friend Stephen, but his was a very different nature. Despite being a planter's son, he was not a 'man of pleasure'. He was withdrawn around women. He was attracted to political controversy, an intense, argumentative young man who lacked Stephen's personal charm. Edward Tilghman of Maryland, who knew Lee while a law student in London, described him as a flaming patriot, 'obstinate and perverse as Lucifer', willing to argue 'against an angel and tell him he did not speak common sense'.[17] Strange to say, despite spending his early years on a plantation, Lee disliked being served by slaves. His hatred of the institution of slavery was in keeping with his professed love of liberty – but he also felt ill at ease with servants whose degraded status meant that they had to be treated with indulgence. With free white servants, a close friend recalled, he felt he could be 'rigid and exact', demanding whatever he wanted.[18] Perhaps that reflects his early removal from the plantation environment, but it also indicates a self-conscious and rather defensive character that must have been in strong contrast to Stephen Sayre's easy charm.

Yet Arthur was destined to go much further than Stephen in his political career. He was one of the first United States diplomats during the War of Independence, serving in France, Prussia and Spain. Even earlier, though, during his London years, he showed a flash of brilliance when he conceived the notion of uniting the causes of Wilkes and of colonial rights into a single organised movement. In 1768, en route to London, he stopped off in Pennsylvania to meet the illustrious John Dickinson, then the most prestigious spokesman for colonial rights. Once in London, he began through Stephen Sayre to correspond with the Boston Sons of Liberty, and he eventually put into place a correspondence network between Massachusetts, Virginia and Pennsylvania. It was in the early 1770s, when Arthur became deeply involved in City politics, that he tried to set up political reform societies throughout the colonies modelled on the London Wilkites. His dream of a united Anglo-American movement for reform was ahead of its time, but the ties he established between leading patriots in Virginia and Massachusetts would play a critical role in the revolutionary politics that led to independence.[19]

Lee had no thoughts of war or American independence when he began all this. It was not a separatist impulse, but rather the opposite, that gave him the notion of uniting the causes of reform in Britain and America. As we have seen, he wanted to settle permanently in London. In 1784, a year after the peace treaty that established forever the new United States, Lee was to look back on his years there with regret. He wrote in his journal: 'Could I be restored to the situation that I enjoyed before the Revolution . . . I might be happy.' England, he thought, was 'the Eden of the world'.[20]

Meanwhile, what did Lee live on when he first reached London? There is no evidence that he practised medicine but, unlike Stephen, Arthur had family to fall back on in London. There was his brother William, who worked as a tobacco merchant handling his family's interests. William Lee married his cousin Hannah Ludwell shortly after he arrived in London. Since Hannah preferred London to America, he sold his Virginia property with a view to settling permanently in the capital. The couple lived on Tower Hill (a popular address for transatlantic merchants as it was adjacent to London's busiest docks).[21] Hannah Ludwell had been living in London with her father and sister Lucy since the early 1760s. Lucy was married to John Paradise, a distinguished English philologist who knew not only Dr Johnson but Benjamin Franklin as well. Lucy Ludwell Paradise was a fashionable hostess who charmed Thomas Jefferson when he met her in London after the Revolution. She was not averse to spending beyond her means, which were considerable, and must have given Arthur very high expectations of a life in the metropolis. And there was Edmund Jenings of Maryland, another cousin to the Lees. Like Arthur and William, he had been educated in England. He finished his training with a stint at the Inns of Court and maintained a leisurely legal practice.[22]

Arthur had wealthy relatives near at hand but he may, nevertheless, have been relying partly on Mr De Berdt's bounty before 1770. When the old merchant died, Arthur's hopes of inheriting the Massachusetts agency came to naught; Benjamin Franklin got it instead, and Arthur had the consolation prize of becoming assistant agent in the event of Franklin's incapacity. On the advice of cousin Edmund Jenings, he now registered as a student at the Inns of Court. He got more deeply involved with the Wilkites; by 1771 he was the secretary of their organisation, the Society of the Bill of Rights. He managed to get a reference to American grievances inserted in the Society's list of pledges for parliamentary candidates. And he and Sam Adams, a Boston Son of Liberty, briefly toyed with the idea of a transatlantic political organisation that would push for reform.[23]

But getting in with Wilkes also somewhat distracted Arthur from the cause of American liberty, for it temporarily put him at cross purposes with the powerful Lord Shelburne, an advocate for the colonies who disapproved of the City politician. The fact was that Arthur, having joined the legal profession, hoped that connections with the Wilkes crowd would eventually land him the Recordership of London. He always kept in mind his goal of settling permanently in the Great City, and his Wilkite friendships seemed to offer opportunities. While he waited for his new plans to bear fruit, he was happy with the life of a City politician. He loved controversy, and got all he wanted. He wrote prolifically for the newspapers, often on American issues, probably equalling Ben Franklin in his journalistic output.[24] He and Stephen Sayre practically lived in coffee houses, hobnobbing with Wilkes and his cronies. Years later he recalled his time at the Inns of Court in strongly nostalgic terms: 'I was placed in chambers in the Temple, which looked into a delightful little garden on the Thames, of which I had the key; I could go in and out at all hours, and have what company I pleased, without being questioned or overlooked.' He recalled with a sigh: 'That is as happy as man without domestic cares, domestic anxiety, and domestic love, could be.'[25]

Arthur Lee certainly fared better than his friend Stephen in the months following the death of Mr De Berdt. With the end of the Artillery Court days came a new, sordid chapter in Stephen's quest for survival in the Great City. Now alone, with no means of support, and 'in great distress', he was soon taken in by a woman named Mrs Pearson. Whether she was a widow or separated from her husband is unclear, but she fed and clothed Stephen and gave him money. For several years he lived at her house on the footing of a husband. He entertained there, giving dinners that included John Wilkes and Arthur Lee, and built up a reputation as a Wilkite and a 'red-hot patriot'.[26] But he had neighbours with nicer standards, for Mrs Pearson lived in Berners Street.

There were plenty of American colonists who deplored Wilkes's personal character as much as they did the injustices perpetrated against him. 'Had a fair view of Alderman Wilkes', wrote one blunt New Yorker on a visit to London, 'he is as much deformed in his face as in his mind' – an unkind reference to Wilkes's conspicuous squint.[27] South Carolinians in particular preferred to support him from afar. This was not only a matter of morals, but also of social rank. Wilkes's strongest supporters were small or middling merchants in the City, the 'Polisson order' John Laurens had looked down upon when he attended the ball for the newly elected lord mayor Wilkes in 1774. Almost none of the aristocracy, and just a smattering of the gentry, associated closely with Wilkes – though they might support his right to represent Middlesex. Most South Carolinians in London followed suit, preferring the more genteel brand of opposition to government espoused by Lord Rockingham and his followers (who included Edmund Burke).[28]

Henry Laurens was characteristically blunt. He referred to Wilkes as a 'wretched miscreant', declaring that he was heartily sick of the 'stupid' practice of 'drinking 45 toasts to the cause of *true liberty* 450 times unnecessarily'. Many of Wilkes's friends among 'the best people', Henry observed, were deserting him.[29] When Henry wrote this, in 1771, his West Indian friend Richard Oliver had just resigned from the main Wilkite political vehicle, the Bill of Rights Society. Oliver, an Antigua sugar planter, had been a founding member of the Society, which had been set up to support Wilkes in his campaign for justice during the Middlesex elections. Stephen had joined it in

Watkin Lewes Esq.ʳ presenting the Addresses from the Counties of Pembroke, Carmarthen & Cardigan, to the Lord Mayor-Alderman Wilkes, & Alderman Oliver in the Tower .

Thus Ancient Britons, gen'rous, bold & free,
Untaught at Court to bend the supple Knee,
Corruption's Shrine with honest Pride disdain,
And only bow to Freedom's Patriot Train.

24 This political cartoon depicts Alderman Richard Oliver, friend of Henry Laurens, and Alderman John Wilkes, standing on the left and right of Brass Crosby, who was lord mayor of London in 1771. Wilkes can be identified by his notorious squint, while the artist has given Oliver a dark complexion, an allusion to his well-known West Indian origins. The figure on the far right is a political supporter who is presenting them with an address.

1769. Within a year or two of its founding, Oliver and others broke away after concluding that Wilkes saw the Society simply as a means of getting funds to pay off his heavy debts.[30]

But now Berners Street was going to have a surfeit of exposure to Wilkes and his kind. Just months after Henry's outburst, one of Wilkes's rakehell associates,

Robert Morris, brought scandal to their very doorsteps. Morris had lured thir-
teen-year-old Frances Harford, an illegitimate daughter of Lord Baltimore,
away from her boarding school in Chelsea. Lord Baltimore was the Proprietor
of Maryland (the entire colony had been given to his ancestor by Charles I). He
was also a notorious libertine. He maintained a harem of 'five white and one
black women', who openly paraded about St James's Park on fine days. This was
evidently not enough, for in 1768 he kidnapped a sixteen-year-old girl from
her father's shop on Tower Hill. Although he managed to evade a rape conviction on a technicality, he thought it best to make himself scarce and fled to the
continent, where he died.[31] Morris, who had been his legal counsel, knew that
Miss Harford had an estate of £30,000. His intention in removing her from
school was to pressure her into marriage, and his first port of call was the home
of Mrs Susanna Vaughan in Berners Street, a lady whose family – like so many
in that neighbourhood – had a fortune founded on slave labour in the West
Indies.[32] From there Morris made his way to the continent, where he pressured
the young lady into marriage. Happily, it was later annulled. 'Honest Mr
Morris,' commented Henry Laurens sarcastically, 'one of the guardians of his
deceased friend's daughter and of the British Constitution.'[33] Henry's cynicism
is understandable; South Carolina's gift to the cause of John Wilkes had
embroiled its assembly in a conflict with the British government which only
ended with the War of Independence.

Berners Street was much too short for Stephen Sayre's relationship with Mrs
Pearson, and the comings and goings of Mr Wilkes and his cronies, to pass
unnoticed. And anyway Stephen knew people who knew the South
Carolinian residents, among them the Allens and Peter DeLancey. His years
with Mrs Pearson mark a rather desperate phase in his London career, when
he had no visible means of support.[34] That he was a 'kept man' probably went
without saying among his neighbours. But Stephen, always ambitious to live
in good society, would be careful not to close any doors on his own advancement. Extramarital relationships were much more openly tolerated in the
eighteenth century than they would be in the inhibited Victorian era, even in
polite society. One can go too far with this, but it was a matter of degree;
James Boswell met a respectable woman who argued to him that a married
woman could commit adultery while pregnant by her husband, since there
would be no fear of bastardy. Boswell was uncomfortable with the idea, but
did not dispute it.[35] Young Tom Jones, in Henry Fielding's 1749 novel of the
same name, does not forfeit his status as the hero of the piece by living for a
time as Lady Bellaston's gigolo lover in London. Such behaviour would be

unthinkable for a David Copperfield or a Nicholas Nickleby. In any event, by 1774, when Stephen had left Berners Street and the American crisis was creating common cause among colonists in London (for a while at least), he was invited to sign the petition organised by Ralph Izard protesting the Coercive Acts, so he was not considered as beyond the pale.

Mrs Pearson would not be the first or the last woman to be exploited by Stephen, and one can't help wondering what the attraction was. By all accounts he was very good looking, but that isn't enough to explain the devotion he inspired in some quarters. The friend of one of his mistresses – a hostile witness, to be sure, but the sole extant testimony to his behaviour in the boudoir – claimed that he treated his paramour like a servant, 'would have no one wait on him but her', pretended to be sensitive and fastidious, and moaned that he 'hated servants about his person'.[36] Only her fair hands, apparently, could serve him his tea and toast and bring him his slippers. Reading between the lines, it sounds like he appealed to her maternal instincts. That would fit in with Stephen's upbringing among seven older sisters, as well as his lifelong pattern of relationships with older women – the 'old duchess', for example, and the woman he eventually married.

Poor Mrs Pearson suffered more than anyone from the association with Stephen, for by 1773 he had deserted her and set up a bank in Oxford Street with a partner named Bartholomew Coote Purdon, using her 'little fortune' to fund his latest project. She was not above breaking his windows and causing a scene in her distress at being abandoned, and two unnamed gentlemen from Berners Street had to bail her out of gaol after she was forcibly taken away.[37] Perhaps there were scenes in Berners Street itself, but Stephen no longer needed her. He had his bank, and in the same year his association with the Wilkites bore fruit when he was elected sheriff of London along with Arthur Lee's merchant brother William. '(Could you think it?) both Americans', commented Ben Franklin on hearing the news.[38]

Stephen had appearances to keep up now. On public occasions – and there were many – he sported a coach, with footmen in livery of silver, white and black, and other finery.[39] His bank, still just starting up, was not income enough. As had happened so many times before, Stephen found a woman to exploit. This time, however, he was able to use his office of sheriff to get himself into a most advantageous position. The woman in question was the celebrated Sophia Baddeley, an actress turned courtesan whose *Memoirs* give a rather frightening insight into Stephen's character after ten years in the Great City.

The Divine Baddeley, whose beauty was so great that George III, after seeing her perform, commissioned a portrait by Johann Zoffany, had fallen on

25 Sophia Baddeley.

hard times by 1773. She had started out as an actress and a singer, appearing at Drury Lane and Vauxhall, but soon discovered that it was less work to be supported by her wealthy admirers among the nobility. These included such grandees as the Dukes of Northumberland and Bolton. By the time Stephen came into her life, however, she was in debt to the tune of £7,000, and this was enough to scare off her wealthy clients. As sheriff, Stephen knew when writs were going to be served against her. If he had no money with which to assist her, he was nevertheless in a position to help her evade her creditors.[40]

Stephen now laid a plan that showed considerable cunning. Mrs Baddeley – lovely, but not the sharpest tack in the box – went regularly to a fortune-teller, a circumstance that he somehow or other found out about. He bribed the fortune-teller to predict that the lady would meet a handsome stranger with a gold chain around his neck in St James's Park. Intrigued, Sophia hurried to the park and was astonished to encounter Stephen Sayre in his sheriff's chain of office, staring at her intently. For some time he followed her as she walked up and down the Mall. The rest followed naturally. He took her home, explained to her that he could as sheriff protect her from having writs served against her, and love ensued. He obtained a house for her in Cleveland Row.[41] This was a fashionable address, bordering on leafy Green Park and just around the corner from St James's Palace. But as was so often was the case in Georgian London, the elegance went hand in glove with sordidness. If Admiral Lord Rodney's house was to be found in Cleveland Row, so was a high-class brothel that offered 'special services' such as flagellation. The saving grace was that the clientele were all of the very best society.[42]

Stephen promised to pay for the house, but in fact he never gave a penny for it. He persuaded Mrs Baddeley's long-time companion, Mrs Steele, to take it in her name (for reputation's sake) – a step Mrs Steele soon regretted. After a while Stephen moved in altogether, not waiting for an invitation. He approached Mrs Baddeley's friends among the nobility for loans on her behalf and pocketed them, claiming he was saving them in order to pay off her

26 The entrance to St James's Palace, seen from Cleveland Row.

debts.[43] Was he in effect becoming her pimp? This had formerly been Mrs Steele's role, and she quickly became jealous.

Sayre was possessive of his new asset. When Mrs Baddeley went out in public he was always with her, ostensibly to intercept any bailiffs trying to present her with writs. She was never abroad without Stephen, and the result was that she was deserted by the 'persons of fashion' who used to visit her. 'Mr Sayre is such a Wilkite,' Mrs Steele warned her friend, 'that when your friends know he is one of your visitors, they will instantly forsake you.' And that proved to be the case. Mrs Baddeley was known as a chatterbox, and her aristocratic clients did not relish having their pillow talk repeated to a City patriot. Stephen's own friends, meanwhile, filled up the drawing room at Cleveland Row, all of them fiery City patriots who disgusted Mrs Steele. Arthur Lee was surely among them, and Wilkes, who could already claim Mrs Baddeley as an old acquaintance. They spoke so disrespectfully of the king that Mrs Steele was obliged to leave the room.[44]

She could leave the house for all Stephen cared, and eventually Mrs Steele did just that. She surely hated Stephen Sayre. Curiously, though, she never once in her lengthy memoirs alluded to the fact that he was an American, although she could not but have known. Presumably it was no more note-worthy than being from Yorkshire. But it probably lay behind her insinuations that he was of mixed race, an imputation to which Americans in particular were susceptible in Georgian England. He was of a 'black complexion', she claimed, and attended a masquerade 'in the character of Mungo', the servile black house servant in *The Padlock* – by all of which she hinted that Stephen was common, and that his low birth took a particularly American form.[45]

Stephen, impervious to Mrs Steele's venom, had used his new office to advantage, obtaining a fashionable mistress, a fashionable address and an augmentation of his income at little trouble or expense to himself. And he built up the credit of his bank by giving Mrs Baddeley its notes to spend around town.[46] Things were going swimmingly for him. In fact, the bank was a greater success than he'd ever expected. Dennis De Berdt junior, now setting up for himself as a City merchant, wrote unhappily to Joseph Reed that Stephen's new public career had stirred up all the old gossip about the De Berdt bankruptcy. When he tried to warn Stephen, he complained to Reed, he was dismissed for his pains; Stephen's vanity 'got the better of every argument'. And Stephen 'appears more mysterious every day', wrote the puzzled Dennis, living as he did in 'grandeur' with no apparent means of support, save the merely political support of Arthur Lee and the Wilkes crowd.[47] Somehow

Stephen prevented all and sundry from learning about his special relationship with Mrs Baddeley. That was as well, for he intended to re-enter polite society as quickly as possible.

When the news of Stephen's prosperity reached Joseph Reed's wife Hetta, she quoted the reaction of a Philadelphia gentleman who declared: 'I see what ignorance and impudence will do in London'.[48] Stephen had been demonstrating what ignorance and impudence would do in London ever since he first got there over ten years earlier. He went from strength to strength, even running (albeit unsuccessfully) as MP for Seaford in Sussex in the general election of October 1774.[49] And now he was going to achieve the security and respectability that had eluded him for so long, for just four months later, in February 1775, he married Miss Elizabeth Noel. She was forty-eight, he was ten years younger. But at thirty-eight he must have felt that his eligibility as a dashing bachelor might soon ebb away. Miss Noel's father was a judge, her family had lands in Lincolnshire and she had a small fortune. She opened some highly placed political connections to Stephen through her family, for she was related to the Wentworths, the Rockinghams and the Verneys.[50] Not much is known about her; Mrs Steele claimed Stephen despised her and only married her for her money. No wonder if Mrs Steele was bitter, for at the time of his marriage Mrs Baddeley was expecting his child. He moved his mistress into Rathbone Place, two streets down from Berners Street and close to his new address over his bank in Oxford Street. But he saw less and less of her, a circumstance which suggests that he was preoccupied with his newly won position in the fashionable world. Mrs Steele's *Memoirs* relate that Sophia Baddeley bore a child named Stephen Sayre junior, but the boy promptly disappears from the pages of history.[51]

Stephen was recapturing, and even exceeding, the position he'd reached at the end of the De Berdt years. Since his expulsion from Artillery Court he had laid his plans carefully. Security, wealth and position at last seemed to be his. But an observer – not a friend, but a shrewd British diplomat – once summed him up as a man who had 'better parts than judgment, enterprising in forming a bold project, but unequal to its execution'.[52]

That proved to be an astute judgement; Stephen could not escape from himself. For one brief shining moment he had finally got it all, but it did not last. His election as sheriff occurred at about the same time as the start of the fatal chain of events that would lead to the War of Independence. That chain of events would also lead to the unravelling of all his achievements. The Boston Tea Party in December 1773 brought on a political crisis that ended in war. In the year leading up to the battles of Lexington and Concord, while he lived with Mrs Baddeley and established his bank, Stephen was also in the thick of the London side of the American crisis. He worked with the Lees and others to whip up the parliamentary opposition and the London merchants in support of the colonies; he went with lord mayor Wilkes to St James's Palace to present the king with a petition in favour of American rights. All this was very much in keeping with his public character as a City patriot and an American. But Stephen could not resist getting drawn into activities that were not so above board. Within a few months of the start of the war, he became the first ever American to be imprisoned in the Tower of London.

On 23 October 1775 Stephen was rudely interrupted while at breakfast at his fashionable house in Oxford Street, placed under arrest on a charge of high treason, and locked up in the Tower. The arrest was based on the testimony of Frank Richardson, a Pennsylvanian who was a lieutenant in the First Regiment of the Foot Guards in London. Richardson, who had known Stephen for some time, claimed that he had had a chance encounter with the New Yorker a few days before in the Pennsylvania Coffee House in Birchin Lane. He asserted that Stephen had taken him to a private room, where he proposed to Richardson that he should assist in a wild plot to kidnap George III as he made his way in his coach to the opening of Parliament on 26 October, and incarcerate him in the Tower. The king was not to be killed but forced to return to his German dominions in Hanover. Richardson claimed that Stephen told him that over £1,000 had already been distributed among the soldiery who policed the City, in order to buy their support, and that lord mayor John Wilkes was in on the whole thing. Now he allegedly wanted Richardson to help, by bribing the Tower garrison to join the plot.[53]

Lieutenant Richardson had carried this story to his commanding officer, who promptly took him to cabinet minister Lord Rochford. The plot sounded improbable, even ridiculous, but plots usually do upon first hearing. What worried Lord Rochford was that the whole thing was coming up at a vulnerable time for government. Ministers wanted to escalate the war in America, and they intended to ask Parliament to approve sending 20,000 troops to put down the rebellion. Stephen's 'plot' threatened only mob action, not an armed invasion, but London mobs, once their blood was up, could be formidable. Their numbers could swell to tens of thousands, more than the red-coated regiments that were supposed to keep them in order. Only seven years earlier, riots had disrupted the City for days when John Wilkes had been arrested and denied his seat in Parliament. Cabinet ministers had had their coach windows broken, the king's own brother had his house damaged, and the crowd had shouted 'No king! Damn the king! Damn the government!'[54]

The mood of the London populace with respect to the war in America was still untested, and ministers were nervous. At the moment both the government and the parliamentary opposition were actively soliciting shows of popular support.[55] Now would be a very bad time for the ministry to look as if it could not keep order at home. Even if Lord Rochford dismissed the unbelievable aspects of the plot – the capture of the Tower and the spiriting of His Majesty out of the kingdom – the prospect of an ugly riot was bad enough. It would certainly weaken the case in the minds of many MPs for sending large numbers of troops out of the kingdom.

Lord Rochford knew that he needed a second piece of evidence to corroborate a charge of treason, but the opening of Parliament was only seven days away. After a worrying weekend, he decided to act. He had Stephen locked in the Tower under a charge of 'treasonable practices'. Iron bars were placed on his windows and he was denied visitors. Arthur Lee was turned away; John Wilkes managed only a bow at Stephen when he glimpsed the American at a window.[56]

Four more days passed. The opening of Parliament came and went as uneventfully as usual. No further evidence of a conspiracy had come to light. Stephen was released two days later and the charges were dropped. The whole story quickly became known throughout Britain and America. The ministry ended up looking both foolish and heavy-handed. After all, the 'plot' sounded too absurd to be believed. 'We have been for a week past in perpetual laughter about the late dreadful plot,' wrote one of Wilkes's cronies.[57] The London newspapers got hold of the story and joined in the laugh. Sayre had been arrested 'upon an information so romantic, so foolish, so absurd, that if they thought the accused could have done what he was charged with, he ought to have been committed to Bedlam, not the Tower'. Sayre's arrest was the 'subject of ridicule in every coffee house in town'. When they were not laughing, the papers were accusing the government of heavy-handedness. 'It is French law', and proved that the present government was 'capable of as violent, arbitrary, and unjust executions of power, as if the Tower of London were actually the Bastille'.[58] Stephen himself, the Lees and many others (including Edmund Burke) claimed that Stephen had been framed by a ministry intent on stifling pro-American dissent in London. He became something of a celebrity.[59] The story was quickly picked up by the English provincial presses and by newspapers in the American colonies. In the colonies, where his character was less well known, he was portrayed as a hero who conducted himself with Roman courage and dignity in the face of ministerial tyranny.[60] His integrity was his shield, reported the *New England Chronicle*, and he entered his prison cell gladly, conscious that it would 'prove a safe asylum for virtue'.[61]

It didn't help the case for the government that the informant, Frank Richardson, was far from a shining character. Born a Quaker, he had imbibed a passion for the British army through mixing with army officers in Philadelphia. By 1772 he was in England, where fellow colonist Edward Tilghman reported that he had died of venereal disease: 'Poor Frank Richardson departed this life a few days since at Bath, according to scandal a martyr to debauchery'. But the rumour of his death proved to be exaggerated. A handsome man, he was involved in a scandal with a married woman and was briefly imprisoned for debt by her enraged husband. In his regiment he was known as a 'rattle' who talked too much on American affairs. He wanted a promotion. If he had concocted the whole story about Sayre, it did him no harm. By 1789 he was a colonel.[62]

In the end the entire affair was dismissed by Lord Chief Justice de Grey, because there was nothing to corroborate Richardson's allegations. Sayre admitted meeting Richardson at the Pennsylvania Coffee House but denied that the 'treasonable' conversation had taken place. As de Grey put it in his summary, Sayre had only to say 'that it was all a jest in the first place, that he had a mind to try Richardson in the next place, that it was idle conversation and he meant nothing in the world by it', for the case to be dismissed.[63] With no further proof of a conspiracy, Sayre (under the toothless anti-terrorism laws of Georgian England) would have to go free.

But in summing up the case of Sayre versus Rochford, Lord Chief Justice de Grey expressed sympathy for Lord Rochford's predicament. He was a cabinet minister. He was obliged as a 'vigilant sentinel of the state' to investigate any threat to the king's safety, however unlikely it seemed. De Grey concluded: 'This cause has turned out to be one of the most important that I ever knew because it very materially affects the safety of the government on one side and the safety of the subject on the other.' It had been Lord Rochford's dilemma to decide where to draw the line. Although he was an experienced politician and diplomat, he appeared for once to have panicked and overstepped his authority.

So what really happened? The episode has remained a mystery. Stephen was indeed involved in certain illegal activities on behalf of the rebellion, and the British government knew this.[64] But an extensive conspiracy of this kind would doubtless have left a trail of evidence. And yet Richardson's testimony has the ring of truth to it. Either the lieutenant was a very skilled liar (as good a liar as Stephen himself), or Stephen really did say something that set him off.

More likely it was Stephen who was the liar, and Richardson was his dupe. Years earlier John Wilkes had made the government look bad when he had successfully claimed that he had been the victim of an illegal arrest. Stephen may have had it in mind to stage something similar, by drawing the North administration into pursuing a groundless action against him for treason. It sounds like a rather overblown publicity stunt. But another former Wilkes supporter, the Reverend John Horne Tooke, attempted that very thing in 1792, when he deliberately tricked authorities into arresting him for treason by leaving a trail of false evidence. Tooke, like Sayre, was locked in the Tower. Ultimately, the government looked both foolish and heavy-handed when the evidence collapsed.[65] It has been argued persuasively that the Sayre affair was a deliberate hoax designed by Wilkes and his cronies to test the constitutionality of the government's recent Proclamation of Rebellion.[66]

Whatever the truth, Stephen had finally outdone himself. His days in London were numbered. His bank failed. Like his friend John Wilkes a decade earlier, Stephen filed a civil suit against Lord Rochford, who by now had retired from the cabinet. Wilkes had won his case and been awarded £4,000, amid public fanfare. Sayre, too, won his case. In the end Lord Rochford was found guilty of refusing bail and instructed to pay Sayre £1,000 in damages. But the payment was never made. Sayre's circumstances were very different from those of Wilkes, because by the time the case came to court, in mid-1776, the American colonies had declared independence. Sayre was now clearly marked out as an American rebel, rather than the romantic colonist making a stand for English liberty that he had appeared to be the previous year. Lord Rochford was let off on a legal technicality.[67]

For the second time Stephen was faced with reconstructing his life in London. Once again he was touched by bankruptcy, and this time his reputation was under a far darker cloud than that which had emerged from the De Berdt debacle. In early 1777 he was imprisoned briefly for debt. When he was free, he left England and went to France to join the new United States diplomatic service that included Benjamin Franklin and the Lee brothers. His prospects, he had decided, now lay with the new nation. When Arthur Lee went on a diplomatic mission to Berlin, Stephen went along as his secretary. At the court of Frederick the Great, Stephen and his erstwhile friend quarrelled bitterly, and an unlikely friendship came to an end. Arthur discharged him.[68] Nothing daunted, Stephen travelled through Denmark, Sweden and Russia, everywhere allowing people to assume that he was deputised by the American Congress. His old egotism did not desert him. In St Petersburg he hoped to 'make a conquest' of Catherine the Great, who, he reasoned, 'may have a curiosity for an American gallant'.[69] Characteristically, he claimed great diplomatic conquests wherever he went (though they did not include the empress of Russia, who, after all, could resist him).[70] Finally, the war over, he returned to New York in 1783. He had not been home for seventeen years.

'I can't bear the thoughts of living in America or starving in England.' Did his old mantra still hold true? Or had his youthful ambition to live in London finally faded? Perhaps, left alone with his thoughts during his confinement in the Tower, Stephen might have had a surfeit of the 'modern Babylon' and turned again to the rural retreats of his American boyhood. But the evidence is that he was not at all changed. After the war Stephen made two efforts to re-establish himself in London. His former friend Arthur Lee had preferred to regret from afar, feeling that to go back there would be far too humiliating after having so publicly shaken the dust of England off his feet in order 'to establish republican liberty' in America.[71] Stephen felt no such scruples. He was back in 1786, three years after the peace. The old familiar pattern ensued; he set himself up variously as a merchant and a banker in Oxford Street. As usual he made a splash. He had an adulterous affair with the daughter of Lord Bute, the king's former favourite; he attracted some bad publicity when Mrs Steele's *Memoirs* were published in 1787. Early that year he was in debtors' prison again, this time for twenty months. Poor Mrs Sayre finally obtained his release. She died shortly after, probably quite worn out.[72] Stephen left for the continent, but he was no quitter. He was back again in London in a few years, hoping to get an appointment as United States consul. When that didn't work, he had to leave to escape his creditors, this time for good. Faced with the certainty of debtors' prison if he stayed in London, he was compelled, at last, to contemplate a life in America.

But Stephen never lost his zest for living. He lived many more years and had many adventures. And his charm never deserted him. In his mid-fifties he married a wealthy Jamaican woman. If his schemes to make money came to be tinged with a hint of desperation, he still kept a handsome mansion and lived well.

And yet Stephen Sayre never entirely got the Great City out of his system. His last crack at a job was for a diplomatic post in London; he was almost eighty years of age.[73] And his youthful transformation from homespun colonial to London 'man of pleasure' proved to be an enduring one. Even American independence could not move him to revert to his roots. To the very last, he was known among his New Jersey neighbours as 'the handsome Englishman'.[74]

CHAPTER SEVEN

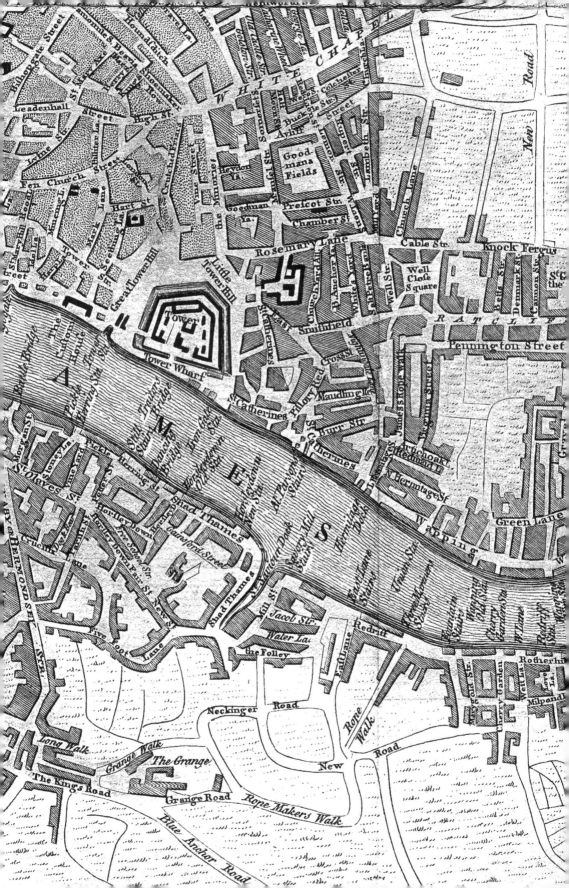

London's American Landscape

'French Dog!' 'French Bastard!' Such were the words that assailed the ears of French visitors as they walked the streets of London. The English were famous for their aversion to foreigners. The eighteenth century was a time when the notion of national character was very much in vogue in Europe, and intellectuals like Montesquieu and Voltaire devoted pages to uncovering national traits. But London's vulgar herd needed no textbook. They already knew that the French were 'over-dressed fawning rogues', the Dutch were a swinish, beer-swilling people who were lazy except where their own self-interest was concerned, and the Italians were would-be assassins who carried stilettos. And even this was more than the average Londoner needed to know, for when in doubt anyone in strange garb could be classed as a Frenchman. Swiss, Germans, Danes, all found themselves labelled 'French dog' (and worse) as they passed through the city. 'Speak your damned French if you dare,' shouted two watermen to a Portuguese gentleman as he walked along the banks of the Thames. 'Thanks to God that I did not understand English,' wrote one Frenchman after another such promenade. One did not need actually to be foreign to come in for abuse. In London the Scots and the Irish were frequently treated with open hostility, and even the occasional riot.[1] In an age when nationalism was on the rise, the ordinary Englishman's idea of what it meant to be English grew stronger as the eighteenth century wore on. The stronger it got, the more he was certain of what he did not like in those who were not English.

The Americans would call themselves a nation in 1776, and by 1783 the rest of the world would agree with them. But just ten years before American independence they had no clear identity in their xenophobic capital. Certainly they were not foreigners; strictly speaking they were British subjects. Most British people, if asked, would class white colonists as fellow Britons.

Viewed up close by Londoners, they could easily be taken for British provincials. Considered from afar, the colonies were presumed by Londoners to be vague extensions of the mother country, the British nation writ large. The perceptive Henry Laurens commented that many Englishmen looked upon the colonies 'as being only, in a distant county of the kingdom', outlying extensions of England.[2] Whether this reflected a spirit of active camaraderie inspired by a history of joint struggles against the French, or just a lazy assumption about far-off places and folk who were known to be part of a wider British world, is less clear. Probably, taking all the people of Britain together, it was a bit of both.[3] Not until after American independence would a demand arise in Britain for books like Hector St John Crèvecoeur's *Letters from an American Farmer*, with its famous essay 'What is an American?'

Without the sort of forthright comments that are available for continentals and Scots, the best empirical evidence for how Londoners saw American colonists just before the Revolution is found in the experiences of the colonists who came there. As we have seen, more and more colonists were in the imperial capital after 1763. The collective experiences of white colonists in London were akin to those of a person moving from the country to the city, rather than those of a foreigner abroad.[4] They worked, studied, conducted business and got married without hindrance. Overall, the experiences of the Laurens family, Joseph Reed, Thomas Ruston, Stephen Sayre, Arthur Lee, even Molsy Bremar with all her problems, show that Londoners expected them to fit in much the same as English provincials, and they pretty much did so. There were of course personal variations in their experiences, and also there were differences based on social level – not all colonists were well to do, or had genteel manners, but then neither did the English people who regularly poured into London from the countryside.

Embryonic notions of certain colonial types were starting to take shape, as we have seen. Metropolitans had developed a distinct, American stereotype of the wealthy plantation owner, to the chagrin of John Laurens. But even American planters like the Laurenses were taken for English when seen without any of the props that indicated their plantation origins, the most common of these being an attending black footman. It is true that the idea of slavery and slave owners as an American thing that metropolitans wished to distance themselves from was growing during the period, partly because the issue was raised by the growing number of slaves in the streets, and partly because the American outcry against British oppression triggered the most obvious defensive response in certain quarters, that Americans themselves were slave-owning tyrants.[5] Yet attitudes had not hardened, and most people were still indifferent. Individuals like Henry Laurens could stay in London and happily ignore any controversy over their plantation lifestyles if they so chose as they went about their daily lives. John Laurens agonised over it, but he didn't have to choose Thomas Day as a companion. Plays like The West Indian show that American planters could be pictured as wayward and charming prodigal sons whose spoilt ways could be corrected by a stint in the metropolis.

It is well known that New England, that witch-hunting, smuggling, Puritan stronghold, was persistently singled out as a troublesome region in the London newspapers and elsewhere.[6] But what were the implications of this for New Englanders in London? Stephen Sayre certainly shed his Long Island Yankee associations as fast as he could, but he wanted to be seen as genteel. There is no evidence that ordinary New Englanders stood out in the streets. John Wilkes himself asserted that there was little difference to be detected 'between an inhabitant of Boston in Lincolnshire, and of Boston in New England'.[7]

For Robert Scipio the situation was more complicated. Black Americans did have to deal with unequal treatment, social obstacles and racism in Georgian London. They lived under a threat of marginalisation which exceeded that of all but the most degraded whites. Theirs was a uniquely vulnerable position in that they might be bought and sold while on English soil, even without the explicit sanction of England's courts. This was enough to set them firmly apart from the English poor. Slaves were probably not seen as British subjects by most.[8] After all, Britons never could be slaves, as the song went. But if some Londoners witnessed their predicament without a qualm, and even participated in the slave market, others came to their aid, not only reformists like Granville Sharp but London's underclass who were prepared to see black slaves as fellow victims.

Just as with their rich plantation masters, the image of black Americans in London was in a state of flux at this time.[9] Robert believed he had a chance to assimilate, even if he needed to shed some of his plantation associations to get on in London. That is clear from the deliberate steps he took to advance himself, importuning Henry to bring him along, and changing his name as soon as he set foot on English soil. Robert's experiences with white fellow servants once in England – closing ranks with the domestic staff in Fludyer Street, and finding a Shropshire lass who had that 'strange partiality shown for them blacks by the lower orders of women' – were not unique.[10]

Blacks were becoming part of the 'British scene' in Georgian London because of America. The complaint made by some white colonists – that 'the common people of *England*' pictured the colonists as 'a compound mongrel mixture of *English, Indian*, and *Negro*' – shows that Londoners expected folk like Robert to be coming off the vessels arriving from the New World, as much as they expected a Henry Laurens or a Stephen Sayre. Not everyone of African descent in London was an American, but they were all understood to be there by virtue of America, either through the slave trade or as incomers from the plantations accompanying their wealthy masters. Whether fresh from Africa or arriving from the colonies, they were presumed to be more or less anglicised. If they represented a threat, it was not cultural but racial – the spectre of 'mongrelisation' that worried some contemporary contributors to Britain's pamphlets and newspapers. Perhaps more could not be expected in a city that openly disliked aliens. French servants in London were regularly abused as agents of a creeping gallicisation that was undermining good old English ways. They supposedly corrupted the dress, manners and eating habits of the wealthy classes they served. They were suspected as enemy spies in wartime (and there were many wars with France). They were caricatured in peacetime as insinuating flatterers who 'multiply like cats' once established in a good English home, scheming to displace honest English employees. If white servants sometimes accepted black plantation slaves as 'one of the gang', they most certainly did not extend this to the French, who were seen as outright competitors for places. Several attempts at collective action were made by English servants during the century in a bid to restrict the employment of French domestics.[11]

The three colonial American types who were taking shape in the minds of metropolitans at the end of the colonial period – the planter, the slave and the Yankee – were to be the progenitors of the American-type characters that appeared on the London stage in the early nineteenth century. As we have seen, the planter and the black house servant had already begun to make an appearance before the Revolution in plays like *The West Indian* and *The Padlock*. By the 1820s and 1830s, when the London stage was feeding an appetite among the British public for plays about American life, 'the clever and enterprising Yankee, the relaxed, horse-racing Southerner, and the singing-dancing plantation Negroes' were established stereotypes with London audiences.[12] These alone were distinct enough in the minds of Londoners to provide the material for caricature. As late as the 1840s there remained a view in London that the manners of America's educated classes were still those of England.[13]

Two conflicting images of the colonies – as a land of planters and slaves, or a land of homespun farmers much like England's own outlying provinces – coexisted in America's capital in the years leading up to independence. Only those with a direct interest in the outcome of the political struggle over colonial rights made any attempt at all to resolve them. The planter image was predominant as more and more absentees like the Laurens family arrived in the streets of the metropolis. It speaks volumes that an English champion of American resistance, writing of the virtues of the New Englanders, was groping to find a name for them that his London readership would recognise. '[T]he Northern *North Americans*', he called them awkwardly, 'poor, laborious, contented with a little, examples of diligence and frugality', homespun types who worked their own modest farms. These, he protested, were a people quite unlike the wealthy planters, who with their 'splendor, dress, show, equipage', and their 'retinue' of 'dark attendants' contributed 'to the general mistake in this country, that the *Americans* are rich'.[14] The planters and their 'dark attendants' stood out in the streets; seeing them, the hazy idea of an American evidently took on some distinct qualities for Londoners, but not the sort this advocate of American rights (a member of the Club of Honest Whigs) approved.

Outside the sphere of politics, there was no portent in London that the Americans were set to become a separate nation or a distinct people by 1776. If anything, London was becoming a place where it was easier for Americans to fit in. Ordinary Londoners might not think very hard about who their fellow Britons across the Atlantic actually were, but they could not fail to know something about them, for by the 1760s London had been the capital of British America for more than 150 years, and the city itself had taken on a distinctly American cast.

If the vision and enterprise of London was transforming America, that wild hinterland was also changing London. It was the New World's plants, edible, smokeable, useful and beautiful, that first left their mark. West Indian sugar brought about a transformation of London's retail sector, and in a city that was always first and foremost a metropolis of merchandise rather than taste it would be a lasting one. Sugar, originally imported into England at great cost from the Mediterranean and seen only on the tables of the wealthy, was by the early eighteenth century found in every British household. Its successful production in England's exploitation colonies in the Caribbean had caused a dramatic and permanent plunge in its price.[15] Outside the home, sweets were at the centre of the rise of recreational shopping. There was a conspicuous expansion of pastry-cooks' shops (the sweets retailers of the Georgian era).

When Daniel Defoe published his stricture on modern retailing, deploring the new-style London shop owners who used elegant shop interiors and plate-glass windows to attract customers (a waste of money, said Defoe!), he used a pastry-cook's shop as an example. London became an exporter of sweets to the countryside. The numbers of confectioners in provincial towns like Norwich and Bristol increased threefold by the end of the century. Elizabeth Raffald invented royal icing, and the tiered wedding cake, modelled after the steeple of St Bride's in Fleet Street, was born. The English took credit for the practice of adding sugar to chocolate. Cocoa beans were from central America; the Spanish first brought them to Europe. The beans were roasted, pounded to a paste and served in hot water with a variety of flavourings, not always sweet. By the eighteenth century drinking chocolate prepared with sugar and milk ('milk chocolate') was served in most London coffee houses. As a nation the English had for centuries been adding sugar to dry wine (hence Falstaff's nickname 'Sir John Sack [Sec] and Sugar'), and it was natural to extend this to the recent arrivals, tea, coffee and chocolate. The advent of cheap sugar from America meant that Georgian Britain was emerging as 'the third great sweets culture', after India and the Islamic empire.[16]

Tobacco gave rise to an altogether new type of shop, dedicated to its consumption. The tobacconists put out exotic signs that decked the London streets with images of Indian kings and queens, or blackamoors' heads.[17] The sight of individuals smoking and snorting tobacco became an everyday one, as did the various implements necessary to the practice, pipes, tobacco stop-pers, pouches, snuffboxes, all new items to stock the shops in a growing consumer society. Smoke visibly clouded the atmosphere of coffee houses, taverns and tobacconists. It became so established a feature of London's public houses that its incidental function as a mask for unsavoury smells was taken for granted, and eventually forgotten altogether. When smoking was banned in London pubs in 2007, after almost four centuries of continuous fumigation by the New World weed, the smells of sweat, stale beer and unclean conven-iences suddenly came to the fore, causing publicans to resort to the medieval expedient of finding alternative scents to mask the unpleasantness.[18]

The mother country had been trying to make a profit from American crops since the start of colonisation in the seventeenth century. Sugar and tobacco were the most obvious success stories, but there were others. It was the British who had introduced rice to South Carolina, probably with the unwilling help of slaves who had experience of rice cultivation back home in Africa. It was a curious choice, because rice was an alien thing to the British in the seventeenth century, and as a nation they were slow to change. In the 1770s Henry Laurens was still fuming that the English poor clung to absurd myths about it. People believed it would make them go blind, he complained. Even in times of food shortages England's labouring classes 'loaded with execrations' the parish official who tried to give them 'that "*outlandish meal*"'. But British merchants made a bundle re-exporting rice to continental markets.[19] By the eighteenth century it was finding its way into genteel Georgian cookbooks as a dessert.

At the docks near the Tower of London sugar and tobacco, deerskins and rice were unloaded and stored, and American merchant sailors came and went in their hundreds. London had been a leading slaving port since the seventeenth century. African faces, another consequence of the rage to cultivate New World cash crops, had become an everyday sight. And London was a major port for another source of cheap colonial labour, for emigrants bound for the West Indies or continental America departed from its wharves on a regular basis. By the eve of the Revolution a couple of thousand people a year were embarking at London for a new life in the colonies. The usual practice was for emigrants to go to the colonies as indentured servants, whereby their passage was paid, and the captain sold them in the colonies for a period of service. It had been frighteningly common in the seventeenth century for unscrupulous captains to kidnap people to sell in the New World, though this had become rare by the 1760s.[20] But other crimes were perpetrated by the

27 The heart of the Port of London. The crowded Pool of London was where most of the shipping on the River Thames was concentrated in the eighteenth century. To the right can be seen the Tower of London, warehouses and wharves.

'night plunderers', 'day plunderers' and 'mudlarks' who comprised the ancient brotherhood of London's dockside thieves. Since the colonisation of America, sugar had become their favourite target, with tobacco and rum close behind.[21] Theft of this kind led to some colourful waterfront scenes. A man filled his apron with forty-two pounds of sugar from a warehouse and tried to run off with it, spilling it in the street when he was caught. A man unloading goods at the docks was caught stuffing handfuls of tobacco into his pockets. When he was let off, the judge warned him 'that if he followed this practice of stealing tobacco, he should be sent to plant it' – a half-jesting allusion to the threat of transportation to the Virginia plantations.[22] The judge's words would have had a real immediacy for the dockside labourer, who regularly saw criminals in chains being packed off to the colonies.

But New World plants were not only the engines of commerce; they also had an aesthetic contribution to make to the face of the city. It was in the early seventeenth century that ornamental gardening began to spread beyond the aristocracy to become a popular pastime, and the word 'flower-garden' entered the English language. The fashion to own exotic plants coincided with the first English settlements in America. Within decades hundreds of new species had reached Britain from the New World. It is not too much to say that America had an 'immense and lasting effect on the horticultural life' of Britain. A healthy market for ornamental American plants was established, and its clearing house was London.[23]

London was an unsurpassed place for plant collecting, a vast port at the crossroads of the sea traffic that traversed the globe.[24] Beautiful gardens distinguished by their American plants sprang up in many parts of the city. Today only the trees remain, a reminder of a time when it was the flora of America, not Asia or India, that were transforming the gardens of Britain. Henry Compton, who was bishop of London during Queen Anne's reign at the start of the century, amassed a famous American collection in his garden at Fulham that was renowned for its trees – black walnuts, magnolias, American honey locusts, some still on the grounds.[25] As bishop of London he could rely on a continuous stream of visitors from America, for he was the head of the Church of England for America throughout the colonial period. Colonial clergymen who came to London for their ordination, bishop's missionaries and commissaries, all could be put to the purpose of conveying new specimens to their lord bishop.

In Upton, Essex, not far from London was the garden of Dr John Fothergill, who wrote so feelingly of the rights of the American colonists during the

28 The bishop of London's Palace at Fulham. Its beautiful trees can be seen clearly in this view from the River Thames.

Stamp Act Crisis. Dr Fothergill was one of London's foremost physicians. He was also a Quaker and a Fellow of the Royal Society, which gave him many American connections. He knew Benjamin Franklin and Arthur Lee, both of them Fellows. He hosted a stream of visiting colonial Quakers, mainly from Pennsylvania, and was involved in philanthropic projects in the colonies such as the Pennsylvania Hospital and the first medical school at the University of Pennsylvania. He let it be known to his London patients that exotic plants were more acceptable to him than fees for his medical services. As he had plenty of West Indian clients, his collection quickly grew. He built a huge complex of greenhouses for his tropical plants, said to contain over 3,000 plant species. His garden was a famous showcase that could be viewed by the public.[26] The man who introduced him to gardening was another Quaker and Fellow of the Royal Society, Peter Collinson. Collinson was a City merchant with extensive trade in America. He was also the London agent for the famous horticulturalist John Bartram of Pennsylvania, who operated a commercial plant nursery on the banks of the Schuylkill river. Collinson acted as middle man for Bartram, who provided exotic plants for the merchant's aristocratic friends.[27] The Dukes of Bedford and Newcastle were just two of the noblemen who subscribed to his 'scheme of seed and plant importation from America'.[28] American trees were Collinson's speciality. When Ben Franklin arrived in

London in 1757 on a mission for the colony of Pennsylvania, he spent his first night at Collinson's home, Ridgeway House in Mill Hill, admiring the exotic American sugar maples and hemlock spruces.[29]

American trees had an important impact on what has been called 'the remaking of the English landscape'. A new generation of gardeners like Capability Brown visualised gardens that fit in with England's scenery. Trees and shrubs (as opposed to the flowers that were so important to formal garden design) were an important part of the new, more natural look. The London plane tree, a hybrid of the American sycamore and the Oriental plane tree, is one of the many surviving American aspects of London that date from the colonial period.[30] These majestic trees are found all over London, lining streets and shading parks. They have sycamore-like, broad leaves, and are hardy enough to withstand the polluted air for which London has long been notorious. They also have flaking bark which sheds London soot, and they are very long-lived. The oldest specimens are at least three hundred years old, and perhaps older.

The gardens of London became tourist attractions to be ranked alongside the Tower, Westminster Abbey and the royal palaces. A sightseer's guide to London published in 1767 recommended the Chelsea Physic Garden, St James's Park, Kensington Gardens, the gardens of Hampton Court and Kew Gardens, in a list that included such glittering attractions as London's theatres, the waxworks at Mrs Salmon's and the lord mayor's Mansion House.[31] The famous Royal Botanic Gardens at Kew date from the Seven Years' War, when the conquest of Canada opened up vast new tracts of wilderness to England's botanists. Designed to be both beautiful and practical, Kew Gardens became the centre of a network of botanical gardens scattered throughout the globe which aimed to cultivate useful plants for the empire's farmers.[32]

Foreign plant collection was one strand of a general interest in exotica of any kind, as the age of discovery led to popular curiosity about the wider world. The Royal Society held learned seminars inspired by newly discovered American animal and plant specimens: rattlesnakes and possums, fossils and flowers, and reports on hitherto unknown creatures like John Laurens's Florida softshell.[33] In 1768 a mastodon's jawbone discovered near the Ohio river sparked off a debate that was at the cutting edge of science. The curious object had been parcelled up and sent to Dr Franklin and Lord Shelburne in London. In an unusually animated meeting of the Royal Society, Franklin and others speculated on how elephant remains got to America, arriving at ideas that presaged the theory of evolution.[34] The jawbone was finally laid to rest in the British Museum. Opened to the public in 1759, the British Museum brought together several select private collections, among them the native art and natural curiosities of America that had been gathered by Sir Hans Sloane, president of the Royal Society. But the London public was not so particular as Sir Hans and his learned Fellows. In an era when there was no photography people would queue up to see almost anything from a foreign clime. Coffee houses sometimes advertised American animals on exhibit to draw crowds – snakes and crocodiles, for example, one supposes no longer alive.[35] In 1775 two live porcupines attracted a stream of curious spectators when they were put on display at the newly completed house of Sir Watkin Williams Wynn in St James's Square. The business of porcupines 'shooting out their quills was foolishness', concluded one nervous visitor afterwards.[36]

By the end of the Seven Years' War in 1763, the change worked on the face of the metropolis by its colonies was everywhere to be seen. At the docks near the Tower ships unloaded American cargoes, and American sailors both black and white poured into the taverns near the waterfront. Emigrants, slaves and convicts were packed into crowded vessels bound for the colonies. In the City one saw the tobacconists, the shops stocked with sugar and sugary goods, the faces of blacks whether slave or free, American, British, or African; the coffee houses with New World names like Jamaica or Pennsylvania, or Carolina, where Henry Laurens and Stephen Sayre went every day, and where one met with travellers to America and (it was well known) could look for a berth if one were inclined to emigrate. One could go to the Old Bailey to watch the trials of criminals who were regularly sentenced to transportation to 'the plantations'. The West End had its own New World luxuries, its visible population of black servants, its ostentatious absentee planters and its fashionable parks where American trees swayed in the breeze. These were the everyday reminders of London's distant American hinterland.

But the Seven Years' War abruptly fixed the attention of the British public on America as never before. This was a popular war, seen as a battle for empire and national wealth, rather than just another dynastic struggle slugged out on the battlefields of Europe. William Pitt the Elder, who in his position as secretary of state presided over it all, aimed to reduce the power of France by taking away her colonies overseas. This time Britain left its ally Prussia to do its fighting on the continent and concentrated instead on victory at sea and in America. The Seven Years' War was a war for empire in Pitt's mind. Nicknamed 'the Great Commoner', he became a popular hero whose policies were seen as championing the interests of England's mercantile and middling classes. His vision was one of wealth and liberty for British subjects every-where; he was idolised by patriotic Americans like Arthur Lee.[37] Pitt's admin-istration touched upon an emerging anti-aristocratic feeling, and stirred a sense of British patriotism on both sides of the Atlantic. Whereas in past wars with France, Britain had sent a token few thousand redcoats to the colonies, now over 20,000 were sent to defeat the French attempt to encircle and suffo-cate England's colonies. America was for the first time a major theatre of war for the British army.

Most of the 750,000 people living in London knew about America from what they saw and heard in the streets and going about their daily business. But if, for the first century of settlement, America could be said to have intruded itself on the notice of most Londoners, news of the Seven Years' War reversed that trend as General James Wolfe and his fellow heroes transported the imagination of the British nation into the heart of the Canadian woods. In the year 1759 even the most illiterate slum dweller in a St Giles rookery could not fail to know that British redcoats triumphed repeatedly over the French, for the City's church bells were 'worn threadbare with ringing for victories' in that 'glorious and ever-memorable year'.[38] It was surely the talk of the town, at every level.

The Seven Years' War literally put America on the map for metropolitans. London newspapers began printing charts of the colonies and New France to accompany their war reports, a thing only occasionally seen before.[39] In late 1755, a year after the outbreak of hostilities in America, the *London Magazine* published a two-page map called 'A NEW CHART of the Vast ATLANTIC OCEAN, Exhibiting the SEAT of WAR Both in EUROPE and AMERICA'. It depicted the British Isles, the island and mainland provinces of British America, and British possessions in Europe and Africa, such as Minorca, Gibraltar and the West African forts and factories connected with the slave trade, all of them ranged around the Atlantic Ocean.[40] This was 'the English Atlantic', as it would come to be called by historians. For Londoners contem-plating the far-off scenes of Anglo-French hostilities, America was fitting in as never before. British heroes were emerging in America, and they began to make their presence felt in London's national monuments.

Westminster Abbey had since the Middle Ages been a kind of showcase for Great Britons, a national burial place not only for Royals but also eminent commoners. After 1763 America's growing importance was reflected in several new marbles. A monument to the memory of Roger Townshend, one of the powerful Townshend family, who was killed by a cannonball at Fort

Ticonderoga in New York, featured a 'sarcophagus supported by two Indians', with a representation of the young commander in his 'expiring moments'.[41] In honour of Lord Howe, another British soldier who fell in an earlier expedition against the fort, the colony of Massachusetts placed a memorial in the Abbey. George Augustus Lord Howe was killed in an abortive attempt to oieze Ticonderoga in 1758. His death was said to have so demoralised the British and American soldiers he was leading that it contributed to the failure of the mission.[42]

But it was the immense monument to General James Wolfe, the hero who had captured Quebec and ended French dominion in Canada in 1759, that took pride of place among the Abbey's new marbles. Wolfe had been killed in action at the moment of victory. Indeed, he was one of the great military heroes of the century.[43] He was seen as a consummate patriot and a virtual martyr in Britain and America.

The nation's post-war patriotic pride spilled over into the world of art. On the continent Britain, great though it was in other respects, had long been regarded as artistically backward. Now a new generation of English artists was prepared to challenge this notion. The founding of the Royal Academy of Arts in London in 1768 by Joshua Reynolds and others was a bid to forge an English school. Emerging as it did in the burst of nationalism that followed the Seven Years' War, this new wave of English art included American themes. The British victory in Canada was naturally a popular subject. In the early 1760s the painter Francis Hayman created four vast canvases celebrating Britain's recent victory over France, commissioned especially for display at Vauxhall Gardens in London. America's importance to Britain was given pride of place with the painting *The Surrender of Montreal to General Amherst*. Hayman's Vauxhall exhibition helped to spark off a popular fashion for history painting. But the death of General Wolfe at Quebec was the most popular subject. It was even performed as a brief tableau at the end of theatrical performances, the actors posing as the dying Wolfe and the various symbolic and real figures who might have been grouped around him.[44] Paintings of the dying hero by notable artists George Romney and Edward Penny soon appeared.

More successful than either of these was the work of Pennsylvania-born Benjamin West. West was the son of a Quaker innkeeper, born just a few miles west of Philadelphia. He began painting at a very young age, seemingly on his own initiative and with little to guide him, and soon earned the applause of his rustic neighbourhood. Eventually he attracted the notice of influential individuals in Philadelphia and was sent to study at the College of Philadelphia.[45] In 1760, at the tender age of twenty-one, West took the bold step of going alone to Rome to study art. From that time on his career went from strength to strength. He made advantageous connections wherever he went, first in Italy and then, three years later, in London.[46] He arrived in London from Rome at the end of the Seven Years' War, and became a founding member of the Royal Academy of Arts in 1768.

West established himself as an exciting new artist in 1771 when his most famous painting, *The Death of General Wolfe*, was exhibited at the Royal Academy. His English audience was electrified by this depiction of what was an epochal moment for Britain and America, the death of General Wolfe at Quebec, 'a British hero on the heights of Abraham in North America expiring in the midst of heroes, and in victory', in West's words. He had not only chosen the perfect subject but he had also taken the bold stroke of breaking with tradition by painting his figures in authentic military dress. The convention in history painting was to depict heroes – even eighteenth-century English heroes – in Roman togas, thus singling them out as ideal universal types rather than everyday people. Although West was not the first artist to dispense with the convention of using classical dress, his *Death of General Wolfe* set the seal on the practice.[47] West claimed historical accuracy for his picture. It is unlikely, though, that Wolfe's officers flocked about him, watching him die while a battle was raging. But other details – for example, the Mohawk Indian with the American ranger by his side – would have given the painting a compelling air of authenticity for Londoners.

There were some very weighty dissenters, however. William Pitt – no longer a government minister but retired as Lord Chatham – remarked that there was 'too much dejection' in the 'dying hero's face' and in the faces of the officers grouped around him, 'who as Englishmen should forget all traces of private misfortunes when they had so grandly conquered for their country'. Chatham was not alone in thinking Wolfe looked too dejected to be a proper British hero. The actor David Garrick appeared at the exhibit one morning and laid himself before the painting in the pose of the dying Wolfe. At first taking on the expression of tragedy shown in the West portrait, he drew applause when he transformed his mien to the look of 'sublime joy' that a British soldier was deemed to feel at the moment of dying for his country.[48] In fact, West had tried to instill in the scene a sense of Divine Purpose by using Anthony Van Dyck's portrait of Christ taken from the Cross as a model for Wolfe. In so doing he waded into controversy, for such was the patriotic

29 'The Death of General Wolfe at Quebec' by Benjamin West.

significance given to Wolfe's state of mind as he lay gasping out his last that no fewer than thirteen versions of his dying words were circulating in Britain.[49] In spite of its illustrious detractors *The Death of General Wolfe* was an overnight success. Its exhibition attracted the largest crowd ever seen in the history of British painting. The engravings were massively popular and reputedly outsold any others of their time.[50] Visiting colonial Americans tried to get hold of them while they were in London.[51] The king commissioned a full copy of the original, and by the following year West had the title of 'Historical Painter to the King'.

In humbler quarters of the Great City the Seven Years' War spiced up America's image by bringing stories of scalpings and Indian tortures into the pubs and taverns. The surge of returning British soldiers seeking jobs after 1763 fuelled the circulation of fantastic-sounding tales about the New World. If the newspapers are any indication, the London public had an insatiable appetite for the lurid details of frontier warfare. Descriptions of Indian methods of torture and blow-by-blow accounts of massacres and atrocities were eagerly gobbled up. The papers dwelt upon the Indian practice of scalping without regard to age or sex. They told of frontier 'murders, rapine and devastation, such as would melt the heart of any human except that of an

Indian'.[52] With around a thousand coffee houses and taverns carrying the London papers, each reaching an estimated twenty readers, these daily gathering places were highly efficient incubators and disseminators of gossip and could spread attention-grabbing horror stories of this kind by word of mouth, reaching far beyond an actual readership to all levels of society.[53]

It is no wonder that the Seven Years' War produced the first ever celebrity American frontier hero. Major Robert Rogers of New England had formed a famous corps of rangers who were the eyes and ears of the British army. Rogers' Rangers were expert at the guerrilla warfare that was waged on the American frontier. Their fighting techniques fascinated British officers like George, Lord Howe, and the young Thomas Gage (later to be the British commander-in-chief at the start of the American Revolution). Howe and Gage adapted the methods used by the rangers for the new, experimental British light-infantry battalions.[54] This was the blend of heroism, adventure and violence that Londoners loved, and when Rogers came to the metropolis in 1765 he was lionised. While there he published *A Concise Account of North America* and his *Journals of Major Robert Rogers*, which included the famous 'General Rules for the Ranging Service'. The 'General Rules' outlined for the first time the unconventional tactics used by the rangers in their wilderness fighting. Guerrilla-style fighters like Rogers helped to create the notion of an 'American way of war', and gave rise to the romantic idea that small forces of American frontiersmen versed in the lore of the wild could rout large but ponderous formations of professional European soldiers.[55] Londoners loved stories like these, of doughty native fighters who could resist oversized professional armies, especially if the professional armies in question were French. The Protestant Camisards of the Cévennes and the guerrillas of Corsica had each become *causes célèbres* in their time.[56] Rogers became the American frontiersman *par excellence*. Although 'Western man' as an American stereotype would not be fully developed until the nineteenth century, Rogers was the prototype whose popularity foreshadowed the enthusiasm of the British public for figures like Kit Carson and Buffalo Bill Cody, and James Fenimore Cooper's Natty Bumppo from the best-selling *Last of the Mohicans*.[57] The *Journals* remained in print in England long after American independence.

It was not only the vulgar herd that had an appetite for stories of America's Wild West. The learned volumes published by booksellers usually focused on the exploration of America and its native peoples, rather than its British towns and settled areas. Robert Rogers's *A Concise Account of North America* contained lengthy descriptions of Indians and western lands. Even William

Burke's *Account of the European Settlements in America*, published in 1757 and destined to go through many reprints, spent a great deal of time on the early discovery of America and the Amerindian peoples. An immensely popular book was Jonathan Carver's *Travels through the Interior Parts of North America in the Years 1766, 1767, and 1768*. Carver, a New Englander, based his work on his own travels in the American west. In 1769, his exploration completed, he came to London to find a publisher, and remained there for the next ten years. He has been called 'one of the most popular and successful American writers in the eighteenth century'. His work, which was eventually translated into many languages, influenced romantic poets such as William Wordsworth and Chateaubriand.[58]

The new interest in America inspired by the Seven Years' War was drawn to those things that made for a compelling contrast with the most modern city on earth: the idea of a vast wilderness with its unique dangers and attractions, its exotic native peoples, its unknown wildlife and plants, all providing a new and untested backdrop against which to view the perennial battle against the old enemy France. There was less interest in the settled colonies. It is no wonder, then, that before the War of Independence the standard icon of America in London was a Native American. In prints and sculptures an American Indian more quickly conjured up the idea of America than the amorphous notion of a colonist, and at the same time summed up the sense of exoticism that the New World evoked.[59] And anyway Londoners were fascinated by Native Americans and had been almost since the discovery of the New World. Pocahontas achieved lasting fame during her brief sojourn in England between 1616 and 1617. Soon after the first English colonies were established in America, American Indians as exotic heroes began to appear on the stage in the works of popular English writers such as John Dryden and Aphra Behn.[60] When four young Indian warriors visited London in 1710 to represent the Iroquois confederacy at the Court of St James, they became a virtual street show, as curious crowds followed them about wherever they went.[61] Twenty years later seven Cherokee chiefs from South Carolina met with the same reception, a 'vast concourse of people' trailing after them as they walked through the city in their native costumes.[62]

The Seven Years' War only whetted the public's appetite for a sight of genuine Native Americans. In 1762, just a year before the conclusion of the peace, three Cherokee braves were brought to London by Henry Timberlake and Thomas Sumter, both officers who had served with Washington's Virginia regiment during the war. The visit had a serious purpose, no less than to pledge Cherokee friendship to the British king in the wake of a savage Anglo-Cherokee war.[63] Like their predecessors, the exotic visitors found themselves followed by crowds wherever they went.

The three Cherokees became celebrities overnight. Gaping onlookers watched them as they toured the Tower of London, the Houses of Parliament and St Paul's Cathedral. Lifelike figures of them were put on display at Mrs Salmon's Waxworks in Fleet Street.[64] People flocked to see them at Vauxhall Gardens, where they got so drunk that they committed certain 'irregularities' that Timberlake forbore to mention in his account of the tour.[65] The *St James's Chronicle* was not so discreet. On their first visit to Vauxhall the Cherokees were apparently regaled with burgundy and claret. Finding these too dry for their taste, they were offered Frontiniac, a sweet muscadine that tastes like elder-flower wine. This they found perfectly acceptable and drank 'very freely'. Three weeks later they were back at the famous Gardens. This time the proprietor knew what was required. The Cherokees swallowed 'by wholesale, bumpers of Frontiniac'. They got very drunk. Accompanied by several prostitutes, they wandered into the orchestra, pushed away the musicians and proceeded to bang on the keys of the organ and scrape at the violins. The crowd, numbering some ten thousand people, clapped wildly, and the Cherokees clapped back. It was not until two or three in the morning that they were ready to leave.

Then disaster struck. The chief of the three, who was dressed in a 'blue silk mantle, edged with a gold-Lace', made for his coach, linking arms with a prostitute. En route he snagged his robe on someone's sword-hilt. In a flash the sword was out and the Cherokee had broken it with his bare hands. His hands were bloodied. Though neither he nor his comrades spoke a word of English, his chagrin was plain to see. He threw himself on the ground in a sulk, and had to be lifted 'neck and heels' into the coach. The coachman, no doubt used to drunken passengers, deftly packed the chief's legs in the door, and they were off.[66] Poor Mr De Berdt, who worked vigorously for the Christian conversion of Native Americans, was horrified when he heard of it. 'We have here three Cherokees,' he wrote, 'but alas they are only introduced to the scenes of folly and vanity, luxury and superstition with which this city abounds, which must give them very wrong ideas of the Christian religion.'[67]

Mr De Berdt's opinion was decidedly in the minority. All this was the sort of showmanship the London crowds loved. Wherever the three Cherokees visited, advance notice was given in the newspapers. One tavern posted a sign reading 'This day the King of the Cherokees and his two chiefs drink tea here.' Although no entry fee was ever charged, there was an uncomfortable similarity to animals on exhibit in a zoo that was not lost on Londoners. An onlooker commented that they were being 'shown like wild beasts'.[68] But not everyone agreed that their uncivilised image was a disadvantage. The ladies of London found them immensely attractive, according to a satirical broadside circulating during their visit. It sported a bawdy song, to be sung 'To the Tune of, *Caesar and Pompey were both of them Horned*', which suggested that the crowds pressing round the Cherokees were heavily biased towards the fair sex:

The Ladies, dear Creatures, so squeamish and dainty,
Surround the great *Canada* Warriors in plenty;
Wives, Widows and *Matrons*, and pert little *Misses*,
Are pressing and squeezing for Cherokee Kisses.

. . .

No more then these Chiefs, with their scalping Knives dread, Sir,
Shall strip down the Skin from the *Englishman*'s Head, Sir;
Let the Case be revers'd, and the Ladies prevail, Sir,
And instead of the Head, skin the *Cherokee* T–l, Sir.
Ye bold Female Scalpers, courageous and hearty,
Collect all your Force for a *grand Scalping Party*.

For Weapons, ye Fair, you've no need to petition,
No Weapons you'll want for this odd Expedition,
A soft Female Hand, the best Weapon I wean is,
To strip down the Bark of a *Cherokee P–s*.
Courageous advance then, each fair *English* Tartar,
Scalp the *Chiefs* of the *Scalpers*, and give them no Quarter.

But it was not all indignity. The author Oliver Goldsmith waited three hours to meet the Cherokees, and was rewarded with a hearty kiss from Ostenaca. (Goldsmith was not amused when his face was left smeared with war paint.) Another of the Cherokees had his portrait painted by Joshua Reynolds.[69] They were received at Court by the young George III.[70] Other visiting Native Americans were marked out for similar polite treatment. When Joseph Brant (or Thayendanegea), the Mohawk leader, came to London in 1775 to discuss the role of the Six Nations in the war in the colonies, Boswell called upon him at his headquarters in Lad Lane, just around the corner from St Paul's Cathedral, and the Duke of Northumberland invited him to Syon House. And the Earl of Warwick commissioned a portrait of him by George Romney.[71]

A NEW HUMOROUS SONG,

ON THE

CHEROKEE CHIEFS.

(arrived in London July 8. 1762)

Inscribed to the LADIES of GREAT BRITAIN.

By H. HOWARD.

To the Tune of, *Cæsar and Pompey were both of them Horned.*

I.

WHAT a Piece of Work's here, and a d—d Botheration !
  Of Three famous Chiefs from the *Cherokee* Nation ;
Who the Duce wou'd ha' thought, that a People polite, Sir,
Wou'd ha' ftir'd out o' Doors to ha' feen fuch a Sight, Sir ?
Are M——rs fo rare in the *Britifh* Dominions,
That we thus fhou'd run crazy for *Canada Indians.*
                    Are M——rs fo rare, &c.

II.

How eager the Folks at *Vauxhall,* or elfewhere, Sir,
With high Expectation and Rapture repair, Sir ;
Tho' not one of them all can produce the leaft Reafon,
Save that M——rs of all Sorts are always in Seafon.
If fo, let the Chiefs here awhile have their Station,
And fend for the whole of the *Cherokee* Nation.
                    If fo, let the Chiefs, &c.

III.

The Ladies, dear Creatures, fo fqueamifh and dainty,
Surround the great *Canada* Warriors in plenty ;
Wives, Widows and *Matrons,* and pert little *Miffes,*
Are preffing and fqueezing for *Cherokee* Kiffes.
Each grave looking Prude, and each fmart looking Belle, Sir,
Declaring, no *Englifhman* e'er kifs'd fo well, Sir.
                    Each grave looking Prude, &c.

IV.

That *Cherokee* Lips are much fofter and fweeter,
Their Touch more refin'd, and their Kiffes repleter ;
The fair ones agree——nay, I mean not to flatter,
For who like the Ladies can judge of the Matter ?
Ye Nymphs then, who like 'm, indulge your odd Paffion,
Be fw——d by the Chiefs of the *Cherokee* Nation.
                    Ye Nymphs then, &c.

V.

Ye Females of *Britain,* fo wanton and witty,
Who love even Monkies, and fwear they are pretty ;
The *Cherokee Indians,* and ftranger *Shimpanzeys,*
By Turns, pretty Creatures, have tickl'd your Fancies ;
Which proves, that the Ladies fo fond are of Billing,
They'd kifs even M——rs, were M——rs as willing.
                    Which proves, that, &c.

VI.

No more then thefe Chiefs, with their fcalping Knives dread, Sir,
Shall ftrip down the Skin from the *Englifhman's* Head, Sir ;
Let the Cafe be revers'd, and the Ladies prevail, Sir,
And inftead of the Head, fkin the *Cherokee* T——l, Sir.
Ye bold Female *Scalpers,* courageous and hearty,
Collect all your Force for a *grand Scalping Party.*
                    Ye bold Female Scalpers, &c.

VII.

For Weapons, ye Fair, you've no need to petition ;
No Weapons you'll want for this odd Expedition ;
A foft Female Hand, the beft Weapon I wean is,
To ftrip down the Bark of a *Cherokee P—s.*
Courageous advance then, each fair *Englifh* Tartar,
Scalp the *Chiefs* of the *Scalpers,* and give them no Quarter.
                    Courageous advance then, &c.

Peace figned with Cherokees See Gent Mag 1762 p. 97   *1762*

Sold by the AUTHOR, oppofite the Union Coffee-Houfe, in the Strand, near Temple-Bar, and by all the Print and Pamphlet-fellers.
[PRICE SIX-PENCE.]
N. B. In a few Days will be publifhed the *Political Bagpiper.* A new Song, with a Head-piece.

30 'A New Humorous Song, on the Cherokee Chiefs Inscribed to the Ladies of Great Britain', a satirical broadside published in 1762.

However they were received, and whatever their purpose in coming, Indians could always be counted on to draw a crowd in Britain. There is no doubt that Georgian fraudsters occasionally cashed in on this, dressing themselves up as Native Americans.[72] In much the same vein, when Eleazar Wheelock's Indian school at Lebanon, Connecticut, decided to send emissaries to England in 1766 on a fundraising expedition, the school's benefactors thought that 'an Indian minister in England might get a bushel of money for the school'. They sent Samson Occom, a Mohegan teacher at the school. In London he was squired around by the evangelist George Whitefield. Occom met Lord Dartmouth and the Countess of Huntington, who were unique among England's worldly Georgian nobility for being sincerely religious. (Occom referred to these two ironically as 'the *religious Nobility*'.) He called on Mr De Berdt at Artillery Court and was inoculated for smallpox by Thomas Ruston. Occom and his companion Eleazar Wheelock went on to tour the British Isles. Despite being relatively anglicised, the 'Indian minister' aroused great public curiosity. He delivered over three hundred sermons while in England. The hopes of the 'Indian school' trustees were amply realised when he raised no less than £11,000.[73] When Occom returned to Connecticut in 1768, he discovered that the money he had raised was to be used to relocate Wheelock's school to New Hampshire, where it became Dartmouth College and lost its identity as a charity school for Indians.[74]

The Georgian interest in exotic peoples went beyond mere curiosity. The age of exploration had sparked off a new scientific interest in the nature of man. Other non-European visitors were received with great interest: the Tahitian Mai, for example, and the West African Sessarakoo.[75] To the intelligentsia of Georgian England, America's native peoples were just as interesting as its flora and fauna. Native Americans were hailed as an example of humankind in a primitive state, people whose natures were undistorted by civilisation. They were the prototype of the noble savage so beloved of Jean-Jacques Rousseau. If they were romanticised, they also yielded material for an early, crude form of anthropology that allowed theorists to speculate on the origins and nature of 'civilised' society and government.

The stadialist theory of human development, refined during the century by French and Scottish intellectuals, propounded that every human society moved progressively through the phases of hunting, pasturage, agriculture and commerce. American Indians and other 'primitive' peoples were held to be on the bottom rung. Europe's great nations, of course, were on the last and highest.[76] A scientific theory of differences among races had not been developed (although some intellectuals toyed with the idea). The biblical version of the common origin of all mankind was still widely accepted, and Enlightenment philosophy saw all human beings as fundamentally the same, but placed by circumstances in the ascending stages of development.[77] It was not until the nineteenth century that 'scientific' theories of innate racial differences were fully articulated, arguing that certain races were superior, and that some inferior races were simply not, and never would be, capable of attaining the same level of civilisation and cultivation as Europeans.

A theory of human development had a scientific ring to it, but it also had a certain entertainment value. Georgian England regarded itself as among the most sophisticated nations on earth. A fashionable debate was carried on throughout the century as to whether this was really a good thing or not. Was the nation at the brink of its greatest era yet, wealthy, free and enlightened? Or had modern luxuries led to a retreat from wholesome English values and towards a sinister moral decline? According to the theory, unchecked modernisation could result in corruption – the same corruption that destroyed the post-republican Roman empire.

As the epitome of modern living throughout the English-speaking world, London was at the centre of the debate. It was variously eulogised by some and deplored by others. It became a fashionable cliché to assert that one's morals were corrupted by a stay there. Jane Austen, on a jaunt to London in the 1790s, wrote jokingly to her sister Cassandra: 'Here I am once more in this scene of dissipation and vice, and I begin already to find my morals corrupted.'[78] Henry Laurens had made fun of the extremes of opinion he found among Londoners themselves. In the course of a single day, he listened to 'one intelligent sensible friend' lament in the morning 'Alas, sir! This country is undone. We shall soon be crushed by our own weight. We are sinking under corruption'; in the evening he rode out with another who exclaimed that 'England was the happiest kingdom upon earth. See, sir, said he, as we were riding around the skirts of the city, and pointing at innumerable new buildings, large and elegant, which are rising in a hundred different places, See the marks of our poverty and distress. Great Britain is yet but in her infancy, and even this great city very far from its zenith.'[79]

Primed by these conflicting pictures of their own character, Londoners were drawn to the comparisons that could be made between their own ultra-sophisticated society and Native Americans living close to nature. Were Native Americans really at the bottom of the totem pole, as the stadialist theory suggested? Or were they actually closer to what nature intended for mankind, examples of humanity in John Locke's famous 'state of nature', their simple lifestyles exposing 'the weaknesses and vices of an effete Europe'?[80] The cult of the noble savage had its heyday in the eighteenth century.

London chauvinism meant that when the wider world came under scrutiny, it often became a foil for exploring English characteristics. If the nations of Europe were commonly found wanting in one respect or another, the forests of America offered a different measure of the national character. America's native peoples and pristine wildernesses variously affirmed a fashionable indictment of modern lifestyles, or provided an exotic and dangerous backdrop against which to test the valour and resourcefulness of a highly civilised nation. The settled American colonies, by contrast, simply could not command the same level of interest in their capital. What would happen, then, when their most famous son came to London in quest of a second career? When Benjamin Franklin reached the empire's capital in 1757, he was not yet an American icon, only another talented provincial trying to make his way in the great city.

CHAPTER EIGHT

Franklin and Son in London

Benjamin Franklin was not the most successful colonial American in London. That distinction must go to his friend Benjamin West, who came to London as a young artist, rose to the position of History Painter to the King, and remained a leading figure in the British art world despite his open support for the American rebellion. Nor was Franklin the most typical. Putting aside the unusual personal abilities that set him apart from others, demography was against him in Georgian London. A self-made Pennsylvanian man of business was very much a minority in a place where ever more black and white colonists from the southern plantations were making their presence felt in the streets. Not until the nineteenth century would he be held up as the epitome of an American, the so-called 'father of all the Yankees'. By then the notion of an American national character had emerged that embodied the middle-class values of success through self-help and democratic manners that Franklin seemed to personify.[1] To be sure, when he arrived in France in 1778 to represent the new United States as American commissioner, Franklin would be feted as the French ideal of all things American, a rustic backwoods philosopher. But the French did not yet know the Americans as well as the British did. 'Franklin might masquerade at Versailles as a noble savage,' commented historian Piers Mackesy, 'but the British knew the political Americans better: a wealthy sophisticated society with a high standard of living, and as aggressive as the British themselves in the pursuit of commercial gain.'[2]

He was not the most successful or the most typical American, but Ben Franklin was assuredly the most famous when he arrived in the Great City in 1757 to serve as agent for the Pennsylvania Assembly. And during the seventeen years he lived in London, momentous years framed by the Seven Years' War and the American Revolution, his fame, if anything, grew.

Franklin had been to London once before, when in his late teens he worked as a printer's apprentice. His older brother James had done the same, returning afterwards to Boston and publishing the *New-England Courant*; a London apprenticeship was an invaluable start for a colonial newspaperman. Like everyone, young Ben revelled in the sights and sounds of the metropolis. He spent so much of his money on plays and amusements that he was unable to save anything for his passage back home. But most of all he was struck by the intellectual life of the capital. Seeking an introduction to Sir Hans Sloane, soon to be president of the Royal Society, the young Franklin posed as a gentleman just arrived from the colonies. He dropped his façade when he met the great man, but the ruse had worked, and Sloane obligingly purchased some American rarities Franklin had brought with him from Pennsylvania. London was stimulating; Ben was not sure which note to strike, but he knew that he wanted to make an impression. He showed off his athletic prowess on the Thames, swimming from Chelsea to Blackfriars and performing various 'feats of activity' that drew an audience. Within days Sir William Wyndham had called upon him and asked him to teach his boys to swim.[3] London brought out a streak of exhibitionism in the teenager, but he did not seriously think of staying.

Back in Philadelphia Ben Franklin began his famous career. Within three years of his return from London, in 1729, he had acquired the *Pennsylvania Gazette*. He formed the Junto, a mutual improvement society of tradesmen and artisans that became a powerful business and social network. He began to publish his *Poor Richard's Almanac*, and entered civic life, helping to form Philadelphia's Union Fire Company, and became clerk of the Pennsylvania Assembly. In 1737 he became postmaster of Philadelphia, a prelude to his appointment as deputy postmaster general of all North America sixteen years later. Franklin was a driving force behind the trend to make Philadelphia the most urbane city in colonial America, convinced that it would become 'the Seat of the American Muses'.[4] He helped to found the American Philosophical Society, the Philadelphia Academy (later the University of Pennsylvania) and the Pennsylvania Hospital.

Yet the enterprising Franklin never lost sight of business in the midst of all this, and in 1748, aged just forty-two, he was prosperous enough to be able to retire after forming a partnership with printer David Hall. He now began to move on a larger stage. He was elected to the Pennsylvania Assembly. In 1754 he attended the Albany Conference, the first-ever meeting of representatives from all the mainland American colonies, where he proposed an innovative

31 Benjamin Franklin, 1767.

plan to unite the colonies under one government for defence. The following year he helped the British General Edward Braddock supply his ill-fated expedition to drive the French out of Fort Duquesne, the disastrous debut to Britain's conquest of French Canada.

Even this does not do justice to Franklin's accomplishments, his philanthropic introduction of lighting and pavements to the streets of Philadelphia, his lending libraries and fuel-efficient stoves, his observations on eclipses and his personal system for preserving virtue. Benjamin Franklin was a true polymath. But the *pièce de resistance* was assuredly his electrical experiments. Franklin was already famous when in 1752 he used a kite to prove that lightning was indeed an airborne electrical current. For this, a truly cutting-edge contribution to science, he was awarded the Royal Society's Copley Medal. Just a few years previously Franklin had conducted experiments that led to the insight that electricity had a positive and a negative nature.[5] His *Experiments and Observations on Electricity*, published in London in 1751, soon appeared in French, Italian, German and Latin. His spectacular kite experiment so captured the public imagination that he became a celebrity. The 'Prometheus' of the modern age, Immanuel Kant eulogised, who could snatch lightning from the sky like the gods.[6] A year after his electrical feat of daring, Harvard and Yale universities presented him with honorary MAs when he toured New England.

Yet it was politics that brought Franklin to London again. Pennsylvania was one of the proprietary colonies, originally granted by the Crown to the aristocratic Quaker William Penn, who guaranteed religious toleration to its inhabitants. By Franklin's time the Penn family had long since given up their unfashionable Quaker connections; they were firmly Church of England and lived in an elegant home in London's Spring Garden.[7] They were still the proprietors of Pennsylvania, but the colony's assembly, which was dominated by the old Quaker party, held the balance of power, and was frequently at loggerheads with them. This shaky relationship came to a head during the Seven Years' War. The Penns refused to pay taxes on their vast landholdings in Pennsylvania. With the defence of the colony an urgent necessity, the two sides were in deadlock over whether the Penns could be exempted from taxes. The quarrel was so intractable that it had delayed the defence of the western half of the colony. Each side blamed the other, the Penns pointing to the avowed pacifism of the Quakers and the Quakers retorting that the Penns refused to contribute to the cost of defence. Benjamin Franklin, by now a leading figure in the Quaker-dominated assembly and a person of substance, was given the task of going to London to resolve the dispute.

Once in London, Ben Franklin handled the negotiations with the Penns with a gaucheness that was entirely out of character. His famous charm and his skill as a pragmatic conciliator, hitherto among his most outstanding characteristics, deserted him. He lost his temper. After a few meetings with proprieter Thomas Penn in 1758, he wrote indiscreet letters home to Pennsylvania likening the proprietor of Pennsylvania to 'a low jockey when a purchaser complained that he had cheated him in a horse', who responded with 'triumphing laughing insolence'.[8] This and other things got back to Penn, who had not in any case been impressed by his meetings with Franklin. Direct negotiations were at an end. The two men avoided each other.[9] Franklin admitted that his usefulness as a go-between for the Assembly and the proprietor was over; whenever he encountered Penn, he wrote, 'there appears in his wretched countenance a strange mixture of hatred, anger, fear and vexation'. For Penn's part, Franklin looked 'like a malicious V. [villain], as he always does'.[10] Ben was not showing his famous skill at handling people. The business was dragged out, in part by Franklin's refusal to deal directly with the Penns' legal adviser, whom he also hated. It ended after several years in a qualified success for Franklin and the Pennsylvania Assembly as the Privy Council determined that the Penns' estates might be taxed, but the family still retained the right to contest future legislation from the Quaker-controlled assembly, something Franklin had sought to take away from them.[11]

The Penn family had not heard the last of Ben Franklin. From the time of the ill-starred meetings with the Penns in 1758 there ensued a ten-year quest by the Pennsylvania agent to relieve them of their proprietorship. His plan was to have the colony's original charter under the Penns revoked and replaced with royal government. Many in Pennsylvania, including his friends, believed that such a change would pose a danger to the liberties of the colony. It was an ill-judged mission, and one that ran counter to the overall colonial resistance to British authority which gathered steam after 1763. Franklin's vendetta against the Penns has been called an obsession. And he himself was obliged to abandon the whole enterprise a full seven years before the War of Independence brought him home from Britain.[12]

So why did Franklin's second stint in London start out so badly? Ben Franklin had some understandable reasons for losing patience with the Penns. But he also knew that the dangerous delay in getting Pennsylvania ready for war was not entirely their fault. His own allies among the pacifist Friends also had a share in the blame. The Penns had their side of the story, as Franklin was aware.[13] Surely there was something more to cut him so deeply, to move him to feel 'a more cordial and thorough contempt for [Penn] than I ever before felt for any man living'.[14] Franklin's behaviour was out of character – but then he was out of the world he knew so well. He was in London for the first time as a man of business with an important commission to fulfil, rather than as a young and anonymous printer's apprentice who had only himself to please.

Back home in Philadelphia, Ben Franklin knew his environment very well. He knew how to get what he wanted, and he usually got it. He had become a powerful man during his years in Pennsylvania, and a dominant figure in the politics of the colony. More intelligent than many of his associates, and a keen reader of other men's natures, he usually accomplished things by a combination of persuasion and manipulation. He was a complicated man, but this was not obvious to those around him. He had a pronounced ability to charm when he wished to – 'I never found a person in my whole life more thoroughly to my mind', wrote a friend and fellow printer.[15] Because his own personal ambition and his genuine civic-mindedness often overlapped, it was not difficult for him to obscure his self-interest under a mantle of disinterested good will. But when he felt it was needed, he was willing to resort to abusive, confrontational – even bullying – speech to get the better of an opponent. 'No governor' but a 'mere Bashaw' was what he called a newly appointed governor of Pennsylvania to his face when discussing the issue of taxing the Penns, thus establishing his superior footing over the head of the province. Governor William Denny took it 'tamely', according to a witness.[16] At the end of his famous *Autobiography*, Franklin offered this insight with respect to his own character: 'Costs me nothing to be civil to inferiors, a good deal to be submissive to superiors'.[17] It was not to be published until the 1790s, but poor Governor Denny would have known what he meant.

When Franklin arrived in London in 1757, he found himself for the first time in many years uncertain of his environment. He 'seems groundless at a loss how and where to begin', wrote one onlooker of his initial negotiations with the Penns.[18] When he did meet with the Penns, he found that the tactics he had for so long used successfully back home did not work. The Penns lived in London, where social connections and closeness to government circles counted for more than hard work or personal charisma. And they had their own power base, which Franklin did not yet fully understand. It must have added to the anticipation of failure – intolerable to a man like him – to suffer proprietor Thomas Penn's aloof and gloating manner. Penn was known as a cold, formal man, and he no doubt communicated to Franklin his conviction that the agent for Pennsylvania was out of his depth in the metropolis, both socially and politically.[19] There, perhaps, was the sting. Thomas Penn had hurt Ben's pride deeply enough for him to forget his philosophy and retaliate. When his insulting remarks about the proprietor became public knowledge, he wrote to Joseph Galloway, 'I might have left his conduct and sentiments to your reflections, and contented myself with a bare recital of what passed; but indignation extorted it from me, and I cannot yet say that I much repent of it. It sticks in his liver, I find; and e'en let him bear what he so well deserves.'[20]

Was Ben Franklin suffering from what a later generation would call 'status anxiety'? When he embarked for London at the age of fifty-one, his success was such that he had comfortably transcended his humble background.[21] He could be confident that he was more able than many better-born men, like the Penns, who rubbed shoulders with him in political and intellectual circles. And yet – he was not quite a gentleman by most people's standards. Throughout his career in Philadelphia, Franklin had never been entirely accepted by the city's elite.[22] Now he had arrived at a place where that really mattered, for in London it was these elite colonists, families like the Laurenses whose lifestyles emulated those of the English gentry, who fit in so readily.

Henry Laurens was a saddler's son but this does not convey his family's actual social standing. His grandfather was a Huguenot who fled France in the seventeenth century to escape religious persecution. Although André Laurens was not wealthy when he arrived in America, he was gentrified and he left his children small legacies. It was Henry's father John who rebuilt the family fortune, establishing a saddler's business that became the largest of its kind in the colony of South Carolina. By the time he retired in his forties he had acquired real estate and slaves, and held various public offices. His connections were sufficient to obtain a place for Henry as a merchant apprentice in London. This was Henry's starting point; it took several years of hard work and the notorious twenty-hour days, but by the time he was in his twenties Henry was able to marry into one of the first families of South Carolina.[23]

The leap from modest but respectable boyhood origins into genteel society was not so wide or high for Henry as it was for Ben Franklin – the son of a soap maker and chandler, a boy whose family background had for generations never been known to go any higher than small farmers or skilled artisans. Ben Franklin's own London apprenticeship had been done on a shoestring and off his own back. When he married at age twenty-four it was to a dowerless and unpretentious woman, Deborah Read, who could not spell but was a thrifty housekeeper.[24]

In London, Franklin did not resemble fellow colonist Henry Laurens so much as he did his British provincial equivalents, men like the famous engraver Thomas Bewick of Newcastle, who is best remembered for his beautifully illustrated *History of British Birds*. The son of a Northumberland tenant farmer, Bewick's career followed a pattern similar to Franklin's. His early years comprehended a patchy childhood education, a youth that displayed conspicuous enterprising qualities, and a stint in London as a young engraver. Once back in Newcastle there ensued the years of hard work leading to success, a rise in social status affirmed by his entry into civic life, and the elevation of his professional reputation to a national level by taking it beyond mere craftsmanship to art (Franklin would achieve this through his scientific discoveries). Both men would write autobiographies that captured the popular imagination. Because of his rustic provincial origins, Bewick, like Franklin, became romanticised as an untutored genius whose knowledge flowed from his natural surroundings. In reality he was a no-nonsense man with a bluff manner and a strong business sense. He was an avid club-joiner in a day when Newcastle's merchants, tradesmen and skilled artisans (much like the members of Franklin's Junto) were keen to associate in clubs that cultivated self-improvement. The members of these Newcastle clubs might be tradesmen but they were also townsmen, men who knew the world and kept in touch with trends in polite knowledge. Although they claimed the status of gentleman, they were a new breed who staked their claim on the cultivation of the mind rather than the outward deportment of England's fashionable classes.[25]

Both Bewick and Franklin (whom Bewick admired) might cut a respectable figure in a genteel London drawing room but they would not blend in like young John Laurens.[26] This did not have to matter – much. Georgian London was the capital of an aristocratic society but it was also a place where middle-class men who had talent and enterprise could climb, sometimes to the very top. Daniel Defoe put this in a nutshell when he caricatured a newly created lord declaiming his pedigree: 'I am *William* Lord *Craven*; my father was *Lord Mayor* of *London*, and my grandfather was the *Lord knows who*.'[27] Franklin knew the opportunities that could be had in London first-hand, through his friend William Strahan. Like Franklin, Strahan was a printer from the provinces. Born in Edinburgh, he moved to London at the outset of his career, became publisher to Dr Johnson and ended up an MP.[28]

The moral of such stories was clear, and a favourite of Franklin. Poor Richard, the fictional author of Franklin's famous almanacs, repeatedly preached the dignity of success through hard work – '*He that has a trade has an estate* and *He that has a calling has an office of profit and honour*'; 'a *ploughman on his legs is higher than a gentleman on his knees*'.[29] But before he reached London, Franklin knew that his own plain birth and education had already put obstacles in the way of his career. Back in Philadelphia he had tried briefly to serve as a justice of the peace, but his lack of formal education showed and he experienced 'one of his first real failures'.[30] And he had never mastered the art of public speaking, something that formed a part of every young gentleman's education. In the Pennsylvania Assembly Joseph Galloway, the son of a wealthy Maryland landowner, whose legal training made him an effective orator, defended many of Franklin's policies.[31] Evidently Franklin's many talents did not include the chameleon-like acting skills of someone like Stephen Sayre, who although a far lesser man could dissemble gentle breeding.

Franklin made sure that his son William would do better by providing him with an education that enabled him to fit into genteel society. William Franklin was illegitimate, the offspring of a liaison between Franklin and an unknown woman. Gossip identified her as Barbara, a lowly maid-of-all-work in the Franklin household. What is certain is that Franklin as a young bachelor, by his own confession, could not resist 'intrigues with low women', and resorted to marriage in part to contain his 'hard-to-be-governed passion of youth'.[32] Deborah accepted the infant William into her home when she married Ben Franklin, though not necessarily with a good grace. Ben Franklin, though, raised the child with care. There is no evidence that Ben intended his son for a printer; he was placed in a school for Philadelphia's gentry families, where he met boys from the local elite. When Ben came up against his own lack of formal learning during his brief service as a justice of the peace, in 1750, he decided to give William the benefit of legal training. He placed him in the law office of Joseph Galloway in Philadelphia, and asked William Strahan in London to have his son admitted to one of the Inns of Court.[33] William Franklin was to have the education and manners of a son of the colonial elite.

Almost seven years passed before William, who accompanied his father on his mission to London in 1757, was able to attend the Middle Temple. At twenty-seven William was rather older than most other students at the Inns, but he did not stay long. Ben Franklin had discovered the ways by which one could expedite a stay at the Inns. His son's name was entered on the rolls several years in advance of his arrival. Ben then ordered the usual law books from London, which William studied from afar in Philadelphia.[34] Just over a year after reaching the metropolis, in November 1758, William Franklin was called to the bar. Even with the cash fines Ben would have had to pay in lieu of the required terms of residence, he had surely found a thrifty means of attaining a prestigious legal qualification for his son. The brief entry in the barrister's ledger for William lists his chamber in Middle Temple Lane, but during his one year of residence he could not have been parted much from his father.[35] Middle Temple Lane was only a short walk away from Craven Street where Ben had taken lodgings, and William was constantly assisting his father as his secretary from the very start of the London mission.[36] Ben's biggest

V. 2

13

A LAW MACARONI.

Pub by Marly Strand Feb.º 16.ᵗʰ 1772 accor to act.

32 A lawyer in his wig and robes, 1772. William Franklin put on his black barrister's gown for the first time when he was called to the Bar on 10 November 1758.

saving had probably been to avoid the hideous expense of supporting a young, unsupervised man set loose in London during the course of his legal studies. But William himself may have lost out, for there is no evidence that he formed the peer friendships that other colonial youths did while at the Temple, friendships that could be useful contacts for life.

William's early departure probably simplified his social life in Middle Temple Hall, because not long afterwards a clique of young Pennsylvanians from the enemy camp began to form. Foremost among these were the Allen brothers, who were to impress Hetta De Berdt with their neglect of their legal studies. They were the sons of William Allen, a staunch supporter of proprietor Thomas Penn. Once a friend of Ben Franklin, William Allen was now his active opponent. While the Franklins were still in London, Peter DeLancey and another New Yorker, Philip Livingston, came to the Inns of Court and joined the Allens' circle. These last two young gentlemen counted as their patron one of the Penns' ubiquitous associates, Lord Stirling. So William would have had a venomous clique of peers to contend with as he made his way around the environs of the Temple. Apparently he looked undaunted in the face of the opposition, for Philip Livingston called him 'the high and mighty William Franklin'.[37]

33 A view of Middle Temple Hall in the mid-eighteenth century.

Unperturbed by the malice of the Allen set at Middle Temple Hall, both Franklins entered wholeheartedly into the fashionable life of London. Ben bought new clothes and new wigs for himself and his son William; he hired a coach, arguing that he had to live up to 'the public character I sustained'. This was in part at the expense of his employers, the Pennsylvania Assembly. He turned a deaf ear to all protests.[38] The Franklins brought two slaves with them, Peter and King (he who would later abscond to Suffolk). William kept by him a well-thumbed copy of *The True Conduct of Persons of Quality*. Father and son were determined to look the part of genteel colonials in London.[39]

And William acted the part. He imitated the lifestyles of the dissipated youths around the Temple by fathering an illegitimate child, born in 1760. As in his own case, the mother has never been known. William Temple Franklin, or Temple, as he was known, spent much of his infancy under the supervision of that very useful family friend William Strahan, who arranged for his care with a succession of nurses. In a striking departure from the candour Ben had shown back in Philadelphia with respect to his own son's illegitimacy, little Temple's existence was a very well-kept secret. When he finally joined Ben Franklin's London household at around nine or ten years of age, he was known simply as William Temple, a ward of Doctor Franklin. Not until Ben returned to America for good in 1775, taking Temple with him, was his relationship to the Franklins openly avowed; even William's wife Elizabeth was taken by surprise.[40] Ben and William understood that London was not a place to be free and easy with public opinion.

If William Franklin sowed his wild oats while in London, within a year of his arrival he had also met the woman he was to marry, the daughter of a wealthy deceased Barbados planter. There has always been a certain mystery associated with Elizabeth Downes. How did William meet and marry a West Indian heiress? What little is known of her fits in with the usual picture of the wealthy absentee in London. She lived in St James's Street, right near the palace and Royal Court. At the tender age of three she had been bequeathed two slaves as her personal servants. She was connected by marriage to the Alleynes, a well-known Barbadian planter family.[41] There were students from her native Barbados at the Inns of Court while William was living in Middle Temple Lane, so they could have provided the introduction, but there is no evidence that William ever made any social inroads at the Temple. He was never really part of the set of American absentees in London. Instead, he met Miss Downes under circumstances that smacked of heiress-hunting, for his first known meeting with her was at the fashionable spa of Tunbridge Wells, where he and his father, together with several English and American friends, had gone for a brief summer holiday in August 1758.[42]

The episode has all the hallmarks of the Georgian practice of fishing for a good match at a popular resort.[43] Ben had left the holiday makers and returned to London by early September, and William wrote informing him that the whole party were still there because of a 'matrimonial affair' that lawyer Richard Jackson was handling and that was not 'quite settled', a matter that Ben apparently knew all about. Mr Jackson, William said, was lingering in Tunbridge Wells because if he left, the other 'parties' in the matrimonial affair 'would not know where to direct to him'.[44] Richard Jackson was a close friend of both Ben and William, who assisted the Franklins in their agency work and whose discretion could be counted on. Was he now negotiating a marriage settlement with the wealthy Alleynes, a family whose connections were quite out of his usual circle and who did not know his London business direction? Within a month of leaving Tunbridge Wells in 1758, William broke off his engagement to the wealthy Philadelphia socialite Betsy Graeme.[45] The marriage with Miss Downes did not take place until four years later, but marriage settlements could be very long drawn-out affairs. William Franklin must have seemed a dubious proposition in 1758, for he had no employment of his own when he met Miss Downes, and it has been speculated that the marriage – which took place about a fortnight after he was appointed governor in 1762 – was conditional on that appointment.[46] By then William had been courting his heiress for some time. She was his 'old flame in St James's Street', according to Mr Bridges, who had been at Tunbridge Wells when the two first met.[47]

If William did indeed go heiress-hunting, how far was his father in on the business? The question has implications for the whole tenor of the Franklins' first mission to London, for the roots of the public breach between father and son that would take place nearly twenty years later have traditionally been traced back to these years. William became a loyalist at the start of the American Revolution in 1775, and the elder Franklin never forgave him. It has been argued that the parting of the ways between the two began during the Franklins' first London mission, when William was beguiled by the fashionable life of the metropolis. Ben supposedly disapproved of William's pretensions to gentility, and the smart wife and government post he acquired in London in order to live up to the part.[48] But this does not square with the pains Ben took over his son's education, which conspicuously encouraged the boy to hope for the better things in life. It is hard to believe that the father intended anything else, and as we shall see Ben did assist his son to climb in the capital.

Back home, William had already been paying court to a member of one of Philadelphia's leading families. Ben had enthusiastically endorsed William's engagement to Betsy Graeme, daughter of a wealthy and prominent Philadelphian who owned a three-hundred-acre deer park (Miss Graeme kept in her possession gushing letters from Ben – 'some of the kindest and fondest' written 'when he wished me to have been a member of his family' – but they did not survive her).[49] There were no democratic scruples evident while that match was a-brewing. And like those other heiress-hunters, Stephen Sayre and Thomas Ruston, William would have to keep up appearances while courting Miss Downes in London. That cost money, and it was Ben who provided it. Although Ben kept a careful record of his son's expenses (with the view that they would one day be repaid; they were, apparently, an investment), he also paid them without much remark, including the care of little Temple. In fact, William's genteel appearance assisted the partnership between the two Franklins in the metropolis, for it was William who represented the colony of Pennsylvania at the Court of St James on behalf of his father the agent.[50]

It is true that the senior Franklin, an ocean away from his wife, showed no taste for the elegant female company courted by his son. Instead, he seemed to be looking for a substitute for the unpretentious family life he had left behind in Philadelphia. During his five-year sojourn in the capital he formed a close relationship with his landlady, a middle-aged widow named Margaret Stevenson, and her teenage daughter Polly. Ben's lodgings in Craven Street were much more than a living arrangement. The Stevenson women, educated but unpretentious, comfortable but not rich, and bereft of a husband and father, were charmed by their new lodger.[51] Polly in particular became deeply attached to Ben, writing to him constantly whenever she was away from Craven Street.

If Ben stayed true to his roots while in the metropolis, does that mean that he wished William would do the same? Just before he embarked for America in August 1762, when William's marriage to his Barbadian heiress was imminent, Ben wrote a farewell letter to his 'dearest child' (as he called Polly) that sounds as if he wished she, and not Elizabeth Downes, were about to become his daughter-in-law. He lamented his departure from one 'whom he once flattered himself might become his own in the tender relation of a child; but can now entertain such pleasing hopes no more'.[52] It is to be hoped that Ben only

'flattered himself' with such a notion once indeed, and that for the briefest of
moments, for William was barely eligible during the Franklins' London
sojourn. He was engaged to Betsy Graeme when he moved into Craven Street
in 1757. No sooner had he broken that off than he began courting Elizabeth
Downes. It could not have been long after that William began his illicit affair
with the mother of Temple, a liaison of which Ben was well aware. If Polly
herself ever had any thoughts of matrimony with respect to William, then Ben
would have been guilty of a most unkind act in encouraging them. In fact it
was Ben, not his son, who seemed most interested in the Stevenson girl. She
was one of the young women with whom he conducted his well-known
'amorous and romantic – but probably never consummated – flirtations'.[53] His
correspondence with her is lengthy, in places flirtatious, and almost entirely
devoid of any mention of William. In 1760, when Polly was going through a
teenage phase of declaring she would never marry, Ben merely twitted her on
her latest caprice without calling to mind any expectations on behalf of his
son.[54] Taken all in all, his correspondence with Miss Stevenson seems hardly
to have been calculated to push his son's suit. It is more likely that in the
farewell letter on that August day in 1762 Ben, out of an overfull heart, was
resurrecting some long-discarded notion of his own of a match between
William and Polly in a gush of tenderness at the prospect of parting perhaps
forever from his 'dearest child'. 'I will call you so,' he protested, 'Why should I
not call you so, since I love you with all the tenderness, all the fondness of a
father?' He would see Polly again sooner than he thought, and his attachment
to the Stevenson girl would prove more enduring than his bond to his son.

The Franklins exploited their London contacts to the full, and nowhere was
this more evident than in William's appointment as governor of New Jersey in
1762. There has been much speculation over how William landed this post
and whether his father helped him.[55] Ben's role in his son's appointment was
indeed enacted very quietly. There was a great deal of secrecy surrounding
the proceedings, because the Franklins did not wish the Penns (who would
certainly oppose it) to get wind of their plan. And there was the matter of
William's illegitimacy to keep quiet. Plenty of people in London knew about
the circumstances of William's birth – the unfriendly Allen crowd at Middle
Temple Hall, for example – but apparently some of those closest to him did not.
Richard Jackson the attorney, with whom he worked closely, only found out
just before the appointment. If Jackson didn't know, then most likely neither
did Elizabeth Downes and her family. Clearly William kept his own set of
friends in London separate from the Inns of Court crowd, and probably also

from anyone associated with the Penns, all of whom knew his background very well. When he applied for the governorship to Lord Bute, who was then prime minister, his application was supported by two of his father's friends, Peter Collinson and Sir John Pringle. Both were members of the Royal Society and influential with his lordship, who had a keen interest in natural history.[56]

But another factor ensuring William's success was that the Franklins found out the post was vacant well ahead of any competition in London. Although Ben Franklin did not understand the power structure in London when he first arrived, he was a quick learner. When he first reached London, he made the faux pas of applying for an interview with William Pitt, still secretary of state in 1757. But a cabinet minister did not meet with a colony agent; Franklin soon realised that he must conduct his business through Pitt's undersecretary, William Wood. Wood was another provincial (from Ireland) who had overcome his 'mean birth' to take up a challenging post at the centre of government. It was he who alerted the American that the governorship of New Jersey was vacant.[57]

The Franklins' caution was probably well advised, for the Penns were furious when they heard of William's appointment. Wrote John Penn to Lord Stirling: 'It is no less amazing than true, that Mr William Franklin, son of Benjamin Franklin, of Philadelphia, is appointed to be governor of the province of New Jersey! The warrant for his commission was ordered to be made out last Wednesday. The whole of this business has been transacted in so private a manner, that not a tittle of it escaped until it was seen in the public papers; so that there was no opportunity of counteracting, or, indeed, doing one single thing that might put a stop to this shameful affair.' Penn went on: 'If any *gentleman* had been appointed' – his quill probably barely able to keep up with the activity of his thoughts – 'it would have been a different case – but I cannot look upon the person in question in that light, by any means.'[58] And, indeed, William had a close call in this respect, for the fact of his illegitimacy did pose an obstacle in official circles. It is a testimony to his genuine learning and graceful manners that he was able to remove any apprehensions after a rigorous personal interview with Lord Halifax.[59] If John Penn didn't think William seemed like a gentleman, Halifax did. William had undeniable personal abilities, but it must have been an extra reassurance to his lordship that he also had the trappings of colonial gentility: genteel manners, an Inns of Court association and an engagement to a West Indian heiress.

William's appointment was made public sometime after 20 August 1762, and on 27 August he was married to Elizabeth Downes. *She* was unaware of the existence of little Temple. Ben Franklin left London for home a couple of weeks earlier, so was not present for either of these major events in his son's career.[60] He may have left early because he wished to downplay his role in his son's rather sudden prosperity. It was a wise move, for Ben's 'insatiable ambition' as William Allen called it, did indeed excite resentment back home.[61] One Pennsylvanian wrote of his London sojourn:

> I cannot find that his five years negotiation at a vast expense to the province, has answered any other purpose with respect to the public, than to get every point that was in controversy, determined against them. Yet what is this to Mr. Franklin? Has it not afforded him a life of pleasure, and an opportunity of displaying his talents among the virtuosi of various kingdoms and nations? and lastly has it not procured for himself the Degree of Doctor of Laws, and for the modest and beautiful youth, his son, that of Master of Arts, from one of our most famous universities? Let me tell you, those are no small acquisitions to the public, and therefore well worth paying for.[62]

Putting aside the sarcasm, his critic was right. Ben Franklin's second sojourn in London had been a tremendous success. He was given an enthusiastic welcome by the Royal Society, which had made him a Fellow the year before he arrived, and was included in its numerous meetings, dinners and social rounds.[63] The company included Peter Collinson, Dr John Fothergill and the eminent physician Sir John Pringle. The membership of the Royal Society was most eclectic; it included earls and marquesses, but also self-made men with enquiring minds like Franklin. John Canton, for example, who had reproduced some of Franklin's electrical experiments, was the son of a Gloucestershire weaver who earned his living as a schoolmaster in London.[64] The Royal Society, despite its air of distinction, had an earthy, practical character to it. In the days when many areas of scientific enquiry were still in their infancy, the contributions of knowledgeable laymen – mariners, farmers, artisans – were welcomed. This was company Ben felt at home in, intelligent and socially diverse – and it also gave him access to the great, notably Prime Minister Lord Bute.

Dr Fothergill's Club of Honest Whigs, which met every Thursday evening at St Paul's Coffee House near the famous cathedral, was equally congenial. This was one of Franklin's favourite London clubs, and its members welcomed him with open arms. For the Honest Whigs were among those who saw New England and the middling farmlands of the northern colonies as a preserve of bygone English values, and in Franklin they found affirmed all their favourite

34 'House occupied by the Royal Society, Crane Court, Fleet Street', c.1840.

notions of American lifestyles. Canton, Pringle and Collinson were members, as well as other notable figures, men like Richard Price and the scientist Joseph Priestley (famous for discovering carbon dioxide), both of whom would strongly support the American cause during the War of Independence.[65]

The Honest Whigs were heirs to a tradition of radical English political thought stretching back almost a hundred years which argued that England, far from being at its zenith, was in a political and moral decline. Perennial critics of Westminster and the Court, always calling for reform, the self-appointed Jeremiahs had an influence beyond their numbers.[66] Many of the members of the Honest Whigs were dissenters who, as with Dennis De Berdt, had close affinities to New England and saw it as typifying American life. The renowned Unitarian minister Richard Price wrote that the 'happiest state of man' was to be found in Connecticut, 'where the inhabitants consist, if I am rightly informed, of an independent and hardy yeomanry, all nearly on a level, trained to arms, instructed in their rights, clothed in home-spun, of simple manners, strangers to luxury, drawing plenty from the ground'.[67] Even in their own little group the Honest Whigs could not ignore the ugly reality of the slave plantations, for Jamaicans Richard Oliver and Samuel Vaughan, the friends of Henry Laurens, were both members. But they had Dr Franklin among them to counteract that impression.

If Franklin wanted celebrity, that came to him as well. He toured Scotland and became 'Dr Franklin' when the University of St Andrews made him an honorary doctor of laws. Oxford followed suit a few months before the Franklins left for home.[68] In his travels through both Scotland and England he met other well-known philosophers, intellectuals and entrepreneurs – David Hume, Adam Smith, James Watt, Matthew Boulton – all eager to meet 'the best philosopher of America'. In London he had his likeness taken again and again, oil paintings and mezzotints that always depicted him as the 'electrical genius', surrounded by scientific equipment and a lightning-filled sky.[69] Ben and William distributed copies of some of these for sale and as gifts in the colonies.[70] And Ben did not neglect the European continent, where the term 'frankliniste' had been coined in the wake of his scientific discoveries, touring the Austrian Netherlands and the Dutch Republic in 1761.[71] He would give himself a new, artistic gloss in Europe by inventing the armonica, a musical instrument inspired by the plaintive ringing of the rims of wet wineglasses. Mozart would play it, Marie Antoinette would take lessons on it.[72] And Franklin had weighed in as a political writer in London in 1760, with his well-received pamphlet arguing that Britain should retain Canada rather than restore it to the old enemy, France, at the conclusion of the Seven Years' War.

At the time of his arrival in London, Franklin had not gained access to the great and the good as readily as other more well-born colonists. Charles Pinckney, for example, the agent for South Carolina, was received together with his wife at Kew Palace by Augusta, the Princess of Wales, when he arrived in London in the 1750s. This was a private audience, with other members of the royal family present.[73] It was not the colony agency, of course, that was behind an honour of this sort. The Pinckneys were a very wealthy Carolina family.[74] William Allen, the richest and most refined man in Pennsylvania, got closer to Pitt the Elder than Franklin ever did, even sending him a quaint concoction of 'pine bud' tea as a treatment for the gout.[75]

But by making the most of his contacts, Ben Franklin eventually caught up with these genteel fellow colonists. He and William collected shells for Lady Bute, the prime minister's wife, which could only have helped the younger Franklin's application for a governorship.[76] By the time the senior Franklin left London in 1762, he had several opportunities pending for himself. There was a rumour that he would be made governor of Pennsylvania, dependent of course on his successful ousting of the Penns.[77] Or he might be able to get the post of deputy postmaster general in England through his new friend John Sargent, the merchant who handled Pennsylvania's funds in London. That would have meant settling in the metropolis for life.[78] William Strahan wanted Ben to run for Parliament, and urged him to stay with still other attractive proposals.[79]

Yes, Ben meant to return. He warmed to the prospect of becoming 'a Londoner for the rest of my days'.[80] The new career opportunities were exciting, but it was also London itself. He was as enchanted as Stephen Sayre or Arthur Lee. He confided to his Polly: 'Of all the enviable things England has, I envy it most its people. Why should that petty island, which compared to America is but like a stepping stone in a brook, scarce enough of it above water to keep one's shoes dry; why, I say, should that little island, enjoy in almost every neighbourhood, more sensible, virtuous and elegant minds, than we can collect in ranging 100 leagues of our vast forests.'[81]

CHAPTER NINE

'The most cautious man I have ever seen': Ben Franklin's London Career

Ben Franklin would be away from London for just two years, but they were years spent in the thick of Pennsylvanian politics. He spent six months touring Virginia and the northern colonies in his capacity as deputy post-master general, only to find upon his return that John Penn had been installed as the new governor of Pennsylvania. There was of course little love lost between the two men, but Penn would soon come running to Franklin for help. In late 1763, angry frontiersmen who were threatened by Chief Pontiac's uprising massacred a group of friendly Indians, and then headed for Philadelphia intent on killing others who had taken refuge there. Governor Penn, forgetting that Ben was no gentleman, hurried to him in a panic. Franklin organised the city's defence, then met with the mob and talked them into going home. He was a hero, but that would not save him in the impending elections. His ambition to substitute the Penns' proprietary government for royal government led to fierce attacks on him in the press and elsewhere and in 1764, for the first time since becoming an assemblyman, he was not re-elected. Consolation was at hand, because his Quaker party still controlled the assembly, and within five weeks of losing the election he was embarking for England again with a petition asking the Crown for a change of government.[1]

Back in England at last! Franklin was deeply attracted to the centres of power and culture in the metropolis. But on a more personal level what had he hurried back for? What was his home away from home in the Great City? That was an important part of the equation, for Franklin spent his entire seventeen years in London at the home of the widow Margaret Stevenson in Craven Street. There has been inevitable – but fruitless – speculation ever since as to the nature of their relationship. Certainly Mrs Stevenson had many of the advantages of an older woman enumerated by Franklin in his practical and passionless advice 'On how to choose a mistress'. '[O]ld women', Franklin claimed, made better mistresses than young ones; they were more useful than young women, providing 'a 1000 services small and great', and proving 'the most tender and useful of all friends when you are sick'. Still more to the point, 'they are more prudent and discreet in conducting an intrigue to prevent suspicion. The commerce with them is therefore safer with regard to your reputation'. And if you put a basket over her head, you can't tell the difference between an old woman and a young one, he went on gleefully, at least not 'below the girdle'.[2]

We don't know what Mrs Stevenson looked like – whether Ben kept a basket handy or not – but there is no doubt that her manners were more fitted to a London drawing room than those of his plain, provincial wife Deborah. Since Deborah had a phobia about crossing the ocean, there was no likelihood that she would ever arrive to provide a comparison.[3] During his second stay in London, Ben and Margaret Stevenson were sometimes treated as a couple on social occasions.[4] All of this does not amount to proof of adultery, but if they were indeed discreet lovers that would have suited Franklin. Despite all the dissolute noblemen and bawdy wenches who walked the pages of novels like Henry Fielding's *Tom Jones* and Samuel Richardson's *Clarissa*, the eighteenth century was still a period when cohabitation between unmarried men and women was not compatible with respectability. Franklin's career as the foremost colonial spokesman in London would have taken a nosedive if he had openly taken a mistress.

Franklin moved into lodgings at 36 Craven Street in 1757, but when Mrs Stevenson moved to number 7 across the road in 1772, he moved with her.[5] The house at 36 Craven Street is still standing, the only remaining Franklin house in the world. There Franklin rented the entire first floor, which included four furnished rooms.[6] He received visitors in a spacious room with front-facing windows.

Craven Street was in a good location in Westminster. If it was not as genteel as the new developments in the West End and Oxford Street taken by wealthy planter families, it was conveniently central for anyone engaged on government business. It was within walking distance of the government offices in Whitehall, where Franklin's business as a colony agent would take him. The City coffee houses were also just a stroll away. The Pennsylvania Coffee House, where Franklin would have gone to pick up mail, write letters, hear news, and network generally, was in nearby Birchin Lane. Other colony agents chose Craven Street; in 1754 the wealthy South Carolinian

Charles Pinckney and his wife Eliza took an entire house there, fully furnished.[7] Henry Marchant, agent for Rhode Island, had his lodgings there in 1771.[8]

Just around the corner and en route to Whitehall was Charing Cross, where according to Dr Johnson one could find 'the full tide of human existence', and all the news of the city was to be heard. It was here that the pillories stood and royal proclamations were read out. Ben Franklin, turning into Charing Cross from Craven Street, would pass the imposing Northumberland House, a Jacobean mansion topped by the Percy lion, where the young James Boswell went frequently during the period when he hoped the Duke and Duchess of Northumberland would help him to a commission in the Footguards.[9] Northumberland House reflected the area's past grandeur. By Boswell's time the district was more a place of business, attracting those like Franklin who had careers to pursue. London's foremost private school of art, the St Martin's Lane Academy (where William Hogarth had studied as a youth) was in St Martin's Lane, across from Northumberland House. This was the artists' quarter; Joshua Reynolds had a house there.[10] Franklin's friend Benjamin West lived in nearby Panton Square between 1768 and 1775.[11] From the start of his London career, West enthusiastically welcomed a succession of budding American artists who ventured abroad for their training.

Ben turned his lodgings in Craven Street into a home away from home as the household expanded to include various relatives. There were his illegitimate grandson Temple, and his English niece Sally Franklin (both Ben and his wife Deborah had relatives still living in England). Then there were his Boston relations the Williamses, one of whom, his nephew, was blind and came to London hoping to study under the blind music teacher and composer John Stanley. Franklin coaxed Stanley out of retirement to help the young man.[12] Counted among Mrs Stevenson's domestics was 'Nanny', a poor colonial woman whom Deborah Franklin had known in Philadelphia.[13] Martha Harris Johnson, Franklin's niece by his half-sister in Boston, came to London from the English countryside, where she had set up a shop, to call on her philosopher uncle.[14]

On more than one occasion ordinary Pennsylvanians finding themselves in straitened circumstances turned to the colony agent for assistance. Franklin was annoyed when a young woman with two small children appeared on his doorstep back in 1759, claiming that her Philadelphian watchmaker husband was selling up his business and would soon join her. He advanced her four guineas, as she was 'sick and perishing with her children in the beginning of

35 'The American School' by Matthew Pratt, 1765. Matthew Pratt of Pennsylvania was one of the first of many American painters who came to London to study in Benjamin West's studio. In this scene, West stands at the left, and Pratt is at the easel.

winter'. She seemed 'a very helpless silly body', he wrote to Deborah. 'What is to become of her now I know not.'[15] But Mrs Flower, as she called herself, would have had no one else besides the colony agent to turn to for help. In Georgian London one had to belong to a City parish in order to qualify for poor relief. Even the poor from the English countryside who came into London looking for work were obliged to turn to charities set up by their home counties.[16] Franklin was more sympathetic when merchant sailor Seth Paddock of Massachusetts, left penniless after being shipwrecked off the Scilly Isles in 1773, walked to London from Plymouth. His plight moved Franklin to find him a berth home.[17]

In Franklin's London world there was no transplanted Pennsylvanian community that was comparable to the South Carolina planters who had settled in the West End. But in the comings and goings of his household and his agency we catch a glimpse of the sort of ordinary American colonists who, just as much as their well-to-do counterparts, were everywhere in London at this time. It is difficult to know how many white colonial Americans of this type passed through their capital because, like plantation slaves, they appear only by chance in the records, but they were not scarce. Hardworking colonial milliners came to London to stock up on the latest fashions.[18] American merchant sailors must have been continually disembarking at London's Tower docks. In the days when Britain and America were part of one great trading network, thousands of colonial seamen, both black and white, walked the streets of London.[19] Some found themselves before the Old Bailey. Sailor John Gearey was charged with committing highway robbery in the Minories near Tower Docks in 1772. Claiming he was the victim, not the perpetrator, Gearey said in his defence that he was 'a seaman; I was born in America; I have no friends here to appear for me.' Whatever the truth, he was sentenced to death.[20] An American named James Castle was sentenced to transportation at the Old Bailey in 1764 when he was found guilty of shoplifting – in effect, a free trip home.[21] A Philadelphian, Ezekiel Shepherd, complained at the Old Bailey that he was offered the cost of his passage back to America if he would leave quietly so that his wife could marry an Englishman.[22] In 1765 the *Gentleman's Magazine* reported that a 'young American from Carolina' was arrested on suspicion of forgery as he made his way from Bristol to London.[23] These are just a few of the ordinary Americans who ventured to their capital city in the years before independence. The impact of their presence is almost irrecoverable now, but they would have formed a conspicuous part of the everyday London world of prominent colonial merchants and agents like Franklin whose stories have survived.

Franklin was very glad to be back in London in 1764, but the comfort didn't last long. The crisis over the Stamp Act began almost as soon as he was settled in front of his Craven Street fireplace. Rumours that the British government was going to break with all precedent and impose taxes on the colonies had reached him back in Philadelphia, but Franklin's reaction had been nonchalant. After reading the terms of the Stamp Act, he commented to an English friend: 'If it is not finally found to hurt us, we shall grow contented with it; and as it will, if it hurts us, hurt you also, you will feel the hurt and remedy it.'[24] Franklin had always had a broad-minded vision of a joint Atlantic empire of English-speaking peoples, and right now that vision preoccupied him more than the issue of local colonial rights. He was busy with his scheme to give royal government to Pennsylvania. What was particularly worrying was that while he was still back in Philadelphia, he had received a hint that his dispute with the Penns had angered certain people at Whitehall, and could result in the loss of his deputy postmastership.[25] That would be awful. So he arrived in Britain in the autumn of 1764 with his new projects and his new career in mind. The looming crisis over the Stamp Act hardly seemed helpful; he could not have been eager to take the part of an opponent of government.

When the Stamp Act passed just a few months after Franklin returned to London, he was still untroubled. He wrote in a philosophical vein to a friend in Philadelphia: 'We might as well have hindered the sun's setting.'[26] Benjamin Franklin, who had always had an instinct for the popular mood, had got it very wrong. When news of the Act reached the mainland colonies, the reaction was bad. Colonial assemblies passed public resolves saying the tax infringed their rights as Englishmen. A gathering of representatives from most of the colonies assembled in New York City, at an innovative meeting called the Stamp Act Congress, and coined the phrase 'No taxation without representation'. Rioters prevented the Stamp Act from being enforced. Houses were ripped to shreds. Royal officials were personally threatened. The colonists were showing their English spirit. More to the point in England, the colonists created a business crisis by stopping imports of British goods, and threatening not to pay their debts to British merchants. Short of taking up arms, there was little more the colonies could do to express their outrage. In Philadelphia, Franklin's own house was threatened by the mob when his loyalties came under suspicion.

Franklin did an about-face, as quickly as he could. He busied himself with the lobby in London to gain repeal of the Stamp Act. But his initial indifference had not gone unnoticed, and critical onlookers were not easily convinced of his sincerity. Dennis De Berdt, opposing the Stamp Act as agent for Massachusetts, gave it as his opinion that Dr Franklin 'stood entirely neuter till he saw which way the cause would be carried, and then broke out fiercely on the side of America'.[27] In Pennsylvania opponents of the Stamp Act circulated accusations that Franklin not only did little to oppose the Act but actually helped promote it.[28] Franklin knew he had to repair the damage done to his image, and his friends in London helped him. 'He is forever with one member of parliament or other', wrote William Strahan to a Philadelphia correspondent. 'All this while, too, he has been throwing out hints in the public papers.'[29]

But it was not to be so easy. Some continued to suspect Franklin's commitment to American liberty until the start of the Revolution. Even after he had testified for four hours before the House of Commons in February 1766, a Pennsylvanian doubted the published version of his examination, writing 'some people here suspect that this paper contains much more than his examination and greatly exceeds the truth and produces wise answers which he never gave except in his closet'.[30]

36 The old House of Commons. It was destroyed in the Great Fire of 1834.

That was unfair, for Franklin had indeed given a powerful performance before the House of Commons. He had worked closely with ministerial associates Edmund Burke and Richard Jackson to back up the strategy for repeal of the Stamp Act.[31] Prime Minister Lord Rockingham and his administration were keen to avoid an open debate on the principles behind the crisis. The question of whether Parliament had a right to tax its colonies drew one into the labyrinth of constitutional theory; even today historians cannot agree. Most Georgian MPs thought Parliament did. They also thought that to curtail this right would threaten Parliament's hard-won power to control the government's purse strings, a fundamental plank of Britain's constitutional monarchy. For this reason Lord Rockingham's administration sought a repeal on economic grounds. The Stamp Act was bad for business; it obstructed the flow of trade. The government intended to accompany the repeal with a Declaratory Act asserting Parliament's right to legislate for the colonies in all cases whatsoever, as a sop to the hardliners. Ben Franklin took the same pragmatic view of the conflict. Shortly after reaching London in 1764, he suggested to Lord Dartmouth that to avoid a confrontation, the government should simply suspend the Act and then repeal it at the first convenient moment.[32] Franklin, too, did not want the conflict to escalate.

When Franklin testified before the House of Commons in February 1766, he was one of more than thirty colony agents and experts who were called as witnesses to endorse a picture of economic stagnation caused by the Stamp Act.[33] Most of the other colony agents were there as well. The names of Dennis De Berdt and Stephen Sayre appeared in the roll call on 3 February.[34] But Franklin shared the role of star speaker, along with a prominent City merchant. Franklin appeared before the bar in the House of Commons on 13 February 1766. His performance took the form of a four-hour question-and-answer exchange, with himself playing the part of expert witness, but it was carefully rehearsed. He emerged from it as the leading spokesman for America in England, and an American hero.[35] His answers to the lengthy questions on the colonies, their lifestyles and their attitude towards their mother country, which were published on the continent (they were even translated into French and German[36]) were probably the first time in history that Europe was confronted with the views and opinions of such a thing as an 'American people'.

So how did Franklin depict his fellow colonists? In his testimony the mainland American colonies were thickly peopled with white 'farmers, husbandmen or planters', who married earlier, worked harder and could resist the rampant consumerism of the metropolis. These hardy folk were on the increase, he assured the House. He reprised his famous argument, first published in 1751, that the population of the colonies was growing rapidly on the strength of its limitless land and the industry of its people. Although American colonists bought British goods and clothing 'because the fashion in a respected country', they could easily return to making and wearing their own clothes if they chose. And they would choose, promised Franklin, if forced to pay a Stamp Tax, for they were English enough to insist that they be taxed by their own representatives.[37]

To drive home the case for repeal, Franklin warned that colonial affection for Britain would be lost if Parliament persisted in its attempts to impose taxes. And that could happen quickly, he said ominously. Indeed, it was beginning to happen already. Even now imported British 'superfluities' were becoming 'detested and rejected' by alienated colonial consumers. But the colonists were plain-thinking, reasonable people too, who would not quibble over mere abstractions. If Parliament passed the Declaratory Act proposed by the Rockingham administration, it would 'give them very little concern', for 'they may believe you will never exercise it'.[38]

Behind the description of industrious farmers, the underlying message was clear. The Americans were a growing people. They were a major market for

British goods. It was important not to alienate them. Many British politicians were far from reassured by the picture Franklin painted of a colonial people whose loyalty seemed to come and go so easily, and depended on good will alone. How the hackles of many MPs must have risen as they listened to this. Franklin was called a 'perfect anti-Briton' by one British MP.[39] But the Rockingham administration was delighted, for it endorsed their entire policy. Franklin's evidence chimed in perfectly with their case for repeal on pragmatic grounds. Franklin recalled later that after his testimony he was 'caressed' by the ministry.[40]

Franklin's depiction of his countrymen in his famous testimony reflected the notions of his friends in the Club of Honest Whigs, who saw the colonies as the preserves of a bygone, purer English lifestyle. Several years later Franklin would make this point outright in a London newspaper, asserting that the morals of Americans were 'much purer, much less corrupt, than the general morals of the *English*, a difference naturally to be expected, and always to be expected, in *young* countries and old *ones*'.[41] The American colonists as he portrayed them in his testimony before the House of Commons were a homogeneous people who had money to spend, yet lived simple lifestyles on the margins of the empire that were rustic enough to allow them if they chose to ignore the conventions of style and taste that prevailed in England. If this were true, it would give the colonies the kind of power Franklin wanted to claim for them, of being able to strike back at unpopular British legislation simply by withholding their consumption of British goods.

But Franklin's picture was oversimplified, for the colonial societies and their lifestyles were highly diverse. Slaves comprised a fifth of all colonists; backwoods settlers, urban professionals and artisans, tradesmen, rich Atlantic merchants and small coastwise merchants, owners of great plantations, and the middling farmers celebrated by Franklin made up the rest. The notion that most of these would readily revert to wearing homespun was a fantasy. Britain's American colonists were fully modern people. They wanted to be part of the business and social world of the British empire and the northern Atlantic. Even on the frontier imported consumer goods were snapped up as quickly as possible. Colonists did indeed resort to short-term production of homespun during boycotts of British goods in the 1760s and 1770s, but they weren't really going to give up their silks, velvets and fashion accessories for ever. After independence the new United States would find itself in a ruinous balance of trade with Britain precisely because it could not really do what Franklin was now saying it could do whenever it chose, that is, live without modern consumer goods. And colonial attitudes towards their mother country – its lifestyles, politics and values – varied enormously, as would be evident ten years later in the civil war that was the American Revolution.

But the crisis had passed, even if nothing was resolved. And Franklin himself came out of it with his reputation enhanced. Perhaps it was at this time that he got the notion of going for a government post, along the lines of his friend, undersecretary William Wood. Unluckily, Lord Rockingham was out of office soon after the repeal of the Stamp Act, but early 1768 saw Franklin nevertheless trying to land a government job. He wrote to an under-secretary of the lords of the Treasury that he was willing to spend the rest of his life in London. Government ministers mulled over the possibility of giving Franklin a place at Whitehall as a civil servant, some tantalising hints were dropped to the effect that an offer would soon be made, but in the end nothing came of it. His bid to obtain a government post had failed, and his later successes proved to be all ones that were built on his role as a colonial advocate rather than a government man, a strong card for him to play after his conspicuous part in the repeal of the Stamp Act.[42]

It may be that Ben Franklin really wanted to remain in London for the rest of his life. What is more certain is that he didn't want to go back to America with nothing to show for himself. When he gave up his project of royal government for Pennsylvania in 1768, he appeared to have little reason to stay any longer, but new reasons were not hard to find. He became agent for Georgia in 1768, and the following year he was appointed agent for New Jersey, a move obviously welcomed by his son the governor. The Massachusetts agency followed in 1770. Never before had so many colonial agencies been held by one man. An idea was afloat in New Jersey (where he of course had special influence) to propose that he be made agent for all the colonies, with an income to match.[43]

And there were many other things to keep Ben Franklin busy in London: his numerous clubs, his travel, his scientific interests. He travelled often to the continent, touring France with his friend Dr Pringle in 1767 and 1769. Everywhere there was interest in his electrical experiments. At Versailles he met the king and queen of France. A few years later he ventured to Scotland for a second time and then to Ireland with his friend Richard Jackson. He was still a polymath in his interests. He designed a new alphabet that never caught on.[44] He experimented when he felt like it (which was less and less often as the years went by), toying with various ideas as they occurred to him. He played around with the effect of oil upon waves, carrying a cane with a concealed flask of oil in it on his trips to the countryside, and anointing any passing stream or pond that caught his fancy.[45]

Franklin had few contacts in aristocratic circles.[46] But like many Americans he knew Lord Shelburne. He visited his country house and was consulted on American affairs.[47] He may have hoped (like Arthur Lee) that Shelburne would come into government again one day and be in a position to bestow a post. He knew Sir Francis Dashwood, Lord le Despencer, who was postmaster general but also a notorious libertine. Dashwood helped to found the famous Hell Fire Club, whose members included political figures such as City patriot John Wilkes and future cabinet minister Lord Sandwich, but whose purpose was reputed to be purely recreational: drink, sex, and a little black magic for atmosphere.[48] Whatever else Franklin got up to at the Dashwood home in West Wycombe Park, he was engaged in a respectable literary project with Sir Francis to shorten and rationalise the English prayer book. He dined with Christian VII of Denmark in 1768 when His Majesty was in London.[49] Franklin was a friend of the bishop of St Asaph, frequently staying at his home in Twyford.[50] He became the greatest advocate of the colonies in the press, cultivating the image of a land of homespun farmers. He went to countless Royal Society dinners, and continued to enjoy the intellectual life of his Fellows.

Writing to his son William in 1772, he summed up his life in England thus:

> As to my situation here nothing can be more agreeable . . . A general respect paid me by the learned, a number of friends and acquaintance among them with whom I have a pleasing intercourse; a character of so much weight that it has protected me when some in power would have done me injury, and continued me in an office they would have deprived me of; my company so much desired that I seldom dine at home in winter, and could spend the whole summer in the country houses of inviting friends if I chose it. Learned and ingenious foreigners that come to England, almost all make a point of visiting me, for my reputation is still higher abroad than here; several of the foreign ambassadors have assiduously cultivated my acquaintance, treating me as one of their corps, partly I believe from the desire they have from time to time of hearing something of American affairs, an object become of importance in foreign courts, who begin to hope Britain's alarming power will be diminished by the defection of her Colonies; and partly that they may have an opportunity of introducing me to the gentlemen of their country who desire it. The K[ing] too has lately been heard to speak of me with great regard.[51]

His reputation abroad was indeed high. In France, where some of the intelligentsia romanticised agriculture and the purifying influence of a life spent close to the soil, he was welcomed with open arms. The New World was seen as idyllically rustic, and Franklin, its most famous son, appeared to be a genius born of natural influences. His works were translated into French, and he began writing for the magazine of the Physiocrats, the *Citizen's Calendar*. By the late 1760s its wide readership on the continent began to learn of Dr Franklin's views on Britain's imperial affairs.[52]

Ben Franklin looked to be prospering in every way. He made no bones about broadcasting his success to his son. And others saw him in the same light. Writing to his friend William Strahan years later, Franklin reminisced: 'I remember your observing once to me, as we sat together in the House of Commons, that no two journeyman printers within your knowledge had met with such success in the world as ourselves.'[53]

But under the smooth, shiny surface there were tensions. While Franklin was agent for so many colonies, he also remained deputy postmaster general for America. This was a Crown appointment worth £300 a year. Keeping it left him vulnerable to attacks of hypocrisy and lukewarm commitment to the cause of colonial opposition.[54] In 1768 Ben had to endure another bout of rumours that an unfriendly minister was about to relieve him of his favourite post.[55] It was something he had to live with, the being ever conscious that a move too far in the wrong direction could lead to the loss of his beloved title of postmaster general.

Adding to his already tangled web of commitments was his ambition to get rich through land speculation. In 1766 he became involved in a project that aimed to open a new colony in the Ohio territory. It went through many incarnations, as its dimensions and its partners were changed in a long-drawn-out bid for success. Originating with his son William Franklin and Joseph Galloway in America, it soon became expedient to add British part-ners: Ben Franklin's friends William Strahan and Richard Jackson, some well-placed London bankers and even a few peers of the realm.[56] Soon fellow Pennsylvanian Samuel Wharton came to London to lobby at Court on behalf of the project. He was introduced to everyone of importance through Franklin. Although a Quaker, Wharton quickly assumed the manners of a courtier and wore a sword. He was a determined man, and when in 1775 the rebellion in America made Britain's title to the territory uncertain, he transferred his lobbying efforts to the Continental Congress. He continued to have financial support from British as well as American backers. Franklin remained part of the scheme throughout, which, alas, never came to anything.[57]

The whole endeavour put Ben Franklin at the heart of imperial politics in a way that could only complicate his work as an agent. Over the years a succession of ministers – the supportive Shelburne, the hostile Lord Hillsborough, the cautious Dartmouth – waxed hot or cold over the prospect of new western colonies,[58] Franklin's associates became irritated in the early 1770s when his agency business put him at cross-purposes with government men whose good will was essential for the Ohio project. To get around this problem, Franklin and a fellow associate concocted a scheme whereby he appeared to resign from the company but privately continued to own stock.[59]

Being drawn into manoeuvres of this sort did not improve Franklin's environment. Although his working day carried him to different parts of the City – the coffee houses of Birchin Lane and Threadneedle Street, the lobby of the House of Commons, the offices around Whitehall – that world was close-knit enough to take on the claustrophobic atmosphere of a modern office building. A few years after the indefatigable Samuel Wharton arrived in London, Ben complained to William that he suspected the lobbyist of starting a whispering campaign against him: 'I suspect that through his means some of my other friends are rendered cool to me.' Ben was trying to look as if he didn't care, he told William, but it couldn't have been a comfortable situation. Wharton would have frequented the Pennsylvania Coffee House during the same business hours as Ben and collected his letters from the same mail bag.[60]

Even Franklin's assumption of four colonial agencies brought its own complicated stresses and strains. As in the case of Pennsylvania, each new agency embroiled him in the local politics of the colony in question, albeit to differing degrees. The Atlantic Ocean was not nearly wide enough to allow him to feel away from it all. Gossip travelled quickly in the little world of the metropolis and its colonial seaports, and interested parties came and went, taking note of everything as they did so. A case in point can be found in the correspondence of Hetta De Berdt, who by 1771 was living privately in America as the wife of Joseph Reed. She warned her brother in London not to repeat negative comments she made in her letters about Philadelphia lest they be spread around; 'if anybody asks you how we like Philadelphia, you must say very well.'[61] And *her* letters were not being intercepted by the British government, as Ben's would be in the years leading up to the War of Independence. He was being watched on all sides. He was continually under the hostile scrutiny of the Artillery Court crowd – not only old Mr De Berdt, who suspected Dr Franklin's commitment to the cause of liberty, but also the resentful younger set, Arthur Lee and Stephen Sayre, both of whom had coveted agencies acquired by Ben. In 1770 they attacked him in the newspapers, disinterring the old issue of his son's governorship and accusing the Franklins of courting the favour of the odious Lord Bute.[62] It is not surprising that some time in 1773 Ben made a list of reasons to leave London which included 'Get clear of Ag[enc]ys.'[63] Before he left, one agency in particular would become the biggest thorn in his side.

It was lucky for Ben Franklin that the anti-slavery movement was still many years away, or the contradictions inherent in representing both northern and southern colonies would have become intolerable. As it was, there were rumblings of anti-slavery sentiment in some of the northern colonies. In 1771 (the year after Franklin was appointed its agent) the Massachusetts assembly passed a bill prohibiting the slave trade, only to have it vetoed by their governor. The very next year, while the Somerset Case was in court, Franklin was obliged as agent for Georgia to busy himself seeking the approval of the British Privy Council for that colony's slave code.[64] It is no wonder that during the newspaper blitz surrounding the Somerset Case he limited his journalistic output to a short piece of a few hundred words attacking the slave trade (which he blamed on the British), and outlining a method of gradual abolition that had been suggested to him by a Quaker correspondent in Philadelphia.[65]

Two years earlier Franklin had expressed himself in very different terms on the issue of slavery when he had been compelled to spar with Granville Sharp in the newspapers. Sharp had publicly accused the colonies of hypocrisy, asserting that '[M]en, who do not scruple to detain others in slavery . . . have no real regard for liberty, farther than their own private interests are concerned.'[66] In one of his worst literary efforts, Franklin contended that slavery was the fault of the British, who had started the slave trade in the first place, that slave owning was anyway a minority practice in the colonies, and that colonial laws controlling slaves had to be repressive, because the majority of Africans 'are of a plotting disposition, dark, sullen, malicious, revengeful and cruel in the highest degree.'[67] As one who made a career of collecting colony agencies, he was probably most reluctant to take up publicly the controversy over slavery during his London years. Had the British anti-slavery activism of the 1790s been rolled back by a few decades, it would have made it impossible to represent the colonies as a united front in the metropolis.

By the early 1770s Arthur Lee believed that Ben Franklin dreaded any further 'commotions' in the colonies, fearing they would 'hazard the lucrative posts he possessed' – in other words, his complicated personal arrangements meant that he did not want to rock the boat of Anglo-American relations.[68]

Lee was not objective on the subject of Dr Franklin, but there were others who thought the same. Joseph Reed, back in London to marry Hetta in 1770, commented that the Doctor 'appears extremely reserved, though I am informed that is his general character here'. His 'caution' Reed thought was 'necessary for him in the different characters of an agent and a Crown officer'.[69] The philosopher had got himself into a mighty tricky situation.

In his younger years in Philadelphia, Franklin had been known for a personal charisma that lay behind much of his success. The founder of clubs, learned societies, fire companies and militias, he enjoyed conspicuous popularity with all ranks of people. But as a middle-aged lobbyist in London, he changed. There is no doubt that his famous conviviality was still in evidence in many London settings, particularly his clubs, where in James Boswell's words he often seemed 'all jollity and pleasantry'. He was a very popular guest at the country homes of friends like Sir Francis Dashwood and the bishop of St Asaph. But as the years wore on in the capital, he gained an alternative reputation as reserved. His friend Joseph Priestley noted that strangers often found him so.[70] This reserve was probably an essential ingredient of his character. It had been remarked upon back in the 1750s when he toured Scotland with William; then the son had come across as more 'open and communicative' than the famous father.[71] But by all accounts it deepened considerably in the years following his return to London in 1764. His publisher friend Strahan confided to William Franklin in 1771 that Ben's 'temper is grown so very reserved, which adds greatly to his natural inactivity, that there is no getting him to take part in anything'.[72]

Thomas Coombe, a young Pennsylvanian who came to London for his ordination in 1768, put it another way; Dr Franklin was 'the most cautious man I have ever seen'.[73] When Coombe first arrived in England he wrote to his father that Franklin 'appeared shy and cautious, but this wore away gradually, and upon observing the attention which my preaching gained me, and the notice which was taken of me by some men of letters, he received me upon the footing of a friend'.[74] The caution wore away gradually indeed, for it took Ben two years to venture to confide in the youth. Once the philosopher had opened up a little, he took the trouble to explain a few things to Coombe. He informed him of the circumstances by which his son William had obtained the governorship of New Jersey (it had been a reward for William's military service in King George's War; Ben had had no part in it). He contradicted a hostile rumour (put about by friends of Dennis De Berdt, said Ben) that he had been appointed postmaster general *after* becoming an agent. He was still apparently being haunted by malicious gossip regarding his past. Young Coombe, happy to be taken into Franklin's confidence, put it all down in a letter to his father, warning him that 'these anecdotes will do for no eye but your own'.[75] Ben no doubt hoped that Mr Coombe would broadcast his side of the story all over Philadelphia.

Ben Franklin's situation in London had become Byzantine, obliging him always to tread carefully. If he was guarded, or 'cautious', as his young guest expressed it, that was understandable. But judging by the number of remarks clustered around his second agency, his reticence deepened the longer he stayed. A perceptive biographer of Franklin has noted that his failure to be accepted by the highest social circles in London could not all be put down to snobbery; 'some personal difficulties' were evident as well. The historian Edmund Morgan has suggested 'a failure in dealing with people face to face' that was evident at certain points in his career, beginning with his falling out with the Penns.[76] Whatever that failure was – a subtle personal quality that eludes historical documentation – it seems likely that the 'reserve' so noted by his contemporaries formed part of it. It did not charm.

It is obvious that much of this reserve can be explained by a dread of putting a foot wrong, but other feelings may also have been in play. Franklin had worked long and hard, both for his land schemes and for recognition as the leading colonial spokesman in London. But over the years these projects did not come to fruition quickly, if at all. Success had come much more readily in Philadelphia. Perhaps resentment born of frustration led Franklin to be a little unwise, slighting those whom he believed slighted him. In a letter of 1773 he boasted to his son William of having never exchanged 'three sentences' with Prime Minister Lord North during the occasion of an overnight visit to the home of Sir Francis Dashwood, where both men had been present as guests. North 'seemed studiously [to avoid] speaking to me'. So Benjamin Franklin – who felt himself to be 'as proud as anybody' – avoided him right back. That surely put the prime minister in his place. Ben admitted he 'ought to be ashamed' for indulging such feelings, but he couldn't resist.[77] Perhaps Lord North, who was known for his affability, only saw the reserve so many others saw in the American agent.

Certainly, for all Ben Franklin's associations, clubs and friendships – and his was certainly a gregarious nature – there were groups he conspicuously did not mix with. He disliked John Wilkes and his City cronies at a time when that character and his cause were closely linked to the defence of colonial liberties. He had nothing much to do with the Literary Club, despite knowing

Boswell through the Honest Whigs. This was at a time when most colonists were keen to meet this set, and could do so fairly easily. Franklin could do so more easily than most, for his friend Strahan was Dr Johnson's printer. Yet he is known to have met the author of the famous *Dictionary* only once.[78] For all his own lively wit, he avoided the famous wits of the metropolis.

When Franklin first arrived in London his most important contacts were through the Royal Society and his connection with the Post Office. During seventeen years in the metropolis that did not substantially change. He never really became part of the community of genteel planters and absentees in the West End. In this quarter the enmity that persisted between him and the Penns must have been an inconvenience. The Penns knew everyone. Ralph Izard's little girl played with Miss Sophia Penn.[79] A niece of Lady Penn was married to Lord Shelburne, who befriended so many colonials, including Franklin himself.[80] None of the other Pennsylvanians in London avoided the Penn family, even those whom Franklin counted among his friends. Young Thomas Coombe called upon the proprietor of Pennsylvania soon after reaching London, although he was lodging with Ben at Mrs Stevenson's at the time.[81] Ben's wealthy friend Samuel Powel of Philadelphia, who went on a 'Grand Tour' of Italy and stopped in London, introduced Benjamin West to the Penns, who thereafter patronised the young artist.[82] Any awkwardness subsisting between Ben and the absentee set on account of the Penns would have deepened after he took up the agency for Georgia. Ben's work for that colony involved him in a dispute with its governor, Sir James Wright, who was living in Berners Street in the early 1770s.[83]

For all Franklin's accounts of his happy life in London, there was obviously something wrong. His growing reserve was just one symptom. Another was his constant promises to return to Pennsylvania, which peppered his letters to his wife Deborah. Were these the fruits of a guilty conscience? Or symptoms of a genuine sense of insecurity that resulted in homesickness? This is not to say that his provincial roots were the cause of Ben's sense of malaise in the capital of empire. His friend Benjamin West, with a very similar background, was going from strength to strength as a rising artist in the metropolis. Nor was it necessarily his politics, for Arthur Lee, who was just as outspoken in his defence of colonial rights, had become very much a part of the swirling political and social life of the City. It was his own extensive ambitions that set Ben apart from his two countrymen. He had irons in too many different fires. And London, he found, was a place where his well-laid plans for a second, greater career never quite seemed to pan out.

When Ben included 'Get clear of ag[enc]ys' in his list of reasons to go home in 1773, he had, curiously, excepted his Massachusetts agency. That, it seems, was still a motive to remain. There were some who thought that he had plans to retire to New England, perhaps even to become the governor of Massachusetts if he could swing that. Serving as the Bay Colony's agent in London might be a means to that end.[84] So it seemed there was one more line of advancement to be explored before Ben Franklin was willing to give up and go home. If it succeeded, he could return to America with something really impressive to show for himself. But in taking on Massachusetts, his problems in the metropolis were going to blow up, horribly and irrevocably, in the worst disaster of his life.

Massachusetts by this time was considered by the British government to be the most troublesome colony in America. The headaches it caused government ministers took many forms, and one of these had been the attack on Governor Bernard that old Mr De Berdt, just before his death, had been dragged into. Now the colony wanted to get rid of another governor, the unpopular Thomas Hutchinson, and Ben Franklin did all he could to assist. Sometime in 1772 he got hold of copies of private correspondence that had passed between Thomas Hutchinson and Thomas Whately, an MP. These letters were none of Franklin's business, and to this day no one is certain how he got hold of them. But what he did with them became the stuff of political scandal. He posted them to Thomas Cushing, the speaker of the Massachusetts Assembly. He cautioned Cushing to keep them secret and only to show them to a select group of leading Massachusetts patriots. What the letters supposedly proved was that the British legislation so hated in Massachusetts was all the fault of the diabolical Governor Hutchinson. He had misrepresented the people of Massachusetts to the authorities in London. Franklin may have hoped that Hutchinson would serve as the scapegoat whose sacrifice would make peace between stormy Massachusetts and the centre of empire.[85]

Franklin surely knew that the letters would go public. He told Cushing he would be able to send even juicier letters if 'too much noise' was not made.[86] Indications are that he did not expect very serious consequences from this breach of Hutchinson's privacy. After all, a few years earlier something similar had happened to Hutchinson's predecessor, Governor Bernard, and no one was called to account.[87] But Franklin's position was much shakier than Dennis De Berdt's. Back in 1770 De Berdt had been helped out by the great William Beckford – MP, friend of Lord Chatham and of those troublesome agitators the Wilkites, lord mayor of London and millionaire sugar planter – who leaked some of Bernard's letters himself.[88] And De Berdt was an unthreatening figure whose best years were visibly behind him, not a complicated man with a wide set of transatlantic connections whose motives and loyalties were poorly understood. Since becoming agent for Massachusetts in 1770, Franklin began to be looked upon by the king's ministers as a troublemaker who encouraged the disaffected in the colonies to think that they would eventually be in a position to name their terms to the authorities in London. He angered those in power by writing several popular hoaxes for the London newspapers, poking fun at British colonial policy. While the lobbyist and his friends chuckled over these 'spirited' pieces, ministers fumed.[89] Ben Franklin was a lot more vulnerable than Dennis De Berdt. In Arthur Lee's opinion he was the victim of overweening hubris, imagining that he had 'the ministry at his feet'.[90] Whatever his expectations, he presented the British government with the Massachusetts petition in August 1773, asking that Hutchinson be removed from office.

Meanwhile, the Hutchinson letters were published in Boston. Soon the London papers were speculating on who, exactly, had leaked them. A favourite candidate was John Temple, a former customs inspector from Massachusetts now living in London. His wife was the daughter of Massachusetts patriot James Bowdoin. He would have had access to the letters and the motive to give them to the Massachusetts patriots. The case seemed strong enough for Thomas Whately's brother, a London banker, to challenge Temple to a duel. (Thomas Whately had died a few years earlier.) Whately refused to have a second, but Ralph Izard and Arthur Lee promised Temple that they would be at the scene. Lee was already involved as deputy agent for Massachusetts; Izard was there as a friend of Lee. Both men had closed ranks with Franklin over the whole affair, as it was taking on the nature of another conflict between the British government and a beleaguered colonial assembly.

At 4 p.m. on the appointed day, Lee and Izard went in Izard's carriage to an agreed duelling place near the Serpentine in Hyde Park. Upon arrival they heard pistol shots and soon saw Whately walking towards them, slightly wounded. Izard took Whately home in his carriage, and Lee and Temple headed back to Berners Street. It turned out that Whately had brought no pistols of his own, so the two men had used Temple's. When they had both fired off to no effect, they tossed the pistols away and began duelling with swords. Temple found that Whately was hopelessly inept as a swordsman, so he wounded him slightly (to bring the matter to a conclusion), and the duel was ended.

But it did not end there. Soon a rumour spread around town that Temple had cut Whately from behind while the latter was down. Temple's friends were indignant, but there was nothing for it but to challenge Whately to another duel.[91] Franklin couldn't very well sit by and allow John Temple to risk his life twice. On Christmas Day 1773 he published a piece in the London papers confessing that he had sent the letters to Boston. He never admitted how he got them and he did not apologise. Instead, he asserted boldly that the letters deserved to be made public.[92]

Perhaps his confidence faltered a bit on 11 January 1774, the day scheduled for the Privy Council to consider the petition. He had discovered the evening before that Governor Hutchinson would be represented at the hearing by legal counsel. This was none other than the solicitor-general, Alexander Wedderburn, a friend of the Whately family. The business was not going to roll on wheels, apparently. Franklin was granted a couple of weeks to secure counsel for himself. He may have regretted the postponement, because on 20 January news of the Boston Tea Party reached London. Government ministers were appalled and angry. Everything was suddenly much more loaded. On 29 January 1774 Benjamin Franklin came to Whitehall for what would prove to be one of the worst days of his life.[93]

Just as in the case of Governor Bernard four years earlier, the petition was dismissed as 'groundless, vexatious, and scandalous'. But the bearer of the petition came in for much more. In a tirade that lasted an hour Alexander Wedderburn roasted the Massachusetts agent, openly accusing him of the theft of the letters, and gibing that he would henceforth deem it 'a libel to be called a man of letters'. The solicitor-general charged that Franklin had conspired to remove Hutchinson from office so that he, Franklin, could become the next governor, and that he sought to inflame the innocent, well-meaning farmers of Massachusetts with lies about the British government and its intention towards its American colonies. The trouble in Massachusetts, Wedderburn claimed, had for years been the work of Franklin and a group of patriot ringleaders in Boston. Franklin, said Wedderburn, was 'so possessed with the idea of a great American republic' that he spoke as if he were the ambassador of 'a foreign independent state'. For years he had been encouraging 'them at Boston' to 'go on; for you have nothing to fear from the government here', and giving them an inflated impression of his own importance in the capital.[94] Those present reported that Wedderburn used the 'coarsest language', 'a furious philippic against poor Dr Franklin', as MP Edmund Burke put it.[95]

For the roasting had an audience. Privy Council meetings were attended by the lords themselves, and sometimes by interested onlookers. The duel between Whately and Temple had already given a lurid publicity to the whole business. The sense of crisis surrounding the news of the Boston Tea Party now made it the most exciting show in town. On 29 January the Cockpit was packed.[96] Prime Minister Lord North, Lord Dartmouth, who was secretary for American affairs, Lord Hillsborough and a host of others were present. The gallery, too, was packed with onlookers, including Franklin's good friend Joseph Priestley, Edmund Burke and General Thomas Gage, who would shortly return to Massachusetts to preside over the start of the war at Lexington and Concord. While Franklin's friends watched grimly, most of the audience laughed and cheered Wedderburn on. Franklin's London world, so carefully constructed for so many years, was crumbling around him. Throughout it all, he made no reply, refusing to testify on his own behalf. One American onlooker reported that he looked 'as if his features had been made of *wood*'. 'The muscles of his face had been previously composed,' recalled the spectator, 'so as to afford a placid tranquil expression of countenance, and he did not suffer the slightest alteration of it to appear during the continuance of the speech.'[97] After all his years of caution in the metropolis, Franklin now found himself cornered, exposed, humiliated. He could only resort to his famous reserve.

Two days later Franklin was dismissed from his post as deputy postmaster general. Rumours went around that he was going to be arrested. Things would never be the same. His influence in London as a colony agent was at an end. No doubt digesting all this, he became even quieter. A visitor from Scotland met him at a dinner shortly after the Cockpit fiasco and described him as 'silent and inconversible'.[98]

But still Ben Franklin did not go home to Pennsylvania. Why not? His London career was over. His wife Deborah had been ailing for some years and her health was becoming ever more precarious. She longed to see her husband again before she died. William Franklin's son Temple, who now lived with his grandfather at Craven Street, was fourteen and had yet to meet his true father. Even the king openly wondered why Franklin remained where he was. A few months after the Cockpit incident he asked Lord Dartmouth curiously: 'Where is Doctor Franklin?'[99]

But he was, quite simply, still not ready to give up. In the wake of the tea crisis, the 'great friends of the colonies' in London were urging him to stay and see whether he could be of use to the newly created Continental Congress when its resolutions reached England.[100] The absentee colonial community in

London closed ranks around him as the cause of beleaguered Massachusetts became the cause of them all. Franklin was still the best-known spokesman for America in London. He was invited to sign the petitions organised by Henry Laurens and Ralph Izard to protest the Coercive Acts.

For a brief spell at the end of 1774 Franklin's determination to stay put seemed to be vindicated. He was drawn into a series of secret exchanges with powerful figures in Westminster who were searching about for a solution to a situation that was spinning out of their control. The negotiations had been set in motion by his Quaker friends, Dr Fothergill and merchant David Barclay, both of whom had clout as leaders of the London Quaker community. Franklin never met face to face with anyone in the ministry. His reputation as persona non grata in British governing circles was too well known for a public meeting to be anything but embarrassing to His Majesty's ministers. Instead, he wrote up a list of 'Hints' for a 'durable Union between Britain and the Colonies', in effect ideas for a colonial bill of rights, which was shown to Lords Dartmouth and North, and probably others, between November 1774 and January 1775. Other than a brief meeting with Lord Hyde, a privy councillor who as postmaster general knew Franklin, the agent saw only the go-betweens, Fothergill and Barclay.

But other mysterious approaches were made to the discredited agent. In early November, at one of Franklin's much-loved Royal Society dinners, a friend whispered to him that Mrs Caroline Howe would like to pit her wits against him in a game of chess. Mrs Howe was no less than the sister of George Howe, whose death at Fort Ticonderoga had made him a New England hero. Flattered, Franklin went to see her at her house in fashionable Grafton Street.[101] He soon discovered that the game concealed yet another secret negotiation, this time with Admiral Richard Howe, younger brother of George. Howe felt that his brother's death had given him a personal stake in the fate of the colonies, and he was now considering crossing the Atlantic as a peace commissioner. Might Franklin think of going with him, perhaps as a personal secretary or aide? And Howe wanted to look over Franklin's 'Hints'. Other games of chess ensued, but ultimately Howe did not depart as peace commissioner until 1776, sailing at the head of a British naval fleet and arriving after the Declaration of Independence.[102]

Unsurprisingly, these indirect exchanges with the ministry were tense. When David Barclay hinted that Franklin might be restored to his place as postmaster general, he retorted that the ministry 'would rather give me a place in a cart to Tyburn, than any other place whatever'.[103] And the ministers were disappointed with Franklin's 'Hints', saying that he asked too much for the colonies. But Franklin was not really empowered to speak for the colonies or their new Continental Congress. He could only present these British statesmen with his own ideas of what would calm the troubled waters, ideas that they found too extreme.

Lord North and his secretary for America, Lord Dartmouth, were nevertheless serious in their quest for a political solution. Franklin wrote dismissively of their intentions: 'All the colonies but those of New England, it is given out, may still make peace for themselves, by acknowledging the supreme unlimited power of parliament: But those are absolutely to be *conquered*.'[104] The troublesome New Englanders did indeed seem to be spoiling for a fight; many both in England and in the colonies suspected them of secretly aiming at independence. But North and Dartmouth wanted to make genuine concessions on taxation that they hoped would appeal to moderate elements in the colonies. Yet even they, the king's ministers, had to proceed with discretion. Both Parliament and George III were in a hawkish mood and disinclined to consider compromise. After the fighting began at Lexington and Concord in April, Lord Dartmouth wrote wistfully to William Franklin (still governor of New Jersey), bemoaning the 'fatal effects of General Gage's attempt at Concord', and saying it had undermined his hopes for hitting upon some 'plan of accommodation'.[105]

Franklin's last months in London must have been for him a powerful affirmation of his real importance in the town that had so cruelly rejected him the year before. For none other than Pitt the Elder, now Lord Chatham, also came to his door, literally stopping his coach (clearly marked with the great man's personal coat of arms) for several hours before Mrs Stevenson's house in Craven Street while he engaged the Doctor in matters of state. Chatham was determined to present his own conciliatory proposal to the House of Lords. In a style typical of the man, he had his own ideas of what would do the job and he made no effort to gain support from other parliamentary groups. He made no bones about consulting Dr Franklin, either, whom he openly referred to in the House of Lords as 'one whom all Europe held in high estimation for his knowledge and wisdom'.[106] In a nutshell Chatham proposed that Parliament concede the right to tax the colonies; that it had the right, he had no doubt, but to preserve American loyalties it should be formally given up. On a more immediate and practical note, Chatham suggested that the troops in Boston be withdrawn. The city was a tinderbox. Franklin dreaded that any 'unforeseen quarrel might happen between perhaps a drunken porter and a soldier, that might bring on a riot, tumult and bloodshed, and in its consequences produce a breach impossible to be healed'.[107]

But the great Lord Chatham could hardly get a hearing. Franklin, who was in the stranger's gallery at his personal invitation, said angrily that 'all availed no more than the whistling of the winds'. In a mood of angry despair Franklin concluded that it was absurd for these British lords to rule over 'three millions of virtuous sensible people in America . . . since they appeared to have scarce discretion enough to govern a herd of swine'.[108] Franklin was becoming distinctly disenchanted with the leadership at the centre of empire. Perhaps it was finally time to go home.

To the very end Franklin was being harried by his enemy Mr Whately. Thomas Whately's brother, still not satisfied by a duel and Franklin's humiliation in the Cockpit, brought a lawsuit against the Doctor in order to force him to divulge everything he knew about the affair of the Hutchinson letters. Franklin's lawyers stalled for time, putting off the hearing again and again. But it couldn't be put off forever. On 20 March 1775 Franklin left London for America, knowing his departure would expose him to a charge of contempt of court.[109]

The evidence is that when Benjamin Franklin left London for the last time he hoped and expected to return. He told Arthur Lee he might be back in the autumn.[110] He made arrangements for his lawyer to appeal any further proceedings against him, so that when he returned he would not be subject to arrest. But during his Atlantic crossing the Minutemen of Massachusetts took matters into their own hands by firing the proverbial shot heard round the world. The American Revolution began on 19 April 1775 when British and American soldiers clashed on Lexington Green. Franklin was never going back to London. The world he had known all his life was about to change beyond recognition. The warmongers in London and Massachusetts were about to get more than they bargained for. When the American Revolution began, both sides expected that it would be over in no time. Instead, what lay ahead was eight years of fighting and an empire torn asunder.

But Ben Franklin was about to enter a whole new phase of his career that was if anything more glorious than all that had gone before. By 1776 he was in Paris as Congressional commissioner for the United States. There he was warmly welcomed as the harbinger of the exciting new Republic that was rising in the west. Franklin became a potent symbol of a new age at the ancient Court of Versailles. Parisians were not accustomed to the self-taught scientists that were welcomed into Britain's Royal Society. They granted to

Benjamin Franklin all the mystique of a backwoods philosopher who drew his inspiration from nature.[111] Man of letters Hilliard d'Auberteuil recalled how his appearance astonished the people of Paris. He walked the streets 'clad in the simplest of garments. His eyes were shadowed by large glasses and in his hand he carried a white cane. He spoke little.' 'The people clustered around as he passed and asked, "Who is this old peasant who has such a noble air?" ' D'Auberteuil concluded: 'Everything in him announced the simplicity and the innocence of primitive morals.'[112] Franklin had never known such celebrity in London. He had certainly never been called simple or innocent. The French were captivated by his lack of pretentiousness; in London, where American colonists were better known, people were more apt to see beneath the surface. Just as he had done years ago in Philadelphia, Ben Franklin in Paris was once again able to make the cult of his own personality an ingredient of his success. Save within his own circle of friends at the Club of Honest Whigs and the Royal Society, that sort of cult status had always eluded him in London. As a backwoods philosopher in Paris he climbed much higher and more quickly than ever he had as a gentleman colonist in London. He was now without doubt the most famous American in Europe.

But of course Franklin did more than pose during his seven years in France. He worked tirelessly to get money, military aid and supplies for America from her former enemy. He remains one of the most renowned overseas spokesmen the United States has ever had.

There is an apocryphal tale that Dr Franklin, as he left the Cockpit after his public roasting, happened to find himself next to Wedderburn, and whispered to him: 'I will make your master a little king for this.' Was Franklin really that vindictive – and that egotistical? Not likely, but he would have had to be more than human not to feel a sense of triumph over the British establishment that had rejected him so publicly.

So was there to be no sense of loss for a man who had spent much of his prime living in London as a British subject, with no thought or wish of ever leaving? There was his son William, still governor of New Jersey when the war began. He remained loyal to his king and nation, taking an active part in the British war effort. After the peace William spent his remaining years in England, a virtual exile from his native country. Ben never forgave William for what he saw as a betrayal. Father and son met again briefly in the English port of Southampton in 1785, where Ben stopped on his return journey from France to America. By then the peace had been concluded and William longed to restore the family ties. But there was no warmth in the reunion.

Even the presence of Temple, who had spent the war with his grandfather, did not revive former feelings. When Ben was roused by the ship's captain in the middle of the night to be told that the wind was fair for America, he got up, got dressed and left without awakening his son, taking Temple with him.[113] The two Americans never saw one another again.

Epilogue

Benjamin Franklin was the first of the American activists to leave London under the shadow of civil war. The others would only follow gradually. The start of the fighting at Lexington and Concord did not spark off an abrupt exodus. Its initial effect was the opposite. Crack British troops being chased back to Boston by a mob of farmers looked bad, and now General Gage and his regiments found themselves holed up in the little seaport of Boston. Some MPs thought Lord North's administration would be brought down by the news and a pro-American government would take its place.[1] Arthur Lee predicted confidently that the present ministry could not last more than a few months.[2]

But in a few months it became apparent that the king and his ministers were preparing for full-scale war in America. By September word was out that the government was trying to buy in Hessian troops from Germany to do some of the fighting in the colonies. The British weren't going to be stopped by a few local heroics, courtesy of the Concord militia. If the Congress wanted to fight on, it had little choice but to turn to France – the arch-enemy of old – for help. That would mean declaring independence, for nothing less than the chance of permanently relieving Britain of her American possessions would tempt France into a war. The prospect of American independence filled Arthur Lee with regret. 'My rooted affection for the stock from which we sprung', he wrote wistfully, 'would incline me not to adopt such a measure but as the last resource. Arms have been taken up avowedly to vindicate old, not to establish new rights.'[3] His brother William, too, was hesitant. 'I am afraid a total disconnection between the two countries will be the consequence of these hostile measures,' he wrote.[4]

As a colonial war against a mother country, the American Revolution was unusual in that it did not begin with independence as its goal. From the start of the political conflict in the 1760s the stated objective had been to win greater rights for the colonies within the empire. The crisis that was launched by the Boston Tea Party in 1773 had a dangerous new element of violent confrontation, but even that did not have to mean war. The shooting in Massachusetts could have remained a mere local uprising that would end inconclusively as it had the last two times. Some hoped the defiance of the Minutemen might even be enough to wring concessions from a government that was unwilling to go to greater lengths to exert its authority. In early 1775 both Benjamin Franklin and Arthur Lee toyed with the idea that the colonies should settle for an indecisive conclusion to the latest crisis, and wait until the colonies were bigger, stronger and more consequential before insisting on a final settlement of American rights within the empire.[5] 'We should never forget in the conduct of this business', wrote Arthur Lee in February 1775, 'that we are every day growing stronger. That therefore, any future contest will certainly find us more powerful and probably the circumstances of the times may render the opportunity more favorable.'[6]

Even after the fighting began, last-minute ideas for preserving the empire were bruited about. The Lees considered the possibility that Britain and America could maintain a partial connection, one based on trade, a loose commercial arrangement 'under one king'. This would preserve the empire, ensure that America's burgeoning wealth enriched Britain rather than France, and give the colonies greater self-determination.[7] Franklin had put forward a similar idea during his secret negotiations with the ministry, and once back in Philadelphia he privately suggested it to certain members of Congress. His proposal was that if the American colonies were to pay taxes towards the cost of empire, they should have the same trading privileges as Scotland, which, since the Act of Union in 1707, had been free to trade on an equal footing with England.[8]

On 4 July 1776 all of the halfway drawing-board plans to keep Britain and her colonies together would be swept away in a cleaner, simpler Declaration of Independence. Despite this, the Lees hung on in their London residences for a little while longer. Arthur Lee had already begun secret meetings with the French agent Pierre-Augustin Caron de Beaumarchais, who promised French arms for American troops. He first met Beaumarchais at the lord mayor's Mansion House (where John Wilkes presided until the end of 1775). These dangerous rendezvous were continued at Lee's own lodgings in Garden Court.[9] Understandably, Lee started having fears for his safety. 'A man here in the clutches of bloodthirsty ministers must be cautious what he writes,' he fretted, suggesting that his friends in America should take hostages if he and other American activists in London were arrested.[10]

Sure enough, before long Lee lived under the shadow of British government surveillance. His mail was opened and read by minions at the Post Office. On one occasion it was confiscated and sent to Whitehall for ministerial scrutiny. Lee sent a letter of angry reproach to a cabinet minister, demanding his mail and asserting: 'I have waited this long, out of respect to your Lordship, and in expectation, that, when the letters had been examined, you would have had the goodness to send them as they were addressed.' British sangfroid was preserved; there was no hint either of denial or apology. His lordship directed his secretary to inform Lee that all letters from America had been returned to the Post Office.[11] Not until a year later was Lee appointed United States Commissioner to France. And so, in December 1776, he finally left 'the Eden of the world' to join Franklin in Paris. His brother William Lee soon followed. Early in 1777 he departed for the French seaport of Nantes, where he was to act as a commercial agent for Congress. He too had lived under the shadow of suspicion during his last years in London. In the summer of 1775 he was suspected of involvement in a plot to entice striking British shipwrights to emigrate to New York and work for the American cause. Government under-cover agents investigated the business, but in the end no action was taken.[12]

Stephen Sayre, despite the rude treatment he had received at the hands of Lord Rochford, stayed in London as long as the Lees did. He was not easily deterred from his purpose of fomenting disturbances in the capital. In September 1776 he approached the Duke of Portland with a proposal from an unnamed group, suggesting that if news of a British defeat in America reached the city, the duke and others should lead the country in a massive extra-parlia-mentary protest. The scheme smacked of rebellion. The duke declined the honour.[13] Not long afterwards government intelligence uncovered evidence that Sayre was involved in a plot to assassinate the king.[14] To everyone's relief Sayre finally left for France in February 1777.

Of all the Americans in London at the start of the war, the Lee brothers and Stephen Sayre were bound to be targeted by an exasperated ministry. But the fact that three high-profile American rebels were never prosecuted highlights the remarkable forbearance of the British government towards Americans in London during the War of Independence. To be sure, in August 1775, a few months after the fighting had started on Lexington Green, the colonies were declared in rebellion. The king's speech three months later in October asserted the government's conviction that the rebels sought independence, not simply a guarantee of their English liberties. Despite this, occasional expressions of support for 'American fellow subjects' were to be heard in the capital throughout the war.[15] In a nation that prided itself on its love of liberty, the rule of law prevailed. No open spirit of persecution was directed against Americans in London. No rebels were publicly executed at Tyburn or on Tower Hill. No American heads appeared on Temple Bar (the last Jacobite head was finally taken down in 1772, so a replacement was in order). Americans who openly sided with the rebellion but broke no laws were suffered to live quietly in the imperial capital. An American just returned from London in 1780 reported that while there he had seen a number of veteran American rebels walking 'openly in the city and no notice taken of them by authority'.[16]

If Ben Franklin was the target of ministerial resentment, the same cannot be said for his London friends and household. Mrs Stevenson and her daughter were not political creatures, but his nephew Jonathan Williams was. Williams stayed on at Craven Street until 1776, when he crossed the Channel to serve as a commercial agent in France for the American Congress. Meanwhile, Franklin's old lodgings were taken over by a Massachusetts loyalist, Sampson Salter Blowers, who had come to London to escape the conflagration that was breaking out at home. Franklin had only barely moved out when Blowers moved in. Mrs Stevenson showed no consciousness of sin for renting to a Tory. She wrote happily to Franklin that Blowers was a companion for nephew Jonathan. Mrs Stevenson died in London in 1783. Her grown-up daughter Polly, a widow with young children, moved to Philadelphia after the peace to be with Franklin in his old age.[17] She had indeed become his virtual daughter. She died there in 1795, five years after Franklin.

Franklin's good friend Benjamin West remained in London for the rest of what was to be a very long life. By 1777 he was living in fashionable Newman Street, just around the corner from Berners Street. During the war he continued as Painter to the King, although he spoke openly of his support for the Americans in the defence of their liberties. On one occasion the king declared before his Court that he honoured West for his loyalty to his native country. So secure was West's favour with his Britannic Majesty that there was even talk of offering him a peerage.[18]

John Temple, who had fought the duel with Mr Whately on Franklin's behalf, remained in London as the war escalated, not troubling to hide his sympathy for the rebellion. Temple, like Franklin, had been dismissed from his Crown post of customs officer after the episode in the Cockpit. Once the fighting started, he remained convinced that a reconciliation would take place and that he could have a role to play in it. His ambition seemed to come true when he was appointed to accompany a British peace commission to America in 1778. This commission, which was hastily put together to prevent an American alliance with France, offered too little too late. Temple returned to London, from whence he was appointed, in 1785, the first British consul general to the United States. With family in Massachusetts and a Bostonian mother, John Temple had a fair claim to call himself an American. But in a time of rapid and turbulent change, he had associated himself too closely with the British government. Despite Temple's commitment to the patriot cause, John Adams declared that he had too many British attachments and should 'make no pretensions as an American'. 'He is now an Englishman,' pronounced Adams when Temple was appointed consul general.[19]

There was a bit of unfairness in all this. American Henry Cruger had served as MP for Bristol all through the War of Independence. Despite a rumour that he had sworn allegiance to the United States during the war, he was re-elected to Parliament in 1784. When his opponents protested that as a 'native of America' he was ineligible, their petition was dismissed by the House of Commons. After the peace he was allowed to return to his native New York and run for state senator. There a similar scene ensued; his American opponents protested that as an MP, Cruger had been obliged to take oaths of loyalty to the king throughout the War of Independence. This surely made him a British subject, not an American citizen. But Cruger had a prominent brother in New York who had served valiantly beside George Washington. The protesters were overruled, and Cruger won the election.[20] The uneven fates of a Cruger and a Temple reflect the confusion that reigned in this time of sudden change.

And what of Ralph Izard, who presided over the Berners Street set? Izard was a patriot. Until the end of 1775 he stayed in London, talking to his acquaintances in the government and the opposition, hoping to bring about a reconciliation.[21] He had many friends and relatives on both sides of the conflict, and they opened doors to him in his self-appointed role as peace-maker. But in a civil war in which both sides were bound by many personal ties, they also must have caused him considerable pain.

In late July word of the Battle of Bunker Hill reached London. Among the British dead was Lieutenant Colonel James Abercromby, an old friend. 'Poor Abercromby!', wrote Izard. 'He was a brave and good man; if he had died in any other cause, I should have lamented his loss.' Izard went on: 'He was a volunteer and therefore, he has, I think, met with the fate he deserved.'[22] His words lacked conviction. One hopes that Izard never knew the details of his friend's death. In Boston there was a rumour – unfounded – that Abercromby held the fighting men of Massachusetts in contempt. On Bunker Hill they had a chance to reply with interest. Abercromby was shot down in a hail of bullets and had to be carried off the field, as the New Englanders jeered: 'Colonel Abercromby, are the Americans cowards now?'[23]

Less tragic but more awkward were Izard's relatives, the Gages. General Gage was married to an American, Margaret Kemble. She was the cousin of Izard's wife, Alice DeLancey. When Gage returned to London after the start of the war, he and Izard met in the street. 'He was civil, and hoped to see me,' reported Izard. There was an exchange of visits, but when Izard called upon the general he was not at home. Izard was probably relieved. There is a tradition that cousin Margaret Gage had tipped off the handsome patriot leader Joseph Warren the night before the British marched to Concord. If true – and it has never been proven – she helped to start the war Gage was desperate to prevent. Whatever really happened, Mrs Gage returned to England alone, in advance of her husband, and the two never lived together again.[24] But taken together or separately, General and Mrs Gage cannot have made for very relaxing company.

Still more of Izard's loyalist relations arrived in 1778. Lord Campbell returned from his adventures as the last royal governor of South Carolina, where he had been forced to flee his home. He was wounded while taking part in the British attack against Sullivan's Island in Charleston Harbor. He never fully recovered and died within a few months of reaching London. Lady Campbell (Sarah Izard that was) called upon Mrs John Laurens at her London home in May 1778, much to the surprise of John himself. From his perspective on the battlefields of America, her ladyship's courtesy call upon the wife of a rebel officer seemed an 'unexpected civility'. But things were very different in London. South Carolinians kept coming and going in much the old way, the students making the usual pleasure rounds, the planters and merchants congregating at the Carolina Coffee House. Visiting in that close-knit group often cut across political lines, even with a war in progress.[25]

Yet the war meant hard times for absentee planters like Izard. Carolina's economy was disrupted; credit and sales were rendered uncertain. Slave labour drained away in some areas as slaves fled to the British in hopes of gaining their freedom. Even in far away London, Izard had to make sacrifices. At the end of 1775 he rented out his house in Berners Street and decamped to Richmond. But he couldn't have been that hard up, for earlier in the year he and his wife had made a tour of Italy, leaving the children in England with their nanny. He still took regular jaunts to Bath. And before he could leave England he had to decide what to do with the costly furniture, plate and horses that were his property. Izard finally left for good in 1777, joining the cluster of Congressional agents now residing in France.[26] He was back in South Carolina by the end of the war, where he was elected one of the state's first senators under the new national Constitution.

It has been said that whereas the American Civil War divided thousands of families the American Revolution divided hundreds of thousands,[27] The Bremars as a breed had never shown much solidarity and now they disagreed over the war. Frank, who had shown glimmers of promise, joined the American cause along with a younger brother, Peter. The unattractive John, who had helped to drive his sister Molsy to desperation, took the other side. John Bremar was already in London by 1780, when Henry Laurens was brought there as a prisoner of war. Henry had been captured en route to the Netherlands on the business of the Continental Congress. Even while locked up in the Tower of London, poor Henry could not escape getting dragged into the trials and tribulations of his sister's orphaned children. There was to be no silver lining to his incarceration. Although Henry's visiting rights were closely restricted – young Harry Laurens only with difficulty obtained permission to visit his father – John was allowed in several times. It was the old story. By now he was married to a woman who declared that he neglected both her and his children in his selfish pursuit of the high life in London. Henry lent the struggling brood money several times before he lost patience. After the war, though, he was persuaded to interest himself in John's affairs once more, when he testified that his nephew John Bremar, who was appealing against the confiscation of his South Carolina estate, had wished success to the American cause. John's property was restored to him, but he had once again imposed on Uncle Henry, for Bremar had also applied to the British government for compensation as a suffering loyalist.[28] He was the sort of person whom no one really wanted on their side.

At least Henry's imprisonment was brightened up by the visits of his daughter-in-law Martha Manning Laurens, who brought his granddaughter Fanny to see him. Martha was to die later in France attempting to meet up with John Laurens while he was on his diplomatic mission to the Court of Versailles. Little Fanny, left an orphan after John was killed, returned to South Carolina with her grandfather in 1784.[29] Henry lived out his remaining years on his South Carolina plantation, Mepkin. He never recovered from the loss of his favourite son.

In America the start of fighting forced people everywhere to take sides. Not so in London. Londoners were slow to react to the American Revolution as if it were a foreign war. Most saw it as a provincial uprising that sooner or later would be patched up. Even the Declaration of Independence was widely seen as just a piece of paper aimed at keeping the French happy while they donated military supplies to the rebels.[30] So Americans in London could delay making their minds up if they wished; those who wanted to side with the winning party could wait to see which way the wind blew.

Ralph Izard's relations the Middletons divided over the war without suffering any diminishment of either their affluence or their family loyalties. William Middleton, Ralph Izard's uncle, remained on his Suffolk estate in England until his death in 1775. William junior stayed in England and died in 1829, having lived to become an MP and a baronet. His cousins, Thomas and Arthur, were educated in England but went home to serve in South Carolina's patriot Congress. After the war the extensive Middleton clan continued their transatlantic sociability unabated, much as if the Revolution had never happened.[31]

Some wealthy families were suspected of deliberately taking both sides of the quarrel in order to protect their estates, by sending one branch of the family back to England for the duration of the war. Suspicions of this kind escalated as more and more loyalist refugees arrived in London. In 1782 this was the cause of a notorious duel. Lloyd Dulany, a wealthy Maryland planter who lived in Newman Street, was accused anonymously in the London papers of staying in England 'to take care of' his property, in case England was 'the winning side'. Dulany responded through the papers, publicly challenging the anonymous author to a duel. But not until three years had passed did Bennet Allen, a Maryland clergyman, finally declare himself and take up the challenge. (Allen was proverbial for his vindictiveness. He also used the London papers to take a swipe at William Franklin's dubious parentage, describing him as 'borne of an oyster wench in Philadelphia'.) In the inevitable duel in Hyde Park, Dulany was killed by a single pistol shot. Allen in his defence pleaded that his eyesight was so poor that he never handled firearms and had none of his own; it had been a 'lucky' shot. Despite the fact that an eyewitness had seen him target-practising on the morning of the duel, he got away with a conviction of manslaughter. He had only to plead Benefit of Clergy and the sentence of six months in Newgate prison was commuted to a mere brand on the hand with a cold iron.[32]

During eight years of war the American population in London underwent considerable change. Loyalist refugees poured in from New England, Pennsylvania, New York and Carolina, as the main theatre of war shifted through the width and breadth of the former colonies. Over 7,000 of the estimated 60,000–80,000 loyal colonists who fled Revolutionary America came to England. For most of them London was the first port of call. They were of all social ranks – tradesmen, farmers, merchants, planters, former slaves.[33]

Hundreds of black Americans who had taken up arms for the king came to London at the end of the war. They were just a fraction of the tens of thousands of slaves who had been recruited by either side on a promise of their freedom.[34] Was Robert Scipio still there when these loyal black Americans arrived? If so, he would have found his employability as a black footman reduced, as competitors multiplied for every position. The numbers of black beggars swelled noticeably on the streets of the Great City. Inevitably, their claims to compensation were less successful than those of their white countrymen. Yet for many decades after American independence, London remained a place where black people could find greater social acceptance. In 1805 the Connecticut academic Benjamin Silliman was shocked at the sight of a genteel-looking black man walking arm in arm with a white woman on Oxford Street. The white woman was fashion-ably dressed and 'even handsome', noted Silliman, whose surprised reaction mirrored that of Henry Laurens thirty years earlier.[35] And the old complaint of white American visitors could still occasionally be heard, that some of 'our dear cousins over here' thought that 'Americans are black, certainly not white'. A Pennsylvanian was rasping to his English associates as late as the 1840s, 'The Americans are white, the same colour exactly as the English, and speak the same language, only they speak it a great deal better, in general' – a distinct echo of the colonial experience.[36]

But the black population that had become so conspicuous in England during the eighteenth century was disappearing, and was almost gone by the 1840s. Behind the decline lay several factors. The Atlantic slave trade ended within the British empire in 1807. In the United States fewer blacks joined the merchant marine as the century wore on. By the late nineteenth century segregation in the maritime unions was preventing blacks from sailing alto-gether except in marginal jobs. The result was that opportunities for blacks to move around the English-speaking Atlantic were dwindling. By the time the *Empire Windrush* arrived in England in 1948 with the first of the post-Second World War West Indian settlers, racist attitudes in England had hardened. To many twentieth-century Britons the mere sight of black faces in their cities seemed 'strange and out-of-place'. The West Indian incomers, who had grown up thinking of Britain as their mother country and of themselves as 'kinds of Englishmen', discovered that this was not a view shared by many white Britons.[37] The exotic, multiracial Atlantic world that, with all its injustices, had emerged in Britain's eighteenth-century empire had faded from memory.

Does this mean that if Robert Scipio lived to a ripe old age, he experienced ever greater isolation? Not likely, for well into the first half of the nineteenth century intermarriages between blacks and whites in Britain remained fairly common. The imbalance in the sex ratio in favour of men had persisted. In 1804 the English radical William Cobbett declared: 'No black swain need, in this loving country, hang himself in despair.' We trust that Robert did not. He may have married his Shropshire sweetheart. Perhaps his descendants are among the 'many thousands of British families' of today who have forgotten African roots.[38]

37 Peace is proclaimed at Charing Cross, above, and at Temple Bar, below. The American War of Independence was formally ended on 6 October 1783.

The American Revolution had begun as a local uprising, but it had escalated into a worldwide conflict and, for Britain, the longest war of the century.
On 5 December 1782 in the House of Lords, King George III proclaimed
Britain's acceptance of American independence in his speech opening the
parliamentary session. Elkanah Watson, a seafaring lad from Cape Cod who
was in London on business, pushed his way to the very foot of the throne to
hear the momentous words. In the gallery he saw Benjamin West. And with a
start he found that he was standing next to Lord Howe, brother of the hero
who had died at Fort Ticonderoga twenty-five years earlier. Did Howe reflect
that his brother's death had, after all, been in vain? As for the king, everyone
noticed that he faltered at the words *free and independent States*. But the deed
was done. For those not hardy enough to force their way into the Lords, the
speech was proclaimed at Charing Cross and Temple Bar. 'Religion, language,
interests and affection,' concluded King George, 'may, and I hope will, yet
prove a bond of permanent union between the two countries.'[39]

Despite the king's words, the Parliament that convened to ponder relations
with the new United States was not in a forgiving mood. There were statesmen
in London who regarded Britain and the United States as natural allies. They
favoured ideas such as shared citizenship and free trade between the two
nations. But the majority of MPs wanted to curtail U.S. trade with Britain and
its imperial dominions, arguing that the new nation was now a rival and must
be kept down. And so it was. The new confederation of States found themselves
barred from much of the trade they had enjoyed while loyal subjects of the king.

In the eyes of some the war was a tragedy that could have been avoided.
Instead, bloodshed and destruction ushered in a new nation whose emergence on
the world stage, some contemporaries felt, was premature. If the colonists were
ready to fight for their rights, they were not so ready to become one nation. The
southern colonies found themselves harnessed in an awkward alliance with the
Yankees of New England. Bonds of history and of geography between Britain's
tropical colonies on the American mainland and in the Caribbean were broken.

And the independence of the thirteen colonies that stretched from New
England to Georgia had come about at a time when many colonists were
drawing closer to their mother country culturally and socially. John Adams
could argue that geography made the separation of the mainland colonies
from their distant mother country a natural development. But it interrupted
an equally natural process of integration by Britain's American colonies,
ranged as they were around the margin of the Atlantic, into the larger western
world centred in Europe. It would be the work of many decades for all the

people of the United States, everywhere, to become fully and finally convinced that they had more in common with each other than with the peoples of Britain and its Atlantic empire.

So with the war over and American independence established, what was the new face of the former capital of the colonies? In many respects, things went on as before. For at least thirty years after the peace any American could still find a reason to go there.

Despite the unforgiving commercial legislation passed at the end of the war, London remained America's financial capital for the time to come. London was the world's financial centre. It continued to be *the* major provider of credit and insurance to America throughout the early years of the Republic. And America remained a major British trading partner. London merchants continued to handle the lucrative market for American tobacco and rice (and soon cotton as well) in Europe. American merchants continued to cross the Atlantic on business trips. Wealthy Americans of the eastern seaboard were still very much a part of the social and business networks that had crisscrossed the Atlantic since the eighteenth century.[40] Large numbers of American sailors continued to come and go in the streets of London.

Americans went on buying huge quantities of British goods. Only after the war of 1812 did Americans begin seriously to manufacture for themselves. This meant that for fashion-conscious Americans, London remained the shopping capital of the English-speaking world for decades after independence. As a token of this, London was still at the cutting edge of retail architecture. The first designed shopping streets, purpose built for the leisure shoppers of Regency London, appeared in the early nineteenth century. The crowning glory was the Burlington Arcade, a covered alley lined with shops – in effect, the world's first mall – which opened in 1819.[41] It is still in business, off Piccadilly. Not until the second half of the century did New York begin to boast its own elegant retail palaces like Macy's and Lord & Taylor.

London still led the way in English-language theatre and entertainment. The plays of the West End remained in heavy demand in the United States for many years to come. It was not until the First World War that the trend was reversed, as American stage shows began to catch on in London. The all-engrossing cultural supremacy of Hollywood and American television lay a long way off in the future. And London remained the first port of call for American artists who studied abroad until after 1820, when Italy and France begin to eclipse the former mother country for the sculptors and painters of the new Republic.[42] Although the young American Republic was ambitiously generating its own literary culture, London retained its supremacy as the centre of literature and publishing.

London's great public monuments would not be displaced by any American equivalents for many years. The city of Washington, D.C., was not even thought of until 1791, and only in 1800 was a president installed in the White House. When John and Abigail Adams moved in, the White House and the Capitol Building were still unfinished – the latter was only in the first phase of its lengthy construction. Washington's Botanic Garden (America's reply to London's famous Kew Gardens, launched in 1820) and the landmark Washington Monument would not be completed for several more decades. For awe and splendour, for towering examples of human ingenuity and achievement, Americans must still cross the Atlantic for the foreseeable future.

London's polite society remained the standard for good breeding in the early days of the American Republic. This no doubt is why the wealthy youth of America continued to go to the Inns of Court to finish their education after 1783, despite the divergence of English and American law. As in the colonial days, most of these were from the states south of New England. One of Ralph Izard's sons entered the Middle Temple in the 1790s, where the last American entry was in 1836.[43] Sixty years after independence Ralph Waldo Emerson could still write: 'Our civility England determines the style of, inasmuch as England is the strongest of the family of existing nations and as we are an extension of that people.'[44] Patriotic American visitors chafed under this vestige of British cultural supremacy, complaining that to be taken for English was considered the ultimate gauge of social success in London.[45]

Yet as long as the United States had no big cities of its own, London must serve. At the new nation's outset Americans lived almost entirely in the countryside. By the 1820s only New York could claim to be anything more than a provincial town. In the English-speaking world, London retained its supremacy as the metropolis wherein could be found that critical mass of talent that only cities can bring together.

It was no surprise, then, that things did not change overnight. After all, American independence had taken place years before anyone – even in America – had expected it. In 1759, when Wolfe and his redcoats took Quebec from the French, most American colonists were enthusiastic British patriots. When the shooting started at Lexington and Concord a scant sixteen years later, Americans had no national identity. In London in 1776 Americans were still seen as a medley of tricky Yankees, half-savage frontiersmen, and white plantation owners with their black labourers – mostly the latter. Their colonial legacy continued to dog the new nation's image in her former mother country. The United States was seen as a shaky concern, a band of dissimilar provinces whose premature bid for nationhood would not last long. In England this was treated as common knowledge. James Fenimore Cooper suffered the indignity of hearing it from a teenage girl at a London tea party, who blurted out: ' "Oh, but your Union will soon dissolve." '[46]

But by the second half of the nineteenth century, after the Civil War that Cooper's tea-room companion had anticipated, the case was very much altered. America had become the giant that Benjamin Franklin and others had predicted. With her own booming metropolises America had ceased to require a foothold in Europe. To be sure, the great city of London had to be replaced, not by one, but by three cities. New York, Washington and Boston became, respectively, the financial, political and cultural centres of the United States.

And in a further inversion of the colonial status quo, Ben Franklin became the personification of the American character. Slavery and the planter class had been relegated to the past. The Yankee North now embodied mainstream American values, and Franklin, with his self-made success and democratic manners, seemed the ideal type. Franklin and his friends among the Honest Whigs would have been gratified to see the lifestyles they attributed to New England come to be accepted as the defining characteristics of the American people. The Yankee persona of the nineteenth century was a blend of old English traits and new American ones. Honest and energetic, enterprising and plain-dealing – and white – it seemed to stand for the best of what distin-guished the new nation from Europe.

But the virtues associated with the simple life of farm and frontier had been only a part of the complex character the colonies sustained while still members of the British empire. Perhaps that earlier, half-formed image better reflected a people who could never really be summed up by narrow provincial caricatures like 'enterprising Yankees' or 'innocents abroad'. Americans always were, and always would be, an amalgam of the cosmopolitan and the provincial, the enterprising and the exploitative, the dispossessed and the privileged, decadent and simple, white, black and brown. That was how they had appeared in the streets of the great city of London when it was the capital of America.

Appendix

An unpublished database of Americans in London between 1755 and 1775 was compiled by Julie Flavell for the purposes of a study of the colonial population in London in the late colonial period. Individual colonists in London were identified in a range of sources (see list below) and collected into a database.

Except where sources by their nature include mainland Americans only (Jones, Bedwell, Sachse), West Indians were included as Americans in the data capture.

Descriptive variables entered for each individual record include sex, age (adult or minor), race, occupation, purpose in Great Britain, and colony of origin.

The statistical method known as capture-recapture was applied to the data at an early stage of data capture by Dr Gordon Hay of the Centre for Drug Misuse Research, Glasgow University, in order to generate a statistical estimate of the colonial American population in London. Capture-recapture is a method of estimating population size and characteristics that compensates for incomplete, missing or fragmented data. The results, published in the *Journal of Interdisciplinary History* (JIH) in 2001 (see full citation below), indicate that in the early 1770s alone there were at least 500 white mainland American men in London, more than twice the number appearing in the lists that formed the basis of the calculation.

My estimate of 1,000 wealthy mainland Americans and West Indians in London is based on the assumption that at least half of the estimated population of white adult males in the JIH article were well-to-do colonists from New York, Pennsylvania and the southern colonies. (See Flavell, 'Decadents Abroad', cited below, pp. 33–7 and ff., for a discussion of the preeminence of wealthy absentee colonists within the colonial population in London.)

Wealthy colonists of this type were able to afford to travel to London as families, and commonly did so. For example, one study concludes that there were at least fifty South Carolinian families living in London in the late colonial period (Jack P. Greene, 'Colonial South Carolina and the Caribbean Connection', in *idem* (ed.), *Imperatives, Behaviors, and Identities: Essays in Early American Cultural History*, Charlottesville, Virginia, and London: University Press of Virginia, 1992, p. 84). There are many anecdotal references to wealthy colonial families in London in published and unpublished letters and papers of colonial Americans in London, but as named individuals, women and children are under-represented in such sources. Since the estimate of 250 wealthy Americans in London does not include women or minors, I am factoring them in to reach a suggested total of around 400. This is probably an underestimate, and the figure is certainly closer to 1,000 if one includes the West Indian absentees, who were still reckoned 'Americans' before the War of Independence. (For a recent estimate of West Indian numbers, see Trevor Burnard, 'Passengers Only: The Extent and Significance of Absenteeism in Eighteenth-Century Jamaica', *Atlantic Studies*, Vol. 1, no. 2 [2004], p. 189.)

Total records in Flavell database of Americans in London between 1755 and 1775 = 772.

Publications:

Julie M. Flavell and Gordon Hay, 'Using Capture-Recapture Methods to Reconstruct the American Population in London', *Journal of Interdisciplinary History*, XXXII (Summer 2001).

Julie Flavell, 'Decadents Abroad: Reconstructing the Typical Colonial American in London in the Late Colonial Period', in Leonard J. Sadosky, Peter Nicolaisen, Peter S. Onuf and Andrew J.O'Shaughnessy, eds, *Old World, New World: America and Europe in the Age of Jefferson*, Charlottesville, Virginia, and London: University of Virginia Press, 2010, includes further discussions of the colonial population in the metropolis based on a later stage of data collection.

List of sources consulted in compiling the database:

The Papers of Benjamin Franklin, ed. L. W. Labaree et al., 39 vols, New Haven, Connecticut: Yale University Press, 1959–, vols 9–21 (coverage: 1760–1775).

The Papers of Henry Laurens, ed. George C. Rogers, Jr., et al., 16 vols, Columbia, South Carolina: University of South Carolina Press, 1968–2002, vols 7–9 (coverage: 1771–1774).

E.A. Jones, *American Members of the Inns of Court* (London, 1924) (coverage: 1755–1775).

C.E.A. Bedwell, 'American Middle Templars', *American Historical Review*, July 1920, pp. 680–89 (coverage: 1755–1775).

Register of Emigrants, Treasury Papers (PRO), 1773–1775 (coverage: 1773–1775).

William Sachse, *The Colonial American in Britain*, Madison, Wisconsin: University of Wisconsin Press, 1956 (coverage: 1750–1775).

Henry F. MacGeagh and H.A.C. Sturgess, *Register of Admissions to the Honourable Society of the Middle Temple from the Fifteenth Century to the Year 1944* (London, 1949), 2 vols (coverage: 1755–1775).

Joseph Foster, ed., *The Register of Admissions of Gray's Inn 1521–1889* (London, 1889) (coverage: 1755–1775).

Records of the Honorable Society of Lincoln's Inn, Vol. I: *Admissions from AD 1420 to AD 1799* (Lincoln's Inn, 1896) (coverage: 1755–1775).

R.A. Roberts, ed., *A Calendar of the Inner Temple Records* (London, 1933), Vol. V: 1751–1800 (coverage: 1755–1775).

Lewis Namier and John Brooke, *The History of Parliament: The House of Commons, 1754–1790*, 3 vols London: Her Majesty's Stationery Office, 1964 (coverage: 1755–1775).

Notes

Prelude: An American City in Europe

1. L.H. Butterfield, ed., *Letters of Benjamin Rush*, 2 vols, Princeton, New Jersey: Princeton University Press, 1951, Vol. II, p. 1,016.
2. *Ibid.*, pp. 1,043, 1,050–51.
3. *Ibid.*, Vol. I, p. 72.
4. Catherine Molineux, 'Pleasures of the Smoke: "Black Virginians" in Georgian London's Tobacco Shops', *William and Mary Quarterly*, Vol. LXIV (April 2007), pp. 338, 344.
5. Julie Flavell, 'Decadents Abroad: Reconstructing the Typical Colonial American in London in the Late Colonial Period', in Leonard J. Sadosky, Peter Nicolaisen, Peter S. Onuf and Andrew J. O'Shaughnessy, eds, *Old World, New World: America and Europe in the Age of Jefferson*, Charlottesville, Virginia, and London: University of Virginia Press, 2010.
6. Andrew Jackson O'Shaughnessy, *An Empire Divided: The American Revolution and the British Caribbean*, Philadelphia, Pennsylvania: University of Pennsylvania Press, 2000, pp. xi, 251.

Chapter One: The London World of Henry Laurens

1. Max Edelson, *Plantation Enterprise in South Carolina*, Cambridge, Massachusetts: Harvard University Press, 2006, pp. 216–18.
2. *The Papers of Henry Laurens*, ed. George C. Rogers, Jr., et al., 16 vols, Columbia, South Carolina: University of South Carolina Press, 1968–2002, Vol. 7, pp. 468–87, letters dated between 2 and 6 April 1771.
3. Edelson, *Plantation Enterprise*, p. 222; *Papers of Henry Laurens*, Vol. 7, p. 375.
4. Edelson, *Plantation Enterprise*, p. 231; Gregory D. Massey, *John Laurens and the American Revolution*, Columbia, South Carolina: University of South Carolina Press, 2000, p. 231.
5. *Papers of Henry Laurens*, Vol. 9, p. 317; Vol. 8, p. 4.
6. Kenneth Silverman, *A Cultural History of the American Revolution: Painting, Music, Literature, and the Theatre in the Colonies and the United States from the Treaty of Paris to the Inauguration of George Washington, 1763–1789*, New York: Crowell, 1976; this edition, New York: Columbia University Press, 1987, pp. 38, 60, 92.
7. Richard Barry, *Mr Rutledge of South Carolina*, Salem, New Hampshire: Ayer, 1942; this edition Hawthorn Books, New York, 1971, p. 38; Massey, *John Laurens and the American Revolution*, pp. 6–9; Edelson, *Plantation Enterprise*, pp. 210–11.
8. Edelson, *Plantation Enterprise*, pp. 148–50, 226; Richard S. Dunn, 'The English Sugar Islands and the Founding of South Carolina' in T.H. Breen, ed., *Shaping Southern Society: The Colonial Experience*, New York: Oxford University Press, 1976, p. 55.
9. Edelson, *Plantation Enterprise*, p. 141; *Papers of Henry Laurens*, Vol. 8, p. 150.

10. William R. Taylor, *Cavalier and Yankee: The Old South and American National Character*, Oxford: Oxford University Press, 1993, p. 44.
11. *Papers of Henry Laurens*, Vol. 8, p. 3.
12. Robert Greenhalgh Albion, *The Rise of New York Port [1815–1860]*, Newton Abbot, Devon: David & Charles, 1970; first edition New York: Charles Scribner's Sons, 1939, p. 343.
13. Rosamond Bayne-Powell, *Travellers in Eighteenth-Century England*, London: John Murray, 1951, pp. 2, 13–14, 21, 32.
14. Ian K. Steele, *The English Atlantic, 1675–1740: An Exploration of Communication and Community*, New York and Oxford: Oxford University Press, 1986, p. 6.
15. *Papers of Henry Laurens*, Vol. 8, pp. 6–8.
16. *Ibid.*, p. 4.
17. *St James's Chronicle*, no. 204, 29 June–1 July 1762.
18. Philip D. Morgan, *Slave Counterpoint: Black Culture in the Eighteenth-Century Chesapeake & Low Country*, Chapel Hill, North Carolina, and London: University of North Carolina Press, 1998, pp. 555–6.
19. *Ibid.*, p. 246.
20. Silverman, *A Cultural History of the American Revolution*, pp. 138–9; Gretchen Holbrook Gerzina, *Black London: Life before Emancipation*, New Brunswick, New Jersey: Rutgers University Press, 1995, p. 10; Felicity A. Nussbaum, 'The Theatre of Empire: Racial Counterfeit, Racial Realism' in Kathleen Wilson, ed., *A New Imperial History: Culture, Identity, and Modernity in Britain and the Empire, 1660–1840*, Cambridge: Cambridge University Press, 2004, p. 86.
21. Elizabeth A. Fenn, *Pox Americana: The Great Smallpox Epidemic of 1775–82*, New York: Hill & Wang, 2001, pp. 6, 21–3, 28–9; James Walvin, *Fruits of Empire: Exotic Produce and British Taste, 1660–1800*, New York: Palgrave Macmillan, 1997, p. 56.
22. Massey, *John Laurens and the American Revolution*, p. 13.
23. *Papers of Henry Laurens*, Vol. 8, pp. 42, 44, 47.
24. *Ibid.*, Vol. 8, p. 44.
25. *The London Encyclopædia*, ed. Ben Weinreb and Christopher Hibbert, London: Macmillan, 1983, p. 242.
26. *Boswell's London Journal*, ed. Frederick A. Pottle, Melbourne, London and Toronto: William Heinemann, 1950, pp. 50, 53, 87, 295.
27. *Papers of Henry Laurens*, Vol. 8, p. 134.
28. *Ibid.*, pp. 130, 184.
29. *The London Encyclopædia*, p. 448.
30. Peter Thorold, *The London Rich: The Creation of a Great City, from 1666 to the Present*, London: Viking, 1999; this edition London: Penguin Books, 2001, pp. 112–18, 133.
31. *Papers of Henry Laurens*, Vol. 8, p. 206.
32. John Summerson, *Georgian London*, London: Pleiades Books, 1945; this edition Cambridge, Massachusetts: MIT Press, 1978, p. 165; Thorold, *The London Rich*, pp. 133, 146, 151.
33. Thorold, *The London Rich*, p. 137.
34. Summerson, *Georgian London*, p. 143; *The London Encyclopædia*, p. 61.
35. *Papers of Henry Laurens*, Vol. 8, pp. 23, 52, 107, 178.
36. Maurie D. McInnis, *In Pursuit of Refinement: Charlestonians Abroad, 1740–1860*, Columbia, South Carolina: University of South Carolina Press, 1999, pp. 100–2, 103 fn 12, 112; Edelson, *Plantation Enterprise*, p. 153.
37. William Sachse, *The Colonial American in Britain*, Madison, Wisconsin: University of Wisconsin Press, 1956, p. 189; *Papers of Henry Laurens*, Vol. 9, p. 373; *The Papers of Benjamin Franklin*, ed. L.W. Labaree et al., 39 vols, New Haven Connecticut: Yale University Press, 1959–, Vol. 21, pp. 157–8, fn; Wilmarth S. Lewis, ed., *The Yale Editions of Horace Walpole's Correspondence*, 39 vols, New Haven Connecticut: Yale University Press, 1937–, Vol. 6, p. 63, fn; McInnis, *In Pursuit of Refinement*, pp. 28–9, 66, 116.

38. *The Diary of John Baker, Barrister of the Middle Temple, Solicitor-General of the Leeward Islands*, ed. Philip C. Yorke, London: Hutchinson, 1931, p. 308; Lewis, ed., *The Yale Editions of Horace Walpole's Correspondence*, Vol. 25, p. 184; *The London Magazine. Or, Gentleman's Monthly Intelligencer*, London, 1747–83, Vol. 34 (June 1765), pp. 431–2; McInnis, *In Pursuit of Refinement*, p. 108.

39. *Papers of Henry Laurens*, Vol. 9, pp. 225–6, 394, fn; David Hackett Fischer, *Paul Revere's Ride*, New York and Oxford: Oxford University Press, 1994, pp. 35, 75; Julian Gwyn, *An Admiral for America: Sir Peter Warren, Vice Admiral of the Red, 1703–1752*, Gainesville, Florida: University Press of Florida, 2004, pp. 22–3; Lewis, ed., *The Yale Editions of Horace Walpole's Correspondence*, Vol. 6, p. 63; *ibid.*, Vol. 32, pp. 68, 98; *ibid.*, Vol. 33, p. 104.

40. *Papers of Henry Laurens*, Vol. 8, pp. 23, 107, fn; *ibid.*, Vol. 9, pp. xiii, 376–7, fn.

41. *Papers of Henry Laurens*, Vol. 8, p. 467 fn; *ibid.*, Vol. 9, pp. xiii, 647, fn; Edward A. Jones, *American Members of the Inns of Court*, London, 1924, p. 60.

42. *Papers of Henry Laurens*, Vol. 8, p. 107, fn; Jones, *American Members of the Inns of Court*, pp. 224, 229.

43. *Papers of Henry Laurens*, Vol. 9, p. xiii; James A. McMillin, *The Final Victims: Foreign Slave Trade to North America, 1783–1810*, Columbia, South Carolina: University of South Carolina Press, 2004, pp. 74–5.

44. *Papers of Henry Laurens*, Vol. 8, pp. 231, 307–8; Massey, *John Laurens and the American Revolution*, pp. 9, 14, 36.

45. Jones, *American Members of the Inns of Court*, p. 116; *Papers of Henry Laurens*, Vol. 9, pp. 227–8.

46. *Papers of Henry Laurens*, Vol. 9, pp. 228, 373 fn; Barry, *Mr Rutledge of South Carolina*, pp. 84–5; Robert M. Weir, 'Thomas Boone', *Oxford Dictionary of National Biography*, 60 vols, Oxford: Oxford University Press, 2004, Vol. 6, p. 590; C.E.A. Bedwell, 'American Middle Templars', *American Historical Review*, Vol. 25 (1920), p. 686.

47. *Papers of Henry Laurens*, Vol. 8, p. 148, fn.

48. *Ibid.*, pp. 306–7.

49. Julie M. Flavell and Gordon Hay, 'Using Capture-Recapture Methods to Reconstruct the American Population in London', *Journal of Interdisciplinary History*, Vol. XXXII (2001), pp. 38, 41–3; Henry F. MacGeagh and H.A.C. Sturgess, *Register of Admissions to the Honourable Society of the Middle Temple from the Fifteenth Century to the Year 1944*, London, 1949, 2 vols, Vol. 2, pp. 393–4.

50. Thorold, *The London Rich*, pp. 131–3, 136–7.

51. Andrew Jackson O'Shaughnessy, *An Empire Divided: The American Revolution and the British Caribbean*, Philadelphia, Pennsylvania: University of Pennsylvania Press, 2000, pp. 11, 14.

52. Dunn, 'The English Sugar Islands and the Founding of South Carolina', p. 58.

53. Christopher Iannini, ' "the Itinerant Man": Crevecoeur's Caribbean, Raynal's Revolution, and the Fate of Atlantic Cosmopolitanism', *William and Mary Quarterly*, 3rd series, Vol. LXI (2004), pp. 227–8.

54. The Steads from Berners Street and Lord and Lady Campbell were also part of the set. Massey, *John Laurens and the American Revolution*, p. 41; *The Diary of John Baker*, pp. 16, 195, 308, 333, 428–9, 555; *Correspondence of Mr. Ralph Izard of South Carolina*, ed. Anne Izard Deas, New York, 1844, p. 193; McInnis, *In Pursuit of Refinement*, p. 108.

55. Julie Flavell, 'British Perceptions of New England and the Decision for a Coercive Colonial Policy, 1774–1775' in Julie Flavell and Stephen Conway, eds, *Britain and America Go to War: The Impact of War and Warfare in Anglo-America, 1754–1815*, Gainesville, Florida: University Press of Florida, 2004.

56. Barbara G. Carson, 'Early American Tourists and the Commercialization of Leisure', in Cary Carson, Ronald Hoffman and Peter J. Albert, eds, *Of Consuming Interests: The Style of Life in the Eighteenth Century*, Charlottesville, Virginia: University Press of Virginia, 1994, p. 374; Steele, *The English Atlantic, 1675–1740*, p. 10.

57. Carl Bridenbaugh, 'Colonial Newport as a Summer Resort', *Collections of the Rhode Island Historical Society*, Vol. XXVI (1933), pp. 1–23; Carl Bridenbaugh, 'Baths and

Watering Places of Colonial America', *William and Mary Quarterly*, 3rd series, Vol. 3 (1946), pp. 151-81.

58. See Appendix.
59. Foster Rhea Dulles, *Americans Abroad: Two Centuries of European Travel*, Ann Arbor, Michigan: University of Michigan Press, 1964, pp. 27, 44.
60. McInnis, *In Pursuit of Refinement*, pp. 100, 102.
61. *The Independent*, Friday 14 May 2004, p. 34.
62. Taylor, *Cavalier and Yankee*, pp. 37-8; Edelson, *Plantation Enterprise*, pp. 255-6.
63. McInnis, *In Pursuit of Refinement*, p. 102.
64. *Papers of Henry Laurens*, Vol. 8, pp. 51, 169, 199-201.
65. *Ibid.*, p. 147.
66. *Ibid.*, Vol. 7, p. 328; *ibid.*, Vol. 8, pp. 140, 144, 325, 425, 434, 467.
67. Jeremy Black, *The British Abroad: The Grand Tour in the Eighteenth Century*, Stroud and New York: Alan Sutton, 1992, p. 244; *Papers of Henry Laurens*, Vol. 8, p. 27.

Chapter Two: Upstairs, Downstairs: Master and Slave in Georgian London

1. J. Jean Hecht, *The Domestic Servant Class in Eighteenth-Century England*, London: Routledge & Kegan Paul, 1956, pp. 81, 89, 216, 220.
2. *Ibid.*, pp. 1, 7-8, 80-82, 227.
3. *The Papers of Henry Laurens*, ed. George C. Rogers Jr., et al., 16 vols, Columbia, South Carolina: University of South Carolina Press, 1968-2002, Vol. 4, pp. 632-3, 664-5; Hecht, *The Domestic Servant Class*, pp. 8-9.
4. Hecht, *The Domestic Servant Class*, p. 52.
5. *The Diary of John Baker, Barrister of the Middle Temple, Solicitor-General of the Leeward Islands*, ed. Philip C. Yorke, London: Hutchinson, 1931, p. 15.
6. *Papers of Henry Laurens*, Vol. 4, p. 664; *ibid.*, Vol. 8, p. 489.
7. Hecht, *The Domestic Servant Class*, p. 216.
8. Cited from M. Dorothy George, *London Life in the Eighteenth Century*, first published London: Kegan Paul, Trench, Trubner, 1925; this edition London: Penguin Books, 1987, p. 140; for other examples of contemporary white fears that imported black servants would become refractory, see Folarin Shyllon, *Black People in Britain 1555-1833*, London: Oxford University Press, 1977, pp. 94-5.
9. Hecht, *The Domestic Servant Class*, ch. 8.
10. *Papers of Henry Laurens*, Vol. 9, p. 530.
11. Gretchen Holbrook Gerzina, *Black London: Life before Emancipation*, New Brunswick, New Jersey: Rutgers University Press, 1995, p. 122.
12. Andrea Levy, *Small Island*, London: Review (an imprint of Headline Book Publishing), 2004, pp. 139-40, 329.
13. Gerzina, *Black London*, p. 122.
14. George, *London Life in the Eighteenth Century*, pp. 173, 212, 228-32, 240, 242.
15. *The Diary of John Baker*, pp. 311, 427.
16. *Papers of Henry Laurens*, Vol. 10, p. 97. Dr Sylvia Watts has identified the names of two slaves and an African servant in Shifnal who were probably connected with the Austin family. Charlestown and Benjamin Priouleu are both listed in the Shifnal Baptism Registers. Thomas Africanus was a hired servant at Shifnal. On Africanus, see Shropshire Archives, P246/L/1/38a. I am indebted to Dr Watts for this information.
17. *Papers of Henry Laurens*, Vol. 8, pp. 464, 466, 468; *ibid.*, Vol. 9, p. 150.
18. Christopher Leslie Brown, *Moral Capital: Foundations of British Abolitionism*, Chapel Hill, North Carolina: University of North Carolina Press, 2006, pp. 94-5, 97.
19. *The Diary of John Baker*, pp. 107, 288.
20. *Ibid.*, p. 193; Old Bailey Proceedings Online (www.oldbaileyonline.org, 9 September 2009), 21 October 1767, trial of Thomas Windsor (t17671021-44).
21. Shyllon, *Black People in Britain 1555-1833*, p. 96; Peter Fryer, *Staying Power: The History of Black People in Britain*, London: Pluto Press, 1984, p. 72.

22. W. Jeffrey Bolster, *Black Jacks: African American Seamen in the Age of Sail*, Cambridge, Massachusetts: Harvard University Press, 1997, pp. 19–20; Fryer, *Staying Power*, pp. 68, 75.
23. Gerzina, *Black London*, pp. 23–4, 36; Fryer, *Staying Power*, pp. 68–71.
24. *Papers of Henry Laurens*, Vol. 8, p. 124.
25. Hecht, *The Domestic Servant Class*, pp. 105, 107, 109, 128–30.
26. *Ibid.*, pp. 16–18, 35–7.
27. Douglas A. Lorimer, 'Black Resistance to Slavery and Racism in Eighteenth-Century England', Jagdish S. Gundara and Ian Duffield, eds, *Essays on the History of Blacks in Britain*, Aldershot: Ashgate, 1992, p. 63.
28. Hecht, *The Domestic Servant Class*, p. 31.
29. Shyllon, *Black People in Britain*, pp. 102–4.
30. James Hogg, *The Private Memoirs and Confessions of a Justified Sinner*, London: Longman, 1824.
31. Gerzina, *Black London*, pp. 22, 38–9; Gary B. Nash, *Red, White and Black: The Peoples of Early America*, Englewood Cliffs, New Jersey: Prentice-Hall, Inc., 1974, p. 287.
32. *Papers of Henry Laurens*, Vol. 9, p. 317.
33. Christopher Leslie Brown, *Moral Capital: Foundations of British Abolitionism*, Chapel Hill, North Carolina: University of North Carolina Press, 2006, pp. 95–6.
34. Hecht, *The Domestic Servant Class*, p. 85.
35. *Papers of Henry Laurens*, Vol. 8, pp. 227, 232.
36. Max Edelson, *Plantation Enterprise in South Carolina*, Cambridge, Massachusetts: Harvard University Press, 2006, pp. 228, 230–31; George D. Massey, *John Laurens and the American Revolution*, Columbia, South Carolina: University of South Carolina Press, 2000, p. 15.
37. Massey, *John Laurens and the American Revolution*, p. 233.
38. Edelson, *Plantation Enterprise*, p. 228.
39. *Papers of Henry Laurens*, Vol. 6, pp. 181–2; *ibid.*, Vol. 7, p. 228.
40. *Ibid.*, Vol. 8, p. 696.
41. Hecht, *The Domestic Servant Class*, pp. 89, 160–67.
42. *Ibid.*, pp. 153–5.
43. *Papers of Henry Laurens*, Vol. 8, p. 696.
44. Hecht, *The Domestic Servant Class*, pp. 131–2, 135–6, 155–6.
45. *Papers of Henry Laurens*, Vol. 8, p. 696.
46. Hecht, *The Domestic Servant Class*, pp. 78–80; *The Diary of John Baker*, p. 423.
47. Gerzina, *Black London*, pp. 40–41; see also Shyllon, *Black People in Britain*, p. 39, 94.
48. Jos. Ball to Aron, Stratford 31 August 1754, reprinted in Robin Blackburn, *The Making of New World Slavery: From the Baroque to the Modern, 1492–1800*, London: Verso, 1997, p. 457, p. 504, fn 24. A London house servant, such as Aron had evidently been, would have to be able to read and write. Robert Scipio could do so.
49. *The Papers of Benjamin Franklin*, ed. L.W. Labaree et al., 39 vols, New Haven, Connecticut: Yale University Press, 1959–, Vol. 9, pp. 174–5.
50. Hecht, *The Domestic Servant Class*, pp. 99, 150.
51. An example is one Tobias Pleasant, a black footman who rode behind his master's carriage with a French horn. He had been working for his master for thirty-two years when he testified in a trial at the Old Bailey. Old Bailey Proceedings Online (www.oldbaileyonline.org, 9 September 2009), 6 December 1780, trial of Michael Daniel (t17801206-2). See also an advertisement for a runaway black in Bristol who 'blows the French horn very well.' Shyllon, *Black People in Britain*, p. 12. For more on black musicians in Georgian England, see Fryer, *Staying Power*, pp. 80–85.
52. K.L. Little, *Negroes in Britain: A Study of Race Relations in English Society*, London: Routledge & Kegan Paul, 1947, pp. 167–9.
53. Brown, *Moral Capital*, p. 151.
54. Shyllon, *Black People in Britain*, p. 43; *Papers of Henry Laurens*, Vol. 9, p. 317.
55. Fryer, *Staying Power*, pp. 72–3.

56. Shyllon, *Black People in Britain*, p. 20
57. Lorimer, 'Black Resistance to Slavery and Racism in Eighteenth-Century England', pp. 59–64.
58. Janet Schaw, *Journal of a Lady of Quality; Being the Narrative of a Journey from Scotland to the West Indies, North Carolina, and Portugal, in the Years 1774 to 1776*, ed. Evangeline Walker Andrews and Charles McLean Andrews, New Haven, Connecticut: Yale University Press, 1921; this edition 1939, pp. 22 3.
59. Fryer, *Staying Power*, pp. 60–61.
60. Granville Sharp, *A Representation of the Injustice and Dangerous Tendency of Tolerating Slavery; or of Admitting the Least Claim of Private Property in the Persons of Men, in England* (London, 1769), p. 88.
61. Gerzina, *Black London*, pp. 11, 104, 115.
62. Fryer, *Staying Power*, p. 61.
63. *Ibid.*, pp. 115–16.
64. Gerzina, *Black London*, pp. 116–17.
65. Fryer, *Staying Power*, p. 125.
66. Cited in Shyllon, *Black People in Britain*, p. 24.
67. Brown, *Moral Capital*, pp. 100–1.
68. William M. Wiecek, 'Somerset: Lord Mansfield and the Legitimacy of Slavery in the Anglo-American World', *University of Chicago Law Review*, Vol. 42, no. 1 (1974), pp. 107–8, 110.
69. 'A Conversation *between an* ENGLISHMAN, *a* SCOTCHMAN, *and an* AMERICAN, *on the Subject of* SLAVERY', in Verner W. Crane, ed., *Benjamin Franklin's Letters to the Press, 1758–1775*, Chapel Hill, North Carolina: University of North Carolina Press, 1950, pp. 187–8.
70. Sharp, *A Representation of the Injustice and Dangerous Tendency of Tolerating Slavery*, pp. 81–2, 85–6.
71. John Bernard, *Retrospections of America 1797–1811*, first published New York and London, 1887; this edition New York: Benjamin Blom, 1969, p. 15.
72. The Historical Society of Pennsylvania (HSP), Ebenezer Hazard Journal, 1770–71.
73. Cited in Michael Kammen, 'The Colonial Agents, English Politics, and the American Revolution', *William and Mary Quarterly*, 3rd series, Vol. 22 (1965), p. 252.
74. Wallace Brown, 'The British Press and the American Colonies', *History Today*, Vol. 44 (1974), p. 331; cited from Gerzina, *Black London*, p. 23, and see Catherine Molineux, 'Pleasures of the Smoke: "Black Virginians" in Georgian London's Tobacco Shops', *William and Mary Quarterly*, Vol. LXIV (April 2007).
75. Bernard Bailyn, *Voyagers to the West: A Passage in the Peopling of America on the Eve of the Revolution*, New York: Alfred A. Knopf, 1987, pp. 3, 55, 114, 229; George, *London Life in the Eighteenth Century*, pp. 149–50.
76. Dr John Fothergill, *Considerations Relative to the North American Colonies*, London, 1765, p. 36.
77. *Ibid.*, pp. 42–3.
78. Cited in Trevor Burnard, *Creole Gentlemen: The Maryland Elite, 1691–1776*, New York and London: Routledge, 2002, p. 222.
79. Thomas Ruston Journal, 1762–1765, Library of Congress, Washington, D.C.
80. Cited in Francis D. Cogliano, *American Maritime Prisoners in the Revolutionary War: The Captivity of William Russell*, Annapolis, Maryland: Naval Institute Press, 2001, pp. 42–3.
81. James Otis, *The Rights of the British Colonies Asserted and Proved* (Boston, 1764) in *Pamphlets of the American Revolution, 1750–1776*, Vol. I: *1750–1765*, ed. Bernard Bailyn, Cambridge, Massachusetts: Harvard University Press, 1965, pp. 435–6.
82. Cited in T.H. Breen, 'Ideology and Nationalism on the Eve of the American Revolution: Revisions *Once More* in Need of Revising', *Journal of American History*, Vol. 84, no. 1 (June 1997), p. 32.
83. Walter Isaacson, *Benjamin Franklin: An American Life*, New York and London: Simon & Schuster, 2003, p. 269.

84. Jim Potter, 'Demographic Development and Family Structure' in *Colonial British America: Essays in the New History of the Early Modern Era*, ed. Jack P. Greene and J.R. Pole, Baltimore, Maryland, and London: The Johns Hopkins University Press, 1984, p. 136; John J. McCusker and Russell R. Menard, *The Economy of British America, 1607–1789*, Chapel Hill, North Carolina: University of North Carolina Press, 1985, 1991, p. 219.

85. Joe Klein, 'How the Supremes Redeemed Bush', *Time Magazine*, 7 July 2003, p. 27.

86. Fryer, *Staying Power*, p. 69.

87. Gerzina, *Black London*, ch.4.

88. Wiecek, '*Somerset*: Lord Mansfield and the Legitimacy of Slavery in the Anglo-American World', pp. 102–4.

89. *Papers of Henry Laurens*, Vol. 8, p. 353.

90. *Ibid.*, pp. 342–3.

91. *Ibid.*, p. 286.

92. 'Behind the Plum Line', *Guardian* Saturday 6 September 2003.

93. *Papers of Henry Laurens*, Vol. 10, p. 97; on slaves in Shifnal who were probably connected with the Austin family, see ch.2, note 16 (sources given by Dr Sylvia Watts), above.

94. Wiecek, '*Somerset*: Lord Mansfield and the Legitimacy of Slavery in the Anglo-American World', p. 106, fn.

95. Gerzina, *Black London*, p. 132.

96. *Joshua Johnson's Letterbook, 1771–1774: Letters from a Merchant in London to his Partners in Maryland*, ed. Jacob M. Price, London Record Society, 1974, p. 44.

97. Gerzina, *Black London*, p. 133; *Phillis Wheatley: Complete Writings*, ed. Vincent Carretta, New York: Penguin Books, 2001, p. xxvii; see also Philip D. Morgan, *Slave Counterpoint: Black Culture in the Eighteenth-Century Chesapeake and Lowcountry*, Chapel Hill, North Carolina, and London: University of North Carolina Press, 1998, pp. 246, 461.

98. *Papers of Henry Laurens*, Vol. 8, p. 435.

99. *Ibid.*, Vol. 8, pp. 464, 466, 468.

100. Brown, *Moral Capital*, p. 92; Lorimer, 'Black Resistance to Slavery and Racism in Eighteenth-Century England', p. 69.

101. *Papers of Henry Laurens*, Vol. 8, p. 144, fn; p. 489.

102. *Ibid.*, p. 515.

103. *Ibid.*, p. 696.

104. *Ibid.*, Vol. 9, pp. 249, 264.

105. *Shrewsbury Chronicle*, 26 February 1774; *Papers of Henry Laurens*, Vol. 9, p. 316.

106. I would like to thank Sarah Davis of the Shropshire Archives for checking the Quarter Sessions order book from January 1774 to January 1775 for mention of bigamy cases.

107. *Papers of Henry Laurens*, Vol. 9, p. 317.

108. Kenneth M. Stampp, *The Peculiar Institution: Slavery in the Ante-bellum South*, New York: Vintage Books, 1956, p. 198.

109. Gerzina, *Black London*, p. 34.

110. *Papers of Henry Laurens*, Vol. 9, pp. 316–18, 347–8.

111. Hecht, *The Domestic Servant Class*, p. 145.

112. *Papers of Henry Laurens*, Vol. 8, pp. 1, 128.

113. Sharp, *A Representation of the Injustice and Dangerous Tendency of Tolerating Slavery*, pp. 43–4.

114. Hecht, *The Domestic Servant Class*, pp. 115–16.

115. *Papers of Henry Laurens*, Vol. 8, p. 696.

116. Sharp, *A Representation of the Injustice and Dangerous Tendency of Tolerating Slavery*, p. 45.

117. See, for example, H. Trevor Colbourn, ed., 'A Pennsylvania Farmer at the Court of King George: John Dickinson's London Letters, 1754–1756', *Pennsylvania Magazine of History and Biography*, Vol. 86 (1962), pp. 422–3.

118. Henry Steele Commager, ed., *Britain through American Eyes*, New York: McGraw-Hill, 1974, pp. 169–70.
119. Hecht, *The Domestic Servant Class*, p. 80.
120. *Shrewsbury Chronicle*, 19 March 1774.
121. Old Bailey Proceedings Online (www.oldbaileyonline.org, 9 September 2009), 10 September 1777, trial of Mary Slugg (t17770910-96).

Chapter Three: English Lessons in London: A Tale of Two Teenagers

1. *The Papers of Henry Laurens*, ed. George C. Rogers, Jr., et al., 16 vols, Columbia, South Carolina: University of South Carolina Press, 1968–2002, Vol. 7, p. 328.
2. *Ibid.*, Vol. 8, pp. 86–7.
3. *Ibid.*, p. 87.
4. Gregory D. Massey, *John Laurens and the American Revolution*, Columbia, South Carolina: University of South Carolina Press, 2000, p. 20; *Papers of Henry Laurens*, Vol. 7, p. 328.
5. Douglas Hay and Nicholas Rogers, *Eighteenth-Century English Society*, Oxford and New York: Oxford University Press, 1997, pp. 22–3; *Papers of Henry Laurens*, Vol. 6, p. 530.
6. Julie M. Flavell, 'The "School for Modesty and Humility": Colonial American Youth in London and their Parents, 1755–1775', *Historical Journal*, Vol. 42 (1999), p. 379.
7. Peter Roebuck, *Yorkshire Baronets, 1640–1760: Families, Estates and Fortunes*, Oxford, 1980, p. 53.
8. Flavell, 'The "School for Modesty and Humility" ', pp. 379, 401–3.
9. *Papers of Henry Laurens*, Vol. 8, pp. 326–7.
10. Flavell, 'The "School for Modesty and Humility" ', p. 394.
11. Trevor Burnard, *Creole Gentlemen: The Maryland Elite, 1691–1776*, New York and London: Routledge, 2002, p. 231.
12. John Brewer, 'Commercialization and Politics' in Neil Mckendrick, John Brewer and J.H. Plumb, eds, *The Birth of a Consumer Society: The Commercialization of Eighteenth-Century England*, London: Europa, 1982, p. 214.
13. *Papers of Henry Laurens*, Vol. 8, p. 134.
14. The Historical Society of Pennsylvania (HSP), Chew Papers, Edward Tilghman to Benjamin Chew, Middle Temple, 3 November 1773.
15. The Historical Society of Pennsylvania (HSP), Chew Papers, Edward Tilghman Sr to Benjamin Chew, 1 January 1773.
16. James H. Peeling, 'Tilghman, Edward (Feb. 11, 1750/51–Nov. 1, 1815)', *Dictionary of American Biography*, first edition, 20 vols, New York: American Council of Learned Societies, 1927–36; this edition 10 vols, New York: Charles Scribner's Sons, 1957, Vol. 9, pp. 542–3.
17. Oliver DeLancey to Lady Susannah Warren, New York, 9 January 1764, Gage Papers, East Sussex Record Office, SAS/G/ACC 1201.
18. H. Trevor Colbourn, ed., 'A Pennsylvania Farmer at the Court of King George: John Dickinson's London Letters, 1754–1756', *Pennsylvania Magazine of History and Biography*, Vol. LXXXVI (1962), pp. 422–3. p. 269.
19. Walter Jones to Thomas Jones, Edinburgh, 15 August 1766, Roger Jones Family Papers, Library of Congress (microfilm, Reel 6, Containers 15–16), Washington, DC.
20. Diary of Sylas Neville, cited in Alvin R. Riggs, 'The Colonial American Medical Student at Edinburgh', *University of Edinburgh Journal*, Vol. 20 (1961–2), p. 148; William Sachse, *The Colonial American in Britain*, Madison, Wisconsin: University of Wisconsin Press, 1956, p. 130.
21. *Papers of Henry Laurens*, Vol. 9, pp. 27–9; *ibid.*, Vol. 8, p. 389.
22. Janet Adam Smith, 'Some Eighteenth-Century Ideas of Scotland' in N.T. Phillipson and Rosalind Mitchison, eds, *Scotland in the Age of Improvement: Essays in Scottish*

History in the Eighteenth Century, Edinburgh: Edinburgh University Press, 1970, pp. 108–10; Frederick A. Pottle, ed., *Boswell's London Journal*, Melbourne, London, and Toronto: William Heinemann, 1950, p. 72; Colin Kidd, 'North Britishness and the Nature of Eighteenth-Century British Patriotisms', *Historical Journal*, Vol. 39 (1996), p. 365.

23. Cited in Smith, 'Some Eighteenth-Century Ideas of Scotland', pp. 108–10.
24. David Hackett Fischer, *Albion's Seed: Four British Folkways in America*, Oxford: Oxford University Press, 1989, p. 263.
25. James Fenimore Cooper, *Gleanings in Europe: England*, Albany, New York: State University of New York Press, 1982, pp. 27–8, 96, 269–70.
26. It is a common complaint that actor Leslie Howard did not even try to assume a southern accent when he played Ashley Wilkes in the film of *Gone With the Wind*, but Susan Myrick, who coached Howard on his 'Old South' accent during the filming, recalled that he argued that 'the Southerner of the [eighteen] sixties had a pronunciation that was closer kin to Elizabethan English than is that of the present era [1930s] state diction in England'. Howard, who did not relish the role, was probably looking for excuses, but he may have been closer to the truth than he knew. *White Columns in Hollywood: Reports from the GWTW Set* by Susan Myrick, edited and with an introduction by Richard Harwell, Macon, Georgia: Mercer University Press, 1982, p. 120.
27. *Papers of Henry Laurens*, Vol. 7, pp. 479, 328.
28. *Ibid.*, p. 482.
29. *Ibid.*, p. 475; *Ibid.*, Vol. 8, p. 481; Massey, *John Laurens and the American Revolution*, p. 39.
30. *The Diary of John Baker, Barrister of the Middle Temple, Solicitor-General of the Leeward Islands*, ed. Philip C. Yorke, London: Hutchinson, 1931 p. 17; Massey, *John Laurens and the American Revolution*, p. 41.
31. *London Chronicle*, reel for 1776, no. 2,974.
32. *Papers of Henry Laurens*, Vol. 8, p. 490.
33. HSP, Chew Papers, James Allen to Benjamin Chew, London, 12 December 1764.
34. Cited in Sachse, *The Colonial American in Britain*, p. 54.
35. *Papers of Henry Laurens*, Vol. 8, p. 31; Massey, *John Laurens and the American Revolution*, pp. 28–9; Jeremy Black, *The British Abroad: The Grand Tour in the Eighteenth Century*, Stroud and New York: Alan Sutton, 1992, p. 244.
36. Massey, *John Laurens and the American Revolution*, p. 35.
37. John Laurens to James Laurens, 17 April 1772, cited in Massy, *John Laurens and the American Revolution*, pp. 33–4.
38. *Papers of Henry Laurens*, Vol. 8, p. 547.
39. *Ibid.*, Vol. 9, p. 1; *ibid.*, Vol. 8, pp. 506–9, 567, 569.
40. *Ibid.*, Vol. 8, p. 557. Molsy was certainly in her teens when she fell pregnant, but her exact age cannot be ascertained. A search of the records in the South Carolina Historical Society, including the Laurens family genealogy and newspaper and church records, failed to uncover Molsy's date of birth, as did a check of the search database for the South Carolina Department of Archives and History. I am grateful to Mary Jo Fairchild, Reference Librarian at the South Carolina Historical Society, for undertaking the search for Molsy's record of birth. In 1769, when Molsy's mother died, she was undoubtedly a minor. Despite being Egerton Leigh's sister-in-law, she was referred to as his 'foster-child' who was young enough to require that she be ' "Educate[d] & in all respects train[ed] up . . . as his eldest daughter" '. *Papers of Henry Laurens*, Vol. 8, p. 626. Leigh's actual eldest daughter Martha was born on 5 December 1757. (John DeBrett, *The Baronetage of England*, 3rd edition, Vol. II, London, 1815, p. 797.) Molsy had a brother, Peter, who was born in 1754 (and who was also treated with 'cruelty' by John Bremar, *Papers of Henry Laurens*, Vol. 16, p. 263, fn). Molsy was probably born after him. She was still young enough to attend dancing school with her younger

cousins when she reached London in 1771, and Henry later placed her in a convent school, so she was probably a year or two older than her cousin Martha Leigh. Martha would have been fifteen by January 1773, when Henry heard of Molsy's plight. Molsy was probably seventeen or eighteen years of age.

41. Robert M. Calhoon and Robert M. Weir, ' "The Scandalous History of Sir Egerton Leigh" ', *William and Mary Quarterly*, Vol. XXVI (1969), pp. 49, 53–9.
42. *Papers of Henry Laurens*, Vol. 8, pp. 556, 558–9, 575.
43. *Ibid.*, p. 606.
44. Max Edelson, *Plantation Enterprise in South Carolina*, Cambridge, Massachusetts: Harvard University Press, 2006, pp. 227, 233; Massey, *John Laurens and the American Revolution*, p. 20.
45. *Papers of Henry Laurens*, Vol. 8, pp. 595, 606; *ibid.*, Vol. 10, p. 76.
46. *Ibid.*, Vol. 8, pp. 173, 331; *ibid.*, Vol. 9, pp. 45, 49.
47. Calhoon and Weir, ' "The Scandalous History of Sir Egerton Leigh" ', p. 63; *Papers of Henry Laurens*, Vol. 8, p. 173.
48. *Papers of Henry Laurens*, Vol. 8, pp. 331, 559; *ibid.*, Vol. 9, p. 254.
49. *Ibid.*, Vol. 7, p. 448; *ibid.*, Vol. 8, p. 326; *ibid.*, Vol. 10, p. 20.
50. For example, see Elizabeth Achenbed of Jamaica, aged thirteen, Mary Ann Morgan of Jamaica, aged nine, Catherine and Maria Lewis of Jamaica, aged thirteen and fifteen respectively, Register of Emigrants, Treasury Papers (PRO), 1773–1775. See also Andrew Jackson O'Shaughnessy, *An Empire Divided: The American Revolution and the British Caribbean*, Philadelphia, Pennsylvania: University of Pennsylvania Press, 2000, p. 20. Some Virginian families sent their daughters to English schools. The Baylors sent four of their daughters in the 1760s. Sachse, *The Colonial American in Britain*, p. 51.
51. *Papers of Henry Laurens*, Vol. 8, pp. 562, 569.
52. *Ibid.*, pp. 173, 269.
53. *Ibid.*, pp. 508–9.
54. *Ibid.*, pp. 506–9, 557.
55. *Ibid.*, pp. 506–9, 558.
56. *Ibid.*, pp. 507, 557, 561, 626; Philip D. Morgan, *Slave Counterpoint: Black Culture in the Eighteenth-Century Chesapeake & Low Country*, Chapel Hill, North Carolina, and London: University of North Carolina Press, 1998, pp. 324–5.
57. *Papers of Henry Laurens*, Vol. 8, pp. 507, 558, 560.
58. *Ibid.*, pp. 558, 575, 594–5.
59. Unfortunately, Molsy's deposition no longer exists. The depositions from the Mayor's Court (CLA/024) only survive for the periods 1641–1738 and 1803–1835 (with gaps in each sequence). There are no records of depositions for 1773. I am grateful to Bridget Howlett, senior archivist, London Metropolitan Archives, for this information.
60. *Papers of Henry Laurens*, Vol. 8, pp. 625–7, 654, 688; Massey, *John Laurens and the American Revolution*, p. 37.
61. *Papers of Henry Laurens*, Vol. 8, p. 606.
62. *Ibid.*, pp. 571, 595; *ibid.*, Vol. 9, pp. 41, 45, 254.
63. *Ibid.*, Vol. 9, pp. 25, 74.
64. *Ibid.*, p. 562.
65. *Ibid.*, Vol. 8, p. 595; *ibid.*, Vol. 10, pp. 76–7, 121.
66. *The Diary of John Baker*, p. 428; J. Jean Hecht, *The Domestic Servant Class in Eighteenth-Century England*, London: Routledge & Kegan Paul, 1956, pp. 19–20.
67. Calhoon and Weir, ' "The Scandalous History of Sir Egerton Leigh" ', pp. 47, 50, 63.
68. *Papers of Henry Laurens*, Vol. 8, p. 626.
69. *Diary and Autobiography of John Adams*, Vol. 2, 1771–1781, ed. L.H. Butterfield, Cambridge, Massachusetts: Harvard University Press, 1961, pp. 117–18.
70. Calhoon and Weir, ' "The Scandalous History of Sir Egerton Leigh" ', pp. 70–71.

Chapter Four: Young and Rich in Fleet Street: The Decadents Abroad

1. Gregory D. Massey, *John Laurens and the American Revolution*, Columbia, South Carolina: University of South Carolina Press, 2000, pp. 35–6.
2. Walter Crosby Eells, *Baccalaureate Degrees Conferred by American Colleges in the 17th and 18th Centuries*, U.S. Department of Health, Education, and Welfare: Office of Education, Circular no. 528, May 1958, pp. 4–8.
3. Julie M. Flavell, 'The "School for Modesty and Humility": Colonial American Youth in London and their Parents, 1755–1775', *Historical Journal*, Vol. 42 (1999), p. 403.
4. Julie Flavell, 'Decadents Abroad: Reconstructing the Typical Colonial American in London in the Late Colonial Period', in Leonard J. Sadosky, Peter Nicolaisen, Peter S. Onuf and Andrew O'Shaughnessy, eds, *Old World, New World: America and Europe in the Age of Jefferson*, Charlottesville, Virginia, and London: University of Virginia Press, 2010, pp. 34–6.
5. Julie Flavell, unpublished database of Americans in London between 1755 and 1775 (see Appendix) shows 123 West Indian students at the Inns of Court for that period, compared to 106 mainland American students.
6. David Lemmings, *Professors of the Law: Barristers and English Legal Culture in the Eighteenth Century*, Oxford: Oxford University Press, 2000, pp. 108, 113, 114; John F. Roche, *Joseph Reed: A Moderate in the American Revolution*, New York: Columbia University Press, 1957, p. 13.
7. Lemmings, *Professors of the Law*, pp. 70, 108; The Inner Temple Admissions Database, 17 March 2008, www.innertemple.org.uk
8. Lemmings, *Professors of the Law*, pp. 66–70.
9. *Dear Papa, Dear Charley: The Peregrinations of a Revolutionary Aristocrat, as told by Charles Carroll of Carrollton and his Father, Charles Carroll of Annapolis, with Sundry Observations on Bastardy, Child-Rearing, Romance, Matrimony, Commerce, Tobacco, Slavery, and the Politics of Revolutionary America*, ed. Ronald Hoffman, Sally D. Mason and Eleanor S. Darcy, Chapel Hill, North Carolina, and London: University of North Carolina Press, 2001, 3 vols, Vol. I, pp. 1–2, 14.
10. Hoffman et al., eds, *Dear Papa, Dear Charley*, Vol. I, pp. 136, 137, 149.
11. *Diary and Autobiography of John Adams*, Vol. 2, 1771–1781, ed. L.H. Butterfield, Cambridge, Massachusetts: Harvard University Press, 1961, p. 117.
12. H. Trevor Colbourn, ed., 'A Pennsylvania Farmer at the Court of King George: John Dickinson's London Letters, 1754–1756', *Pennsylvania Magazine of History and Biography*, Vol. LXXXVI (1962), p. 243.
13. *Ibid.*, pp. 249, 251.
14. *Ibid.*, p. 251.
15. Hoffman et al., eds, *Dear Papa, Dear Charley*, Vol. I, pp. 303–4. The original text reads 'Coke Little', by which is probably meant 'Coke upon Littleton', a standard legal text. I am grateful to Professor Peter Marshall for drawing this to my attention.
16. The Historical Society of Pennsylvania (HSP), Ebenezer Hazard Journal, 1770–1771; V.A.C. Gatrell, *The Hanging Tree: Execution and the English People, 1770–1868*, Oxford: Oxford University Press, 1994, pp. 137–8.
17. The *Papers of Henry Laurens*, ed. George C. Rogers, Jr., et al., 16 vols, Columbia, South Carolina: University of South Carolina Press, 1968–2002, Vol. 9, p. 644; *ibid.*, Vol. 10, pp. 11, 87.
18. Massey, *John Laurens and the American Revolution*, pp. 44, 45.
19. *Papers of Henry Laurens*, Vol. 10, p. 34.
20. Lemmings, *Professors of the Law*, pp. 25, 27, 223.
21. *Ibid.*, pp. 143, 223, 225, 307.
22. *Ibid.*, pp. 15, 115, 143.

23. *Ibid.*, pp. 25–7.
24. Hoffman et al., eds, *Dear Papa, Dear Charley*, Vol. I, p. 220; Colbourn, ed., 'Dickinson's London Letters', p. 276.
25. Colbourn, ed., 'Dickinson's London Letters', p. 275; Christopher Hibbert, *The Personal History of Samuel Johnson*, London: Longman, 1971; this edition Newton Abbot: Readers Union, 1973, pp. 82, 88; Henry F. MacGeah and A.A.C. Sturgess, *Register of Admissions to the Honourable Society of the Middle Temple from the Fifteenth Century to the Year 1944*, London, 1949, 2 vols, Vol. 2, p. 356.
26. Granville Sharp, *A Representation of the Injustice and Dangerous Tendency of Tolerating Slavery; or of Admitting the Least Claim of Private Property in the Persons of Men, in England* (London, 1769), p. 88.
27. *The St James's Chronicle, or The British Evening-Post*, 18–20 March 1762, no. 160.
28. Palfrey's London Journal, 1775, Palfrey Family Papers, bMS Am 1704.18 (46), Houghton Library, Harvard University.
29. George Rudé, *Hanoverian London, 1714–1808*, London: Secker & Warburg, 1971, pp. 55–6; Ben Rogers, *Beef and Liberty: Roast Beef, John Bull and the English Nation*, London: Chatto & Windus, 2003, p. 75.
30. *Papers of Henry Laurens*, Vol. 9, p. 622, fn, and p. 645.
31. Benjamin Franklin, *Autobiography and Other Writings*, New York and Oxford: Oxford University Press, World's Classics Paperback, 1993, p. 46.
32. Richard D. Altick, *The Shows of London*, Cambridge, Massachusetts: Harvard University Press, 1978, pp. 52, 55, 57.
33. John Summerson, *Georgian London*, London: Pleiades Books, 1945; this edition Cambridge, Massachusetts: MIT Press, 1978, pp. 44, 58; *The London Encyclopædia*, ed. Ben Weinreb and Christopher Hibbert, London: Macmillan, 1983, p. 212.
34. Esmond Wright, *Franklin of Philadelphia*, Cambridge, Massachusetts: Harvard University Press, 1986, p. 114
35. *Papers of Henry Laurens*, Vol. 10, p. 34.
36. HSP, Chew Papers, Edward Tilghman to Benjamin Chew, London, 17 June 1772; Hoffman et al., eds, *Dear Papa, Dear Charley*, Vol. I, p. 167.
37. William Sachse, *The Colonial American in Britain*, Madison, Wisconsin: The University of Wisconsin Press, 1956, p. 162.
38. Kenneth Silverman, *A Cultural History of the American Revolution: Painting, Music, Literature and the Theatre in the Colonies and the United States from the Treaty of Paris to the Inauguration of George Washington, 1763–1789*, New York: Crowell, 1976, p. 132; Sachse, *The Colonial American in Britain*, pp. 112, 162–4, 173.
39. Maurie D. McInnis, *In Pursuit of Refinement: Charlestonians Abroad, 1740–1860*, Columbia, South Carolina: University of South Carolina Press, 1999, p. 12.
40. *Papers of Henry Laurens*, Vol. 9, p. 648; *ibid.*, Vol. 10, pp. 58–9.
41. *Ibid.*, Vol. 9, pp. 588–9, 631; *ibid.*, Vol. 10, p. 100.
42. *Ibid.*, Vol. 10, p. 52.
43. *Ibid.*, pp. 93–4, 103.
44. Massey, *John Laurens and the American Revolution*, pp. 43–4.
45. *Papers of Henry Laurens*, Vol. 10, pp. 35–6, 77.
46. Peter Rowland, *The Life and Times of Thomas Day, 1748–1789: English Philanthropist and Author*, Lewiston, Queenston and Lampeter: The Edwin Mellen Press, 1996, p. 12.
47. *Ibid.*, p. 54.
48. *Papers of Henry Laurens*, Vol. 10, p. 59.
49. Jenny Uglow, *The Lunar Men: The Friends Who Made the Future 1730–1810*, London: Faber & Faber, 2002, pp. 124, 154.
50. Rowland, *The Life and Times of Thomas Day*, p. 330.
51. *Ibid.*, pp. 21, 27.
52. Massey, *John Laurens and the American Revolution*, p. 53.
53. Rowland, *The Life and Times of Thomas Day*, pp. 54–5, 80.

54. *Papers of Henry Laurens*, Vol. 11, pp. 276–7; Rowland, *The Life and Times of Thomas Day*, p. 82.
55. Gregory D. Massey, 'The Limits of Antislavery Thought in the Revolutionary Lower South: John Laurens and Henry Laurens', *Journal of Southern History*, Vol. 63 (1997), pp. 500, 506–7, 513.
56. Rowland, *The Life and Times of Thomas Day*, pp. 81–2, 383.
57. *Ibid.*, pp. 207–14.
58. Massey, 'The Limits of Antislavery Thought in the Revolutionary Lower South: John Laurens and Henry Laurens', pp. 510–11.
59. Michael Edwardes, *The Nabobs at Home*, London: John Constable, 1991, pp. 52–8.
60. Maria Edgeworth, *The Absentee*, first published 1812; this edition London: Penguin, 1999, pp. 5–6.
61. *The West Indian: A Comedy As it is performed at the Theatre Royal, in Drury-Lane*. By Richard Cumberland. Printed 1771.
62. Silverman, *A Cultural History of the American Revolution*, p. 237.
63. Rebecca Starr, *A School for Politics: Commercial Lobbying and Political Culture in Early South Carolina*, Baltimore, Maryland, and London: The Johns Hopkins University Press, 1998, p. 66.
64. At least two, and probably four West Indians signed – John Ellis, who had encouraged John Laurens's interest in the natural world, John Alleyne of Barbados (who was related to Benjamin Franklin by marriage), and Charles and Peeke Fuller, probably of the Fuller family of Jamaica. The Fullers were a well-known Jamaican planter family, with prominent members resident in London. Peeke was another Jamaican family name. Almost nothing is known of Charles or Peeke Fuller, but Peeke was commissioned as a captain in the 46th Foot on 26 October 1763. I am indebted to Trevor Burnard for information on the Fuller family, and to Stephen Conway for confirmation of the details of Peeke Fuller's commission.
65. *Papers of Henry Laurens*, Vol. 9, p. 648.
66. *Ibid.*, p. 651; *ibid.*, Vol. 10, p. 75.
67. *Ibid.*, Vol. 10, pp. 57–8. John Laurens is best known for his exploits as a military hero of the American Revolution, but his conflict with his father during his latter years in London is told briefly in David Duncan Wallace, *The Life of Henry Laurens. With a Sketch of the Life of Lieutenant-Colonel John Laurens*, New York and London, 1915, pp. 470 and ff., and in greater depth in Massey, *John Laurens and the American Revolution*, chs. 2 and 3.
68. *Proceedings and Debates of the British Parliaments Respecting North America, 1754–1783*, ed. R.C. Simmons and P.D.G. Thomas, 6 vols, White Plains, New York: Kraus International, 1982, Vol. 5, p. 347.
69. Massey, *John Laurens and the American Revolution*, p. 22.
70. Crane, *Benjamin Franklin's Letters to the Press*, pp. 281–2. Crane attributes this article to Franklin, but it was probably written by American MP Henry Cruger, who had become incoherent with rage when he tried to respond to Grant in the House of Commons.
71. *Papers of Henry Laurens*, Vol. 9, pp. 651–2.
72. Rowland, *The Life and Times of Thomas Day*, p. 80.
73. *Ibid.*, p. 87; *The Papers of Benjamin Franklin*, ed. L.W. Labaree et al., 39 vols, New Haven, Connecticut, and London: Yale University Press, 1959–, Vol. 21, p. 453.
74. *Papers of Henry Laurens*, Vol. 10, p. 81.
75. Julie M. Flavell, 'Government Interception of Letters from America and the Quest for Colonial Opinion in 1775', *William and Mary Quarterly*, 3rd series, Vol. LVIII (2001), p. 417.
76. *Ibid.*, p. 417.
77. James Hutchinson to Isreal Pemberton, London, 20th.12 mo., 1775, and same to same, 6 mo. 12th. 1776, James Hutchinson Papers, American Philosophical Society.

78. *Papers of Henry Laurens*, Vol. 9, p. 647; *ibid.*, Vol. 10, p. 335; Flavell, 'Government Interception of Letters from America', p. 416.
79. On mention of Henry Laurens in the London newspapers, see, for example, the *Morning Post and Daily Advertiser*, no. 863, 2 August 1775.
80. *Papers of Henry Laurens*, Vol. 10, pp. 33, 362, 512.
81. Sachse, *The Colonial American in Britain*, p. 189; Mary M. Drummond, 'Middleton, William (1748–1829)' in Lewis Namier and John Brooke, *The History of Parliament: The House of Commons, 1754–1790*, 3 vols, London: Her Majesty's Stationery Office, 1964, Vol. 3, p. 137; *Biographical Directory of the South Carolina House of Representatives*, Vol. 3: *The Commons House of Assembly, 1775–1790* by N. Louise Bailey and Elizabeth Ivey Cooper, Columbia, South Carolina: University of South Carolina Press, 1981, pp. 458–9, 494–5.
82. Massey, *John Laurens and the American Revolution*, p. 65.
83. *Ibid.*, p. 53.
84. *Papers of Henry Laurens*, Vol. 10, p. 452; Massey, *John Laurens and the American Revolution*, p. 56.
85. *Papers of Henry Laurens*, Vol. 10, pp. 452–3; Massey, *John Laurens and the American Revolution*, pp. 56–7.
86. *Papers of Henry Laurens*, Vol. 10, p. 617.
87. Massey, *John Laurens and the American Revolution*, p. 58.
88. For an excerpt of John Laurens's letter to his uncle on the circumstances of his marriage, see Wallace, *The Life of Henry Laurens. With a Sketch of the Life of Lieutenant-Colonel John Laurens*, p. 465.
89. Sachse, *The Colonial American in Britain*, p. 192; *Chain of Friendship: Selected Letters of Dr John Fothergill, 1735–1780*, ed. Betsy C. Corner and Christopher C. Booth, Cambridge, Massachusetts: Harvard University Press, 1971, pp. 471–2, fn.
90. *Papers of Henry Laurens*, Vol. 11, pp. 277–8.
91. Wallace, *The Life of Henry Laurens. With a Sketch of the Life of Lieutenant-Colonel John Laurens*, p. 471.
92. Cited from *ibid.*, p. 489.
93. *Papers of Henry Laurens*, Vol. 11, p. 204; Massey, 'The Limits of Antislavery Thought in the Revolutionary Lower South', p. 511.
94. Massey, *John Laurens and the American Revolution*, p. 92.
95. Cited from Frank Edward Ross, 'Laurens, John (Oct. 28, 1754–Aug. 27, 1782)', *Dictionary of American Biography*, Vol. 6, pp. 35–6.
96. Philip K. Goff, 'Laurens, John (28 Oct. 1754–25 or 27 Aug. 1782)', *American National Biography*, 24 vols, New York and Oxford: Oxford University Press, 1999, Vol. 13, p. 263.
97. Massey, 'The Limits of Antislavery Thought in the Revolutionary Lower South', pp. 518, 524; on Read, see Anne King Gregorie, 'Read, Jacob (1752–July 16, 1816)', *Dictionary of American Biography*, Vol. 8, p. 425.
98. Massey, 'The Limits of Antislavery Thought in the Revolutionary Lower South', pp. 528, 529; *Papers of Henry Laurens*, Vol. 16, p. 555.

Chapter Five: A Long Island Yankee in the City

1. George Rudé, *Hanoverian London 1714–1808*, London: Secker & Warburg, 1971, pp. ix, xi, 4.
2. John Alden, *Stephen Sayre, American Revolutionary Adventurer*, Baton Rouge, Louisiana, and London: Louisiana State University Press, 1983, p. 7.
3. T.H. Breen, ' "Baubles of Britain": The American and Consumer Revolutions of the Eighteenth Century', *Past and Present*, no. 119 (May 1988), pp. 78–80.
4. Alden, *Stephen Sayre*, pp. 1–3.
5. Ian K. Steele, *The English Atlantic 1675–1740: An Exploration of Communication and Community*, New York and Oxford: Oxford University Press, 1986, pp. 140, 149–50.

6. John Shy, *Toward Lexington: The Role of the British Army in the Coming of the American Revolution*, Princeton, New Jersey: Princeton University Press, 1965, p. 144, 385; Alden, *Stephen Sayre*, p. 7.

7. William Alexander Duer, *The Life of William Alexander, Earl of Stirling*, New York: Collections of the New Jersey Historical Society, Vol. 2, 1847, pp. 27–8.

8. Duer, *The Life of William Alexander*, p. 50.

9. Joseph Reed to Charles Pettit, London, 25 June 1770, Joseph Reed Papers (BV Reed, Joseph), New-York Historical Society. Used by courtesy of The New-York Historical Society.

10. Duer, *The Life of William Alexander*, pp. 9–10, 46, 50 fn.

11. *Ibid.*, p. 12; Edith, Lady Haden-Guest, 'Morris, Staats Long (1728–1800)' in Lewis Namier and John Brooke, eds, *The History of Parliament: The House of Commons, 1754–1790*, 3 vols, London: Her Majesty's Stationery Office, 1964, Vol. 3, pp. 168–9.

12. Duer, *The Life of William Alexander*, pp. 51, 55, 58, 67–8, 74, 87–8.

13. *Ibid.*, p. 10; Alden, *Stephen Sayre*, p. 8; William Sachse, *The Colonial American in Britain*, Madison, Wisconsin: University of Wisconsin Press, 1956, pp. 99, 101, 104.

14. Alden, *Stephen Sayre*, p. 8; Stephen Sayre to Joseph Reed, London, 19 June 1769, Joseph Reed Papers (BV Reed, Joseph).

15. Stephen Sayre to Joseph Reed, St Croix, 20 February 1765, Joseph Reed Papers (BV Reed, Joseph).

16. Rudé, *Hanoverian London 1714–1808*, p. 54; for examples of well-to-do English and Portuguese merchants living in the Yard, see Old Bailey Proceedings Online (www.oldbaileyonline.org, 9 September 2009); 18 February 1778, trials of Matthew Jones et al. (t17780218-45), and 9 September 1772, trial of William Row (t17720909-20); see Old Bailey Proceedings Online (www.oldbaileyonline.org, 9 September 2009); 9 January 1788, trials of Isaac Jesuran Alvarez et al. (t17880109-56), for an example of a trader who kept a counting house only in Tokenhouse Yard; on living arrangements in general for merchants, see also (and cited from) *Joshua Johnson's Letterbook, 1771–1774: Letters from a Merchant in London to his Partners in Maryland*, ed. Jacob M. Price, London Record Society, 1974, p. xxii.

17. Sachse, *The Colonial American in Britain*, p. 24.

18. Jonathan R. Dull, *A Diplomatic History of the American Revolution*, New Haven, Connecticut, and London: Yale University Press, 1985, pp. 14–18; John J. McCusker and Russell R. Menard, *The Economy of British America, 1607–1789*, Chapel Hill, North Carolina: University of North Carolina Press, 1985, 1991, p. 36; T.O. Lloyd, *The British Empire, 1558–1983*, Oxford: Oxford University Press, 1984, p. 57.

19. Richard Tames, *A Traveller's History of London*, London and Adlestrop: The Windrush Press, 2002, p. 13; John Summerson, *Georgian London*, London: Pleiades Books, 1945; this edition Cambridge, Massachusetts: MIT Press, 1978, pp. 266–7.

20. Joseph Addison and Richard Steele, *The Spectator; With Notes and a General Index*, 2 vols, Philadelphia, Pennsylvania: published by J.J. Woodward, 1836, no. 69; Saturday, May 19, 1711, 'Visit to the Royal Exchange – Benefit of extensive Commerce', p. 114.

21. *The London Encyclopædia*, ed. Ben Weinreb and Christopher Hibbert, London: Macmillan, 1983, p. 508; Summerson, *Georgian London*, pp. 62–3.

22. *The Papers of Henry Laurens*, ed. George C. Rogers, Jr., et al., 16 vols, Columbia, South Carolina: University of South Carolina Press, 1968–2002, Vol. 8, p. 269.

23. Bernard Bailyn, *Voyagers to the West: A Passage in the Peopling of America on the Eve of the Revolution*, New York: Alfred A. Knopf, 1987, p. 276; Robert Greenhalgh Albion, *The Rise of New York Port [1815–1860]*, Newton Abbot: David & Charles, 1970, p. 265.

24. Josiah Quincy, Jr., *Memoirs of the Life of Josiah Quincy, Junior, of Massachusetts: 1744–1775* (Boston, 1874), p. 249; Eric Stockdale, *Middle Temple Lawyers and the American Revolution*, Eagan, Minnesota: Thomson-West, 2007, p. 51.

25. John and Linda Pelzer, 'The Coffee Houses of Augustan London', *History Today*, Vol. 32 (October 1982), pp. 40–47.

26. Michael Kammen, *A Rope of Sand: The Colonial Agents, British Politics, and the American Revolution*, Ithaca, New York: Cornell University Press, 1968, this edition New York: Vintage Books, 1974, p. 16; *The London Encyclopædia*, p. 943; Alison G. Olson, *Making the Empire Work: London and American Interest Groups, 1690–1790*, Cambridge, Massachusetts: Harvard University Press, 1992, p. 97; Sachse, *The Colonial American in Britain*, pp. 17–18; Peter Fryer, *Staying Power: The History of Black People in Britain*, London: Pluto Press, 1984, p. 60.

27. Esmond Wright, *Franklin of Philadelphia*, Cambridge, Massachusetts: Harvard University Press, 1986, p. 217.

28. Rudé, *Hanoverian London 1714–1808*, p. 54; Summerson, *Georgian London*, p. 64.

29. Price, 'Who Cared about the Colonies? The Impact of the Thirteen Colonies on British Society and Politics, circa 1714–1775', in Bernard Bailyn and Philip D. Morgan, eds, *Strangers within the Realm: Cultural Margins of the First British Empire*, Chapel Hill, North Carolina: University of North Carolina Press, 1991, p. 417.

30. Julie M. Flavell and Gordon Hay, 'Using Capture-Recapture Methods to Reconstruct the American Population in London', *Journal of Interdisciplinary History*, XXXII (2001), p. 42; Julie Flavell, 'Decadents Abroad: Reconstructing the Typical Colonial American in London in the Late Colonial Period' in Leonard J. Sadosky, Peter Nicolaisen, Peter S. Onuf, and Andrew J.O'Shaughnessy, eds, *Old World, New World: America and Europe in the Age of Jefferson*, Charlottesville, Virginia and London: University of Virginia Press, 2010, pp. 35–6.

31. John Adams to Abigail Adams, 3 August 1776, in Paul H. Smith et al., eds, *Letters of Delegates to Congress, 1774–1789*, 14 vols to date, Washington, D.C.: Library of Congress, 1976–, Vol. 4, p. 611.

32. Flavell and Hay, 'Using Capture-Recapture Methods to Reconstruct the American Population in London', p. 43. Henry Laurens knew the Vaughans, a West Indian family with Boston connections. Merchant Samuel Vaughan was married to Sarah Hallowell of Boston. (*Papers of Henry Laurens*, Vol. 8, p. 327, and 'Journal of Josiah Quincy, Jun., During his Voyage and Residence in England from September 28th, 1774, to March 3d, 1775', *Proceedings* of the Massachusetts Historical Society, Vol. 50 (1916–17), p. 443, fn.) He also knew Richard Oliver of Antigua, who became an MP and whose Massachusetts connections are mentioned in O'Shaughnessy, *An Empire Divided: The American Revolution and the British Caribbean*, Philadelphia, Pennsylvania: University of Pennsylvania Press, 2000. Significantly, the only student from Massachusetts at the Inns of Court when John Laurens attended was William Vassall, whose family had prominent connections in the West Indies. (*Papers of Henry Laurens*, Vol. 8, p. 121; Andrew Jackson O'Shaughnessy, *An Empire Divided*, p. 18; Edward A. Jones, *American Members of the Inns of Court*, London, 1924, p. 212)

33. *Papers of Henry Laurens*, Vol. 9, pp. 377–8; Julie Flavell, 'British Perceptions of New England and the Decision for a Coercive Colonial Policy, 1774–1775' in Julie Flavell and Stephen Conway, eds, *Britain and America Go to War: The Impact of War and Warfare in Anglo-America, 1754–1815*, Gainesville, Florida: University Press of Florida, 2004, pp. 106–8; Staffordshire Record Office, Dartmouth MSS, D(W)1778/II/1165, Richard Oswald, 'Sketch of an Examination at the Bar of the House', enclosure in a letter of Oswald to Lord Dartmouth, 27 February 1775; Dartmouth MSS, D(W)1778/II/1139, Richard Oswald, 'Thoughts on the State of America', enclosure in a letter of Oswald to Lord Dartmouth, 9 February 1775.

34. John M. Murrin, 'A Roof without Walls: The Dilemma of American National Identity' in Richard Beeman, Stephen Botein and Edward Carter II, eds, *Beyond Confederation: Origins of the Constitution and American National Identity*, Chapel Hill, North Carolina: University of North Carolina Press, 1987, p. 343.

35. *The Writings and Speeches of Edmund Burke*, Vol. III: *Party, Parliament, and the American War, 1774–1780*, ed. Warren M. Elofson and John A. Woods, Oxford: Clarendon Press, 1996, p. 219.
36. Flavell, 'British Perceptions of New England and the Decision for a Coercive Colonial Policy, 1774–1775', p. 105.
37. Joseph A. Conforti, *Imagining New England: Explorations of Regional Identity from the Pilgrims to the Mid-Twentieth Century*, Chapel Hill, North Carolina, and London: University of North Carolina Press, 2001, pp. 271–83.
38. Cited in T.H. Breen, 'Ideology and Nationalism on the Eve of the American Revolution: Revisions *Once More* in Need of Revising', *Journal of American History*, Vol. 84, no. 1 (June 1997), p. 32.
39. John Bernard, *Retrospections of America 1797–1811*, first published New York and London, 1887; this edition New York: Benjamin Blom, 1969, p. 31.
40. E.A. Wrigley, 'A Simple Model of London's Importance in Changing English Society and Economy 1650–1750', *Past and Present*, no. 37 (1967), p. 49; Daniel Statt, *Foreigners and Englishmen: The Controversy over Immigration and Population, 1660–1760*, Newark, Delaware: University of Delaware Press; London and Toronto: Associated University Presses, 1995, pp. 29–30; Robin Gwynn, *The Huguenots of London*, Brighton and Portland, Oregon: Alpha Press, 1998, p. 4.
41. Thomas Chandler Haliburton, *The Attaché, or Sam Slick in England*, first published 1844; this edition Stroud, Gloucestershire: Nonsuch Publishing, 2005, p. 35.
42. Andrew Oliver, ed., *The Journal of Samuel Curwen, Loyalist*, Cambridge, Massachusetts: Harvard University Press, 2 vols, 1972, Vol. 1, pp. 118, 162, 184, 187.
43. Francis Hodge, *Yankee Theatre: The Image of America on the Stage, 1825–1850*, Austin, Texas: University of Texas Press, 1964, p. 41; Bernard, *Retrospections of America 1797–1811*, pp. 37–8.
44. David Hackett Fischer, *Albion's Seed: Four British Folkways in America*, Oxford: Oxford University Press, 1989, pp. 57–9.
45. R.H. Lee, *Life of Arthur Lee, LL.D.*, 2 vols, Boston, 1829; reprinted, Freeport, New York: Books for Libraries Press, 1969, Vol. II, p. 391.
46. Stephen Sayre to Joseph Reed, Boston, 3 September 1766, Joseph Reed Papers (BV Reed, Joseph).
47. Lawrence Stone, *The Family, Sex and Marriage in England 1500–1800*, London: Penguin, 1977, pp. 377–9, cited at p. 377.
48. Sachse, *The Colonial American in Britain*, p. 125.
49. J. Jean Hecht, *The Domestic Servant Class in Eighteenth-Century England*, London: Routledge & Kegan Paul, 1956, pp. 210–11.
50. Royall Tyler, *The Contrast*, 1787.
51. Hecht, *The Domestic Servant Class in Eighteenth-Century England*, p. 85.
52. E.J. Burford, *Royal St James's: Being a Story of Kings, Clubmen and Courtesans*, London: Robert Hale, 1988, p. 116.
53. Lawrence Stone, *Uncertain Unions: Marriage in England 1660–1753*, Oxford: Oxford University Press, 1992, pp. 128–9.
54. Thomas Ruston to Job Ruston, London, 4 February 1767, Thomas Ruston Collection, Library of Congress; Stone, *The Family, Sex and Marriage in England 1500–1800*, p. 317.
55. Alden, *Stephen Sayre*, p. 19.
56. John F. Roche, *Joseph Reed: A Moderate in the American Revolution*, New York: Columbia University Press, 1957, p. 18.
57. 'Letters of Dennys De Berdt, 1757–1770', *Publications of the Colonial Society of Massachusetts*, Vol. 13 (1917), pp. 410–12, 419, 426, 431, 436–7; Kammen, *A Rope of Sand*, pp. 30, 78.
58. Colin Bonwick, *English Radicals and the American Revolution*, Chapel Hill, North Carolina: University of North Carolina Press, 1977, pp. 52, 190–95; Kammen, *A Rope of Sand*, pp. 76–8, 201.
59. Bonwick, *English Radicals and the American Revolution*, pp. 44–5.

60. Dr John Fothergill, *Considerations Relative to the North American Colonies*, London, 1765, p. 36.
61. T.O. Lloyd, *The British Empire 1558–1983*, Oxford: Oxford University Press, 1984, pp. 87–8.
62. 'Letters of Dennys De Berdt', pp. 428, 436–8.
63. Peter Rowland, *The Life and Times of Thomas Day, 1748–1789: English Philanthropist and Author*, Lewiston, Queenston and Lampeter: The Edwin Mellen Press, 1996, p. 83.
64. 'Letters of Dennys De Berdt', p. 136.
65. *Ibid.*, p. 319.
66. Alden, *Stephen Sayre*, p. 16; Stephen Sayre to Joseph Reed, St Croix, 20 February 1765, Joseph Reed Papers (BV Reed, Joseph).
67. Francis Wharton, ed., *The Revolutionary Diplomatic Correspondence of the United States*, 6 vols, Washington, D.C.: Government Printing Office, 1889, Vol. I, p. 139.
68. Alden, *Stephen Sayre*, p. 7, fn; Stephen Sayre to Joseph Reed, London, 10 March 1769, and Stephen Sayre to Joseph Reed, London, 19 June 1769, Joseph Reed Papers (BV Reed, Joseph).
69. Alden in his biography of Sayre (p. 9, fn) mistakenly gives the De Berdts' address as Artillery Row in the West End, which still exists. Artillery Court does not; it was off Chiswell Street, between Bunhill Row and City Road, leading into the entrance of the old Artillery Ground (Stockdale, *Middle Temple Lawyers and the American Revolution*, p. 111).
70. Joseph Reed to Charles Pettit, London, 7 May 1770, Joseph Reed Papers (BV Reed, Joseph).
71. *Ibid.*, London, 25 June 1770, Joseph Reed Papers (BV Reed, Joseph).
72. Roche, *Joseph Reed: A Moderate in the American Revolution*, p. 19.
73. Stone, *The Family, Sex and Marriage in England 1500–1800*, pp. 283, 324, 328–9.
74. Stephen Sayre to Joseph Reed, St Croix, 20 February 1765, Joseph Reed Papers (BV Reed, Joseph); Roche, *Joseph Reed: A Moderate in the American Revolution*, pp. 19–20.
75. Cited in Alden, *Stephen Sayre*, p. 19.
76. Stephen Sayre to Joseph Reed, London, 3 July 1768, Joseph Reed Papers (BV Reed, Joseph); William B. Reed, *The Life of Esther De Berdt Reed*, Philadelphia, Pennsylvania 1853, this edition New York: Arno Press, 1971, pp. 122–6; 'Stephen Sayre' in Clifford K. Shipton, *Sibley's Harvard Graduates: Biographical Sketches of those who attended Harvard College*, 18 vols, Boston: The Massachusetts Historical Society, 1873–, Vol. 14 (1756–1760), p. 206.
77. Reed, *Life of Esther De Berdt Reed*, pp. 105–6.
78. Kammen, *A Rope of Sand*, pp. 129–30; 'Letters of Dennys De Berdt', p. 299.
79. Joseph Reed to Charles Pettit, London, 7 May 1770, Joseph Reed Papers (BV Reed, Joseph).
80. Roche, *Joseph Reed: A Moderate in the American Revolution*, p. 18; 'Stephen Sayre' in James McLachlan, *Princetonians, 1748–1768: A Biographical Dictionary*, Princeton, New Jersey: Princeton University Press, 1976, p. 205.
81. *Life of Esther De Berdt Reed*, pp. 179–80; Stockdale, *Middle Temple Lawyers and the American Revolution*, p. 91.
82. Stockdale, *Middle Temple Lawyers and the American Revolution*, p. 82.
83. The Historical Society of Pennsylvania (HSP), Chew Papers, James Allen to Benjamin Chew, London, 12 December 1764, and Andrew Allen to Benjamin Chew, 2 July 1763, London.
84. *Life of Esther De Berdt Reed*, pp. 179–80.
85. Stockdale, *Middle Temple Lawyers and the American Revolution*, pp. 83, 85.
86. Duer, *The Life of William Alexander*, pp. 67–8.
87. John Watts to Sir James Napier, New York, 9 August 1764, in *The Letterbook of John Watts (1762–1765)*, Collections of the New York Historical Society, 61 (1928), p. 278; see also John Watts to Sir William Baker, New York, 13 May 1763, and John Watts to Sir William Baker, New York, 11 August 1764, *ibid.*, pp. 142, 282.

88. Thomas Ruston Journal, 1762–1765, Library of Congress, Washington, D.C., and Thomas Ruston to Mrs Ann Ruston, London, 4 February 1766, Thomas Ruston Collection, Library of Congress, Washington, D.C.

89. Thomas Ruston to Job Ruston, London, 4 July 1768, Thomas Ruston Collection, Library of Congress, Washington, D.C.

90. Thomas Ruston to Job Ruston, London, 4 July 1768, Thomas Ruston Collection, Library of Congress.

91. Julie M. Flavell, 'The "School for Modesty and Humility": Colonial American Youth in London and their Parents, 1755–1775', The Historical Journal, Vol. 42 (1999), p. 389.

92. Alden, Stephen Sayre, pp. 9, 11; Records of the Honorable Society of Lincoln's Inn, Vol. I: Admissions from 1420 to 1799 (Lincoln's Inn, 1896), p. 452, lists John Nelthorpe of Little Grimsby, Lincolnshire, 1 March 1762. On Charlotte Nelthorpe, see Nelthorpe of Scawby in Lincolnshire Pedigrees, ed. Rev. Canon A.R. Maddison, Vol. II (London, 1903), p. 705. Her father was Baronet of Barton and Scawby, as was her brother John. The cousin John Nelthorpe at Lincoln's Inn was one of the Nelthorpes of Little Grimsby, see Lincolnshire Pedigrees, Vol. II, p. 703. He was at Lincoln's Inn with Peter DeLancey.

93. Stephen Sayre to Joseph Reed, St Croix, 5 December 1764, Joseph Reed Papers (BV Reed, Joseph).

94. Stephen Sayre to Joseph Reed, St Croix, 20 February 1765, Joseph Reed Papers (BV Reed, Joseph); Alden, Stephen Sayre, p. 9. William Neate the merchant traded to New York and Pennsylvania. Sayre did business with the merchant house of Neate & Co. on behalf of De Berdt (Sayre to Reed, London, 19 June 1769, Joseph Reed Papers, BV Reed, Joseph).

95. Alden, Stephen Sayre, p. 22.

96. Stephen Sayre to Joseph Reed, London, 29 March 1768, and Stephen Sayre to Joseph Reed, 3 July 1768, Joseph Reed Papers (BV Reed, Joseph).

97. Stone, The Family, Sex and Marriage in England 1500–1800, pp. 377–9.

98. Rosamond Bayne-Powell, Travellers in Eighteenth-Century England, London: John Murray, 1951, pp. 62–3.

99. Frederick A. Pottle, ed., Boswell's London Journal 1762–1763, Melbourne, London and Toronto: William Heinemann, 1950, pp. 49–50, 135–61.

100. Kammen, A Rope of Sand, pp. 120–21; Alden, Stephen Sayre, pp. 14–15.

101. Charles Townshend Papers (RH 4/98), on microfilm in the Scottish Record Office, Edinburgh. Originals are in the William L. Clements Library. 'Answers to Q.s Mr. Sayre' is on reel 9: 'Papers mainly relating to America, including report of examinations before the Parliamentary committee for American affairs, 1766' (8/44/34). On 3 February 1766 'Stephen Sayre' was ordered to attend next day as a witness, but there is no evidence he was called upon to testify. R.C. Simmons and P.D.G. Thomas, eds, Proceedings and Debates of the British Parliaments Respecting North America, 1754–1783, White Plains, New York: Kraus International, 1982, Vol. II, p. 134. I am grateful to Peter Thomas for drawing this reference to my attention.

102. 'Letters of Dennys De Berdt', p. 318; Alden, Stephen Sayre, p. 17.

103. 'Letters of Dennys De Berdt', p. 453.

104. Portions of the pamphlet simply reprinted two of De Berdt's letters to Shelburne and Dartmouth. 'Letters of Dennys De Berdt', p. 438, fn.

105. Stephen Sayre, The Englishman Deceived, A Political Piece: Wherein some very important Secrets of State are briefly recited, and offered to the Consideration of the Public London, 1768, pp. 49–51.

106. For example, the Gentleman's Magazine, a popular London publication, printed 'A Song sung at Boston, in New-England', in which rustic New Englanders sang their willingness to 'Eat the crust of the tree, And away to the fig-leaf again', rather than pay unconstitutional taxes (1765). Stephen's pamphlet enjoyed a brief period of celebrity in London, inflating his ego so much that Hetta wrote, 'I begin to fear the effect this applause may have on his mind' (Life of Esther De Berdt Reed, p. 129).

107. Louis W. Potts, *Arthur Lee, A Virtuous Revolutionary*, Baton Rouge, Louisiana, and London: Louisiana State University Press 1981, p. 73; 'Letters of Dennys De Berdt', p. 302, fn.
108. Alden, *Stephen Sayre*, pp. 30–31; Kammen, *A Rope of Sand*, p. 177.
109. Arthur Lee to Richard Henry Lee, 18 September 1769, Paul P. Hoffman, ed., *Lee Family Papers 1742–1795*, Microfilm Publications, University of Virginia Library, 1966–, Roll 1.
110. Dennis De Berdt to Joseph Reed, 8 February 1768, Joseph Reed Papers (BV Reed, Joseph); 'Stephen Sayre' in Shipton, *Sibley's Harvard Graduates*, Vol. 14 (1756–1760), p. 205.
111. Joseph Reed to Charles Pettit, London, 8 June 1770; Joseph Reed to Charles Pettit, London, 7 May 1770; Joseph Reed to Charles Pettit, London, 25 June 1770, Joseph Reed Papers (BV Reed, Joseph).
112. Alden, *Stephen Sayre*, p. 25.

Chapter Six: 'The Handsome Englishman'

1. *The London Encyclopædia*, ed. Ben Weinreb and Christopher Hibbert, London: Macmillan, 1983, p. 446.
2. Peter D.G. Thomas, *Revolution in America: Britain & the Colonies 1763–1776*, Cardiff: University of Wales Press, 1992, pp. 7–8.
3. George Rudé, *Wilkes and Liberty: A Social Study of 1763 to 1774*, Oxford: Clarendon Press, 1962, pp. 176, 179; H.T. Dickinson, *Liberty and Property: Political Ideology in Eighteenth-Century Britain*, London: Weidenfeld & Nicolson, 1977; this edition London: Methuen, 1979, pp. 205, 211–13; John Brewer, 'Commercialization and Politics', in Neil Mckendrick, John Brewer and J.H. Plumb, eds, *The Birth of a Consumer Society: The Commercialization of Eighteenth-Century England*, London: Europa Publications, 1982, pp. 231–3.
4. Peter D.G. Thomas, *John Wilkes: A Friend to Liberty*, Oxford: Clarendon Press, 1996, p. 14.
5. *Ibid.*, p. 4.
6. Horace Walpole, *Memoirs of the Reign of King George III*, ed. Derek Jarrett, 4 vols, New Haven and London: Yale University Press, 2000, Vol. I, p. 117.
7. Dickinson, *Liberty and Property*, p. 215.
8. Thomas, *John Wilkes*, pp. 82–3, 93.
9. Pauline Maier, 'John Wilkes and American Disillusionment with Britain', *William and Mary Quarterly*, Vol. 20 (1963), p. 379; Louis W. Potts, *Arthur Lee, A Virtuous Revolutionary*, Baton Rouge, Louisiana, and London: Louisiana State University Press, 1981, p. 161.
10. Colin Nicolson, *The 'Infamas Govener': Francis Bernard and the Origins of the American Revolution*, Boston, Massachusetts: Northeastern University Press, 2001, p. 187.
11. *Ibid.*, pp. 187–90, 198–9.
12. Michael Kammen, *A Rope of Sand: The Colonial Agents, British Politics and the American Revolution*, Ithaca, New York: Cornell University Press, 1968; this edition New York: Vintage Books, 1974, pp. 182, 233; Thomas, *Revolution in America: Britain & the Colonies 1763–1776*, pp. 11, 25–31.
13. Nicolson, *The 'Infamas Govener'*, p. 206; Potts, *Arthur Lee*, pp. 75–8.
14. Potts, *Arthur Lee*, p. 101.
15. *Ibid.*, pp. 21–31, 33–5, 38, 45–50; R.H. Lee, *Life of Arthur Lee LL.D*, 2 vols, Boston, 1829; reprinted, Freeport, New York: Books for Libraries Press, 1969, Vol. II, p. 392.
16. Potts, *Arthur Lee*, pp. 56, 60, 67, 73–5, 82, 92, 99–100; L.H. Butterfield, *Letters of Benjamin Rush*, 2 vols, Princeton, New Jersey: Princeton University Press, 1951, Vol. I, p. 72; Alvin Richard Riggs, 'Arthur Lee and the Radical Whigs, 1768–1776', Yale University, Ph.D., 1967; copyright by A.R. Riggs, 1968. Filmed by University Microfilms, Inc., Ann Arbor, Michigan, p. 93.

17. The Historical Society of Pennsylvania (HSP), Chew Papers, Edward Tilghman to Benjamin Chew, London, August 18, 1772.

18. Lee, *Life of Arthur Lee*, Vol. I, p. 183; Potts, *Arthur Lee*, pp. 11, 30.

19. Potts, *Arthur Lee*, pp. 52–3, 61, 88; Lee, *Life of Arthur Lee*, Vol. I, p. 244; Riggs, 'Arthur Lee and the Radical Whigs', pp. 80, 93; John Sainsbury, *Disaffected Patriots: London Supporters of Revolutionary America 1769–1782*, Kingston and Montreal: McGill-Queen's University Press 1987, pp. 49–50.

20. Lee, *Life of Arthur Lee*, Vol. II, p. 391; Potts, *Arthur Lee*, p. 33.

21. William Lee was following a family tradition by handling the business end of his family's tobacco interests in London. Since the beginning of the eighteenth century there had been a Lee among the City merchants. William Lee also had West Indian trading interests; see William Sachse, *The Colonial American in Britain*, Madison, Wisconsin: University of Wisconsin Press, 1956, p. 124.

22. *Ibid.*, pp. 50, 68, 124; Esmond Wright, *Franklin of Philadelphia*, Cambridge, Massachusetts: Harvard University Press, 1986, p. 287; William Howard Adams, *The Paris Years of Thomas Jefferson*, New Haven, Connecticut, and London: Yale University Press, 1997, pp. 201, 224; Potts, *Arthur Lee*, pp. 20, 82; *The Papers of Benjamin Franklin*, ed. L.W. Labaree et al., 39 vols, New Haven, Connecticut: Yale University Press, 1959–, Vol. 21, p. 216, fn.

23. Potts, *Arthur Lee*, pp. 82, 86; John Sainsbury, 'The Pro-Americans of London, 1769 to 1782', *William and Mary Quarterly*, Series 3, Vol. 35 (1978), p. 431.

24. Potts, *Arthur Lee*, p. 84; Riggs, 'Arthur Lee and the Radical Whigs', pp. 5, 8, 93; Sainsbury, *Disaffected Patriots*, p. 49.

25. *Life of Arthur Lee*, Vol. II, pp. 391–2. Lee lived at No. 2 Garden Court in the Middle Temple.

26. Elizabeth Steele, *The memoirs of Mrs Sophia Baddeley. Late of Drury-Lane Theatre* (Dublin, 1787, 3 vols), Vol. 3, pp. 177–8, 195; British Library (BL) Add. MS. 30866. Eight Diaries of J. Wilkes. See, for example, entry for 9 February 1772.

27. The Historical Society of Pennsylvania (HSP), Ebenezer Hazard Journal, entry dated 8 May 1771.

28. Rebecca Starr, *A School for Politics: Commercial Lobbying and Political Culture in Early South Carolina*, Baltimore, Maryland, and London: The Johns Hopkins University Press, 1998, pp. 66–9; on the connections of Ralph Izard with the Rockinghams, see Julie M. Flavell, 'American Patriots in London and the Quest for Talks, 1774–1775', *Journal of Imperial and Commonwealth History*, Vol. 20 (1992), pp. 354–5.

29. *The Papers of Henry Laurens*, ed. George C. Rogers, Jr., et al., 16 vols, Columbia, South Carolina: University of South Carolina Press, 1968–2002, Vol. 8, pp. 121, 129.

30. Thomas, *John Wilkes*, pp. 112, 122–4; Starr, *A School for Politics*, pp. 66–9.

31. E.J. Burford, *Royal St James's: Being a Story of Kings, Clubmen and Courtesans*, London: Robert Hale, 1988, p. 61.

32. I am grateful to Peter D.G. Thomas for information regarding the Vaughan family of Goldengrove.

33. *Papers of Henry Laurens*, Vol. 8, p. 329.

34. John Alden, *Stephen Sayre, American Revolutionary Adventurer*, Baton Rouge, Louisiana, and London: Louisiana State University Press, 1983, p. 33. Alden stops short of assuming that Sayre was supported by Mrs Pearson. Arthur Lee, as a wealthy planter's son, fitted in more easily with the Berners Street set. He was hired by Henry Laurens and Ralph Izard to write a political pamphlet against Sir Egerton Leigh, and in the same year he went on a tour of Europe with Ralph Izard and his wife; see Potts, *Arthur Lee*, pp. 122–3, 128.

35. Lawrence Stone, *The Family, Sex, and Marriage in England 1500–1800*, London: Penguin, 1977, pp. 505–7.

36. Steele, *The memoirs of Mrs Sophia Baddeley*, Vol. 3, p. 199.

37. *Ibid.*, Vol. 3, pp. 194–5.

38. Cited in Alden, *Stephen Sayre*, p. 38.
39. Alden, *Stephen Sayre*, p. 39.
40. Steele, *The memoirs of Mrs Sophia Baddeley*, Vol. 3, p. 183.
41. *Ibid.*, Vol. 3, pp. 148, 172–3.
42. Burford, *Royal St James's*, p. 167.
43. Steele, *The memoirs of Mrs Sophia Baddeley*, Vol. 3, pp. 173–5, 195–8, 201.
44. *Ibid.*, Vol. 3, pp, 167, 174, 177–8, 185, 192.
45. *Ibid.*, pp. 148, 193.
46. *Ibid.*, p. 196.
47. Dennis De Berdt, Jr., to Joseph Reed, 24 July 1774, and Dennis De Berdt, Jr. to Joseph Reed, 8 October 1774, Joseph Reed Papers (BV Reed, Joseph), New-York Historical Society.
48. William B. Reed, *The Life of Esther de Berdt Reed*, Philadelphia, 1853; this edition New York: Arno Press, 1971, p. 186.
49. As early as 1772, when Stephen was still living off the bounty of Mrs Pearson in Berners Street, he had ambitions to become a Member of Parliament, presumably through the Wilkite connections he was cultivating. Stephen Sayre to Ezra Stiles, London, 20 July 1772, Ezra Stiles Papers, Microfilm, from the originals at Yale University, 1976, reel 3 (1769–1779).
50. Alden, *Stephen Sayre*, pp. 49–51.
51. Steele, *The memoirs of Mrs Sophia Baddeley*, Vol. 3, pp. 211–15.
52. Cited in Alden, *Stephen Sayre*, p. 124.
53. Alden, *Stephen Sayre*, pp. 70–71; Sayre vs. Rochford et al., Treasury Solicitor, TS 11/542, fols. 4–6, The National Archives: PRO, London.
54. Thomas, *John Wilkes*, pp. 76, 83.
55. Sainsbury, *Disaffected Patriots*, pp. 98–9; James F. Bradley, *Popular Politics and the American Revolution in England: Petitions, the Crown, and Public Opinion*, Macon, Georgia: Mercer University Press, 1986, pp. 50–58.
56. Alden, *Stephen Sayre*, pp. 77–9.
57. *Ibid.*, pp. 82, 85.
58. *Public Advertiser*, 26 October 1775, no. 14,374.
59. Alden, *Stephen Sayre*, p. 85.
60. *Ibid.*, p. 77.
61. Cited in 'Stephen Sayre', Clifford K. Shipton, *Sibley's Harvard Graduates: Biographical Sketches of those who attended Harvard College*, 18 vols, Boston: The Massachusetts Historical Society, 1873–, Vol. 14 (1756–1760), p. 210.
62. Alden, *Stephen Sayre*, pp. 70, 96; HSP, Chew Papers, Edward Tilghman to Benjamin Chew, 6 August 1772; Sayre vs. Rochford et al., Treasury Solicitor, TS 11/542, fols. 173–5.
63. Sayre vs. Rochford et al., Treasury Solicitor, TS 11/542, fol. 159.
64. For at least a year before the incident, the correspondence of suspicious Americans in London, particularly the Lees, had been intercepted by the government (Julie M. Flavell, 'Government Interception of Letters from America and the Quest for Colonial Opinion in 1775', *William and Mary Quarterly*, 3rd series, Vol. LVIII (2001), pp. 408–9). They and their political cronies in the City of London – some of whom openly supported the colonial rebellion as the cause of true 'English liberty' – were indeed engaged in illegal activities. They sent military advice and intelligence to the rebels in Massachusetts, the scene of the fighting. They arranged for shipments of weapons to the rebels from neutral countries such as Holland. By September 1775 Arthur Lee had made contact with a French agent in London (Potts, *Arthur Lee*, p. 152). William Lee illegally encouraged striking shipwrights in England to emigrate to the colonies. Government agents tried, and failed, to incriminate those who had tampered with the strike (Sainsbury, *Disaffected Patriots*, pp. 104–5).
65. Derek Wilson, *The Tower of London: A Thousand Years*, London: Hamish Hamilton, 1978; this edition London: Allison & Busby, 1998, pp. 222–3.

66. James Lander, 'A Tale of Two Hoaxes in Britain and France in 1775', *Historical Journal*, Vol. 49 (2006), pp. 995–1,024.
67. Alden, *Stephen Sayre*, pp. 89–91.
68. *Ibid.*, pp. 100–1.
69. BL, The Auckland Papers (Correspondence and papers, political and private, of William Eden, First Baron Auckland), Add. MS. 34, 413 (Vol. II), Paul Wentworth to the Earl of Suffolk, Paris, 15 May 1777, fol. 457.
70. 'Stephen Sayre' in Shipton, *Sibley's Harvard Graduates*, Vol. 14 (1756–1760), pp. 210–13.
71. Lee, *Life of Arthur Lee*, Vol. II, p. 393; Potts, *Arthur Lee*, p. 278.
72. Alden, *Stephen Sayre*, pp. 150–57.
73. 'Stephen Sayre' in Shipton, *Sibley's Harvard Graduates*, Vol. 14 (1756–1760), pp. 214–15.
74. Alden, *Stephen Sayre*, p. 198.

Chapter Seven: London's American Landscape

1. Rosamond Bayne-Powell, *Travellers in Eighteenth-Century England*, London: John Murray, 1951, pp. 63, 64, 114; Daniel Statt, *Foreigners and Englishmen: The Controversy over Immigration and Population, 1660–1760*, Newark, Delaware: University of Delaware Press; London and Toronto: Associated University Presses, 1995, pp. 184, 187–9, 191.
2. Eliga H. Gould, *The Persistence of Empire: British Political Culture in the Age of the American Revolution*, Chapel Hill, North Carolina, and London: University of North Carolina Press, 2000, pp. 117–21, 142–3, 210; *The Papers of Henry Laurens*, ed. George C. Rogers, Jr., et al., 16 vols, Columbia, South Carolina: University of South Carolina Press, 1968–2002, Vol. 8, p. 130.
3. On the greater awareness in Britain of the colonies as a result of the Seven Years' War, and its significance for British attitudes towards Americans, see Paul Langford, 'Manners and Character in Anglo-American Perceptions, 1750–1850' in Fred M. Leventhal and Roland Quinault, eds, *Anglo-American Attitudes: From Revolution to Partnership*, Aldershot and Burlington: Ashgate, 2000, pp. 76–90; P.J. Marshall, 'Presidential Address: Britain and the World in the Eighteenth Century: II, Britons and Americans', *Transactions of the Royal Historical Society*, 6th series, Vol. IX (1999), pp. 1–16; Peter Marshall, 'Who Cared about the Thirteen Colonies? Some Evidence from Philanthropy', *Journal of Imperial and Commonwealth History*, Vol. 27 (1999); Stephen Conway, 'From Fellow-Nationals to Foreigners: British Perceptions of the Americans, circa 1739–1783', *William and Mary Quarterly*, 3rd series, Vol. LIX (2002). For a summary of the views of British politicians that the American colonists were part of a wider British nation, see P.J. Marshall, *The Making and Unmaking of Empires: Britain, India and America c.1750–1783*, Oxford: Oxford University Press, 2005, pp. 172–4.
4. Langford, 'Manners and Character in Anglo-American Perceptions, 1750–1850', pp. 79–81.
5. Christopher Leslie Brown, *Moral Capital: Foundations of British Abolitionism*, Chapel Hill, North Carolina: University of North Carolina Press, 2006, pp. 113–34.
6. Wallace Brown, 'The British Press and the American Colonies', *History Today*, Vol. XXIV (1974), p. 333; Troy O. Bickham, 'Sympathizing with Sedition? George Washington, the British Press, and British Attitudes during the American War of Independence', *William and Mary Quarterly*, 3rd series, Vol. LIX (2002), p. 101; Solomon Lutnick, *The American Revolution and the British Press, 1775–1783*, Columbia, Missouri: University of Missouri Press, 1967, p. 35. When the *London Magazine* ran a serialised 'Short Account of the British Plantations in America' starting in 1755, only New England was depicted as a region with deviant traits, based on its fanatical religious views, its persecution of Quakers and its witchcraft trials. No attempt was made to assign the white populations of the other colonies any regional character at all, even in the middle colonies where the 'Account' noted the mixed European origins of the settlers. 'A Short

Account of the British Plantations in America', serialised in the *London Magazine*, vols 24–6 (1755–1757), beginning July 1755, p. 307. The account of the settlement of New England is in the *London Magazine*, Vol. 25 (1756), pp. 29 and ff.

7. Cited in Gould, *The Persistence of Empire*, p. 143.
8. Christopher L. Brown, 'Empire without Slaves: British Concepts of Emancipation in the Age of the American Revolution', *William and Mary Quarterly*, Vol. LVI (1999), p. 285.
9. Peter Fryer, *Staying Power: The History of Black People in Britain*, London: Pluto Press, 1984, pp. 71–2; for one assessment of attitudes towards race in eighteenth-century Britain, see *ibid.*, Ch. 7, 'The Rise of English Racism'.
10. Jean Hecht, 'Continental and Colonial Servants in Eighteenth-Century England', *Smith College Studies in History*, Vol. XL (1954), pp. 45–7.
11. Fryer, *Staying Power*, pp. 151–61; Hecht, 'Continental and Colonial Servants in Eighteenth-Century England', pp. 14–15, 19, 23, 46.
12. Francis Hodge, *Yankee Theatre: The Image of America on the Stage, 1825–1850*, Austin, Texas: University of Texas Press, 1964, p. 197.
13. *Ibid.*, p. 260; Christopher Mulvey, *Transatlantic Manners: Social Patterns in Nineteenth-Century Anglo-American Travel Literature*, Cambridge: Cambridge University Press, 1990, pp. 19–24.
14. Dr John Fothergill, *Considerations Relative to the North American Colonies*, London, 1765, pp. 41–3. 'North America' was often used to refer to all the colonies on the continent of North America, as opposed to the West Indies.
15. James Walvin, *Fruits of Empire: Exotic Produce and British Taste, 1660–1800*, Basingstoke: Macmillan, 1997, pp. 117–19.
16. Tim Richardson, *Sweets: A History of Temptation*, London: Bantam Press, 2002, pp. 186, 189–90, 198, 194, 201; Reay Tannahill, *Food in History*, London: Penguin, 1973; revised edition, 1988, pp. 241–2.
17. Catherine Molineux, 'Pleasures of the Smoke: "Black Virginians" in Georgian London's Tobacco Shops', *William and Mary Quarterly*, Vol. LXIV (2007), p. 344.
18. Ben Clerkin, 'Pubs could pump in scent of freshly-mown lawns to mask smell of stale beer and sweat', *Daily Mail*, 5 August 2007. Medieval herb strewers used to spread aromatic plants like lavender over floors.
19. Peter H. Wood, 'Black Labor – White Rice: Colonial Manpower and African Agricultural Skill in Early Carolina', in T.H. Breen, ed., *Shaping Southern Society: The Colonial Experience*, New York: Oxford University Press, 1976, pp. 151, 154–5; *The Papers of Henry Laurens*, ed. George C. Rogers, Jr. et al., 16 vols, Columbia, South Carolina: University of South Carolina Press, 1968–2002, Vol. 9, p. 578.
20. George, *London Life in the Eighteenth Century*, pp. 147–51; Bernard Bailyn, *Voyagers to the West: a Passage in the Peopling of America on the Eve of the Revolution*, New York: Alfred A. Knopf, 1987, pp. 114, 229, 308–9.
21. John Herbert, *The Port of London*, London: Collins, 1947, p. 16.
22. Old Bailey Proceedings Online (www.oldbaileyonline.org, 2 June 2009), February 1719, trial of John Dickson and Robert Killison (t17190225-4); Old Bailey Proceedings Online (18 November 2008), 17 January 1746, trial of Thomas Bozeley (t17460117-29).
23. Prudence Leith-Ross, *The John Tradescants: Gardeners to the Rose and Lily Queen*, London: Peter Owen, 1984, p. 18; Maggie Campbell-Culver, *The Origin of Plants: The People and Plants that Have Shaped Britain's Garden History since the Year 1000*, London: Headline Book Publishing, 2001, pp. 11, 13, 144, 149, 155; Richard Drayton, *Nature's Government: Science, Imperial Britain and the 'Improvement' of the World*, New Haven, Connecticut, and London: Yale University Press, 2000, pp. 6, 9, 16–17, 26, 33.
24. Richard D. Altick, *The Shows of London*, Cambridge, Massachusetts: Harvard University Press, 1978, p. 12.
25. Campbell-Culver, *The Origin of Plants*, p. 155.

26. *Chain of Friendship: Selected Letters of Dr John Fothergill 1735–1780*, ed. Betsy C. Corner and Christopher C. Booth, Cambridge, Massachusetts, Harvard University Press, 1971, Introduction, pp. 4, 9, 14, 15, 18, 19, 20, 24, 30.
27. Thomas P. Slaughter, *The Natures of John and William Bartram*, New York: Alfred A. Knopf, 1996; this edition New York: Vintage Books, 1997, pp. 82–4; Andrea Wulf, *The Brother Gardeners: Botany, Empire and the Birth of an Obsession*, London: Windmill Books, 2009, Chs. 4 and 5.
28. Douglas Chambers, *The Planters of the English Landscape Garden: Botany, Trees and the Georgics*, New Haven, Connecticut, and London: Yale University Press, 1993, pp. 81, 86–7, 94, 95.
29. Eleanor Robbins, 'Franklin's Botanical Interests', in 'Benjamin Franklin of Craven Street', a Royal Society of Arts-Benjamin Franklin House Symposium, 15 October 1999, p. 30.
30. Chambers, *The Planters of the English Landscape Garden*, pp. 81, 92–5; Campbell-Culver, *The Origin of Plants*, pp. 74, 144.
31. *A Companion to every Place of Curiosity and Entertainment in and about London and Westminster* (London, 1767), Table of Contents.
32. Campbell-Culver, *The Origin of Plants*, p. 150; Drayton, *Nature's Government*, p. 87.
33. William Sachse, *The Colonial American in Britain*, Madison, Wisconsin: The University of Wisconsin Press, 1956, pp. 157, 159.
34. *The Papers of Benjamin Franklin*, ed. L.W. Labaree et al., 39 vols, New Haven, Connecticut: Yale University Press, 1959-, Vol. 14, pp. 25–8.
35. Brown, 'The British Press and the American Colonies', p. 330.
36. Andrew Oliver, ed., *The Journal of Samuel Curwen, Loyalist*, Cambridge, Massachusetts: Harvard University Press, 2 vols, 1972, Vol. I, p. 67.
37. Gould, *The Persistence of Empire: British Political Culture in the Age of the American Revolution*, pp. 65, 68, 70; Howard H. Peckham, *The Colonial Wars, 1689–1762*, Chicago, Illinois, and London: University of Chicago Press, 1964, p. 155; Kathleen Wilson, 'Empire of Virtue: The Imperial Project and Hanoverian Culture, c.1720–1785' in Lawrence Stone, ed., *An Imperial State at War: Britain from 1689 to 1815*, London: Routledge, 1994, pp. 146–51.
38. Horace Walpole, cited in Nicholas Rogers, 'Brave Wolfe: The Making of a Hero' in Kathleen Wilson, ed., *A New Imperial History: Culture, Identity and Modernity in Britain and the Empire, 1660–1840*, Cambridge: Cambridge University Press, 2004, p. 240.
39. Maps of the colonies were rare in British newspapers until around 1755. Brown, 'The British Press and the American Colonies', p. 330.
40. *London Magazine* (London, 1747–1783), Vol. 24 (November 1755), pp. 511–12.
41. *A Companion to every Place of Curiosity and Entertainment in and about London and Westminster*, p. 129.
42. Bellamy Partridge, *Sir Billy Howe*, London: Longmans, Green, 1932, p. 3.
43. Rogers, 'Brave Wolfe: The Making of a Hero', pp. 239–43.
44. Holger Hoock, *The King's Artists: The Royal Academy of Arts and the Politics of British Culture 1760–1840*, Oxford: Clarendon Press, 2003, p. 7; John Brewer, *The Pleasures of the Imagination: English Culture in the Eighteenth Century*, London: HarperCollins, 1997, p. 226; Wilson, 'Empire of Virtue', p. 150; Rogers, 'Brave Wolfe: The Making of a Hero', pp. 240–41.
45. James Thomas Flexner, *America's Old Masters*, New York: Viking Press, 1939; this edition New York: Dover, 1967, pp. 22, 26, 34–5, 42–4.
46. Susan Rather, 'Benjamin West's Professional Endgame and the Historical Conundrum of William Williams', *William and Mary Quarterly*, Vol. LIX (2002), p. 850.
47. Silverman, *A Cultural History of the American Revolution*, pp. 26, 175–9.
48. Flexner, *America's Old Masters*, pp. 66–7.
49. Rogers, 'Brave Wolfe: The Making of a Hero', pp. 250, 252.
50. Flexner, *America's Old Masters*, p. 67.

51. Whitfield J. Bell, Jr., 'Thomas Parke's Student Life in England and Scotland, 1771–1773', *Pennsylvania Magazine of History and Biography*, LXXV (1951), p. 254; *The Journal of Samuel Curwen*, Vol. 1, p. 132.
52. Brown, 'The British Press and the American Colonies', pp. 326, 329.
53. Bickham, 'Sympathizing with Sedition? George Washington, the British Press, and British Attitudes during the American War of Independence', pp. 105–6.
54. *Reminiscences of the French War: Robert Rogers' Journal and a Memoir of General Stark*, reproducing the edition published in Concord, New Hampshire, in 1831 by Luther Roby; this edition published by The Freedom Historical Society, Freedom, New Hampshire, 1988, p. 199; Peter E. Russell, 'Redcoats in the Wilderness: British Officers and Irregular Warfare in Europe and America, 1740 to 1760', *William and Mary Quarterly*, Vol. XXV (1978), p. 645.
55. Richard Slotkin, *Regeneration through Violence: The Mythology of the American Frontier, 1600–1860*, Middletown, Connecticut: Wesleyan University Press, 1973, pp. 227–9; John Ferling, 'The New England Soldier: A Study in Changing Perceptions', *American Quarterly*, Vol. 33 (1981), pp. 37–40; Douglas Edward Leach, *Roots of Conflict: British Armed Forces and Colonial Americans, 1677–1763*, Chapel Hill, North Carolina, and London: University of North Carolina Press, 1986, p. 165.
56. Robert Louis Stevenson, *Travels with a Donkey in the Cevennes*, first published 1879; this edition London, 1909, pp. 132, 189; Peter Martin, *A Life of James Boswell*, London: Weidenfeld & Nicolson, 1999, pp. 204–9.
57. Mulvey, *Transatlantic Manners*, pp. 49–57.
58. Sachse, *The Colonial American in Britain*, p. 170; Daniel E. Williams, ' "Until they are contaminated by their more refined neighbours": The Images of the Native American in Carver's *Travels through the Interior* and its Influence on the Euro-American Imagination', in Christian F. Feest, ed., *Indians and Europe: An Interdisciplinary Collection of Essays*, Aachen: Alano Verlag, 1989, pp. 195–9, 207–9.
59. Linda Colley, *Britons: Forging the Nation 1707–1837*, London and New Haven, Connecticut: Yale University Press, 1992; this edition London: Vintage, 1992, p. 141.
60. Altick, *The Shows of London*, p. 46.
61. Eric Hinderaker, 'The "Four Indian Kings" and the Imaginative Construction of the First British Empire', *William and Mary Quarterly*, 3rd series, Vol. LIII, no. 3 (July 1996), pp. 490, 497.
62. Brown, 'The British Press and the American Colonies', pp. 328, 332.
63. John Oliphant, 'The Cherokee Embassy to London, 1762', *Journal of Imperial and Commonwealth History*, Vol. 27 (1999), p. 1.
64. *A Companion to every Place of Curiosity and Entertainment in and about London and Westminster*, p. 60.
65. Altick, *The Shows of London*, p. 47.
66. *The St James's Chronicle, or the British Evening-Post*, no. 206, 3–6 July 1762; no. 207, 6–9 July 1762; no. 208, 8–10 July 1762; no. 217, 29–31 July 1762.
67. 'Letters of Dennys De Berdt, 1757–1770', *Publications of the Colonial Society of Massachusetts*, Vol. 13 (1917), p. 424.
68. Cited in Altick, *The Shows of London*, p. 47.
69. Oliphant, 'The Cherokee Embassy to London, 1762', p. 13; Altick, *The Shows of London*, p. 47.
70. *The St James's Chronicle, or the British Evening-Post*, no. 207, 6–9 July 1762.
71. Stephanie Pratt, 'Joseph Brant (Thayendanegea)' in *Between Worlds: Voyagers to Britain, 1700–1850*, ed. Jocelyn Hackforth-Jones, London: National Portrait Gallery Publications, 2007, pp. 57–62.
72. Several instances of Native American visitors to London in the 1760s are mentioned in Liza Picard, *Dr Johnson's London*, London: Weidenfeld & Nicolson, 2000; this edition London: Phoenix Press, 2001, p. 253. Other than the well-known three Cherokees, these may have been hoaxes. In 1762 Goldsmith satirised the gullibility of the London public in their rage to see genuine Indians in *The Citizen of the World*, suggesting

that frauds were not uncommon (Altick, *The Shows of London*, p. 49). For an account of two Mohawk warriors who visited London in 1765, see John Jewitt, 'Extraordinary Arrivals: Native American Visitors to London, 1710–1844'; Thesis submitted for the degree of Master of Arts, Department of History, University of Kent at Canterbury, 1998.

73. 'Letters of Dennys De Berdt', p. 323, fn; Thomas Ruston to Job Ruston, London, 3 April 1766, Thomas Ruston Collection, Library of Congress; Sachse, *The Colonial American in Britain*, pp. 112–14, and cited from Sachse.

74. Deborah L. Madsen, *American Exceptionalism*, Edinburgh: Edinburgh University Press, 1998, pp. 43–4.

75. 'Introduction' by Jocelyn Hackforth-Jones in *Between Worlds: Voyagers to Britain, 1700–1850*, ed. Hackforth-Jones, pp. 14–15.

76. Jack P. Greene, *The Intellectual Construction of America: Exceptionalism and Identity from 1492 to 1800*, Chapel Hill, North Carolina: University of North Carolina Press, 1993, p. 117.

77. Reginald Horsman, *Race and Manifest Destiny: The Origins of American Anglo-Saxonism*, Cambridge, Massachusetts: Harvard University Press, 1981, pp. 46–7.

78. Claire Tomalin, *Jane Austen: A Life*, New York and London: Viking, 1997; this edition London: Penguin Books, 2000, p. 135.

79. *Papers of Henry Laurens*, Vol. 8, p. 323.

80. Horsman, *Race and Manifest Destiny*, pp. 104–5.

Chapter Eight: Franklin and Son in London

1. Carla Mulford, 'Figuring Benjamin Franklin in American Cultural Memory', *New England Quarterly*, Vol. 72 (1999), pp. 417–18, 423–5.

2. Piers Mackesy, *The War for America, 1775–1783*, Cambridge, Massachusetts: Harvard University Press, 1964; this edition Lincoln, Nebraska, and London: University of Nebraska Press, 1993, p. 36.

3. Joyce E. Chaplin, *The First Scientific American: Benjamin Franklin and the Pursuit of Genius*, New York: Basic Books, 2006, pp. 27, 32; Ian K. Steele, *The English Atlantic 1675–1740: An Exploration of Communication and Community*, New York and Oxford: Oxford University Press, 1986, p. 142; Franklin, *Autobiography and Other Writings*, pp. 50–51.

4. Kenneth Silverman, *A Cultural History of the American Revolution: Painting, Music, Literature, and the Theatre in the Colonies and the United States from the Treaty of Paris to the Inauguration of George Washington, 1763–1789*, New York: Crowell, 1976; this edition New York: Columbia University Press, 1987, pp. 47–9, Franklin cited from Silverman, p. 10; Carl Bridenbaugh, *Rebels and Gentlemen: Philadelphia in the Age of Franklin*, New York: Reynal & Hitchcock, 1942; this edition Westport, Connecticut: Greenwood Press, 1978, pp. x, 103, 106, 111–13, 175.

5. J.A. Leo Lemay, 'Franklin, Benjamin (6 Jan. 1706–17 Apr. 1790)', *American National Biography*, Vol. 8, pp. 385, 386.

6. Chaplin, *The First Scientific American*, pp. 132–6.

7. Franklin, *Autobiography and Other Writings*, p. 173.

8. H.W. Brands, *The First American: The Life and Times of Benjamin Franklin*, New York: Anchor Books, 2000, p. 301.

9. Robert Middlekauff, *Benjamin Franklin and his Enemies*, Berkeley, Los Angeles, and London: University of California Press, 1996, pp. 67, 73–4.

10. Cited in Esmond Wright, *Franklin of Philadelphia*, Cambridge, Massachusetts: Harvard University Press, 1986, p. 117, and Brands, *The First American*, pp. 302, 303.

11. Brands, *The First American*, pp. 314–15.

12. Middlekauff, *Benjamin Franklin and his Enemies*, pp. 85–90, 107, 114.

13. *Ibid.*, pp. 36–9; Cecil B. Currey, *Road to Revolution: Benjamin Franklin in England 1765–1775*, Gloucester, Massachusetts: Peter Smith, 1978, pp. 25, 31.

14. Cited in Middlekauff, *Benjamin Franklin and his Enemies*, p. 66.
15. Cited in J.A. Cochrane, *Dr Johnson's Printer: The Life of William Strahan*, London: Routledge & Kegan Paul, 1964, p. 107.
16. I am indebted to Robert Middlekauff for his astute assessment of Franklin's character, which I have drawn upon for my own account. See Middlekauff, *Benjamin Franklin and his Enemies*, pp. 108–13.
17. Franklin, *Autobiography and Other Writings*, p. 180.
18. Currey, *Road to Revolution*, p. 38.
19. Middlekauff, *Benjamin Franklin and his Enemies*, pp. 34, 109–10, 112–13.
20. Benjamin Franklin to Joseph Galloway, London, 7 April 1759, *The Papers of Benjamin Franklin*, ed. L.W. Labaree et al., 39 vols, New Haven, Connecticut: Yale University Press, 1959–, Vol. 8, p. 309.
21. Middlekauff, *Benjamin Franklin and his Enemies*, pp. 111, 112.
22. Sheila L. Skemp, *William Franklin, Son of a Patriot, Servant of a King*, New York and Oxford: Oxford University Press, 1990, pp. 6–7; Wright, *Franklin of Philadelphia*, p. 151; Middlekauff, *Benjamin Franklin and his Enemies*, p. 112.
23. Gregory D. Massey, *John Laurens and the American Revolution*, Columbia, South Carolina: University of South Carolina Press, 2000, pp. 6–8; Daniel J. McDonough, *Christopher Gadsden and Henry Laurens: The Parallel Lives of Two American Patriots*, Selinsgrove, Pennsylvania: Susquehanna University Press and London: Associated University Presses, 2000, pp. 14–15.
24. Brands, *The First American*, pp. 109, 113–19.
25. Thomas Bewick, *My Life*, edited and with an introduction by Iain Bain, London: The Folio Society, 1981, pp. 13, 16; John Brewer, *The Pleasures of the Imagination: English Culture in the Eighteenth Century*, London: HarperCollins, 1997, pp. 500–3, 508–10, 521; Franklin, *Autobiography and Other Writings*, p. 62.
26. Bewick, *My Life*, p. 118, mentions Franklin in terms of admiration.
27. Daniel Defoe, *The Complete English Tradesman in Familiar Letters*, 2 vols, London: first edition 1726; second edition with Supplement 1727; reprinted New York: Augustus M. Kelly, 1962, Vol. I, p. 312.
28. Cochrane, *Dr Johnson's Printer*, pp. 1–6, 190.
29. Franklin, *Autobiography and Other Writings*, pp. 267, 270.
30. Skemp, *William Franklin*, p. 14.
31. Middlekauff, *Benjamin Franklin and his Enemies*, pp. 87–8.
32. *Ibid.*, p. 97; Franklin, *Autobiography and Other Writings*, p. 70.
33. Skemp, *William Franklin*, pp. 4, 8–9, 12, 14.
34. *Papers of Benjamin Franklin*, Vol. 4, p. 78.
35. I am grateful to Professor Wilfrid Prest of the University of Adelaide for explaining the means by which a would-be barrister was able to 'compound' – i.e. pay a cash fine in lieu of terms and vacations supposedly resident in commons in order to qualify for call – and for providing me with information on the entry for William Franklin in the relevant Bar ledger MT.3/BAL 1 (Barristers' ledger 1747–60; the entry for Franklin appears on p. 112). Franklin's entry was unusually brief, which fits in with the impression that he did not participate much in the life of the Middle Temple.
36. Skemp, *William Franklin*, pp. 29–32.
37. William Alexander Duer, *The Life of William Alexander Earl of Stirling*, New York: Collections of the New Jersey Historical Society, Vol. 2, 1847, pp. 67–8.
38. Skemp, *William Franklin*, p. 29.
39. Bridenbaugh, *Rebels and Gentlemen*, p. 187; Walter Isaacson, *Benjamin Franklin: An American Life*, New York: Simon & Schuster, 2003, p. 188.
40. Cochrane, *Dr Johnson's Printer*, pp. 93, 108; Skemp, *William Franklin*, pp. 38, 179; Isaacson, *Benjamin Franklin: An American Life*, p. 221.
41. R.C. Simmons, 'Colonial Patronage: Two Letters from William Franklin to the Earl of Bute, 1762', *William and Mary Quarterly*, 3rd series, Vol. LIX (2002) pp. 124–5; Vernon

O. Stumpf, 'Who Was Elizabeth Downes Franklin?', *Pennsylvania Magazine of History and Biography*, Vol. 94 (1970), pp. 533–4.

42. Elizabeth Downes was the sister-in-law of Thomas Alleyne (sometimes spelled 'Allen') of Barbados (Simmons, 'Colonial Patronage: Two Letters from William Franklin to the Earl of Bute, 1762', p. 125). On 26 August 1758 the West Indian John Baker, a friend of the Mannings and the Laurenses, described an assembly of fashionable people at Tunbridge Wells that included 'Mr Allen of Barbadoes', his wife and his wife's sister 'Miss Donne' (*The Diary of John Baker, Barrister of the Middle Temple, Solicitor-General of the Leeward Islands*, ed. Philip C. Yorke, London: Hutchinson, 1931, p. 115). Baker's Tunbridge Wells company on that day in August was unusual in that it included several individuals who are nowhere else in his diary; 'Hunter of Virginia' – William Hunter, who shared with Ben Franklin the post of deputy postmaster general of America, and who was then in England for his health (*Papers of Benjamin Franklin*, Vol. 9, p. 363); and 'Mr Bridges', Richard Jackson's brother-in-law. Richard Jackson ('Mr Jackson, a lawyer') was there as well, and one 'Franklin, the son of Philip Franklin'. This 'son of Philip Franklin' was surely William himself. Ben Franklin, who was never part of Baker's set, was not yet a household name in England in the 1750s, as Thomas Penn liked to point out (Chaplin, *The First Scientific American*, pp. 177–8). The two Franklins, Jackson, Hunter and Bridges had gone to Tunbridge Wells in August for a short stay (*Papers of Benjamin Franklin*, Vol. 8, pp. 131–2).

43. Lawrence Stone, *The Family, Sex and Marriage in England, 1500–1800*, London: Penguin, 1977, pp. 316–17.

44. *Papers of Benjamin Franklin*, Vol. 8, p. 132.

45. Martha C. Slotten, 'Elizabeth Graeme Ferguson: A Poet in "The Athens of North America" ', *Pennsylvania Magazine of History and Biography*, Vol. CVIII, no. 3 (1984), p. 262; Skemp, *William Franklin*, p. 37.

46. Simmons, 'Colonial Patronage: Two Letters from William Franklin to the Earl of Bute, 1762', p. 125.

47. Cited in Stumpf, 'Who Was Elizabeth Downes Franklin?', p. 533.

48. For a recent example see Isaacson, *Benjamin Franklin: An American Life*, pp. 203–4.

49. Skemp, *William Franklin*, p. 24; cited from Slotten, 'Elizabeth Graeme Ferguson: A Poet in "The Athens of North America" ', p. 262, fn.

50. Isaacson, *Benjamin Franklin: An American Life*, p. 189; Skemp, *William Franklin*, p. 31.

51. Brands, *The First American*, p. 278.

52. *Papers of Benjamin Franklin*, Vol. 10, p. 142.

53. Isaacson, *Benjamin Franklin: An American Life*, pp. 162–5.

54. *Papers of Benjamin Franklin*, Vol. 9, p. 102.

55. William's biographer Sheila Skemp provides a brief overview of scholarly views on Ben's role in his son's appointment, and concludes that 'there is no question but what Ben was pleased with his son's success.' – *William Franklin*, p. 40. See also Simmons, 'Colonial Patronage: Two Letters from William Franklin to the Earl of Bute, 1762', pp. 123–34.

56. Simmons, 'Colonial Patronage: Two Letters from William Franklin to the Earl of Bute, 1762', pp. 129–31.

57. *Ibid.*, pp. 127–8.

58. Duer, *The Life of William Alexander*, p. 70.

59. Skemp, *William Franklin*, p. 41.

60. Simmons, 'Colonial Patronage: Two Letters from William Franklin to the Earl of Bute, 1762', pp. 125, 131.

61. Eric Stockdale, *Middle Temple Lawyers and the American Revolution*, Eagan, Minnesota: Thomson-West, 2007, p. 84.

62. *Papers of Benjamin Franklin*, Vol. 10, p. 113.

63. Wright, *Franklin of Philadelphia*, p. 114.

64. Chaplin, *The First Scientific American*, p. 130.

65. Wright, *Franklin of Philadelphia*, p. 115.
66. H.T. Dickinson, *Liberty and Property: Political Ideology in Eighteenth-Century Britain*, London: Weidenfeld & Nicolson, 1977; this edition London: Methuen, 1979, pp. 192, 197.
67. Richard Price, 'Observations on the Importance of the American Revolution, and the Means of making it a Benefit to the World' (1784), reprinted in Bernard Peach, ed., *Richard Price and the Ethical Foundations of the American Revolution*, Durham, North Carolina: Duke University Press, 1979, p. 208.
68. J.A. Leo Lemay, 'Franklin, Benjamin (6 Jan. 1706–17 Apr. 1790)', *American National Biography*, 24 vols; New York and Oxford: Oxford University Press, 1999, Vol. 8, p. 387.
69. Chaplin, *The First Scientific American*, pp. 164–9.
70. *Papers of Benjamin Franklin*, Vol. 10, p. xv.
71. Lemay, 'Franklin, Benjamin', p. 387; Currey, *Road to Revolution*, p. 87.
72. Chaplin, *The First Scientific American*, pp. 169–71.
73. Maurie D. McInnis, *In Pursuit of Refinement: Charlestonians Abroad 1740–1860*, Columbia, South Carolina: University of South Carolina Press, 1999, pp. 9–10.
74. Michael Kammen, *A Rope of Sand: The Colonial Agents, British Politics, and the American Revolution*, Ithaca, New York: Cornell University Press, 1968; this edition New York: Vintage Books, 1974, p. 20.
75. Stockdale, *Middle Temple Lawyers and the American Revolution*, p. 88.
76. Simmons, 'Colonial Patronage: Two Letters from William Franklin to the Earl of Bute, 1762', pp. 129–30.
77. Middlekauff, *Benjamin Franklin and his Enemies*, pp. 98, 104.
78. David T. Morgan, *The Devious Dr Franklin: Benjamin Franklin's Years in London*, Macon, Georgia: Mercer University Press, 1996, p. 72. Franklin knew Sargent through his work as agent of Pennsylvania, but as well as this Sargent had a packet franchise and carried mail to the West Indies and New York, so he was also another useful post-office connection; David Hancock, *Citizens of the World: London Merchants and the Integration of the British Atlantic Community, 1735–1785*, Cambridge and New York: Cambridge University Press, 1995, pp. 224–5, 314.
79. Edmund S. Morgan, *Benjamin Franklin*, New Haven, Connecticut, and London: Yale University Press, 2002, p. 127; Cochrane, *Dr Johnson's Printer*, p. 106.
80. Cited in Currey, *Road to Revolution*, p. 53.
81. *Papers of Benjamin Franklin*, Vol. 10, p. 232.

Chapter Nine: 'The most cautious man I have ever seen': Ben Franklin's London Career

1. Edmund S. Morgan, *Benjamin Franklin*, New Haven, Connecticut, and London: Yale University Press, 2002, pp. 130–32, 137–40.
2. 'Old Mistresses Apologue' in Benjamin Franklin, *Autobiography and Other Writings*, New York and Oxford: Oxford University Press, World's Classics Paperbacks, 1993, pp. 244–5.
3. Morgan, *Benjamin Franklin*, p. 112.
4. For examples of this, see a letter of Benjamin Franklin to Polly Stevenson, 15 June 1765, *The Papers of Benjamin Franklin*, ed. L.W. Labaree et al., 39 vols, New Haven, Connecticut: Yale University Press, 1959–, Vol. 12, p. 182, and other letters between Ben and Polly in 1765 and 1766 in *ibid.*, Vols 12, 13.
5. Esmond Wright, *Franklin of Philadelphia*, Cambridge, Massachusetts: Harvard University Press, 1986, pp. 110, 216.
6. *Papers of Benjamin Franklin*, Vol. 7, p. 369.
7. Eliza Lucas Pinckney, *The Letterbook of Eliza Lucas Pinckney, 1739–1762*, ed. Elise Pinckney, Columbia, South Carolina: University of South Carolina Press, 1997, p. 80.

8. William Sachse, *The Colonial American in Britain*, Madison, Wisconsin: The University of Wisconsin Press, 1956, pp. 19, 99.
9. *The London Encyclopædia*, ed. Ben Weinreb and Christopher Hibbert, London: Macmillan, 1983, pp. 142, 570–71; *Boswell's London Journal 1762–1763*, ed. Frederick A. Pottle, Melbourne, London, and Toronto: William Heinemann, 1950, pp. 4, 11, 73.
10. Holger Hoock, *The King's Artists: The Royal Academy of Arts, and the Politics of British Culture 1760–1840*, Oxford: Clarendon Press, 2003, p. 6; *The London Encyclopædia*, pp. 754, 756.
11. *The London Encyclopædia*, p. 598.
12. David T. Morgan, *The Devious Dr Franklin: Benjamin Franklin's Years in London*, Macon, Georgia: Mercer University Press, 1996, pp. 94, 174.
13. *Papers of Benjamin Franklin*, Vol. 17, p. 167.
14. *Ibid.*, Vol. 16, p. 212.
15. *Ibid.*, Vol. 9, p. 38; see also *ibid.*, Vol. 12, p. 169.
16. Peter Clark, 'Migrants in the City: The Process of Social Adaptation in English Towns, 1500–1800' in Peter Clark and David Souden, eds, *Migration and Society in Early Modern England*, London: Hutchinson, 1987, pp. 281–2.
17. *Papers of Benjamin Franklin*, Vol. 20, p. 513.
18. For examples from Virginia, South Carolina and Philadelphia, see Sachse, *The Colonial American in Britain*, pp. 119–20, 127, and William B. Reed, *The Life of Esther De Berdt Reed*, Philadelphia, 1853; this edition New York: Arno Press, 1971, p. 157.
19. Jesse Lemisch, 'Jack Tar in the Streets: Merchant Seamen in the Politics of Revolutionary America', reprinted in *In Search of Early America: The William and Mary Quarterly 1943–1993*, Richmond, Virginia: The Institute of Early American History and Culture, 1993, p. 112; on the East End of London and its seafaring community, see Marcus Rediker, *Between the Devil and the Deep Blue Sea*, Cambridge: Cambridge University Press, 1987, ch. 1.
20. Old Bailey Proceedings Online (www.oldbaileyonline.org, 31 March 2009), September 1772, trial of John Gearey (t17720909–24).
21. Old Bailey Proceedings Online (www.oldbaileyonline.org, 31 March 2009), September 1764, trials of James Castle and Matthew Farmer (t17640912–39).
22. Old Bailey Proceedings Online (www.oldbaileyonline.org, 31 March 2009), September 1768, trial of Robert Woodman (t17680907–85).
23. *Gentleman's Magazine and Historical Chronicle*, Vol. XXXV (1765), p. 346.
24. Cited in Wright, *Franklin of Philadelphia*, p. 185.
25. Robert Middlekauff, *Benjamin Franklin and his Enemies*, Berkeley, Los Angeles, and London: University of California Press, 1996, pp. 100–1.
26. Wright, *Franklin of Philadelphia*, pp. 188, 190.
27. *Life of Esther De Berdt Reed*, p. 107.
28. Eric Stockdale, *Middle Temple Lawyers and the American Revolution*, Eagan, Minnesota: Thomson-West, 2007, p. 89.
29. Cited in Wright, *Franklin of Philadelphia*, pp. 192–3.
30. British Library, Add. 20733, Correspondence of John Almon, 1766–1805, Hugh Williamson to John Almon, Philadelphia, 11 December 1766, ff. 145–146.
31. B.R. Smith, 'The Committee of the Whole House to Consider the American Papers (January and February, 1766)', M.A. thesis, Sheffield University, 1956, pp. 270, 272–3. There is no evidence that Franklin actually met Prime Minister Lord Rockingham and members of the cabinet during the weeks of preparation, as did the other star speaker, Barlow Trecothick. *Ibid.*, pp. 95–6.
32. Michael Kammen, *A Rope of Sand: The Colonial Agents, British Politics, and the American Revolution*, Ithaca, New York: Cornell University Press, 1968; this edition New York: Vintage Books, 1974, p. 119.
33. *Ibid.*, p. 121; Morgan, *The Devious Dr Franklin*, pp. 110–11.
34. R.C. Simmons and P.D.G. Thomas, eds, *Proceedings and Debates of the British Parliaments Respecting North America 1754–1783*, 3 vols, Millwood, New York,

London, and Nendeln, Liechtenstein: Kraus International Publications, 1982–3, Vol. II (1765–1768), pp. 134–5.
35. Kammen, *A Rope of Sand,* p. 121.
36. Wright, *Franklin of Philadelphia,* p. 197.
37. Franklin, 'Observations concerning the Increase of Mankind' (1751); Simmons and Thomas, eds, *Proceedings and Debates of the British Parliaments Respecting North America, 1754–1783,* Vol. II (1765–1768), pp. 237, 238–42, 244,
38. Simmons and Thomas, eds, *Proceedings and Debates of the British Parliaments Respecting North America, 1754–1783,* Vol. II (1765–1768), pp. 238, 241, 242.
39. *Ibid.,* Vol. II, pp. 235, 238.
40. Franklin, *Autobiography and Other Writings,* p. 179.
41. Crane, ed., *Benjamin Franklin's Letters to the Press,* p. 58.
42. Morgan, *The Devious Dr Franklin,* pp. 126, 148.
43. *Ibid.,* pp. 128, 158–60.
44. Cecil B. Currey, *Road to Revolution: Benjamin Franklin in England 1765–1775,* Gloucester, Massachusetts: Peter Smith, 1978, pp. 70, 85–7, 90.
45. Wright, *Franklin of Philadelphia,* pp. 214–15, 217; H.W. Brands, *The First American, The Life and Times of Benjamin Franklin,* New York: Anchor Books, 2000, pp. 324, 448.
46. Wright, *Franklin of Philadelphia,* pp. 151, 216.
47. Currey, *Road to Revolution,* p. 96.
48. Peter D.G. Thomas, *John Wilkes: A Friend to Liberty,* Oxford: Clarendon Press, 1996, p. 4. Dashwood was postmaster general and a Fellow of the Royal Society, so Franklin would have known him on both counts.
49. Currey, *Road to Revolution,* pp. 92, 98–9.
50. Wright, *Franklin of Philadelphia,* p. 216.
51. *Papers of Benjamin Franklin,* Vol. 19, pp. 258–9.
52. Currey, *Road to Revolution,* pp. 87–90.
53. Cochrane, *Dr Johnson's Printer,* pp. 204–5.
54. Wright, *Franklin of Philadelphia,* pp. 153, 209.
55. Sheila Skemp, *William Franklin, Son of a Patriot, Servant of a King,* New York and Oxford: Oxford University Press, 1990, p. 119.
56. Wright, *Franklin of Philadelphia,* pp. 211–12.
57. Sachse, *The Colonial American in Britain,* pp. 105–6, and *Papers of Benjamin Franklin,* Vol. 16, p. 200; Currey, *Road to Revolution,* p. 390; Louis W. Potts, *Arthur Lee, A Virtuous Revolutionary,* Baton Rouge and London: Louisiana State University Press, 1981, p. 255.
58. Wright, *Franklin of Philadelphia,* pp. 211–12.
59. Currey, *Road to Revolution,* p. 391; *Papers of Benjamin Franklin,* Vol. 18, p. 65.
60. *Papers of Benjamin Franklin,* Vol. 20, p. 305.
61. *Life of Esther De Berdt Reed,* p. 166.
62. Kammen, *A Rope of Sand,* p. 149.
63. Franklin's Use of 'Prudential Algebra', 3 August 1773, *Papers of Benjamin Franklin,* Vol. 20, p. 319.
64. Morgan, *The Devious Doctor Franklin,* p. 199.
65. Crane, ed., *Benjamin Franklin's Letters to the Press,* pp. 222–3.
66. Granville Sharp, *A Representation of the Injustice and Dangerous Tendency of Tolerating Slavery; or of Admitting the Least Claim of Private Property in the Persons of Men, in England,* London, 1769, pp. 81–2, 85–6.
67. 'A Conversation *between an* ENGLISHMAN, *a* SCOTCHMAN, *and an* AMERICAN, *on the Subject of* SLAVERY', in Verner W. Crane, ed., *Benjamin Franklin's Letters to the Press, 1758–1775,* Chapel Hill, North Carolina: University of North Carolina Press, 1950, pp. 186–92.
68. R.H. Lee, *Life of Arthur Lee, LL.D.,* 2 vols, Boston, 1829; reprinted Freeport, New York: Books for Libraries Press, 1969, Vol. I, p. 257.

69. Joseph Reed to Charles Pettit, 7 May 1770, Joseph Reed Papers (BV Reed, Joseph) New-York Historical Society.
70. Wright, *Franklin of Philadelphia*, p. 216; Middlekauff, *Benjamin Franklin and his Enemies*, p. 2.
71. Skemp, *William Franklin*, p. 35.
72. *Papers of Benjamin Franklin*, Vol. 18, p. 65.
73. Historical Society of Pennsylvania (HSP), Thomas Coombe Papers, Thomas Coombe, Jr., to his father, 6 June 1770.
74. HSP, Thomas Coombe Papers, Thomas Coombe, Jr. to his father, 4 August 1770.
75. *Ibid*.
76. Wright, *Franklin of Philadelphia*, p. 151; Morgan, *Benjamin Franklin*, p. 129.
77. *Papers of Benjamin Franklin*, Vol. 20, p. 305.
78. Middlekauff, *Benjamin Franklin and his Enemies*, p. 5.
79. Annette Laing (independent scholar), 'Unbroken Unions: Transatlantic Personal Relationships and Identity among the South Carolinian Gentry in the Age of the American Revolution', unpublished paper presented at the Omohundro Institute of Early American History and Culture, Seventh Annual Conference, University of Glasgow, 10–15 July 2001. I am grateful to Dr Laing for allowing me to consult her paper.
80. Middlekauff, *Benjamin Franklin and his Enemies*, p. 106.
81. HSP, Thomas Coombe Papers, Thomas Coombe, Jr. to his father, August 11, 1769.
82. Carl Bridenbaugh, *Rebels and Gentlemen: Philadelphia in the Age of Franklin*, New York: Reynal & Hitchcock, 1942; this edition Westport, Connecticut: Greenwood Press, 1978, pp. 207–12.
83. Morgan, *The Devious Doctor Franklin*, pp. 184–6.
84. *Ibid*., pp. 121–2, 161–2, 188. William Franklin had hinted to his father in 1769 that there was support for him in the Bay Colony as the next governor of Massachusetts; *Papers of Benjamin Franklin*, Vol. 16, pp. 129–30.
85. Wright, *Franklin of Philadelphia*, pp. 224–5.
86. Morgan, *The Devious Dr Franklin*, pp. 221–2.
87. Potts, *Arthur Lee*, pp. 75–8.
88. Andrew Jackson O'Shaughnessy, *An Empire Divided: The American Revolution and the British Caribbean*, Philadelphia, Pennsylvania: University of Pennsylvania Press, 2000, p. 105; John Sainsbury, *Disaffected Patriots: London Supporters of Revolutionary America 1769–1782*, Kingston and Montreal: McGill-Queen's University Press, 1987; p. 38.
89. W. Isaacson, *Benjamin Franklin: An American Life*, Simon & Schuster, 2003, pp. 274–5.
90. *Life of Arthur Lee*, Vol. I, p. 270.
91. *Ibid*., pp. 270–71.
92. Morgan, *The Devious Dr Franklin*, p. 224.
93. *Ibid*., pp. 224–6.
94. *Papers of Benjamin Franklin*, Vol. 21, pp. 58–9, 61.
95. Brands, *The First American*, pp. 470–74.
96. *Papers of Benjamin Franklin*, Vol. 21, pp. 38–9.
97. Brands, *The First American*, pp. 470, 472, 475; *Papers of Benjamin Franklin*, Vol. 21, p. 41.
98. Alexander Carlyle, *Autobiography of the Reverend Dr Alexander Carlyle*, second edition, Edinburgh and London: William Blackwood, 1860, p. 437.
99. Isaacson, *Benjamin Franklin: An American Life*, pp. 279, 282–3.
100. *Papers of Benjamin Franklin*, Vol. 21, pp. x, 286.
101. *Ibid*., p. 363, fn.
102. *Ibid*., pp. 363, 589; *ibid*., Vol. 22, p. 599, fn.
103. *Ibid*., Vol. 21, p. 584.
104. *Ibid*., pp. 521–2.

105. Julie Flavell, 'British Perceptions of New England and the Decision for a Coercive Colonial Policy, 1774–1775', in Julie Flavell and Stephen Conway, eds, *Britain and America Go to War: The Impact of War and Warfare in Anglo-America, 1754–1815*, Gainesville, Florida: University Press of Florida, 2004, pp. 107–8. Letter of Lord Dartmouth to Franklin cited in Julie M. Flavell, 'Government Interception of Letters from America and the Quest for Colonial Opinion in 1775', *William and Mary Quarterly*, 3rd series, Vol. LVIII, no. 2 (April 2001), p. 414.

106. *Papers of Benjamin Franklin*, Vol. 21, p. 582.

107. *Ibid.*, p. 570.

108. *Ibid.*, pp. 577, 583.

109. *Ibid.*, pp. 197–8, 201, xxxv.

110. *Ibid.*, p. 535.

111. Joyce E. Chaplin, *The First Scientific American: Benjamin Franklin and the Pursuit of Genius*, New York: Basic Books, 2006, pp. 260–61.

112. Wright, *Franklin of Philadelphia*, pp. 267–9; cited in *ibid.*, p. 270.

113. Middlekauff, *Benjamin Franklin and his Enemies*, p. 209.

Epilogue

1. Solomon Lutnick, *The American Revolution and the British Press, 1775–1783*, Columbia, Missouri: University of Missouri Press, 1967, p. 63.

2. The Historical Society of Pennsylvania (HSP), Powell-Dickinson Papers, Arthur Lee to John Dickinson, London, 30 May 1775.

3. [Arthur Lee] to Robert Carter Nicholas, 22 September 1775, Colonial Office Papers, CO5/40, fols. 17–21, the National Archives, Kew: PRO.

4. William Lee to Richard Henry Lee, 22 September 1775, Worthington Chauncey Ford, ed., *Letters of William Lee, 1766–1783*, Brooklyn, New York, 3 vols, 1891, Vol. I, p. 174.

5. Jack N. Rakove, *The Beginnings of National Politics: An Interpretive History of the Continental Congress*, Baltimore, Maryland, and London: Johns Hopkins University Press, 1982, p. 9.

6. HSP, Powell-Dickinson Papers, [Arthur Lee] to John Dickinson, 13 February 1775.

7. HSP, Powell-Dickinson Papers, [unsigned] to John Dickinson (in William Lee's hand), London, not dated, but the contents indicate that it was written some time between February and October 1775.

8. *The Papers of Benjamin Franklin*, ed. L.W. Labaree et al., 39 vols, New Haven, Connecticut: Yale University Press, 1959–, Vol. 22, pp. 118–19; *ibid.*, Vol. 21, pp. 556–7.

9. Louis W. Potts, *Arthur Lee, A Virtuous Revolutionary*, Baton Rouge and London: Louisiana State University Press, 1981, p. 152.

10. Arthur Lee to John Dickinson, London, 4 September 1775; [unsigned] to Col. Landon Carter, London, Sept. 23, 1775 [Copy]; Paul P. Hoffman, ed., *Lee Family Papers 1742–1795* (Microfilm Publications, University of Virginia Library, 1966–), roll 2.

11. Arthur Lee to George Germain, 22 December 1775, Colonial Office Papers, CO5/154, fol. 205; John Pownall to Arthur Lee, 23 December 1775, CO5/154, fols. 206–207d, the National Archives: PRO.

12. John Sainsbury, *Disaffected Patriots: London Supporters of Revolutionary America 1769–1782*, Kingston and Montreal: McGill-Queen's University Press, 1987, pp. 104–5.

13. Ross J.S. Hoffman, *The Marquis: A Study of Lord Rockingham, 1730–1782*, New York: Fordham University Press, 1973, p. 337.

14. British Library, Add. MS. 34, 413 (Vol. II), The Auckland Papers (Correspondence and papers, political and private, of William Eden, First Baron Auckland), fols. 240–41, 242–3.

15. John Sainsbury, 'The Pro-Americans of London, 1769 to 1782', *William and Mary Quarterly*, 3rd series, Vol. 35 (1978), pp.436–43.

16. Lewis Einstein, *Divided Loyalties: Americans in England during the War of Independence*, London: Cobden-Sanderson, 1933, pp. 359–63.

17. *Papers of Benjamin Franklin*, Vol. 22, p. 28; Mary Beth Norton, *The British-Americans: The Loyalist Exiles in England, 1774–1789*, Boston: Little, Brown, 1972; this edition London: Constable, 1974, p. 237; Esmond Wright, *Franklin of Philadelphia*, Cambridge, Massachusetts: Harvard University Press, 1986, pp. 323, 347, 353.

18. James Thomas Flexner, *America's Old Masters*, New York: Viking Press, 1939; this edition New York: Dover Publications, 1967, pp. 68, 78.

19. Einstein, *Divided Loyalties: Americans* pp. 83–90, 106–12.

20. *Felix Farley's Bristol Journal*, 10 April 1874; Henry C. Van Schaack, *Henry Cruger the Colleague of Edmund Burke in the British Parliament* (New York, 1859), pp. 37–9. I am grateful to Professor Peter Marshall for drawing my attention to the details of Cruger's final parliamentary election.

21. Julie M. Flavell, 'American Patriots in London and the Quest for Talks, 1774–1775', *Journal of Imperial and Commonwealth History*, Vol. 20, no. 3 (1992), pp. 335–69.

22. *Correspondence of Mr. Ralph Izard of South Carolina*, ed. Anne Izard Deas, New York, 1844, p. 109.

23. Thomas J. Fleming, *Now We Are Enemies: The Story of Bunker Hill*, New York: St. Martin's Press, 1960, pp. 184, 257.

24. *Correspondence of Mr. Ralph Izard*, p. 189; David Hackett Fischer, *Paul Revere's Ride*, New York and Oxford: Oxford University Press, 1994, pp. 75, 96–7, 386–7.

25. M. McInnis, *In Pursuit of Refinement: Charlestonians Abroad, 1740–1860*, Columbia, South Carolina: University of South Carolina Press, 1999, pp. 33, 66, 110, 302; *The Papers of Henry Laurens*, Vol. 13, p. 250; on the South Carolina community in London during the war, see Annette Laing, 'Unbroken Unions: Transatlantic Personal Relationships and Identity among the South Carolinian Gentry in the Age of the American Revolution', unpublished paper presented at the Omohundro Institute of Early American History and Culture, Seventh Annual Conference, University of Glasgow, 10–15 July 2001.

26. *Correspondence of Mr. Ralph Izard*, pp. vii, 173.

27. Cecil B. Currey, *Road to Revolution: Benjamin Franklin in England, 1765–1775*, Gloucester, Massachusetts: Peter Smith, 1978, p. 359.

28. *The Papers of Henry Laurens*, ed. George C. Rogers, Jr., et al., 16 vols, Columbia, South Carolina: University of South Carolina Press, 1968–2002, Vol. 15, pp. 382, 620–21; *ibid.*, Vol. 16, pp. 2–3, 262–3 fn, 392, 408, 640 fn.

29. Gregory D. Massey, *John Laurens and the American Revolution*, Columbia, South Carolina: University of South Carolina Press, 2000, pp. 165–6.

30. Stephen Conway, 'From Fellow Nationals to Foreigners: British Perceptions of the Americans, Circa 1739–1783', *William and Mary Quarterly*, 3rd series, Vol. LIX (2002), pp. 85–8.

31. Mary M. Drummond, 'Middleton, William (1748–1829)' in Lewis Namier and John Brooke, *The History of Parliament: The House of Commons, 1754–1790*, 3 vols, London: Her Majesty's Stationery Office, 1964, Vol. 3, p. 137; McInnis, *In Pursuit of Refinement*, pp. 28–9, 66–7, 104.

32. Old Bailey Proceedings Online (www.oldbaileyonline.org, 18 November 2004), 5 June 1782, trial of Bennet Allen, Robert Morris (t17820605-1); J. Bennett Nolan, *Benjamin Franklin in Scotland and Ireland, 1759 and 1771*, Philadelphia, Pennsylvania: University of Pennsylvania Press, 1938, p. 27; Rosamond Bayne-Powell, *Travellers in Eighteenth-Century England*, London: John Murray, 1951, p. 156.

33. Norton, *The British-Americans: The Loyalist Exiles in England, 1774–1789*, pp. 8, 68; see also Maya Jasanoff, 'The Other Side of Revolution: Loyalists in the British Empire', *William and Mary Quarterly*, 3rd series, Vol. LXV (2008), pp. 205–32; Gretchen Holbrook Gerzina, *Black London: Life before Emancipation*, New Brunswick, New Jersey: Rutgers University Press, 1995, pp. 134–6.

34. Peter Fryer, *Staying Power: The History of Black People in Britain*, London: Pluto Press, 1984, p. 191; Gerzina, *Black London*, pp. 134–6.

35. *Ibid.*, pp. 21–2.

36. Henry Steele Commager, ed., *Britain through American Eyes*, New York: McGraw-Hill, 1974, p. p. 381; Richard D. Altick, *The Shows of London*, Cambridge, Massachusetts: Harvard University Press, 1978, p. 276.

37. Fryer, *Staying Power*, pp. 191–5, 235, 372–5; W. Jeffrey Bolster, *Black Jacks: African American Seamen in the Age of Sail*, Cambridge, Massachusetts: Harvard University Press, 1997, pp. 216, 218, 229–32.

38. Fryer, *Staying Power*, pp. 234–6.

39. Commager, ed., *Britain through American Eyes*, pp. 14–16.

40. Frank Thistlethwaite, *America and the Atlantic Community: Anglo-American Aspects, 1790–1850*, first edition 1959; this edition New York: Harper & Row, 1963, pp. 6–8.

41. John Summerson, *Georgian London*, London: Pleiades Books, 1945; this edition Cambridge, Massachusetts: MIT Press, 1978, p. 265.

42. Foster Rhea Dulles, *Americans Abroad: Two Centuries of European Travel*, Ann Arbor, Michigan: University of Michigan Press, 1964, pp. 20, 87.

43. J.G. De Roulhac Hamilton, 'Southern Members of the Inns of Court', *North Carolina Historical Review*, Vol. 10 (1933), pp. 273–80; C.E.A. Bedwell, 'American Middle Templars', *American Historical Review* (July 1920), pp. 688–9; McInnis, *In Pursuit of Refinement: Charlestonians Abroad*, p. 33.

44. Cited in Howard Temperley, *Britain and America since Independence*, Basingstoke, Hampshire and New York: Palgrave, 2002, p. 4.

45. Paul Langford, 'Manners and Character in Anglo-American Perceptions, 1750–1850' in Fred M. Leventhal and Roland Quinault, eds, *Anglo-American Attitudes: From Revolution to Partnership*, Aldershot and Burlington: Ashgate, 2000, pp. 81, 82, 86.

46. James Fenimore Cooper, *Gleanings in Europe: England*, Albany, New York: State University of New York Press, 1982, p. 290.

Further Reading

The momentous years surrounding the American Revolution have been the subject of numerous political histories. Robert Middlekauff, *The Glorious Cause: The American Revolution, 1763–1789* (New York and Oxford: Oxford University Press, 1982) is a highly readable narrative of events on both sides of the Atlantic up to and including the War of Independence. For those interested in British attitudes towards the American colonies during the Seven Years' War and the era of the American Revolution, *The Persistence of Empire: British Political Culture in the Age of the American Revolution* by Eliga H. Gould (Chapel Hill: University of North Carolina Press, 2000) goes beyond political history to discuss popular attitudes and how they were changed by the growth of Anglo-American conflict during these pivotal years. Christopher Brown, *Moral Capital: Foundations of British Abolitionism* (Chapel Hill: University of North Carolina Press, 2006) provides an excellent account of how the debate over American rights and liberties sharpened public awareness in Britain of the wrongs of slavery. A book which puts the conflict of the Revolution in the context of the wider British empire is P.J. Marshall's *The Making and Unmaking of Empires: Britain, India and America c.1750–1783* (Oxford: Oxford University Press, 2005). The story of how the West Indian colonies, still classed as part of America at the end of the Seven Years' War, had severed their connections with the mainland colonies by the end of the American Revolution is told in Andrew O'Shaughnessy, *An Empire Divided: The American Revolution and the British Caribbean* (Philadelphia: University of Pennsylvania Press, 2000).

Georgian London is a topic that is never exhausted. M. Dorothy George's *London Life in the Eighteenth Century*, first published over half a century ago, remains an excellent readable social history. George Rudé, *Hanoverian London 1714–1808* (first published London: Secker & Warburg, 1971; Stroud, Sutton Publishing Ltd, 2003) is a lively and authoritative social and political history. Peter Thorold, *The London Rich: The Creation of a Great City, from 1666 to the Present* (London: Viking, 1999) devotes several chapters to the West End during the Georgian Era, and discusses the wealthy West Indian absentees who settled there. *Georgian London* by John Summerson (first published London: Pleiades Books, 1945; revised edition by New Haven and London: Yale University Press, 2003) is a fascinating architectural history of the city in a period when it was taking on the shape of the London we know today. For those who would like to read about Georgian London in the words of one who lived there, *Boswell's London Journal, 1762-1763* (edited by Frederick A. Pottle, Yale University Press, 2004) by James Boswell provides an insider's account of a single young man's life in the Great City that gives a flavour of the experiences of young colonials at the Inns of Court.

On the black community in London, Gretchen Gerzina's *Black London: Life before Emancipation* (New Brunswick: Rutgers University Press, 1995) is a highly readable account of the thriving African community in the imperial capital during the eighteenth century. Peter Fryer, *Staying Power: The History of Black People in Britain* (London: Pluto Press, 1984) charts the black presence in Britain over four centuries. Simon Schama's *Rough Crossings: Britain, the Slaves, and the American Revolution* (London: BBC Books, 2005) tells the story of black Loyalists in the aftermath of the war.

For books on colonial Americans in their mother country, William L. Sachse's *The Colonial American in Britain* (Madison: University of Wisconsin Press, 1956) was published many decades ago but remains a readable overview on the subject. A book which tells the stories of the American political activists in London before the Revolution is John Sainsbury, *Disaffected Patriots: London Supporters of Revolutionary America 1769-1782* (Kingston and Montreal: McGill-Queen's University Press, 1987). Biographies of colonial Americans who lived in London are a good window into their world. There are far too many biographies of Benjamin Franklin to mention here; all of them include his career in the metropolis, but one which focuses on his London years is David T. Morgan's *The Devious Dr Franklin, Colonial Agent: Benjamin Franklin's Years in London* (Macon: Mercer University Press, 1996). Other biographies of colonists who lived in London in the years leading up to the Revolution include Gregory D. Massey, *John Laurens and the American Revolution* (Columbia: University of South Carolina Press, 2000), John Alden, *Stephen Sayre, American Revolutionary Adventurer* (Baton Rouge and London: Louisiana State University Press, 1983), and Louis W. Potts, *Arthur Lee, A Virtuous Revolutionary* (Baton Rouge and London: Louisiana State University Press, 1981).

Books on topics that could only be touched upon briefly in my work, but which readers may wish to explore in more depth, include Fred Anderson's fascinating *Crucible of War: The Seven Years' War and the Fate of Empire in British North America, 1754–1766* (New York: Alfred A. Knopf, 2000). Troy O. Bickham, *Savages within the Empire: Representations of American Indians in Eighteenth-Century Britain* (Oxford: Oxford University Press, 2005) is a thorough and interesting account of how Native Americans were seen at the centre of empire during the Georgian Era. Alden T. Vaughan, *Transatlantic Encounters: American Indians in Britain, 1500–1776* (Cambridge: Cambridge University Press, 2006) tells the stories of Native American visitors to Britain throughout the colonial period. An enjoyable book on Benjamin West and other early American artists in England is James Thomas Flexner, *America's Old Masters* (first published New York: Viking Press, 1939; revised edition New York: Dover Publications, 1967). For those who wish to read more about the impact of American plants on the gardens of England during the eighteenth century, Andrea Wulf's *The Brother Gardeners: Botany, Empire and the Birth of an Obsession* (London: Windmill Books, 2009) is an absorbing account of the Georgian fascination for New World plants.

Index

Abba (slave) 33–4
Abel, Carl Friedrich 147
Abercromby, James 239–40
absentee planters *see* planters, absentee
Act of Union (1707) 70
Adam (slave) 53
Adams, Abigail 247
Adams, John 2, 82, 86, 118, 127, 239, 245, 247
Adams, John Quincy 53
Adams, Louisa Catherine Johnson 53
Adams, Samuel 150
Addison, Joseph 123
African Americans 4, 13–14
    see also black population; servants, London; slaves, American
Albany Conference 190–1
Allen, Andrew and James 24, *24*, 136–7, 197
Allen, Bennet 242
Allen, William 199, 205, 207
Allen family 153, 203
Alleyne family 200, 201
American Civil War 25, 46, 47, 147, 241, 248
American Philosophical Society 190
American Revolution *see* American War of Independence
American War of Independence 1, 4, 23–5, 42, 49, 55, 82, 83, 85, 92, 101, 102, 104, 107, 116, 118, 149, 153, 158, 171, 180, 181, 189, 193, 201, 218, 232, 235–45
    peace proclaimed *244*, 245
    refugees in London from 242
Americans, colonial
    bad behaviour of 'Carolina set' 96
    bad reputation of young Americans in London 71–2, 83

believed to be black, mixed race 48, 49–50, 119, 128, *152*, 157, 243
considered to be English, British 70, 71, 165–6, 168–70
and education 66–8
lack of distinctive accents 71, 128–9
lack of national identity 22–3, 165–6, 247
as refugees from Revolutionary America 242
stereotypes of 168–9
Americans, development of national character 189, 248
Amsterdam 67
Anglo-Cherokee war 182
Annapolis, Maryland 53
Anson, George, 1st Baron Anson 11
Ansonborough, Charleston, South Carolina 8, 38–9, 52, 56, 84
Antigua 21, 72
Appleby, George 20, 32, 52–8
Appleby family 58
architecture
    Georgian 10–11
    nineteenth-century 246
Argyll, General John Campbell, 4th Duke of 19
armonica (invention of Benjamin Franklin) 207
army 145
    as profession 66, 74, 117–18
artists 246
Augusta, Princess of Wales 207
Austen, Jane 73
    on London 186
    Mansfield Park 20, 22, 66, 80, 81
    Pride and Prejudice 75, 80, 129–30, 137
    Sense and Sensibility 18, 19, 66, 67, 68
Austin, George 20, 32, 52, 55, 71

Austin, George, Jr. 71
Austin family 54, 55, 74
Austria 122
Aylesbury, Lady 19

Bacchus (slave) 53
Bach, Johann Sebastian 147
Baddeley, Sophia 154–9, *155*
    Memoirs 154
Bahamas 4
Baker, John 28, 33, *41*, 82
Ball family 10, 11
Baltimore, Frances Calvert, 7th Earl 153
Baptists 132
Barbados 4, 22, 45, 200
Barbara (putative mother of William
    Franklin) 197
Barber, Francis 91
Barclay, David 230
Barnwell, Elizabeth (Betsey) 76
Bartram, John 173
Bartram, William 64, 93
basket-women 30–1, *31*
Bath 131, 161, 240
Bathurst, Richard 91
Beaumarchais, Pierre-Augustin
    Caron de 236
Beckford, William (1709–70) 22,
    146, 226–7
Beckford, William, (1760–1844) 22
Beckford family 24, *24*, 44
Bedford, John Russell, 4th Duke of 173
Beef, Jack 28–9
beggars, black 243
    see also black population; slaves,
        American
Behn, Aphra 181
Bengal 103
Beresford, Mrs Richard 19
Beresford family 137
Bermuda 4
Bernard, Sir Francis 146–7, 148, 226, 228
Berners Street set 18–21, 24, 29, 34, 39, 61,
    67, 76, 79, 101, 105, 109, 119, 137,
    151–4, 225, 238, 239, 240
Bewick, Thomas 195–6
    History of British Birds 195
Bicknell, Charles 88–9, 99
    elder brother 99, 101
bigamy 57–8
Bill of Rights Society 151–2
Birmingham 50, 73, 77, 100
'Black Jack' (slave) 33
black population
    of London 34, 243–4

    of mainland colonies 50
    see also slaves, American
Blowers, Sampson Salter 238
boarding schools 67–8, 69, 104
Bolton, Duke of 155
Boone, Sarah (Tattnall, Peronneau) 20–1
Boone, Thomas 20–1
Boston, Massachusetts 2, 19, 23, 46, 48,
    50, 55, 104–5, 118, 146, 190, 211,
    235, 248
Boston Massacre 145–6
Boston Tea Party 55, 104, 158, 228, 229, 236
Boswell, James 16, 70, 95, 96, 139,
    153, 183, 211, 223, 224–5
Boulogne, France 80
Boulton, Matthew 207
Bowdoin, James 227
Braddock, Edward 191
Brailsford, Samuel 20, 25, 29, 92
Brailsford family 18, 20, 21, 67, 76, 122
Brant, Joseph (Thayendanegea) 183
Bremar, Francis (Frank) 75, 81, 241
Bremar, John 75–6, 81, 241
Bremar, Mary (Molsy) 74–82, 98–9, 112,
    166, 241
Bremar, Peter 241
Bremar family 79, 241
Bridges, Thomas 201
Bristol 2, 55, 73, 213, 239
Britain
    electoral system 144
    liberty and prosperity of 122
Brompton, Kent 109–10
Brown, Lancelot 'Capability' 174
Brown Decision (1954) 50
Brown University (earlier College of
    Rhode Island) 84
Bunker Hill, Battle of 108, 239–40
Burke, Edmund 95, 127, 141, 146, 151,
    160, 215, 228, 229
Burke, William, *Account of the European
    Settlements in America* 181
Bute, John Stuart, 3rd Earl of 119, 143,
    163, 204, 205, 222
Bute, Mary, Countess of 208

Cambridge, University of 18, 54, 67, 72,
    84, 85
Camisards 180
Campbell, Lady William (née Sarah Izard)
    19, 240
Campbell, Lord William 19, 240
Canada 4, 207
    British defeat of French in 107, 117, 119,
        133, 174, 177, 191

Canton, John 205, 206
Cape Cod, Massachusetts 245
Caribbean islands 23, 245
  see also West Indies
Carolina Packet 74, 78, 81
Carroll, Charles, of Annapolis 85, 89
Carroll, Charles, Barrister 53
Carroll, Charles, of Carrollton 85–6, 87,
  88, 89, 95
Carson, Kit 180
Carver, Jonathan, Travels through the
  Interior Parts of North America in
  the Years 1766, 1767, and 1768 181
Castle, James 213
Catherine II (the Great), Empress of
  Russia 163
Catholics 85–6, 131–2
Cato (Appleby slave) 32, 53–4, 56, 59, 91
Cato (Dickinson slave) 91
Cévennes 180
Chambers, Sir William 18
Charles I, King 29
Charles II, King 17
Charleston, South Carolina 7, 9, 13, 19, 20,
  22, 53, 55, 74, 75, 77, 82, 137
  Harbor 240
Charlotte, Queen 16, 131
Charming Polly (brig) 53
Chateaubriand, François-René de 181
Chatham, Lord see Pitt, William
Cherokees, in London 181–3, 184
Chesapeake 48
chimney sweeps 32, 33
chocolate 170
Christian VII, King of Denmark 219
Church, as profession 66, 73, 117
Church of England 132
The Citizen's Calendar 220
Clarke, Reverend Richard (schoolteacher)
  16, 21, 25–6, 43, 72
Clay, Joseph 53–4
clergymen, colonial 172
Club of Honest Whigs 169, 205–7, 217,
  225, 233, 248
  idealise life in northern colonies 169,
  205, 207, 217, 248
Cobbett, William 244
cocoa beans 170
Cody, Buffalo Bill 180
Coercive Acts (1774) 104–5, 154
coffee 170
coffee houses, London 17, 26, 28, 29, 39,
  40, 48, 72, 87, 93, 96, 101, 113, 126,
  136, 147, 150, 160, 170, 175, 180
  as business meeting places 124–5

Carolina Coffee House 25, 29, 32, 110,
  124, 125, 175, 240
Georgia Coffee House 125
Grecian Coffee House 95
Jamaica Coffee House (later Jamaica
  Wine House) 3, 125, 175
New England Coffee House 125
New York Coffee House 125
Pennsylvania Coffee House 125, 159,
  161, 175, 210, 221
  as social and cultural centres 94–5
St Paul's Coffee House 205
Virginia and Baltick Coffee House 125
Virginia and Maryland Coffee House 125
colleges, in America 84
Collinson, Peter 173–4, 204, 205, 206
colonial rights 48–9, 105–6, 127, 149, 169,
  213, 225
Columbia University (earlier King's
  College) 84
Compton, Henry, bishop of London 172
Congregationalists 132
Connecticut 127, 207
Constitution, U.S. 2
consumer goods, British, imported by
  American colonists 216–18
Continental Congress 1, 70, 111, 113, 162,
  220, 229, 231, 235, 241
Cook, Captain James 65, 108
Coombe, Thomas 223–4, 225
Cooper, James Fenimore 59, 71, 248
  Last of the Mohicans 180
  The Spy 82
Corsica 180
Cowper, William 47
Crèvecoeur, J. Hector St John de 4
  Letters from an American Farmer 166
cricket 25
crime, at London docks 171–2, 213
Crosby, Brass 152
Cruger, Henry 239
Cushing, Thomas 226

Dance, George 123
Dartmouth, William Legge, 2nd Earl of
  140, 185, 215, 221, 229, 230, 231
Dartmouth College 84, 132, 185
Darwin, Erasmus 100
Dashwood, Sir Francis, Baron Le
  Despencer 145, 219, 223, 224
Day, Thomas 99–101, 107, 112, 133, 167
  'Fragment of an Original Letter on the
  Slavery of the Negroes' 102
  Sandford and Merton 102–3
  see also 'The Dying Negro'

294 INDEX

De Berdt, Dennis 131–41, 143, 147, 148,
150, 151, 182, 185, 207
as agent for Massachusetts 134, 136,
139–40, 214, 216, 226–7
idealises life in northern colonies 131,
132, 133, 207
De Berdt, Dennis, Jr. 135, 142, 157
De Berdt, Esther (Hetta) (later Reed)
135–6, 141–2, 148, 158, 197,
221, 223
De Berdt, Mrs 141–2
De Berdt family 134–42, 162
de Grey, William, Lord Chief
Justice 161
Deans, Robert 16, 28, 35, 55
Deans family 35, 39
Declaration of Independence (1776) 1, 2,
4, 86, 148, 230, 236, 241–2
Declaratory Act, proposed 215, 216
Defoe, Daniel 27, 170, 196
Moll Flanders 116
DeLancy, Elizabeth (née Beresford) 19
DeLancey, Peter 19, 137, 153, 199
DeLancey family 19, 22, 109, 119
Delaware 86
Denmark 162
Denny, William 194
Dickens, Charles 3
A Christmas Carol 125
David Copperfield 154
Nicholas Nickleby 154
The Old Curiosity Shop 52
The Pickwick Papers 120
Dickinson, John 86–7, 89–90, 149
Letters from a Farmer in
Pennsylvania 86
dissenters, religious 132, 136, 207
Draper, Sir William 19
Dryden, John 181
Dublin 123
duels 227, 242
Dulany, Daniel, Jr. 49
Dulany, Lloyd 242
Dutch, reputation of among English 165
Dutch Republic 207
'The Dying Negro' (poem) 101

East India Company 103
Edgeworth, Maria, The Absentee 103–4
Edinburgh 70, 196
Edinburgh University 137
American students at 1, 69, 84
medical students at 69, 147
education 66–8, 69, 100–1, 104, 201–2
electoral system 144

Elizabeth I, Queen 122
Ellis, John 64–5, 108
Emerson, Ralph Waldo 128, 247
emigrants to colonies 48, 171–2
Empire Windrush, MV 243
Endeavour, HMS 65
Enfield 134
Enlightenment, philosophy of 186
Eton College 147
exotica, collections of 174–5
extramarital relationships 153–4, 210

Falmouth 11–14, 59
Harbour 12
Fenwick family 19
Ferguson, Elizabeth Graeme see Graeme,
Elizabeth
Fielding, Henry 96
Tom Jones 153–4, 210
Fielding, Sir John 29, 96
First World War 246
Fischer, Johann Caspar Ferdinand 147
Florida 4, 120
Flower, Mrs 211–12
Fonthill Abbey, Wiltshire 22
foodstuffs 10
Foot Guards, First Regiment 159
foreigners, English aversion to 165, 168
Fort Duquesne 191
Fort Necessity 117
Fort Niagara 117–18
Fort Ticonderoga 3, 176–7, 230, 245
Fothergill, Dr John 132–3, 172–3, 205, 230
France 54, 85, 111, 112, 122, 149, 176, 181,
189, 219–20, 235, 237, 239, 246
Franklin, Benjamin 189–99, 191, 209–34,
235–8
as agent for Georgia and New Jersey
218, 222, 225
as agent for Pennsylvania Assembly 189,
190, 202, 222
at Albany Conference 190–1
as American hero 189, 217, 233
on American sheriffs of London 154
appears before Privy Council 228–9
athletic prowess 190
at coffee house 125
and Peter Collinson 173–4
on colonial Americans as a people
216–17
as deputy postmaster for America 190,
209, 213, 220, 223, 229, 230
dispute with Penn family 192–5, 208–9,
213, 224, 225
education 116–17

electrical experiments 192, 218
on England 208
as epitome of an American 189, 248
estrangement from William 201–2,
233–4
failure to obtain British government
post 218
as Fellow of the Royal Society 205
first arrival in London 173–4, 187
flirtations 203
and Mrs Flower 211–12
in France 189, 218, 232–3
growing fame 189, 190
growing reputation for reserve and
caution 223–5
'Hints' for union between Britain and
colonies 230–1
on his life in England 219
honorary doctorates 207
and intellectual life in London 190
as journalist 150, 220, 222
and land speculation 220–1
and leaked Hutchinson letters
226–8, 232
Learned Society 95
on London servants 27, 41–2
and Massachusetts agency 141, 150, 218,
222, 226–7
and mastodon's jawbone 174–5
Monday Club 125
and Ohio project 220–1
in Paris 218, 232–3, 237
and Pennsylvanian politics 209
personality 193–4, 223–4
in Philadelphia 190, 193–4, 196
and Pitt 204, 231
as political writer 207, 222
as polymath 190–2, 218–19
and Pontiac uprising 209
portraits of 207
as printer's apprentice in London
190, 193
in protest against Coercive Acts
105, 230
receives Copley Medal from Royal
Society 192
reputation in France 219–20, 232–3
returns to America (1775) 232, 235
scheme for royal government for
Pennsylvania 209, 213, 218
on slavery 47–8, 50, 107, 222
social status in London 195–6, 224–5
and Stamp Act Crisis 213–16
and Margaret and Polly Stevenson
202–3, 209–10, 238

testimony to House of Commons
214–17
travels 218
and U.S. diplomatic service 162
various accomplishments 190–1
Autobiography 194, 196
*Experiments and Observations on
Electricity* 192
'On how to choose a mistress' 209–10
Poor Richard's Almanac 190, 196
see also Franklin, Deborah; Franklin,
William
Franklin, Deborah (née Read) 195, 197,
210, 211, 212, 225, 229
Franklin, Elizabeth (née Downes) 200–5
Franklin, James 190
Franklin, Sally 211
Franklin, William 91, 96, 197–205, 207,
208, 224
called to bar 197
as governor of New Jersey 203, 204, 222,
223, 231, 233
as heiress-hunter 201–3
illegitimacy 200, 203, 204, 242
and Ohio project 220
personality 223
Franklin, (William) Temple 200, 202, 203,
205, 211, 229, 234
Frederic (Laurens slave) 113
Frederick II (the Great), King of
Prussia 162
French
intellectuals 185
as servants in London 167
as visitors to London 165
see also France
French and Indian War *see* Seven Years'
War
frontiersmen, American 180
Frost, Robert 128

Gage, Margaret (née Kemble) 240
Gage, Thomas 19, 180, 229, 231, 235, 240
Gage family 240
Galloway, Joseph 194, 196–7, 220
Garden, Alexander 63, 64, 65, 73
gardening
landscape 174
ornamental 172–4
gardens, London 174
Garrick, David 2, 95, 96, 178–9
Gearey, John 213
Geneva 26, 50, 52, 54, 55, 67, 72–3, 80, 89,
97, 98, 108
Gentleman's Magazine 40, 213

gentlemen, manners of 68–70, 129, 130
George III, King 16, 25, 105, 130, 143, 154,
        157, 159, 179, 182, 183, 231, 235
    alleged plot against 159–62, 237
    Benjamin West in favour with 238
    proclaims British acceptance of
        American independence 245
George (Laurens slave) 113
George (Manning slave) 32, 110
Georgia 20, 112, 218, 222
Germans, Germany 4, 235
Gervais, John Lewis 25
Gibbes family 76
Gibbon, Edward 96
Gibson, Mel 82
Goldsmith, Oliver 2, 95, 96, 183
Gordon Castle, Morayshire, Scotland 118
Graeme, Elizabeth (Betsy) 201, 202, 203
Grafton, Augustus Henry Fitzroy, 3rd
        Duke of 146
Grand Tour 4, 67, 225
Grant, James 106–7
Gravesend 77, 96, 105
Great Fire of London (1666) 90, 122–3
Greene, Nathanael, 112
Gresham, Thomas 122
Griffin, Christina (née Stewart) 70
Griffin, Cyrus 70
Grimké, John Faucheraud 54
guerrillas 180

Halifax, George Montagu Dunk, 2nd
        Earl of 204
Hall, David 190
Hamilton, Alexander 113
Hampton Court 17
Harford, Frances 153
Harvard University 84, 192
Hawkins Petrie & Co. 75
Hayman, Francis 96, 177
    The Surrender of Montreal to General
        Amherst 177
heiress-hunting 131, 137–9, 148, 200–2
heiresses, West Indian 200, 204
Hell Fire Club 145, 219
Henry VIII, King 12, 31
Hilliard d'Auberteuil, Michel-René 232
Hillsborough, Wills Hill, 1st Earl of 141,
        146, 147, 148, 221, 229
Hogarth, William 211
Hollywood 246
Howe, Caroline 230
Howe, George Augustus Lord 177, 180,
        230, 245
Howe, Richard, 4th Viscount Howe 230

Howe, Sir William 245
Huguenots 54, 72, 195
human development, stadialist theory
        of 185–7
Hume, David 70, 207
Huntingdon, Countess of (Selina
        Hastings) 185
Hutchinson, Thomas 109, 226–8, 232
Hyde, Thomas Villiers, 1st Lord 230

India 170
Indians (American) see Native Americans
Ingersoll, Jared 108
inoculation 14–15, 185
investors, colonial 119–20
Ireland 218
Irish, unpopularity of 165
Islamic culture 170
Italians, reputation among English 165
Italy 178, 246
Izard, Alice (née DeLancey) 18–19, 240
Izard, Elizabeth 19
Izard, Ralph 18–20, 24–5, 24, 41, 72, 119,
        136–7, 154, 247
    aristocratic connections 19
    education and early years 18–19
    family and friends in England
        19–20, 240
    in London after outbreak of American
        Revolution 239–41
    marries Alice DeLancey 18–19
    organizes petition against Coercive
        Acts 105, 230
    returns to America 240–1
    settles in Berners Street 19
    and Temple-Whately duel 227
Izard family 22, 23, 25, 242

Jackson, Richard 201, 203, 215, 218, 220
Jacobs, Jonathan 137
Jamaica 4, 21, 33–4, 207
Jamestown, Virginia 4
Jefferson, Thomas 2, 150
Jenings, Edmund 150
Johnson, Joshua 53
Johnson, Martha Harris 211
Johnson, Samuel 2, 91, 94–6, 96, 196,
        211, 225
    Literary Club 94–5, 224
Jones, Walter 69
July (Manigault slave) 32

Kant, Immanuel 192
Kerr, James 45
kidnapping 171

King (slave of William Franklin) 42,
44, 91, 200
King, Martin Luther 144
King's Bench, court of 88
Kinloch, Francis 16
Kitty (Deans' maid) 35
Knowles, John 16

La Rochelle 54
Laird, Captain 45
land speculation 119–20, 148, 220–1
landscape gardening 174
Lascelles family 22
Laurens, André 195
Laurens, Eleanor (née Ball, 1731–70)
7–8, 10, 75
Laurens, Eleanor (Nelly, 1755–64) 8
Laurens, Frances Eleanor (Fanny) 241
Laurens, Henry (1724–92) 7–23, 9, 25–6,
50, 120, 126
arrival in England 11–12, 34
and black people in London 243
and Carolina Coffee House 125
and Cato (Appleby slave) 53–4
and coffee houses 175
death of wife 7–8
on English myths about rice 171
and English view of colonies 166, 167
imprisoned in Tower of London 60
and John's education and career 64–6,
72–3, 96–8, 100, 106
joins absentee planter set in London 11
looks for suitable schools for sons 16, 72
management of plantation and house
slaves 38–9
and Molsy Bremar 74–82, 124
on Robert Morris 153
origins and career 9–10, 195
plans trip to England 8–9
as prisoner of war 241
and protest against Coercive
Acts 105, 230
references to Robert 12–13, 28, 29, 37,
39, 51, 56–7
returns to America, and political career
60, 81, 87, 88, 241
rise in social status 195
and Robert's arrest 55–60
and slavery 102
on Soubise 43
as successful merchant and planter
7–8, 10–11
taken for Englishman in France 70
takes rooms in Fludyer Street 16, 35
travels in England 73–4

travels to Geneva 50–1, 54, 55
on varying opinions of London 186
on Wilkes 151–2
Laurens, Henry, Jr. (Harry, 1763–1821)
7–8, 16, 21, 22, 26, 50, 52, 55, 71,
72, 73, 80, 97–8, 112, 241
Laurens, James (1720–84) 8, 75, 77–81,
88, 109
Laurens, James (Jemmy, 1765–75) 8,
12, 14, 16, 26, 50–1, 55, 65, 97,
109–11, 112
Laurens, John (Jacky, 1754–82)
as American hero 111–13
arrival in England 12
on choice of profession 73
at Clarke's school, Chelsea 16, 26, 71
and Thomas Day 99–103, 107
death 241
decides to study law 84–5
early interest in natural world 63–6, 73,
112, 174
and Harry 97–8
Henry's concern for 71, 96–7
and Jacob Read 96
and Jemmy 97, 109–11
as law student 87–9, 95, 97–9
and Egerton Leigh 99
and London society 196
at Lord Mayor's Ball 92, 151
marriage to Martha Manning and
return to America 111
and Molsy Bremar 81–2, 98–9
at school in Geneva 50–1, 55, 72–4, 80
sent to England to finish education 8
and slavery 101–2, 167
and smallpox 14
and stereotype of American planters 83,
101–2, 104, 112–13 166
and War of Independence 104–9
wish to return to America 108–9
Laurens, John (Jean Samuel)
(1696–1747) 195
Laurens, Martha (née Manning) 111,
240, 241
Laurens, Martha (Patsy, 1759–1811) 8,
14, 75, 101, 109
Laurens, Mary (Polly, 1770–94) 8, 109
Laurens, Robert Scipio 96, 107, 112
after war 243–4
arrested for burglary 55–7
attempts to assimilate 13–14, 167
begs to be taken to England 8–9, 59
and black community in London 34
changes of name 13, 28, 58, 59, 60, 167
charged with bigamy 57–8

duties as servant to Henry Laurens 28, 50, 51–2
errands in London 29–32
Henry on 12–13, 28, 29, 51, 56–7, 37.39
market value to Henry 58–9
and moral temptations 26, 27, 96
on sea journey to England 11
in Shropshire 50–1, 52–3, 55, 59
and Mary Slugg 60–1
and slave stereotypes, 13
and smallpox inoculation 14–15, 58
travels to Geneva with Henry 54
and workmates 35–7
Laurens family 7–26, 45, 71, 116, 166, 195
law
    as profession 66, 67, 73, 84, 88–9, *90*, 99–100, 137, 197
    students of 84–9
A Law Macaroni 198
Lee, Arthur 147–51, 157, 163, 166, 173, 208, 219, 221
    after Declaration of Independence 236
    on American independence 235, 236
    appointed U.S. Commissioner to France 237
    defence of colonial rights 225
    and Franklin 222–3, 227, 232
    hatred of slavery 149
    and imprisonment of Sayre 160
    on mission to Berlin 162
    as patriot 148, 151
    and Pitt 176
    and Temple–Whately duel 227
Lee, Richard Henry 148
Lee, Robert E. 147
Lee, William 72, 148, 149–50, 154, 235, 237
Lee family 147, 159, 160
Leigh, Sir Egerton 74, 77–82, 99, 112, 124
Leigh, Martha (née Bremar) 74, 76, 79–81, 99
Leigh family 76–7, 98–9
Lennox, Charlotte Ramsay 95
Leslie, William 2
Levy, Andrea, *Small Island* 30
Lexington and Concord, battles of 104, 159, 229, 231, 232, 235, 237, 240, 247
Linnaeus, Carolus 63
Lisle, David 45
literary world, in London 2, 94–6, 224–5, 247
Liverpool 2
Livingston, Philip 199
Locke, John 187

London
    American artists in 211, 246
    benefits of stay in 69
    black population 34
    as business capital of the world 123, 246
    gardens 174
    housing boom 17
    literary set in 2, 94–6, 224–5, 247
    lord mayors of 123
    mixed origins of population 128
    opportunities of 115–16
    ordinary colonists in 212–13
    as shopping capital of English-speaking world 246
    as source of moral corruption 186
    theatre 9, 168, 174, 246
London (streets, buildings)
    Artillery Court 134, 135–41, 147, 148, 151, 158, 185, 221
    Artillery Ground 134
    Bank of England 19, 79, 120, 121–2, *121*, 124, 125, 137
    Banqueting House 29
    Berkeley Street 18
    Berners Street 18, 19–21, 29, 32, 34, 39, 67, 81, 105, 109, 119, 137, 152, 153–4, 158, 225, 238, 240
    Birchin Lane 110, 125, 159, 210, 221
    Bishop's Palace, Fulham 172, *173*
    Board of Trade 119, 120, 140
    Bond Street 18
    British Museum 3, 175
    Broad Street (later Broadwick Street) 22
    Buckingham House 16
    Burlington Arcade 246
    Carolina Coffee House, Birchin Lane 25
    Chancery Lane 88, 93, *94*, 95, 97, 99
    Charing Cross 32, 211, *244*, 245
    Chelsea 14, 26, 60, 153, 190
        Clarke's school 14, 16, 21, 25–6, 43, 71, 72
    Chelsea Physic Garden 174
    Cheshire Cheese 95
    Chiswell Street 134
    Cleveland Row 156–7, *156*
    Conduit Street 18, 44
    Cornhill 17, *121*, 122, 124, 125
    Court of St James's 2, 130, 181
    Covent Garden 70, 96
    Crane Court 63, 93, *206*
    Craven Street 197, 202, 203, 209–11, 229, 231, 238
    Devereux Court 95
    Devil Tavern 95
    Downing Street 16

Drury Lane 155
Falcon tavern 106
Fenchurch Street 45
Fleet Market 93
Fleet Prison 93
Fleet Street 29, 30, 90, 91, 93, 94–5, *95*,
    10*6*, 170
Fludyer Street (formerly Axe Yard) *15*,
    16–17, 18, 19, 26, 30, 51, 55, 97, 167
Garden Court 236
George and Vulture 125, *126*
Grafton Street 230
Green Park 156
Greenwich 72, 109–10
Grosvenor Square 17
Hackney 137
Hampton Court 174
Harley Street 18
Hatton Garden 44, 91
Horse Guards Parade 16
House of Commons 99, 144, 146,
    148, *215*, 221
House of Lords 106, 231, 245
Houses of Parliament 2, 182
Hyde Park 21, 227, 242
Inns of Court 21, 24, 67, 68, 73, 84, 85,
    86, 89, 92–3, 108, 119, 127, 135,
    137, 138, 150–1, 197, 199,
    200, 247
Kensington Gardens 174
Kew Gardens 18, 174, 247
Kew Palace 207
King Street 30
King's Bench Prison 144, 148
King's Bench Walk 95
King's Road 17
Lad Lane 183
Lincoln's Inn Fields 93
Mansion House 3, 123–4, *124*, 236
Marylebone 17, 21–2
Mayfair 17, 44
Middle Temple 84, 91–3, 105, 108,
    197–200, *199*, 203, 247
Middle Temple Lane 95, 197–200
Mincing Lane 45
Minories 213
Mitre 95
Monument 137
Moorfields 134
New Road (later Euston Road) 17
Newman Street 238, 242
Newman's Court 125
Northumberland House 211
Old Bailey 34, 60–1, 175, 213
Old Broad Street 125

Oxford Street 17, 154, 158, 159, 163,
    210, 243
Paddington 17
Pall Mall 44, 76
Panton Square 211
Parliament Street 16
Pool of London *171*
Portugal Street 119
Prince's Street *121*
Rackstraw's Museum of Anatomy 93
Rathbone Place 158
Ridgway House, Mill Hill 174
Robinhood Tavern 105
Royal Academy of Arts 177, 178
Royal Cockpit 16, 229, 232
Royal Exchange 17, 19, 122–3,
    123, 125
Royal Parks 3, 17
St Bride's, Fleet Street 170
St Christopher-le-Stocks *124*
St Dunstan's Church 93
St George's Fields 145
St James's Palace 16, 156, *156*, 159
St James's Park 16, 29, *78*, 79, 153,
    156, 174
St James's Square 3
St James's Street 200
St Martin's Lane Academy 211
St Mary Axe 110
St Michael's Alley 3
St Paul's Cathedral 29, 182, 183, 205
Salmon, Mrs, waxworks 3, 93, *94*, 95,
    174, 182
Serpentine 227
Soho Street 22
Spring Garden 192
Strand 29, 32, 87, *95*, 139
Syon House 183
Temple Bar 29, 90, 92, 238, 244, 245
Threadneedle Street 19, 121, *121*, 122,
    124, *124*, 125, 221
Tokenhouse Yard 120–1, 127
Tower Docks 213
Tower Hill 150, 153, 238
Tower of London 17, 113, 143, 171, *171*,
    182, 241
Tyburn 238
Union Court 74, 79, 81
Vauxhall 155
Vauxhall Gardens 9, 177, 182
Westminster Abbey 3, 16, 97, 176–7
Westminster Hall 50, 51, 87
Westminster School 97
Whitehall 4, 16, 29, 30, 140, 141,
    210, 221

Wimpole Street 22
see also coffee houses, London
London Chronicle 72
London Magazine 176
Long Island 118, 129
Lord Mayor's Ball 92
Louis XV, King of France 218
Louisbourg, Siege of 19
Loyalists 109
Ludwell, Hannah (later Lee) 149–50
Lunar Society 100
Luttrell, Henry 144
Lynch, Thomas 82

Mackesy, Piers 189
McQueen, Alexander 21
McQueen, Mrs 21
Madison, James 1
Mahon, Charles Stanhope, Lord 92
Mai (Tahitian) 185
Manchester 100
Manigault, Peter 32
Manning, John 71, 72
Manning, Martha see Laurens, Martha
    (née Manning)
Manning, William 22, 98, 99, 111
Manning family 22, 32, 40, 71, 97, 110, 122
Mansfield, William Murray, Earl of, Chief
    Justice 46–7, 51, 53, 54
Marchant, Henry 211
Marie Antoinette, Queen of France 207
Marie, Queen of France 218
maritime unions, segregation in 243
marriage
    arranged 135
    to heiresses 131, 137–9, 148, 200–2
    interracial 37, 57, 244
Marseilles 54
Maryland 21, 48, 68, 85, 146
    owned by Lord Baltimore 153
Massachusetts 25, 104–5, 127, 133, 136,
    139–41, 149, 177, 230, 239
    agency 141, 142, 147, 148, 150, 218,
        222, 226
    Assembly 146, 226
    considered troublesome colony 226, 228
    and Hutchinson letters 226–8
    Minutemen 232, 236, 239–40
Massey, 'Mulatto Sam' (Laurens slave) 38
May Day procession 36
medicine, as profession 73, 84
Medmenham Abbey 145
Melville, Herman 128
Mepkin, South Carolina 241
merchants and businessmen 144

American 126–7, 128
    in London 121–7
'The Middle Temple Macaroni' 91, 91
Middlesex elections 151–2
    petitions against outcome 143, 144
Middleton, Arthur 24, 242
Middleton, Thomas 242
Middleton, William 242
Middleton, William, Jr. 242
Middleton family 19, 23, 109
Minutemen see Massachusetts, Minutemen
Mississippi, river 119
Mississippi Company 148
Montesquieu, Charles, Baron de 165
    The Spirit of the Laws 122
Moreton, John see Laurens,
        Robert Scipio
Morgan, Edmund 224
Morgan, John 136
Morland, Sir Samuel 131
Morris, Robert 153
Morris, Staats Long 119, 138
Moultrie family 16, 22
Mountmorres, Hervey Redmond Morres,
        2nd Viscount 92
Mozart, Wolfgang Amadeus 207
mulattoes 37

'Nanny' (in Stevenson household) 211
Nantes 54, 237
Napoleon I, Emperor 122
Napoleonic Wars 23
Native Americans 141, 181–5,
        186–7, 209
Navy, Royal 36–7, 66
Neate, William 138
Nelthorpe, Charlotte 138
Nelthorpe, John 138
Nelthorpe, Lady 138
Netherlands 241
    Austrian 207
New England 4, 23, 49, 108, 116, 127, 192,
        205, 207
    and Coercive Acts 105
    and colonial sectionalism 23, 127
    cultural heyday of 128
    rustic image 23, 116, 127–9, 131–2,
        169, 205, 207
    as troublesome region 167, 231
    see also Club of Honest Whigs; De
        Berdt, Dennis; New Englanders
New England Chronicle 161
New Englanders 169
    at battle of Bunker Hill 240
    English, British origins 49, 128

nonconforming 132
prejudice against 127 9
as refugees in London 242
New France 176
New Hampshire 127
'A New Humorous Song on the Cherokee
    Chiefs' 184
New Jersey 118, 203, 204, 218, 223
New York 2, 21, 49, 116, 126–7, 163, 214,
    242, 247, 248
  Lord & Taylor 246
  Macy's 246
  Wall Street 127
New Yorkers 71
New-England Courant 190
Newcastle 195–6
Newcastle, Duke of 173
Newport, Rhode Island 23
Niagara 140
noble savage, cult of 186 7
Noel, Elizabeth (later Sayre) 158, 163
North, Frederick, Lord 105, 107, 162, 224,
    229, 230, 231, 235
The North Briton 143, 146
Northumberland, Elizabeth Seymour,
    Duchess of 211
Northumberland, Hugh (Smithson)
    Percy, 1st Duke of 155,
    183, 211
Nova Scotia 4, 118

Occom, Samson 185
Ohio project 220–1
Ohio river 174
Old Sarum, Wiltshire 144
Oliver, Richard 151, *152*, 207
Ostenaca (Cherokee chief) 183
Otis, James 49, 128
Ovid (slave) 44
Oxford 55, 73
  University of 67, 72, 84, 85, 92, 207

packet ships 11–12
Paddock, Seth 212
The Padlock 13, 157, 168
Paine, Thomas 4
Palmer, Miss 148
Paradise, John 150
Paradise, Lucy Ludwell 150
Paris 232–3, 237
  Peace of (1763) 17, 119
Parsons, Martha (Trezevant, Bostock) 79
Parsons family 74, 79, 81
pastry-cooks' shops 169–70
The Patriot 82

Patriot movement 1, 25, 60, 69, 74, 86,
    108, 109, 148, 149, 226, 227, 239,
    247
Pearson, Mrs 151, 153, 154
Pendennis Castle 12
Penn, John 204, 209
Penn, Lady Juliana Fermor 225
Penn, Sophia 225
Penn, Thomas 192–3, 194, 199
Penn, William 192
Penn family 192–5, 204, 208, 213, 224, 225
Pennsylvania 4, 42, 48, 49, 105, 119, 126,
    136, 149, 173, 174, 242
  Assembly 189, 190, 192, 193, 196, 200
  and Franklin's scheme for royal
    government 209, 213, 218
  University of (earlier Academy of
    Philadelphia; College of
    Philadelphia) 2, 84, 96, 136,
    173, 190
Pennsylvania Gazette 190
Pennsylvania Hospital 173
Pennsylvanians, in London 108, 136–7,
    159, 189, 205, 211–12, 220, 223–5,
    243
Penny, Edward 177
Percy family 211
Peronneau family 21
Peter (slave of Benjamin Franklin) 42, 200
Petric, Jacky 25 6
Philadelphia 1, 21, 48, 134, 142, 161, 178,
    193, 195, 196, 211, 214, 221
  College of 2, 84, 96, 178
  Congress 105
  Hospital 190
  Union Fire Company 190
Physiocrats 220
Pierce, Edwards 80, 81
Pinckney, Charles 207, 211
Pinckney, Eliza 211
Pinckney, Thomas 105
Pinckney family 207
Pitt, William, 1st Earl of Chatham (Pitt the
    Elder) 2, 175–6, 178, 204, 208, 226,
    231–2
  in Seven Years' War 132
placemen 100, 145
plantation colonies
  conditions in 103–4, 207
  metropolitan image of 48–9
    as decadent, tyrannical 101–4,
    166–7
    as mixed race 49, 168–9
    products of 48, 126, 169–72
plantation slaves 32, 48, 213

planters, absentee
  at American resorts 23
  in London 33–4, 127, 133, 138, 168, 169,
    240, 242
    metropolitan image 22, 23, 49, 50, 83,
      91, *91*, 103, 104, 166–7, 168–9
    origins of 22–3,133
    numbers 23
  and mainland American absentees 22–3
plants
  collectors and collecting 172–4, 174
  New World 169–74
Pocahontas 181
Pontiac, Chief 209
Pontiac uprising 120, 209
Portland, William Henry Cavendish
      Bentinck, 3rd Duke of 237
Portland, HMS 77
Post Office (British) 225
poverty, among white people in London
      30–2
Powel, Samuel 225
Pratt, Matthew, 'The American School' *212*
Presbyterians 132, 134
press gang 36–7
Price, Richard 206, 207
Priestley, Joseph 100, 206, 223, 229
Princeton, New Jersey 129
  battle of 2
Princeton University (formerly College of
      New Jersey) 84, 117–18, 135
Pringle, Sir John 204, 205, 206, 218
Privy Council 47, 51, 147, 193, 222, 228–9
  at Cockpit 229, 232, 233
Proclamation of 1763 120
Proclamation of Rebellion (1775) 108, 111,
      162
professions, gentlemanly 65–6
prostitution 32, 36, 72, 87, 137, 139, 145,
      156, 182
Protestant Dissenting Deputies 132
Protestantism 132
Prussia 122, 149, 175
Public Advertiser 107
Public Ledger 44
Purdon, Bartholomew Coote 154
Puritans 128

Quakers 4, 132, 161, 173, 177, 192, 193,
      209, 220, 222, 230
Quebec 120
  capture of 3, 177, 178, *179*, 247
Queensberry, Catherine Hyde, Duchess
      of 43
Quincy, Josiah 49

racial differences, theories of 185–6
racism 36, 243
Raffald, Elizabeth 170
Rawlins, Steadman 22
Rawlins family 22
Read, Jacob 96, 105, 113
Reed, Joseph 135, 136, 138, 139, 141–2,
      157, 158, 166, 221, 223
religion 131–2
  see also Catholics; dissenters, religious;
      Protestantism
religious persecution 131
retailing, in London 170
Reynolds, Joshua 2, 95, 177, 183, 211
Rhode Island 211
rice 170–1
Richardson, Frances (Frank) 159, 161–2
Richardson, Samuel, *Clarissa* 210
Richmond, Charles Lennox, 3rd Duke of
      19, *41*
Richmond, Surrey 240
riots
  in Boston 55, 105
  in London 145, 159, 160, 165
  in New York 214
Rochford, William Henry Nassau De
      Zuylestein, 4th Earl of 159–62
Rockingham, Charles Watson-Wentworth,
      2nd Marquess of 151, 215, 216, 218
Rockingham family 158
Rodney, Admiral George 156
Rogers, Robert 180
  A Concise Account of North America 180
  'General Rules for the Ranging Service'
      180
  Journals of Major Robert Rogers 180
Rogers' Rangers 180
Roman empire 186
Rome 178
Romney, George 177, 183
Rousseau, Jean-Jacques 103, 185
  Émile 100
Royal African Company 51
royal icing 170
Royal Navy 36–7, 66
Royal Society 63, 64, 93, 173, 174,
      190, 204, 205, *206*, 219, 225,
      230, 232
  Copley Medal 192
rum 172
Rush, Benjamin 1–3, 4, 148
Rush, James 1
Russia 122, 162
Ruston, Thomas 49, 137, 148, 166,
      185, 202

Rutgers University (earlier Queen's College) 84
Rutledge, John and Edward 113

St Albans, 8th Duke of 138
St Andrews, University of 207
St Asaph, bishop of *see* Shipley, bishop Jonathan
St Croix 138
St George's Fields Massacre 145–6
St James's Chronicle 182
St Kitts 22, 28, 29, 34
St Mawes Castle 12
St Petersburg 162
Salmon, Mrs 3, 93, *94*, 95, 174, 182
Sampson, George 121–2
Sandwich, John Montagu, 4th Earl of 106, 219
Sargent, John 208
Savannah, Georgia 53
Sayre, Stephen 115–21, *117*, 126–7, 129–30, 131, 134–42, 143, 147–9, 150, 151, 153–4, 166, 197, 202, 208, 221
    and alleged plot against George III 159–62
    and Arthur Lee 162
    career and adventures after the war 162–3
    and coffee houses 175
    disliked by Mrs Steele 157
    The Englishman Deceived 140–1
    imprisoned 159–60, 162, 163
    leaves London for France 237
    as sheriff of London 154, 155–6, 158
    and Stamp Act Crisis 216
    strives for gentility 167
    travels 162–3
    see also Baddeley, Sophia
Sayre, Stephen, Jr. 158
Schuylkill river 173
Scots, Scotland 118–19, 185, 207, 218
    trading privileges with England 236
    unpopularity of 69–70, 127–8, 143, 165
Scott, Dred 46
Seaford, Sussex 158
seamen, colonial, in London 213, 246
Second World War 243
    black West Indians in London during 30
servants, London 13–14
    amusements of 40
    beating of 39, 40–1, 58
    black preferred to white 59
    mistaken for their masters 130
    quarters in West End houses 35

seen as insolent 27, 39
solidarity with black servants and slaves 36–8
tipping of 39–40, 42
see also slaves, American, in London
Sessakaroo 195
Seven Years' War 4, 17, 23, 106, 117, 132, 174, 189, 192, 207
    and metropolitan views of America 175–81
Sharp, Granville 45, 46, 47, 50, 58, 59, 107, 222
Shaw, George Bernard, *Pygmalion* 130
Shelburne, Sophia, Countess of 148
Shelburne, William FitzMaurice, 2nd Earl of 119, 140, 148, 150, 174, 219, 221, 225
Shepherd, Ezekiel 213
Shifnal, Shropshire 51, 52–3, 59–60, 73–4
    Aston Hall 52–3, 55, *56*, 57, 71
Shinnecock Indians 116
Shipley, bishop Jonathan 219, 223
Shrewsbury Chronicle 55
Shrewsbury Flying Waggon 12
Shropshire 50–1, 54
Shropshire, John 34
Sierra Leone 25
Silliman, Benjamin 243
Six Nations 183
slavery, slave trade 4, 7, 10, 22, 25, 34, 38, 40–1, 44–7, 51, 53, 57–8, 101–3, 133, 149, 166–7, 243, 248
    anti–slavery campaign 83
    Franklin and 47–9, 50, 107, 222
    London as slaving port 171
    Massachusetts and 222
Slavery Abolition Act (1833) 47
slaves, American
    advertised for sale or wanted for purchase 44
    classical names given to 13
    demand for 52
    Sir John Fielding on 29
    and interracial marriage 37, 57, 244
    in London 4, 13–14, 28–38, 91, 166
    market value 58–9
    mentioned in records 32–3, 37
    metropolitan stereotypes of 13, 36, 40–1, 42, 59, 168
    as part of London scene 168
    and poor white people in London 30–2
    population in colonies 217
    runaway 42, 44, 53, 54, 92–3, 113, 240
    'Town Negroes' 38–9, 52, 84
    see also servants, London

Sloane, Sir Hans 175, 190
Slugg, Mary 60–1
smallpox 14–15, 58, 185
Smith, Adam 207
Society of the Bill of Rights 150
Solander, Daniel 65
Somerset, James 46–7, 50, 51, 53
Somerset case 46–7, 50, 51, 52, 54, 89,
    101, 222
Sons of Liberty, Boston 49, 146–7,
    149, 150
Soubise, Julius 43, *43*
South Carolina
    absentee community in London 9–11,
        18–22, 26, 32, 34, 35, 48, 52, 63,
        64, 73, 76, 85, 96, 109, 131, 146,
        153, 212
    agency of 207
    Assembly 112, 146, 153
    attitude to slavery in 102
    booming economy 10
    Campbell (last royal governor) and
        19, 240
    Cherokees from 181–3
    emigrants to 48
    Henry Laurens returns to 81, 87, 241
    Leighs in 77, 81, 82
    Liberty Boys 146
    Provincial Congress 60, 242
    rebel movement in 106, 109
    slaves in 112–13
    Vice-Admiralty Court 74
    wildlife 63–4
    see also Berners Street set; Izard, Ralph
South Carolina Gazette 21
Southampton (English port) 233
Southampton, Long Island 116
Spain 149
The Spectator 68
Spooner, Charles 34
stagecoaches 12
Stamp Act Congress 214
Stamp Act Crisis (1765) 133–4, 139–40,
    141, 147, 173, 213–16, 218
Stanley, John 211
Stead, Benjamin 19, 25, 29
Stead family 18, 19
Steele, Mrs 156–7
    Memoirs 158, 163
Stepney, 'Daddy' (Laurens slave) 38
stereotypes of Americans 4, 13, 83, 133,
    166, 168, 180
    see also Americans, colonial; New
        England; New Englanders;
        plantation colonies; planters,

absentee; slaves, American; West
    Indians
Stevens, Margaret (Peggy) 76
Stevenson, Margaret 202–3, 209–10, 225,
    231, 238
Stevenson, Mary (Polly) 202–3, 208, 238
Stewart, Charles 46, 50, 51, 53
Stewart, George (slave) 91–2
Stirling, William Alexander, Earl of
    118–19, 137, 199
Strahan, William 196, 197, 200, 208, 214,
    220, 223, 225
Stratford Hall, Virginia 147
Stratford-upon-Avon 55, 73
Strawberry Hill, Twickenham 19
Strong, Jonathan 45–6
students, colonial, in London 84–9
'sturdy beggars' 31–2
sugar 175
    West Indian 169–70, 172
Sullivan's Island 240
Sumter, Thomas 181
Susquehanna Company 119
Sweden 162
Switzerland 26, 50, 52, 54, 55, 67, 72

Talbot, Miss 148
taxation 231, 236
    of colonies 106, 133, 144, 145, 213–15
tea 170
    taxation of 145
Temple, John 227–9, 238–9
Thames, river 19
theatre, London 9, 168, 174
Thelwall, Robert Carter 138
Thoreau, Henry David 128, 144
Tilghman, Edward 68–9, 95, 148–9, 161
Timberlake, Henry 181
tobacco 48, 170–1, 172, 175
Tooke, John Horne 162
Tories 69, 109, 238
Toulon 54
tourism, tourists, colonial American 4, 23,
    122, 174
'Town Negroes' 38–9, 52, 84
Townshend, Charles 119, 140, 145
Townshend, Roger 176–7
Townshend Acts 145, 146, 148
trade, between Britain and America 3, 169,
    245, 246
transportation 11–12, 172, 213
    of criminals 57, 130–1
travel books 180–1
Traquair, James Stewart, 6th Earl of 70
trees, American 174

The True Conduct of Persons of Quality 200
Tunbridge Wells 201

Upton, Essex 172–3
Ursulines 80

'vails' 39–40, 42
Van Dyck, Anthony 178
Vaughan, Samuel 207
Vaughan, Susanna 153
Vaughan family 45
Verney family 158
Versailles 218, 232, 241
Virginia 21, 48, 49, 131, 134, 146, 149
Voltaire 165

Walpole, Horace 19, 145
warfare, metropolitan appetite for stories of 179–80
Warren, Joseph 240
Warren, Admiral Sir Peter 19
Warwick, Earl of 183
Washington, D.C. 247, 248
    Botanic Garden 247
    Capitol Building 247
    Washington Monument 247
    White House 53, 247
Washington, George 1, 111–12, 181, 239
Watson, Elkanah 245
Watt, James 100, 207
Watts, John 137
Wedderburn, Alexander 228–9, 233
wedding cakes, tiered 170
Wedgwood, Josiah 100
Wentworth family 158
West, Benjamin 2, 177–9, 189, 211, *212*, 225, 238, 245
    The Cricketers 24–5, *24*, 136
    The Death of General Wolfe 178–9, *179*
The West Indian (play) 104, 167, 168
West Indians, in London 13, 30, 32–4, 45, 51, 91, *91*, 113, 127, 151, 173
    black 30, 43
    classed as Americans 21–3, 48–9, 105
    education 76, 85
    heiresses 200, 204
    and petition against Coercive Acts 105
    post-Second World War settlers 30, 243
    and slavery bill 53
West Indies 4, 21, 23, 25, 48, 56, 58, 134, 153

Wharton, Samuel 220, 221
Whately, Thomas 226–8
Whately, William 227–9, 232, 238
Wheelock, Eleazar 132
    Indian school, Lebanon, Connecticut 185
Whigs 69, 71
    see also Club of Honest Whigs
White, John 111
White, William 74, 78–9
Whitefield, George 185
Whittington, Richard 115, 130
Wild West 180–1
Wilkes, John 2, 143–53, *152*, 224
    and alleged plot against George III 159–62
    and Arthur Lee 148–51
    champions constitutional reform in England 143, 144–5
    disliked by Americans in London 151
    imprisoned in King's Bench Prison 144
    imprisoned in Tower of London 143
    as Lord Mayor 151, 236
    and Stephen Sayre 157, 159, 160
    and Wilkites 149–51, 154, 157, 227
    'Essay on Woman' 145
William and Mary, College of 84
Williams, Jonathan 238
Williams, Josiah 211
Williams family 211
Williams Wynn, Sir Watkin 175
Winchester 71
Windsor, Thomas 34
Winson Green 52, 55, 73, 97, 109
Wolfe, James 176, 177, 178–9, 247
women, colonial, in London 69, 76
Wood, William 204, 218
Wordsworth, William 181
Wormeley, Ralph 24, *24*
Wren, Sir Christopher 90
Wright, Sir James 19–20, 225
Wright, James, Jr. 19–20
Wright family 18, 22, 23, 109
Wyndham, Sir William 190

Yale University 84, 192
Yankees 48, 116, 127, 130, 245
    as embodiment of national values 248
    see also New Englanders
York 123
Yorkshiremen 128

Zoffany, Johann 154